ON TO BERLIN

ON TO BERLIN

Battles of an
Airborne Commander
1943-1946

James M. Gavin

THE VIKING PRESS NEW YORK

Published in 1978 by The Viking Press
625 Madison Avenue, New York, N.Y. 10022
Published simultaneously in Canada by
Penguin Books Canada Limited

LIBRARY OF CONGRESS CATALOGING IN PUBLICATION DATA
Gavin, James Maurice, 1907–
    On to Berlin.
    Includes index.
    1. World War, 1939–1945—Regimental histories—
United States—82nd Division.   2. United States.
Army. 82nd Division.   3. World War, 1939–1945—
Aerial operations, American.   I. Title.
D769.346 82nd.G38   940.54'12'73   77–10475
ISBN 0–670–52517–0

Printed in the United States of America
Set in Linotype Times Roman

ACKNOWLEDGMENTS:
    Astor-Honor, Inc. From Patton: Ordeal and Triumph by
Ladislas Farago. Copyright © 1964 by Ladislas Farago.
Reprinted by permission of Astor-Honor, Inc., New York
    Houghton Mifflin Company: Two maps—Figs. 15 and 17—
from The Damned Engineers by Janice Holt Giles. Copyright
© 1970 by Janice Holt Giles. Reprinted by permission of
Houghton Mifflin Company
    Harold Matson Co., Inc. Map—Fig. 11—from The Struggle
for Europe by Chester Wilmot. Copyright 1951 by Chester Wilmot.
Published by Harper & Row, and reprinted by
permission of Harold Matson Co., Inc.

To Jeanne and our five daughters,
Barbara, Caroline, Patricia, Aileen, and Chloe

Foreword

I had just passed my tenth birthday when the United States entered World War I. I was living in Mount Carmel, Pennsylvania, where I sold morning and evening newspapers. My favorite corner was at Third and Oak streets, which was the main intersection in our small town.

Soon after we entered the war, the government began a vigorous campaign to sell war bonds (they were called Liberty Bonds). Parades and rallies were organized, and there was much enthusiasm. I followed the war closely in the daily newspapers; of course, we did not have radio or television in those days. Across the street from my favorite corner was a shoe store. The proprietor, a patriotic man, placed a large map of Europe in the store window. On the map he depicted the Western Front where the Allied armies were locked in battle with the Germans. From there he drew a route to Berlin. As bonds were sold, he marked the route to indicate our progress to Berlin. The over-all title he gave to his map was "On to Berlin." I followed it with great interest, never realizing, of course, that someday I, too, would go "on to Berlin."

Acknowledgments

I would like especially to thank Mr. William H. Cunliffe and his colleagues in the National Archives for their invaluable help with research for this book. "Invaluable" is a much overused word, but their assistance was exactly that. They located many important cables and had a number of suggestions concerning other sources that might prove useful. I am also grateful to Ms. Yen Tsai Feng, Assistant Director of Research, Boston Public Library (now Librarian, Wellesley College), and the staff of the Boston Athenaeum for their great help, and to my capable secretary, Mrs. Hazel Shaner, whose memory of my files is unfailing and precise. Finally, I would like to thank my patient wife, who understood my distractions and preoccupations during the time I was researching and writing this book. In addition, she helped in proofreading critical parts of it.

Contents

Photo sections following page 50
and page 192

MAPS

Introduction

This is the story of an odyssey, from its beginning in Casablanca, proceeding to Tunisia, Sicily, Italy, Normandy, Holland, the Ardennes, the crossing of the Elbe, and finally the Allied victory parade up Unter den Linden in the heart of Berlin itself. I was fortunate to be a member of the 82nd Airborne Division all the way and more than fortunate to bring it home for the victory parade up Fifth Avenue.

As a parachutist, I became involved in any number of small-unit actions immediately following landings. And having found this a good way of learning how to survive on the battlefield, I continued to associate myself closely with small-unit engagements. In addition, as a parachutist, I was involved in a number of high-level planning conferences, since frequently parachute units were under the command of higher headquarters. This, in turn, put me directly in touch with a number of senior officers and higher headquarters staffs. Thus, early in the war I became aware of the personal feelings that seemed to involve many of the senior commanders, their attitudes toward one another and the difficulties they encountered in trying to carry out complex plans involving the forces of two or more nations. Finally, from the spring of 1945 on, when we were alerted to parachute into Berlin, I was constantly involved with the Berlin problem. Later I was to serve as the senior U.S. officer on the Berlin Kommandantura. Since the war I have discussed the problem of Berlin many times, and I have never been able to satisfy myself as to why we did not seize it. Now I know that we should have seized it.

Although the U.S. Air Corps had parachuted a machine gun and crew in 1923, the concept of airborne warfare was entirely neglected in the United States until World War II. The Russians, however, picked up the idea, and between wars they staged a number of massive drops.

They viewed the airplane as a means of delivering lightly armed partisans behind enemy lines. Even as late as the end of World War II they had not been able to solve the organization, management, and weapons problems that would permit them to use large airborne formations effectively. As a Russian paratrooper colonel explained to me on Tempelhof airfield in Berlin in the summer of 1945, "We just couldn't make sense out of all those men and airplanes." The Germans, on the other hand, saw the possibility of combining parachutes and gliders into large organizations on a division scale. As a beginning they organized hundreds of sports glider clubs as a means of circumventing the Versailles Treaty. They then organized the first airborne combat division.

The United States experimented with its first parachute platoon in the summer of 1940. By the summer of 1941 it had three battalions of paratroopers that it organized under a Provisional Parachute Group. I completed parachute training in August 1941, and shortly thereafter I joined the staff of the Provisional Parachute Group. I was responsible for the development of doctrine, training, equipment, organization. The problems were many, and although we studied the German airborne battles that had been fought in Europe, we knew that we had to go well beyond their achievements if we were to make a decisive contribution to winning the war.

The first U.S. battalion that went to war was the 2nd Battalion of the 503rd Infantry Regiment, later to be the 509th. It was commanded by a very capable and courageous soldier, Colonel Edson D. Raff. In early November 1942, it took off from England to land in North Africa as part of Operation TORCH, the large-scale American landings that extended from Algiers to Casablanca. When the battalion left England, it did not know whether its mission would be a peaceful one or would meet with hostility. Actually, its reception was mixed, but it did a fine job. At the same time it made it clear that we had a long way to go before we could use parachutes and gliders on the scale of a field army. This is the story of the development of that new arm, not in the training centers in the United States but in the crucible of war itself—in Europe.

ON TO BERLIN

The world was at war in the early 1940s. By the summer of 1942 the German empire extended from the Pyrenees to the outskirts of Moscow and, with the exception of Switzerland and Sweden, from the Mediterranean to the Arctic. It had been an impressive diplomatic and military performance, and there was good reason for many Americans to doubt that we, with the British, could successfully engage and destroy the German colossus. For some time we had been supplying the British with destroyers, airplanes, and arms and ammunition.

The impact of Pearl Harbor was immediate and dramatic. At the very moment when we were desperately eager to step up training, all training involving airplanes ceased. The airplanes disappeared. There was nothing to jump from. The War Department seemed little interested in us. All eyes were on the West Coast and the Pacific. There was a hiatus of many months during which little was done, except for physical training and tower jumping. By 1942, when we were formally at war, we were still short of trained manpower, weapons, tanks, airplanes, and warships. Our professional military people looked with some foreboding on our prospects of winning a war.

In 1941 I had been a member of the Department of Tactics at the Military Academy at West Point. Normally, tactical officers concern themselves more with the discipline of the Corps of Cadets than with teaching. However, I became deeply interested in the Germans' conquest of Europe and their use of a new arm—parachute-glider troops—and I taught as many classes as possible in the new and evolving tactics that could be learned from the European war. I had access to many of the original documents relating to the German airborne operations in Holland. I also read avidly the reports from our military attaché in Cairo,

Colonel Bonner Fellers, on the German parachute and glider operations in Crete. The whole concept of vertical envelopment was an exciting one, and it would seem to offer us a new dimension of tactics if we entered the war.

In August 1941 I volunteered as a paratrooper and was sent to the Parachute School at Fort Benning, Georgia. Except for being banged around a bit, I completed my training unscathed and as a young parachute captain reported to the 503rd Parachute Infantry as a company commander. In a couple of weeks I was moved to our highest airborne headquarters, the Provisional Parachute Group, then headed by Brigadier General William Lee. My new job, as Plans and Training Officer, gave me an exciting opportunity to experiment and develop new techniques for large-scale parachute-glider operations.

The problems were without precedent. Individuals had to be capable of fighting at once against any opposition they met on landing. Although every effort was being made to develop the communications and techniques to permit battalions, companies, and platoons to organize promptly, we had to train our individuals to fight for hours and days, if necessary, without being part of a formal organization. Equipment had to be lightweight and readily transportable. Weapons had to be hand-carried. This meant that larger weapons had to be broken down into individual loads, such as mortars and parachute-dropped artillery. To simplify our logistics problem, we had to use the same ammunition as the regular divisions, but we had to break it down into man-size loads. Finally, since entry into combat was to take place in the midst of the enemy, a new scheme for issuing combat orders and coordinating the efforts of all the troops had to be developed. All these problems brought into sharp focus the most important problem of all—how to train the individual paratrooper.

Since the beginning of recorded history, soldiers have been drilled repetitively to de-emphasize their individual behavioral traits and force them to adapt to larger combat formations. Perhaps the greatest efficiency in transforming each individual, squad, platoon, and so forth into a cog in a larger machine was demonstrated in the armies of Frederick the Great, and although machine weapons had changed all this, between World War I and World War II countless hours were spent on wheeling about and moving squads to the right and to the left, as though they were preparing to fight the wars of a century ago.

All this had to be discarded as we sought to train the paratroopers to the highest peak of individual pride and skill. It was at this time that the use of nameplates was adopted, the purpose being to emphasize the importance of an individual's personality and reputation. To the soldiers of another generation, it seemed to suggest too little discipline and too much initiative given to individual soldiers. We were willing to take a chance that this would not have a disrupting effect on larger formations. It did not, and there were many occasions in combat when the paratroopers were mixed up with regular ground formations and paratroop officers, and NCOs effectively took over the command of larger formations of other units. Aside from the impact of this type of training on the airborne formations themselves, it had a tremendous significance to the Army as a whole. The morale of the airborne units soared, especially after their first combat, when they could see for themselves the results of their training.

In the spring of 1942 Brigadier General William Lee and I, as his Plans and Training Officer, went to Washington to discuss the creation of our first airborne division. The Washington staff seemed rather skeptical about the whole idea. However, after some discussion it was agreed that we could start the organization of an airborne division provided certain stipulations were met. The division had to be one that had already completed basic training, and it could not be a regular Army or National Guard division; the States would not want the National Guard made airborne. It was also stipulated that the division should be one that was then stationed where flying weather was generally good and near one or more airfields. The one division that met all these requirements was the 82nd Division stationed at Camp Claiborne, Louisiana. It had been activated on April 25, 1942, and was under the command of Brigadier General Omar Bradley. Plans were made at once to convert it to an airborne division by adding two parachute regiments to it, making one of the infantry regiments glider-borne, and replacing all heavy equipment throughout the division with lighter substitutes that could be carried by glider and parachute. From the division a cadre was set aside for the 101st Airborne Division. The two new parachute regiments assigned to the 82nd were the 504th and 505th.

Early in July 1942 the 505th Parachute Infantry Regiment was activated at Fort Benning, Georgia. I was assigned as its first commanding officer. Its training program was just about as tough and demanding as we could make it. The troopers responded well. However, despite the rigors of their training, they always seemed to have enough energy left to get into fights in Phenix City, Alabama, and its environs during time off.

One particular incident I remember well involved a roadside inn called Cotton Fish Camp. It seems a trooper had been mistreated at the inn. The following night several squads of troopers from the 505th Parachute Infantry decided to take over the place. They deployed some distance away in a skirmish line in good combat style and began to close in on the roadhouse. Rumor of their intentions had preceded them, however, and as they got close to the inn they found themselves confronted by the State Police. They were all promptly arrested. The following morning twenty-seven of them were in the main Post guard house at Fort Benning. To me, a young regimental commander, that was a disastrous turn of events. I called on the Provost Marshal in person and assured him that if he would let me take the men out of the guard house I could handle them myself. At first he was somewhat reluctant to sanction such an irregular proposal, but I finally convinced him that the paratroopers were a special kind of soldier, just too full of imagination and ideas, and that I knew how to handle them. I marched them back to camp and that evening took the entire regiment on an all-night march down through the canebrakes in the bottoms of the Chattahoochee River. It was a Saturday night, and we maneuvered one battalion against two through the night. At daylight we were resupplied by parachute. Sunday evening I marched them back to camp. Later in the evening I noticed quite a few of them in dress uniforms, wearing polished boots, on their way to the bus stop to go to Phenix City. Some time later one of them drew a sketch of a campaign ribbon for the battle of Cotton Fish Camp.

Early in 1943—it must have been about February—I had a phone call from Post Headquarters. The Post Commander was anxious to sell a lot of war bonds, and he asked me to send a representative of the regiment to a meeting at Post Headquarters. I sent Captain Barney Oldfield, the Public Relations Officer of the 505th. He had worked for *Variety* and had had extensive public relations experience. At the meeting it was announced that the Post Commander wanted to have an Easter Sunday breakfast during which they would try to sell war bonds to those attending. Persuading soldiers to come to a breakfast at which they would be urged to buy war bonds was not a very promising project, but there it was.

Evidently the meeting droned on for some time inconclusively before Oldfield announced that he had an idea. He said that he knew Gypsy Rose Lee, who was then appearing in *Star and Garter* in New York, and that he would be happy to telephone her and ask her to come to Fort Benning after the Saturday night performance. She had no show on Sunday. He suggested that they have the breakfast in the Post gym because they were sure to get a lot of people there. Before she appeared on stage, they would have her take off her clothes, and they would then cover her from top to bottom with war bonds, the higher-priced bonds being strategically placed on her anatomy. Members of the audience would then be asked to bid on the bonds, and as they bought them, they would be removed from her body.

Everyone was enthusiastic about the idea. Barney Oldfield called Gypsy Rose Lee, and she accepted the invitation. The word spread around the Post like wildfire, and it was doubtful that the gymnasium would be able to hold the crowd that would certainly be there. All went well until about a week before the affair, when the Post Commander got wind of it. "What is this?" he demanded. "A strip-tease artist attending an Easter morning breakfast in the Post gym?" He stopped it at once. It fell to Oldfield to call Gypsy Rose Lee and explain that they were withdrawing the invitation. She seemed to understand. Oldfield told me later, "I just went off and got under a flat rock." But that was not our last brouhaha with Post Headquarters at Fort Benning.

Not long after this I received a complaint from the Office of the Post Commander. The Regimental Adjutant of the 505th came into my office and told me that one of our troopers had been arrested for having sexual intercourse with a young lady on the lawn of the courthouse in Phenix City. The Regimental Adjutant was asked by Post Headquarters, "What is he going to do about it?"—meaning me. "Well," I replied, "in view of the fact that that young man will be asked to give his life for his country in the next few months, I suggest we give him a medal." I heard nothing further of it.

One of our sister divisions at Fort Benning was the 2nd Armored, commanded by General George Patton. It was a fine division with high unit pride. Inevitably small collisions occurred in the bars and fleshpots of Phenix City, but many friendships were made, and later we were glad to see one another in Sicily.

Meanwhile, visitors came and went. Among the first to visit us was General Frederick M. ("Boy") Browning. He was the senior British airborne officer, a dapper, handsome, charming man, who in combat turned out to be a first-class soldier in every respect. His visit was followed by that of Secretary of War Henry L. Stimson, and later, Chief of Staff George C. Marshall and Winston Churchill, who were visiting Fort Jackson, South Carolina. We were told that the Chief of Staff wanted all the visitors in the stands, including, of course, Churchill and Marshall, to be given walkie-talkies with which they would hear the commands being given by the jumpmasters in the airplanes at the time of the drop. The air armada had to take off from Pope Field at Fort Bragg, North Carolina, about 120 miles north of Fort Jackson, approximately two hours ahead of the arrival of the distinguished visitors. The level of training would permit aircraft to fly only in a V of threes, each V following the other in tandem, making an air column about 75 miles long, with considerable confusion at the tail end caused by changes in behavior of the aircraft up front. To put this column into the air in such form as to have it arrive precisely over the drop zone, allowing for wind conditions both en route and during the drop, was a rather chancy business. But it turned out well and the visitors seemed pleased.

The one thing that couldn't be done was to provide radios on the same frequency and with the ability to pick up the jumpmasters' commands. We spent most of the night before the demonstration experimenting with numerous radios both in the airplane and on the ground, and their performance simply wasn't up to what was required. We checked back with the War Department, and they insisted that the Chief of Staff had seen such a thing done at Fort Benning a month or two before and he wanted a repeat performance. We checked the Airborne School at Fort Benning; they knew nothing about it. We finally settled on having a trooper concealed in the woods on the far side of the drop zone; as he saw the first man jump, he gave the proper commands.

The jump was a dramatic affair. The field the troopers were to land on was small, about the size of a football field, and it was hard-packed clay. Along one side were bleachers in which sat Prime Minister Churchill, General Marshall, Field Marshal Sir John Dill, and a number of junior officers. As the long air armada could be seen approaching over the horizon at a low altitude, one could feel the tension and excitement. The first three planes came over the field; troopers tumbled out of them and landed right in front of the audience. In fact, I was a bit concerned that some of them might land in the stands. They quickly recovered the bundles containing their machine guns, mortars, and demolitions, threw these weapons over their shoulders, and ran by the stands to occupy combat positions off the field. It was obvious to everyone that the troopers themselves were in a high state of excitement, and the feeling transmitted itself at once to everyone present. When one planeload dropped about half a mile short of the drop zone, the announcer simply dismissed it as a patrol that was following the prepared plan. It was the most successful drop, both in size and accuracy, we had ever made. The Prime Minister and his party seemed pleased with what they had seen.

The 505th Parachute Regiment had moved to Fort Bragg on March 9, 1943, and there had joined the 82nd Airborne Division. Although our training had been intense and the troops were in fine physical condition, the regiment was far from ready for combat. A short time after our arrival at Fort Bragg we had a visitor from the United Kingdom, Sir Anthony Eden. After he inspected a 505th Honor Guard, he looked directly into my eyes, grasped my hand, and said with a slight touch of emotion, "Good luck." As fleeting as the moment was, I have never known another exactly like it. He knew something that I didn't know, and it scared me just a bit and made the moment one I would never forget. He knew that we, green as we were, in four months' time would take on the battle-seasoned Wehrmacht by spearheading the assault onto the island of Sicily.

The 82nd Airborne Division departed from Fort Bragg in late April 1943. After an uneventful Atlantic crossing it was off Casablanca on May 10, and the first man stepped ashore at 3:15 P.M. The division moved to a staging area north of the city, where it remained for three days. That was followed by a move by truck and rail to Oujda in western Algeria, near the Spanish Moroccan border. This move also was uneventful, except for some complaints from Eisenhower's headquarters that the troops had been shooting insulators off the telephone lines that paralleled the railroad tracks, thus interfering with the communications of the higher headquarters. We arrived in Oujda on schedule, pitched a tent camp, and settled down to two months of intensive training preparatory to parachuting into Sicily.

A day or so after our arrival, General Matthew Ridgway, the Division Commander of the 82nd Airborne Division, told me that we were to parachute into Sicily on the night of July 9. Since there was sufficient airlift for only one reinforced regimental combat team, he had decided to give the mission to the 505th Parachute Infantry. It would have with it the 456th Parachute Artillery Battalion, the 3rd Battalion of the 504th Parachute Infantry, and B Company of the 307th Airborne Engineers. The landing was to be made under a full moon, close to midnight. I have always remembered looking at the moon that night as it rose, knowing that the second time it was full we would jump into combat. Even today I never see a full moon rise without thinking of its combat meaning. A few weeks later arrangements were made for me to fly to Malta and there join an R.A.F. fighter pilot on a reconnaissance of the drop zones, on the night of June 9, one month before D-day. Knowing the exact date of our mission gave a tremendous stimulation to our desire to train, but we soon learned that there was little time available for training.

The division was placed under the command of General Mark Clark's Fifth Army, with headquarters in Oujda. A division review was held for him on May 19. On May 26 I had my first meeting with General George Patton, under whose command our regimental combat team would be in Sicily. Patton commanded the U.S. Seventh Army. I also visited the staff of the 1st Infantry Division, the division that we were to join when contact was made after the landing. On May 27 General Ridgway and I visited General Bradley's II Corps headquarters in Relizane. Concurrently with this necessary travel and with training, intensive studies were being made of the enemy dispositions on the island.

I met with General Terry Allen and the staff of the 1st Infantry Division on June 6 for a final briefing. Having spent years learning how to issue an appropriate battle order, I was looking forward to hearing the seasoned and legendary Terry Allen tell us what to do. When his staff got through explaining what was expected of us, he concluded by saying, "I don't want any God-damned bellyaching. I want you to do your job and let me know what you are doing." So much for the five-paragraph field order.

The high command was concerned about the attitude of the Spanish in Morocco, so in early June a division review was staged for Lieutenant

General Luis Orgaz, High Commissioner in Spanish Morocco. Among others present were General Auguste Nogues of French Morocco and Major General Francisco Delgado Serrano of Spanish Morocco. A final review was held on June 16, and it was for General Dwight D. Eisenhower. A veteran, Lieutenant John McNally, who participated in that review as a sergeant and then went on to live through all our battles as a parachutist, wrote about the review: "There was no cheering crowd, no waving handkerchiefs, just the Division, almost lost in the empty expanse. It was our greatest moment. Sometimes I think that the men who marched there for the last time that day are the real winners, with this, their brief, bittersweet moment of glory."

But the event that all of us remembered best was the send-off talk given us by General Patton. His talks on such occasions were usually quite good, earthy, and I was impressed. One thing he said always stuck with me, for it was contrary to what I had believed up to that moment, but when I had been in combat only a short while, I knew he was right. Speaking to all of us late one afternoon as we assembled in the North African sunset, he said, "Now, I want you to remember that no sonuvabitch ever won a war by dying for his country. He won it by making the other poor dumb sonuvabitch die for his country."

Patton went on to discuss the tactics that we should employ in fighting the Germans and the Italians, stressing the Italians. The point that he wanted to make was that we should avoid a direct assault on an enemy position but seek to envelop his flanks. However, in doing so, the General used terms applicable to sexual relations. He did so in a very clever manner, emphasizing the point that when one arrived in the rear of one of their positions, the Italians would invariably quickly try to switch to a new position to protect themselves, and at that moment would become vulnerable to our attack from the rear. It was not so much what he said as how he said it that caused us to remember the points he wanted to make—though I did feel somewhat embarrassed at times, and I sensed that some of the troops felt a bit embarrassed, too. Ladislas Farago in his book *Patton: Ordeal and Triumph* describes the reaction of the troops to Patton's talks. "They laughed at the elaborate pornography of his pep talks, but also blushed." Yet the General made his points, and the troops remembered them as much for the very language he used as for their content.

In order to understand the battle of Sicily, one should know the chain of events that led to this moment in history. It is important to understand the personalities involved as well. For this was the beginning of combined American-British amphibious-airborne operations, and the lessons learned were to be applied to the combined arms battles that were to follow. In addition, the personalities of the participants were to play a role as important to the outcome of the war as the troops and their weapons—and perhaps even more important.

The Americans had landed in northwest Africa in November 1942. French North Africa was a pawn in the struggle between the Vichy government and the Allies. Since the British were not acceptable and would be opposed by the French if they attempted to land, it was the Americans who made the initial landings under the command of Lieutenant General Dwight D. Eisenhower. Thereafter, they were reinforced by the British. The troops were consolidated into an army under the command of British General Sir Kenneth A. N. Anderson, and the advance began toward Tunisia. It had been anticipated that they would coordinate their advance with that of Field Marshal Sir Bernard Law Montgomery, who was driving Field Marshal Erwin Rommel ahead of him in North Africa. Eisenhower hoped to seize the port city of Tunis and thus deny that facility to Rommel and the Afrika Korps.

But the Germans appreciated its importance. They improvised a defense as rapidly as they could. Field Marshal Albert Kesselring visited Tunis on November 28, 1942, and issued detailed instructions for its defense. Newly arrived German troops were thrown into the breach, and when the Allies, their supply lines overextended and adequate air support lacking, finally collided with the Germans, heavy fighting ensued. Eisenhower's early optimism began to wane, and he reported on December 3, "We have gone beyond the sustainable limit of air capabilities in supporting ground forces in a pell-mell race for Tunisia." From then on, the battle continued spasmodically up and down the Tunisian front until Rommel intervened with a major attack against the Americans at Kasserine Pass. Here the Americans suffered a serious setback, following which the Commander of the American II Corps, Major General Lloyd R. Fredendall, was relieved of command. Although his removal was justified on what were considered to be valid grounds, the fact is that many American officers thought he had been sacrificed to the whims of the senior British general, General Alexander. Fredendall had wanted to have the American units employed intact, but he found himself having to provide battalions that were shuttled about to satisfy Alexander's apprehensions, which were all too often based on faulty intelligence. His removal seemed to be a small incident at the time, just one of the numerous reliefs from command regarded as inevitable in the American involvement in the war. Nevertheless, when I dealt with the staff of the U.S. II Corps later, there was widespread resentment over the attitude of the British.

The moment the U.S. II Corps had been committed in Tunisia, Patton was desirous of leading it against Rommel. Commander Harry Butcher, Eisenhower's aide, reported Patton as having said to him, "I cried my heart out when Ike gave the job to Lloyd Fredendall, and besides, those mealy-mouthed limies couldn't have pushed me around. I would have stood up to that sonuvabitch Anderson."[1] Actually, Patton was to be given command of II Corps—he assumed command at 10:00 A.M. on March 6 at a time when the Corps was already engaged in battle. It was not long before he had a confrontation with the British. The Luftwaffe had operated seemingly at will over the heavily engaged U.S. II Corps, and in early April Patton complained about it. Air Vice Marshal Sir Arthur Coningham responded to Patton's complaint with the message, "It can only be assumed that II Corps personnel concerned are not battleworthy in terms of present operations." This was infuriating to Patton, as it would be to any combat commander, and it was insulting as well. Patton did not hesitate to say so. Coningham asked that his message be withdrawn and canceled, but this did not satisfy Patton. Coningham made a personal call on him to express his regrets, and in response Patton politely wrote a "My dear Coningham" note that seemed to settle the matter, but instances of this sort had a cumulative and lasting effect.

In the midst of all this, early in 1943 the Combined Chiefs of Staff in London decided on a plan for the invasion of Sicily. Recognizing the need for a major port for each army, it assigned, as a combat objective, the port facilities of Palermo to the United States Seventh Army, and it was in that area that they were to make a landing. The British Eighth Army was given the mission of seizing the port of Siracusa. The ultimate objective of the amphibious attack was to seize Messina at the northeast

---

[1] Ladislas Farago, *Patton: Ordeal and Triumph.* New York: Ivan Obolensky, Inc., 1964.

corner of the triangular island, thus cutting off the German and Italian forces from the mainland.

The commanding generals, Patton of the United States Seventh and Montgomery of the British Eighth, who were to carry out this plan, did not participate in the planning, and when they first heard of its details, they had strong complaints to make. Field Marshal Montgomery first complained of a lack of information about the plan in April. As he learned of the plan he became very much disturbed, and at a meeting in Algiers on May 22 he outlined his ideas for a plan he believed could be carried out successfully. In his presentation he stated, "The areas selected for the landings must be inside fighter cover, a good port must be seized quickly, good airfields must be secured for the air force." The seizure of a port was particularly important, and he added: "You have no port, and the total force could not be maintained for long only through the beaches." This seemed eminently sound; however, to obtain adequate airfields he would have had to spread his army on considerable frontage from Siracusa toward Gela. This he refused to do because, in his opinion, it involved too great a tactical risk. The first suggestion, therefore, was that a U.S. division, the battle-experienced U.S. 9th Infantry Division, be taken from General Patton's Seventh Army and assigned to Field Marshal Montgomery's Eighth Army. One could imagine how well this went down with the American staffs.

Out of all these discussions, which were most complex and at times impassioned, taxing all the diplomatic skill of General Eisenhower, came a plan to abandon the attack on Palermo and launch Patton's Seventh Army on the immediate left flank of the British Eighth Army. Seeking a rationalization of the plan, Field Marshal Alexander, the overall commander, justified it on the grounds that there would probably be good weather in July; thus the seas would not be running too high and the availability of the newly developed two-and-a-half-ton amphibious truck, developed by the Americans, would help solve the Americans' problems. I should add that there was no port of any significant size in the American landing area. Finally, as the official American history described it, "Patton's army would be the shield in Alexander's left hand; Montgomery's army the sword in his right," but to the American staff officers, Patton was thrown ashore without adequate port facilities to provide the left-flank guard for Montgomery, while he did his thing and captured Messina. Some of Patton's associates urged him to protest, but he refused.[2] To him it was an order, and he would do his "Goddamnedest to carry it out."[3]

[2] The presence of the two German Panzer Divisions in Sicily and the denial of this information to the paratroopers were of critical importance. Any inquiry about Germans being on the island was responded to with the statement, "There may be a few German technicians." The intelligence summaries of the North African Theater of Operations, today in the National Archives in Washington, state the same thing. The summaries do not point up the German presence until about D+3 or D+4. However, they worried Montgomery and he knew that they were there, and this was one of the important reasons that he wanted Patton to protect his left flank; thus the American plan to seize Palermo was abandoned.
[3] Samuel Eliot Morison, *History of United States Naval Operations in World War II, Sicily—Salerno—Anzio, January 1943–June 1944*. Boston: Little, Brown and Company, 1954.

Sicily

Sicily, a triangular-shaped island of 9926 square miles of mountainous, inhospitable land, is the steppingstone between Africa and Europe. Too small in size and resources to be an independent nation, yet too large to be ignored, it has played a key role in the affairs of the Western world since the dawn of history. Strategically placed in the narrowest part of the Mediterranean, it has been accurately described as "a palimpsest of history."[1] Greeks, Romans, Carthaginians, Moors, Norsemen, and Spaniards, among others, have all occupied the island during the course of their wars. "Always raped but never loved" was the way one writer described it. The latest invaders had been the Germans, and now we, the Allies, were to be next.

Sicily has always had a way of making history. It has been the arena in which major strategic policies of great powers have been resolved by the outcome of tactical confrontations. The Allies in 1943 were about to undertake a major coalition campaign, the most difficult of all forms of warfare. An American army commanded by an American general was to fight side by side with a British army commanded by a British general, with the over-all campaign planned, administered, and managed by an Allied staff. It was to be the crucible from which would come the tactics, the administrative methods and procedures, and, finally, the personal relationships that would affect the outcome of the entire war.

The generals, from Eisenhower on down, and all the senior staffs, learned their lessons side by side, and it was these lessons that they applied to the problems that confronted them later in the war. And this was important, for it was going to be a war in which, all too frequently, the Allies would be confronted by superior German forces. Never was

[1] M. I. Finley and Dennis Mack-Smith, *A History of Sicily*. New York: The Viking Press, 1968.

the principle of war, "Economy of Means," more important. The Allies had to be particularly skillful in using their inferior numbers in such a way as to maximize the troops and resources available at the decisive time and point of every battle. To move broadly and attack on all fronts was to invite lack of success on any front. On the other hand, to take a calculated risk on a broad front while concentrating the bulk of one's forces for a single decisive battle was in itself risky. But this was the dilemma that constantly confronted the staff planners for the remainder of the war. Inevitably the solutions that they applied reflected the lessons they were about to learn in Sicily.

Sicily had also played a significant role in the German effort in World War II. In support of Rommel's campaigns in North Africa, it had provided an excellent array of air bases. Their numbers increased, and by the time of the Allied assault there were thirty airfields and landing strips in use. Interestingly enough, the growing importance of air power made those very air bases prime targets for attack and seizure by the Allies. Hence, they had to be well defended.

The defense of the island was charged to General Alfredo Guzzoni, Commanding General of the Italian Sixth Army. General Guzzoni had been in retirement for two years, he was sixty-six years of age, and he had never been in Sicily. The Italian component of the defense consisted of twelve divisions, six in fixed coastal defense positions and six mobile divisions. Of the latter, two very good divisions, the Livorno and the Napoli, were in the area of the Allied assault landings. From the outset the Italians alone divined the Allied intentions very well—they were convinced that the landings would take place on the southeastern corner of Sicily. To the Germans, however, the situation seemed to be quite a bit more complex.

The Germans remembered all too well the British Eighth Army sending reinforcements to Greece in the spring of '41. With the Afrika Korps disposed of, wouldn't it be logical for the Eighth Army to return to the Balkans to what Winston Churchill had referred to as "the soft underbelly" of Europe? Furthermore, the command facilities and logistic bases near Cairo would be well placed to support such an undertaking. To lead the Germans to believe that this was exactly what was going to happen, the British devised an elaborate and remarkable hoax.

On April 20, 1943, the British launched the dead body of a "Major Martin" from a submarine less than a mile from the beach at Huelva,

Spain.[2] Attached to his wrist was an attaché case containing a number of sealed envelopes. These in turn contained documents and correspondence to key British personages in Cairo. The correspondence skillfully made clear the British intention of landing in Greece and possibly in Sardinia. The British Naval attaché in Madrid requested the return of the papers from the Spanish Ministry of Marine, and they were returned in time; however, not before the Spaniards had succeeded in extracting and photographing the documents as absolutely genuine. But, in the face of this strong evidence, as though a national intuition in matters such as this were inherited in their genes, the Italians were unconvinced. They still believed that Sicily was the logical and inevitable steppingstone to Italy. On May 14 Admiral Karl Doenitz, having just returned from a meeting with Mussolini, met with Hitler to discuss the Duce's views. He told Hitler that Mussolini expected the landings to take place in Sicily. He recorded the meeting in his diary: "The Fuehrer does not agree with the Duce that the most likely invasion point is Sicily. Furthermore, he believes that the discovered Anglo-Saxon order confirms the assumption that the planned attack will be directed mainly against Sardinia and the Peloponnesus."

So taken by the hoax was Hitler that two weeks *after* the Sicilian landings had taken place he still believed that the main landings were to take place in Greece. Indeed, on July 25 he sent his favorite general, Rommel, to Greece to take command of all German forces there. In the meantime the 1st Panzer Division had been moved all the way from France to the small Greek town of Tripolis, well located to counterattack the landings when they took place. In late May the Naval high command ordered the laying or the completion of three new minefields off Greece. Finally, in early June a whole group of German motor torpedo boats was sent *from* Sicily to the Aegean Sea.

Sardinia and Sicily, however, were another problem. The deception being perpetrated on the Germans and, it was hoped, on the Italians was to cause them to believe there would be a diversionary attack on Sicily. The Allies wanted the Germans to believe that this was a diversion to conceal the main landings that were to take place on Sardinia. There was a certain logic in this as it appeared to the Axis command, for an Allied occupation of Sardinia would place the Allies in close range of

[2] Ewen Montagu, *The Man Who Never Was,* rev. ed. Philadelphia: J. B. Lippincott Co., 1967; J. C. Masterman, *The Double Cross System.* New Haven, Conn.: Yale University Press, 1972.

Rome. Thus, an Allied occupation of Sardinia might place in jeopardy the German formations on Sicily and in Southern Italy, particularly if the Allies were to follow a Sardinian success with a landing near Rome.

To help convince the Germans that this might happen, the Allies hinted at times that that was exactly what they were thinking of doing. I remember on the occasion of my first visit to General Patton's headquarters at Relizane, near the coast of North Africa, seeing a map of Sardinia tacked on the wall just inside the entranceway. His headquarters was in a school surrounding a guarded courtyard. But the map could be seen by civilian workmen within the courtyard passing by the door. I asked about it and was told that it was part of the cover plan. The Germans couldn't afford to ignore Sardinia, but the Italians consistently maintained that Sicily, not Sardinia, was the target. Field Marshal Kesselring visited Sicily in May 1943 to discuss defensive arrangements. He finally reached an agreement to furnish four German divisions. Only two were ready at the time of the Allied landings: the 15th Panzer Grenadier Division located in the western part of the island, and the Hermann Goering Division, officially named the Hermann Goering Panzer Fallschirmjaeger Division (The Hermann Goering Armored Parachute Division), part of the German Luftwaffe, which was to establish its headquarters at Caltagirone.

In mid-May a final meeting was held by Field Marshal Kesselring to thrash out the details of the defense of the island with General Guzzoni and subordinate commanders. Kesselring describes its conclusion in his memoirs:

> In my final briefing of the German Divisional Commanders I drummed into their heads one point on which Guzzoni and myself saw eye to eye.
> "It makes no difference," I told them, "whether or not you get orders from the Italian Army at Enna, you must go into immediate action against the enemy the moment you ascertain the objective of the landing fleet."
> I can still hear General Conrath of the Hermann Goering Panzer Division growl in reply:
> "If you mean to go for them, Field Marshal, then I'm your man."

The Hermann Goering Division had its headquarters in Caltagirone, twenty-five miles east of Gela. As fate would have it, many of the American paratroopers were to land between that German division and the amphibious landings on Gela and Scoglitti beaches. The 1st U.S. Infantry Division was to land near Gela, and the 45th Infantry was to land near Scoglitti. The 505th Parachute Infantry was to land scattered across the fronts of both divisions with a concentration in the direction of Gela— not precisely in the manner in which it had planned to land.

In July 1943 the Allies were to be the latest invaders of Sicily, and we, the 505th Parachute Regimental Combat Team, were to spearhead the invasion. The fateful day of July 9, 1943, seemed to rush upon us, so busy were we with last-minute preparations, and almost before we realized it, we were gathered in small groups under the wings of our C-47s ready for loading and take-off. Appearing from a distance every bit like Strasbourg geese, the airplanes were so loaded with parachute bundles suspended beneath them that they seemed to drag the ground. Because of security restrictions, it had not been possible to inform every trooper of our destination until just before take-off. Then each was given a small slip of paper which read:

> Soldiers of the 505th Combat Team
> Tonight you embark upon a combat mission for which our people and the free people of the world have been waiting for two years.
> You will spearhead the landing of an American Force upon the island of SICILY. Every preparation has been made to eliminate the element of chance. You have been given the means to do the job and you are backed by the largest assemblage of air power in the world's history.
> The eyes of the world are upon you. The hopes and prayers of every American go with you. . . .
>
> James M. Gavin

The plan was simple. (*Figs. 1, 2.*) Taking off from Tunisia in a long column of aircraft, we were to fly via the island of Linosa to Malta. There we were to dogleg to the left, coming in on Sicily's southwestern shore. This was an important point—the island was to come into sight on the right side of the approaching aircraft. The orders were that every man would jump even though there might be some uncertainty in his mind as to his whereabouts. No one but the pilots and crews were to return to North Africa.

Individual equipment was given a final check, and loading began. The equipment consisted of a rifle or carbine, rations, water, knife,

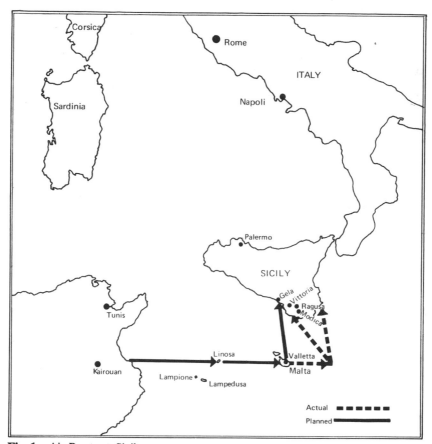

Fig. 1   Air Route to Sicily

grenades, compass, and here and there a bazooka. The bazookas were most important, since they were the only weapons the troopers were carrying that would enable them to engage the German armor on reasonable terms. The pilots were revving up their engines and we were ready to roll down the runway when an airman from the weather station ran up to the door of the plane yelling for me. "Colonel Gavin, is Colonel Gavin here?" "Here I am," I answered, and he yelled, "I was told to tell you that the wind is going to be thirty-five miles an hour, west to east." He added, "They thought you'd want to know."

Well, I did, but there was nothing I could do about it. Training jumps had normally been canceled when the wind reached about fifteen

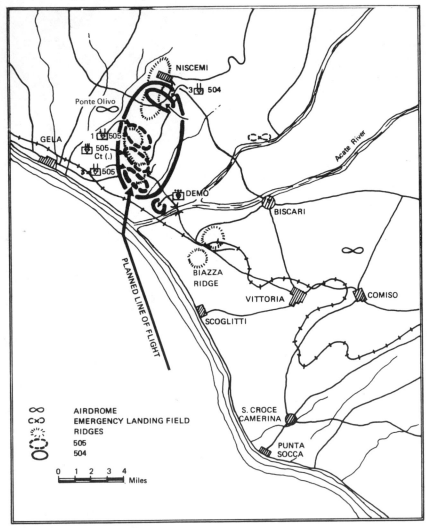

Fig. 2   Attack Plan, Sicily

miles an hour, in order for us to minimize injuries. Few of us had ever jumped with winds more than twenty-five miles an hour. But we couldn't change plans now. Besides, there were many other hazards of greater danger in prospect than the thirty-five-mile-an-hour wind.

At about this time in my troubled thinking another individual

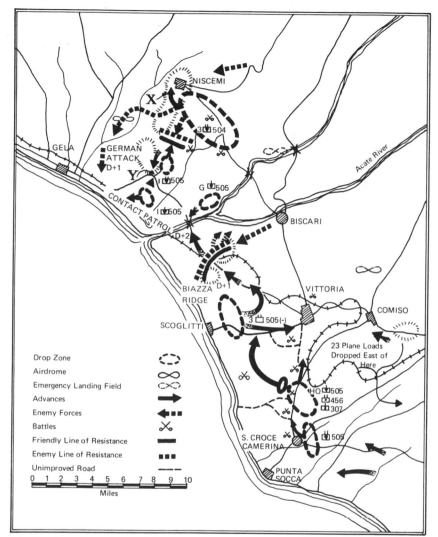

Fig. 3   Actual Landings, Sicily

staggered to the door of the plane with a huge barracks bag on his
shoulder. He heaved it through the door onto the floor of the plane,
saying as he did so, "I was told to give this to you or your S-1." (S-1,
personnel officer, is responsible for the administrative handling of
prisoners.)

I asked, "What in the hell is it?"

He replied, "They are prisoner-of-war tags. You're supposed to put one on every prisoner you capture, and be sure to fill it out properly."

This was no time for argument, when we were within seconds of roaring down the runway, so I merely replied, "O.K."

About an hour after departure the personnel officer, Captain Alfred W. Ireland, threw them into the Mediterranean.

Due to the high winds, the entire air armada was blown far east of its intended landing zones. (*Fig. 3.*) Some pilots made landfall along the eastern coast of Sicily and, having done so, turned back to find their way around to the southwest coast. Several planeloads actually jumped in front of the British Army. The troopers were from the 3rd Battalion and Regimental Headquarters. The first problem they encountered, to their surprise, was that the British had a different countersign. The American countersign was "George Marshall"—that is, when one met an unknown person that night, one was supposed to challenge by saying "George." The response from a friend was expected to be "Marshall." Otherwise, a shooting engagement took place. To the dismay of the American paratroopers, they found that "George" was greeted by a fusillade of fire. One big, burly, redheaded Irishman, well over six feet tall, in the Regimental Demolitions Platoon, talked to me about his experiences afterward. When first challenged, he was shot at, so he decided to hide and to grab any British soldier he could get close to and explain his predicament. Soon a British soldier came by. He jumped out and pinned his arms to his sides and told him who he was. Thus, he learned the British countersign and survived. That detachment fought side by side with the British for several days, but was finally put aboard a boat and sent to the American landing beaches near Gela.

The 2nd Battalion, commanded by Major Mark Alexander, was the next farthest to the east to land. It landed about fifteen miles east of Gela, near the town of S. Croce Camerina, a town that figures prominently in Thucydides' account of the Peloponnesian Wars. As Major Alexander's plane was crossing the Mediterranean, he stood at the door and watched its progress, looking for familiar landmarks. The red warning light to be ready to jump came on, and his troopers stood up and readied themselves. Suddenly, while they were still over the ocean, the green light came on. The men tried to push him out the door, but he succeeded in fighting them off. He then went forward to ask the pilot, "What in the hell are you doing?" The pilot replied, "The co-pilot was in too much of a hurry." They continued a bit farther, crossed the coast, receiving considerable tracer fire, and the battalion jumped.

Although they landed amid a number of huge pillboxes and areas organized for defense, they were quite successful in reorganizing the battalion. The Italian pillboxes were formidable affairs, several stories high, with apertures here and there, and so sited as to overlook other pillboxes. The troopers quickly learned that the way to reduce them was to keep firing at the slits until a trooper could get close enough to throw a grenade into them. The battalion fought most of the night and by daylight had assembled a majority of its men. It then moved toward the coast near a village overlooking the town of Marina di Ragusa, and they organized an all-around defense for the night.

In the meantime they began to receive machine-gun and sniper fire from high ground near where they had been earlier. A British cruiser showed up off the coast, and Mark Alexander found that he had a lieutenant who could use a flashlight and communicate with the cruiser, using the Morse code. They requested fire support on the slope to the north of their positions. As Mark Alexander reported it later, "The cruiser immediately laid in two salvos. The first must have come in about seventy-five feet over our heads, and you can believe me when I say that the whole slope went up in flames. I called for a cease-fire, and we received no more harassment from snipers the rest of the night." At daylight, July 11, his battalion turned north and moved in the direction of S. Croce Camerina, using donkeys, donkey carts, wheelbarrows to help carry the weapons and ammunition. At noon his battalion captured S. Croce Camerina and later that afternoon captured Vittoria. They rejoined the 82nd Airborne Division on July 12. In the meantime those of us who had landed closer to the target areas had been having a busy time of it.

My own flight with the Regimental Headquarters group was uneventful until Linosa was due. It was not to be seen. Malta, which was to be well lighted to assist our navigators, could not be seen either. Suddenly ships by the score became visible in the ocean below, all knifing their way toward Sicily. Obviously, we were off course, since our plan called for us to fly between the American fleet on the left and the British on the right. In fact, the Americans told us that we would probably be shot down if we flew over them. We continued on, finally dog-legging to the left on the basis of time calculation. Soon the flash of gunfire could be seen through the dust and haze caused by the preinvasion bombing, and finally the coast itself could be seen off to the right. Unfortunately, many of the planes overflew the Malta dogleg, and the island first became visible on the left, thus causing confusion and widespread dispersion of the troopers.

We turned inland; the small-arms fire increased; the green light over the jump door went on, and out we went. The reception was mixed. Some of us met heavy fighting at once, others were unopposed for some time, but all were shaken up by the heavy landings on trees, buildings, and rocky hillsides.

I managed to get together a small group and start across country, searching for the combat team objective. I had with me Captain Al Ireland, the combat team personnel officer, and Captain Ben Vandervoort, the combat team operations officer, and three other troopers. The cross-country going was rough, but we pressed on. Soon we came face to face with our first enemy.

It happened about an hour after we had landed. I was moving ahead with about twenty troopers. I was leading, and Vandervoort was alongside. I had been picking up troopers as I moved along through the shadows in the olive groves, over stone walls, darting across moonlit roads, going in what I hoped was the direction of our objective. There had been occasional bursts of small-arms fire, sometimes quite close, but so far we had not seen an actual enemy. Suddenly there were foreign voices, then the sound of a man whistling some distance away. As he got closer, it sounded like "O Sole Mio." I had my group stay down, and I moved up to a stone wall that paralleled the road he was coming along. It was a lone man, walking down the middle of the road, hands in the pockets of his baggy uniform pants. After twenty years of military service I was about to meet The Enemy face to face. I stuck my head up over the stone wall. It seemed a long way up, but it was about an inch, just enough to clear my carbine over the top of the wall.

I gave him my best Italian, *"Alto."* He stopped in his tracks. Vandervoort rushed through an opening in the wall with a .45 in one hand and a knife in the other.

"I'll take care of him," Van said. I wasn't sure what he meant, but I said, "No, let's get the hell out of the middle of the road. Let's get over into the shadows and maybe we can get some information out of him."

There was still some doubt as to whether we were in Sicily, Italy, or the Balkans, although the odds strongly favored the first.

About half a dozen of us surrounded him, and I tried the few Italian words I knew.

"Dove Palermo?"

No reply. He seemed too scared or too bewildered to answer.

"Dove Siracusa?"

I figured that if he would point in the general direction of either or both of these two cities, which were at opposite ends of the island, we could get our first fix on where we were. Since he acted as if he had never heard of either, for a moment it seemed that perhaps we were not even in Sicily. But he was obviously very scared. We had heard that the Germans had scared the wits out of the natives with their stories about the atrocities committed by American parachutists. They spread the news that we were long-term convicts who had been granted our freedom in exchange for becoming paratroopers. This was given credence by the practice in many parachute units of having all the men shave their heads. After the battle of Sicily was over, the Sicilians told us the shaved heads were one of the things that had convinced them that the Germans were right.

But to get back to Giuseppe, or whatever his name was, I hadn't been able to get anything out of him—neither his name, where he was from, nor where he thought we were. I reluctantly decided that we would have to take him along. Vandervoort had taken an intelligence course and knew how to handle a prisoner in a situation like this. The idea was to take the belt out of the prisoner's trousers and to cut the buttons off his fly so that he would have to hold up his trousers when he walked.

Van put his .45 in its holster, pressed his knife against the Italian's chest, and said, "I'll take care of the bastard."

The Italian was muttering, *"Mamma mia, Mamma mia,"* over and over again. His concern was understandable. The moonlight was shining on the knife blade, and it looked as though it were a foot long. He took off his belt and dropped it. Then Van went into Phase Two of the operation and reached for his fly with one hand, bringing the knife down with the other.

A scream went up that could be heard all the way to Rome. The atrocities of the paratroopers and the stories the Italian had heard about Ethiopia must have flashed through his mind; he was being castrated. He screamed louder, grabbing the knife blade with his right hand. The blood ran down his hand as we fell in a kicking, yelling, fighting mass, and he got away. I do not know how he did it, but one second he was with us and the next he was gone. I was madder than hell. I asked Vandervoort, "What in the hell did you think you were doing?"

Vandervoort didn't answer. I decided that we had better get going. By now we had probably alerted any enemy for miles around.

We crawled into the night. Although some men were suffering from jump injuries, they drove themselves toward the cascading flame and white phosphorus of bursting shells that could be seen on the distant horizon. The sight of the shellbursts was reassuring, since it meant that we were in Sicily. That is where the battle was to be fought. And we were "moving toward the sound of the guns," one of the first battle axioms I had learned as a cadet at West Point.

But human flesh could do only so much, and the night was demanding. By count at daylight there were six of us. I approached two farmhouses, but at both of them the natives were terrified and would hardly talk. I continued on in a direction I figured would take us toward our objective. Suddenly, as we came over the crest of high ground, there was a burst of small-arms fire.

We hit the ground. There was a sickening thud of near misses kicking dirt into my face. I reacted instinctively as I had been taught in the infiltration course by hugging closely to the ground. In no time I realized that I would not continue to live doing that; I had to shoot back. I started firing with my carbine, and it jammed. I looked to Vandervoort about six feet to my left; he was having the same trouble. About fifty yards away an officer stood looking at us through low-hanging branches of an olive tree. He was wearing leather puttees and reddish-brown breeches, both plainly visible beneath the branches. Captain Ireland gave him the first squirt of his tommy gun, and he went down like a rag doll. I began to fire my carbine singleshot. The leading trooper, who had gone down at the first fusillade, writhed and rolled over. He appeared to be dead, practically in the enemy position. Their fire increased, and there was a loud explosion like that of a small mortar shell. I decided that there was at least a platoon of enemy and that our best prospects were to try to work around it. I yelled to Vandervoort, Ireland, and the troopers to start moving back while I covered. It worked.

We had a close call and nothing to show for it but casualties, and our prospects were not very bright. I continued to move cross-country in a direction that would take me around the area where we had had the fire fight. We could hear intense firing from time to time, and we were never sure when we would walk into another fire fight or how we would get into the fight since we couldn't tell friend from foe. Then there was the problem of enemy armor. I decided to look for a place where tanks would be unlikely to travel and where we could get good cover to hole up until dark. I wanted to survive until dark and then strike across country again to the combat team objective. It was the high ground east and north of Gela, and there, with the help of God, I hoped to find troopers, and an enemy to fight. For that is what I had come three thousand miles and thirty-six years of my life for—the moral and physical challenge of battle.

At midmorning we came to the place. It was crisscrossed by several irrigation ditches. Along one of them was a thicket of underbrush. The ditch was cut out of the side of a gently sloping hill, and from its edge there was a good view for about half a mile across cultivated land. The ditch I picked was almost dry; the others had a lot of water in them. It did not appear to be a place where a tank would travel by choice. I took stock of the situation, and it wasn't good. Among us we had two carbines that jammed, one tommy gun, a pistol, and an M-1. We were holed up like hunted animals. Tired, wounded, hungry, but too sick at heart to eat, we apprehensively scanned the countryside for any sign of friend or foe. Occasional bursts of rifle and machine-gun fire could be heard in the distance.

It had been a long day. We waited and waited for the setting sun. Soon the Sicilian sun was low in the sky and quickly disappeared like a ball of fire into a cauldron. We began to get things together so as to be able to move out. Water was a first need; it was almost gone. For food we had a few cartons of K rations and some concentrated things in an escape kit. An escape kit was a small plastic box, about six inches square and an inch thick, that contained the essentials for escape and survival behind enemy lines. I felt I had been a failure on my first day in combat and had accomplished nothing. I was determined to find my regiment and engage the enemy, wherever he might be. We went into the Sicilian night, heading for what we hoped was Gela, somewhere to the west. It was a relief to be moving instead of sitting and worrying. Sitting and worrying had been the hardest of all, and I had done a lot of it.

After about an hour we were challenged by a small group of wounded and injured of the 505th under the command of Lieutenant Al Kronheim. We traded morphine Syrettes for their M-1 rifles and ammunition and continued to the west. About 2:30 we were challenged by a machine-gun post of the 45th Division, and at last we had re-entered our own lines. We learned that we were about five miles southwest of Vittoria. In about another mile we came to the main paved road from the beach to Vittoria, passing by a number of foxholes and dead Italian soldiers. By then I had about eight troopers with me. We heard the sound of armor coming and at once got off the road and concealed ourselves on both sides. I cautioned the troopers not to fire if it was a friendly tank. Everybody was so excited, however, that when the first tank appeared, there was a fusillade; it seemed as though everyone fired on it. It was an American tank, fortunately buttoned up, and no one was hurt.

We then went on to the edge of Vittoria, where I was able to borrow a jeep. I had heard rumors that there were more paratroopers a few miles away in the direction of Gela. I continued on toward Gela and to my surprise came across the 3rd Battalion of the 505th, in foxholes in a tomato field and just awakening. The battalion commander, Lieutenant Colonel Edward Krause, whose nickname was "Cannonball," was sitting on the edge of a foxhole, dangling his feet. I asked him what his battalion was doing. He said that he had been reorganizing the battalion and that he had about two hundred and fifty troopers present. He had landed nearby and had rounded everybody up. I asked him about his objective, several miles to the west near Gela, and he said that he had not done anything about it. I said we would move at once toward Gela and told him to get the battalion on its feet and going. In the meantime I took a platoon of the 307th Engineers, commanded by Lieutenant Ben L. Wechsler. Colonel Krause said that there were supposed to be Germans between where he was and Gela and that the 45th Division had been having a difficult time.

Using the platoon of Engineers as infantry, we moved at once on the road toward Gela. We had hardly started when, as we went around a bend in the road, a German motorcycle with an officer in the sidecar drove up in the midst of us. We put our guns on him. He threw up his hands, said he was a medical officer, pointed to his insignia, and told us he wanted to be released at once. We weren't about to release him. He was the first live German we had ever seen in combat, and we noticed that he had grenades in the sidecar. Reasoning that an armed medic should not be let loose, we took the motorcycle and sidecar from him and started him to the rear on foot, disarming the driver also. The medic said they had been moving down from Biscari toward Vittoria. We could hear a great deal of firing, so we continued.

By then it was broad daylight, about 8:30 A.M. In less than a mile we reached a point where a small railroad crossed the road. On the right was a house where the gatekeeper lived. There was a striped pole that could be lowered to signal the automotive and donkey-cart traffic when a train approached. Just ahead was a ridge, about half a mile away and perhaps a hundred feet high. The slope to the top was gradual. On both sides of the road were olive trees and beneath them tall brown and yellow grass, burnt by the hot Sicilian summer sun. The firing from the ridge increased. I told Lieutenant Wechsler to deploy his platoon on the right and to move on to seize the ridge. In the meantime I sent word to Cannonball to bring his battalion up as promptly as he could.

We moved forward. I was with Wechsler, and in a few hundred yards the fire became intense. As we neared the top of the ridge, there was a rain of leaves and branches as bullets tore through the trees, and there was a buzzing like the sound of swarms of bees. A few moments later Wechsler was hit and fell. Some troopers were hit; others continued to crawl forward. Soon we were pinned down by heavy small-arms fire, but so far nothing else.

I made my way back to the railroad crossing, and in about twenty minutes Major William Hagen joined me. He was the Battalion Executive for the 3rd Battalion. He said the battalion was coming up. I asked where Cannonball was, and he said that he had gone back to the 45th Division to tell them what was going on. I ordered Hagen to have the troops drop their packs and get ready to attack the Germans on the ridge as soon as they came up. By that time we had picked up a platoon of the 45th Division that happened to be there, part of a company from the 180th Infantry. There was also a sailor or two who had come ashore in the amphibious landings. We grabbed them also.

The attack went off as planned, and the infantry reached the top of the ridge and continued to attack down the far side. As they went over the top of the ridge, the fire became intense. We were going to have a very serious situation on our hands. This was not a patrol or a platoon action. Mortar and artillery fire began to fall on the ridge, and there was considerable machine-gun fire. I was worried about being enveloped on the right; some of the 45th Infantry Division should have been down on the left toward the beaches, but the right was wide open, and so far I had no one I could send out to protect that flank. If the German column was coming from Biscari, the tactical logic would have suggested that they bypass me on the right and attack me from the rear. At that time I had a few engineers I kept in reserve, and two 81 mm. mortars. They were commanded by a young officer, Lieutenant Robert May, who had been my 1st sergeant almost a year earlier when I had commanded C Company of the 503rd Parachute Infantry. He sent two or three troopers off to the right as a security patrol. Later a Mountain Pack 75 mm. artillery piece from the 456th Parachute Artillery joined me, then another. Occasionally troopers, having heard where we were, would come in from the direction of Vittoria. I began to try to dig in on the back of the crest of the ridge. The ground was hard shale, and I made little headway. The entrenching shovel was too frail, so I used my helmet to dig; it wasn't much better. But we needed protection from the mortar fire that was becoming quite heavy, and I kept digging.

The first wounded began to crawl back over the ridge. They all told the same story. They fired their bazookas at the front plate of German tanks, and then the tanks swiveled their huge 88 mm. guns at them and fired at the individual infantrymen. By this time the tanks could be heard, although I could not see any because of the smoke and dust and the cover of vegetation. Hagen came in, walking and holding his thigh, which had been badly torn by fire. Cannonball had gone forward to command the attack. It did not seem to be getting anywhere, however, as the German fire increased in intensity and our wounded were coming back in greater numbers.

The first German prisoners also came back. They said they were from the Hermann Goering Parachute Panzer Division. I remember one of them asking if we had fought the Japanese in the Pacific; he said he asked because the paratroopers had fought so hard. Ahead of us, mixed with the olive trees, were low grapevines that covered men on the ground quite completely. I went back a few hundred yards to check the 81 mm. mortars and to see what other troopers had joined us. A few had. Lieutenant May had been hit by mortar fragments. I talked to the crews of the two Pack 75 mm. artillery pieces and told them we were going to stay on the ridge no matter what happened. We agreed that they should stay concealed and engage the less heavily armored underbellies of the tanks when they first appeared at the top of the rise. It was a dangerous tactic, but the only thing we could do, and tanks are vulnerable in that position. I was determined that if the tanks overran us we would stay and fight the infantry.

I went back to try to dig my foxhole. By then it had become evident that I would never get deep enough, so I decided to dig the front end about eighteen inches and the back end about a foot; then if I sat down in it and put my head between my knees, a tank could roll over me without doing too much damage to me. So I continued from time to time, when circumstances permitted, to try to get farther into the ground.

At the height of the fighting the first German Messerschmitts appeared overhead. To my surprise, they ignored us and attacked the small railroad gatekeeper's house repeatedly. They must have thought that was the Command Post; it was indeed a logical place for it to be. They did not attack any of us near the top of the ridge. A few more troopers were still coming in. Now, added to the enemy small-arms fire, was the tank fire.

A member of the regimental staff who was with me, Captain Al Ireland, suggested that he go back to the 45th Division and get help. It was the best idea I had heard all day. I had been so busy handling the tactical crisis I had on my hands that the possibility had never entered my mind. The mortar fire continued in intensity, and moving along the back of the ridge to check the security on the right and the position of a 75 mm. the troopers were dragging up, I found myself lying on the ground bouncing from the concussion. The best way to protect yourself from the concussion was to place your palms flat on the ground as though you were about to start doing pushups, and thus absorb the shock of the ground jolts.

In front of us, beyond the vineyard and about four hundred yards to the right, was a small group of buildings. Slowly, very slowly, a German tank became visible. We first saw the right track of the tank come around the corner of a stone house. Then we saw the muzzle of the gun. A Tiger tank is an awesome thing to encounter in combat. Weighing more than sixty tons, armed with an 88 mm. gun and machine guns, it was far more formidable than anything we had ever seen, and we had nothing in our own armored forces to compare with it.

The artillery paratroopers decided that they would take a chance and engage it directly with a 75 mm. gun. The 75 was an artillery piece that could be broken down into several loads and packed on mules. It was the only artillery piece the parachutists could get in 1943. No one had ever intended that the 75 would be an antitank gun, certainly not against the front of a Tiger. Nevertheless the paratroopers snaked their gun up the ridge until they were plainly visible and could get a direct line of sight on the tank. Field artillery in the front lines, shades of Gallant Pelham at Fredericksburg. The tank inched forward, the driver probably hoping that we did not see him. It was obvious that his problem was to get far enough out so he could swing the gun at us and then fire directly, but in order to do this he had to get at least half of the tank exposed. It continued to move out, slowly, very slowly. The crew of our 75 mm. were on their knees and lying down, with the gun loaded and ready to fire.

Suddenly there was a tremendous explosion in front of the gun. The tank had fired and hit the ground just in front of the gun, knocking the troopers like tenpins in all directions. I was standing just at the left rear, watching the action, and I was knocked down, too. Probably I hit the ground instinctively. The troopers got up and ran off like startled quail. A second later they realized, to their embarrassment, what they were doing, and they ran back to the gun. They fired one round that hit the tank, or the corner of the building. In the smoke and dust the tank backed out of sight.

That was the last we saw of it. To my amazement, none of the gun crew was hurt. Tanks began to work their way forward off to our left, coming directly up through the vineyard. Although the tank we fired at had backed up, I got the impression that the tank activity was increasing and that we were facing a pretty heavy attack that would come over the ridge at any moment. Back to digging, with little progress.

Two troopers came from my left rear in an Italian track-laying personnel carrier. They were equipped with rifles and wanted to go over the top of the ridge to engage the Germans. I suggested that they not do it, warning them that they would be knocked out, but they insisted they could take care of themselves. They added that they wanted to "scare the Krauts" into thinking that we too had armor.

They had hardly gotten over the top of the ridge when a direct hit exploded the vehicle in flames. All the next day it was still there, smoking, with two skeletons in the front seat, one of them with a direct hit through his body, the trooper on the driver's side. An ambulance that must have been from the 45th Division showed up, and a doctor from the 505th took it over. He drove it over the ridge—he was on the running board. It too was engaged in fire, and he was knocked to the ground.

I had established an aid station with medics who were off to the left, a couple of hundred yards away. They were bandaging casualties and giving them morphine and sulfa. The fire continued in considerable volume into midafternoon. About this time Cannonball came over the ridge and said that all his battalion was killed, wounded, or pinned down and ineffective. I told him we were going to stay at the top of the ridge with what we had and fight the German infantry that came with the tanks. He said that we didn't have a chance, that we'd be finished if we tried to stay there. He went to the rear.

About four o'clock a young ensign, who had parachuted with me the first night, came up with a radio and said he could call for naval gunfire. I was a bit nervous about it, because we didn't know precisely where we were, and to have the Navy shoot at us would only add to the danger and excitement of what was turning out to be quite a day. We tried to fix our position in terms of the railroad crossing over the road, and he called for a trial round. It came down precisely where the tank had disappeared. He then called for a concentration, and from then on the battle seemed to change. I kept thinking of Shiloh, Bloody Shiloh. General Grant, sheltered under the riverbank, his command overrun, refused to leave the field, counterattacked, and the battle was won.

In about an hour I heard that more troopers were coming, and at six o'clock I heard that Lieutenant Harold H. Swingler and quite a few troopers from Regimental Headquarters Company were on the road. Swingler had been a former intercollegiate boxing champion; he was a tough combat soldier. He arrived about seven o'clock. In his wake appeared half a dozen of our own Sherman tanks. All the troopers cheered loud and long; it was a very dramatic moment. The Germans must have heard the cheering, although they did not know then what it was about. They soon found out.

By now no more wounded were coming back. A heavy pall of dust and acrid smoke covered the battlefield. I decided it was time to counterattack. I wanted to destroy the German force in front of us and to recover our dead and wounded. I felt that if I could do this and at the same time secure the ridge, I would be in good shape for whatever came next—probably a German attack against our defenses at daylight, with us having the advantage of holding the ridge. Our attack jumped off on schedule; regimental clerks, cooks, truck drivers, everyone who could carry a rifle or a carbine was in the attack. The Germans reacted, and their fire increased in intensity. Just about two hundred yards from the top of the ridge Swingler crawled up on a cut through which the paved road ran and saw a German Tiger tank with the crew standing outside, looking at it. He dropped a grenade among them and killed them, and thus we captured our first Tiger. There were several bazooka hits on the front plate with holes large enough to put one's little finger into them, but they went in only about an inch or so. The sloped armor on the Tiger was about four and a half inches thick. Soon we overran German machine guns, a couple of trucks, and finally we captured twelve 120 mm. Russian mortars, all in position with their ammunition nearby and aiming stakes out. Apparently the troopers had either killed, captured, or driven off the German crews. The attack continued, and all German resistance disappeared, the Germans having fled from the battlefield. It was quite a few years before I learned the German side of the operation.

Major General Paul Conrath, commanding the Hermann Goering Parachute Panzer Division, was in an excellent position on the night of July 9–10. (*Fig. 4.*) Achieving complete surprise, he had assembled his division in the vicinity of Caltagirone, roughly twenty-five miles from the disembarkation beaches of two U.S. divisions—the 1st U.S. at Gela and the 45th U.S. at Scoglitti. Although he was not aware of it, the 82nd Airborne Division was to land between his division and the amphibious landings. His location appeared to be an ideal one, far enough back to be free of any naval gunfire that might interfere with his launching of his first counterattack, yet close enough to strike swiftly and powerfully once the whereabouts of the Allied landings were determined. If he had known the details of the Allies' plans, he could not have picked a better location to assemble his division. The road net was ideal, and parallel roads went directly toward the beaches, the western road passing through Niscemi and joining the beach road at the bristling Y. The eastern road passed through Biscari, joining the road paralleling the beaches not far from Ponte Dirillo, five miles east of the Y. In anticipation of the landings taking place near Gela, the Axis forces had just completed a map maneuver several days before the actual landings. Unfortunately for the Germans, the 15th Panzer Division played a leading role in the exercises and then was sent off to the western part of the island. One of its tank battalions, the 235th, remained near Caltagirone. As a prudent battle commander should, General Conrath had already made plans for the disposition of his forces in the event of landings on

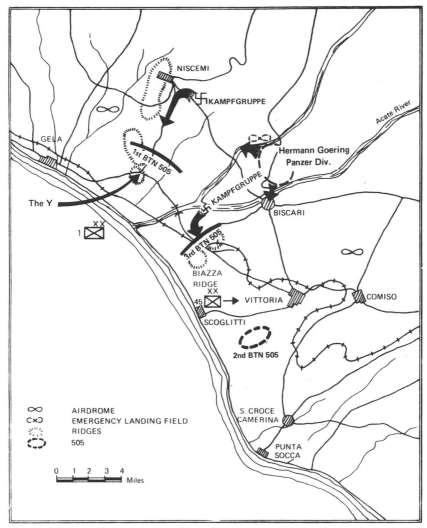

Fig. 4 German Counterattack and Meeting Engagement in Sicily

Gela and Scoglitti beaches. He organized two main battle groups (*Kampfgruppen*). The right battle group was to attack through Niscemi across the Ponte Olivo airfield and over Piano Lupo and drive the Allied forces in that sector into the sea. The left, or eastern, battle group was to move directly toward the beaches and Biazza Ridge via Biscari. That column consisted of:

1st Panzer Grenadier Regiment (2 battalions)
1 armored artillery battalion
1 armored Tiger Tank Company (17 MK VI tanks—60 tons
    mounting 88 mm. guns)

General Conrath got the first information about possible landings from the Axis 6th Army Headquarters. He alerted his command at 10:00 P.M. on July 9 and then decided to jump off without delay. Trouble began at once. Practically all the telephone communications went out. The parachute troops were cutting the wires wherever they found them. As the Office of the Chief of Military History, Washington, D.C., has expressed it in *Axis Tactical Operations in Sicily*: "Since telephone connections were poor to begin with and the Allied paratroopers had cut many of the lines during the night, the units apparently failed to receive any orders." Conrath had no communication with any adjoining Italian commands, such as the Livorno Division on his right, which was most important to him, and none with Corps headquarters.

Not only were his telephone communications badly disrupted, but parachutists began to attack his columns wherever they met. For example, Lieutenant Peter J. Eaton of the 3rd Battalion, 504th Parachute Infantry, had landed two miles northwest of Biscari. His was the battalion that had the mission of blocking the movement of the Germans toward the beaches. Immediately after landing he organized three planeloads, about thirty-six troopers. By daylight more had been gathered up, and he had approximately fifty men. He proceeded toward Niscemi. At noon he encountered two Italian vehicles towing 57 mm. antitank guns. Eaton's men killed the crews and captured the weapons. They then dug themselves in on the Niscemi-Biscari highway, mined the road, and covered it with their newly acquired antitank guns. At 12:30 P.M. a column of troops, approximately a battalion in size, approached, accompanied by a small tank. Eaton's men destroyed the tank and dispersed the enemy troops. Other parachute lieutenants attacked the German column wherever they came in contact with it. As reported in the postwar interrogations, these tank elements stopped in confusion when they were harassed by Allied planes or attacked by paratroopers. Repeatedly, the division commander, in person, had to keep the untrained troops and inexperienced and admittedly not very capable commanders from panicking.

Despite his personal efforts, the first day, July 10, ended with the eastern column of the Hermann Goering Division unable to move much farther than halfway to the beaches. Field Marshal Kesselring received a report of this situation through the Luftwaffe channels, and he was furious. Hitler also learned of the situation and got in touch with Kesselring, demanding that the Allied forces be thrown back into the sea. After some delay Kesselring got through to the Sixth Army and through them ordered the Hermann Goering Division back into the attack early on July 11. It was this attack that I met on Biazza Ridge early that morning.

The senior German general with the Sixth Army was General Fridolin von Senger. He seemed to play a roving role, visiting various German units from time to time and speaking in the name of General Guzzoni, Commanding General of the Italian Sixth Army. Although the Germans paid lip service to serving under Italian command, their troops actually were controlled by their own German generals. In the situation confronting the Sixth Army on the second day of the fighting, General Guzzoni became worried about the progress of the 45th Division in the vicinity of Vittoria and decided to withdraw the Hermann Goering Division. Before orders could reach the division, however, Von Senger visited the battlefield south of Biscari late in the afternoon of July 11. He sensed an opportunity that a Rommel would have made the most of—a chance to cut into the rear area of the 45th Division, whose leading elements, thanks to the work of the paratroopers around Vittoria and S. Croce Camerina, were quite far inland, thus destroying that division. He hoped to coordinate this attack with that of Battle Group Schmalz, which was then fighting in front of the British. Despite General Guzzoni's intentions, therefore, he ordered an attack to the east, in the direction of Vittoria. It was this attack that we encountered at Biazza Ridge.

In their postwar interrogation report, the Germans claimed to have made a vigorous attack only to be met head-on by American parachutists. It was later in the day that the Americans counterattacked and destroyed the German command. A number of Germans and some vehicles fled across the Ponte Dirillo. As reported by the Office of the Chief of Military History, Washington, D.C., in *Axis Tactical Operations in Sicily,* the remainder "became panicky and fled in disorder. Some officers succeeded in bringing them to a stop just short of Biscari, where they took up defensive positions." The regimental commander went to the headquarters of the Hermann Goering Division, under which he commanded a battle group, to explain his actions. The postwar interrogation report comments cryptically, "He was relieved and subsequently court-martialed." Finally, the disaster that befell his eastern column caused General Conrath to change his plans entirely and to pull back his column near Gela, which on July 11 had been meeting with significant success. As reported in the official history of the war, "The paratrooper stand on Biazza Ridge prompted Conrath to change his plans. Learning of the heavy losses being sustained by his infantry-heavy force, he decided, apparently on his own initiative, to break off contact with the Americans near Gela."[3] So the troopers at Biazza Ridge did make a contribution to the accomplishment of the regimental mission, which was to block the movement of the German forces near Gela. In a roundabout way perhaps, and in a way that none of them realized at the time, it is now clear that they accomplished just that. What was happening at Gela?

General Conrath sensed that the main Allied effort on his front would be directed against Gela. From where his division was located around Caltagirone, a road led to Niscemi and then directly to the beaches, meeting the beach road at the Y, then toward Gela. To the northwest was a hill mass, Piano Lupo, 172 meters high. It dominated the entire area, including the Ponte Olivo airfield. Farther west and between the town of Gela and the airfield, the country was very flat and ideal for tanks. It was, no doubt, for this reason that General Conrath placed the bulk of his armor in his western column. His western battle group consisted of:

   2 tank battalions (about 90 MK III and MK IV tanks—30 to 40
       tons respectively)
   2 armored artillery battalions
   1 armored reconnaissance battalion (less one company)
   1 armored engineer battalion (less one company)

He used the troops of the reconnaissance and engineer battalions as infantry.

They moved out as planned during the night of July 9–10, as soon as the landings near Gela had been verified. Very shortly, they encountered the first paratroopers, and from then on they fought a protracted battle all day, July 10. As General Conrath moved into the attack, he hoped to coordinate his plans with the Italian Livorno Divi-

---

[3] *U.S. Army in World War II, Mediterranean Theater of Operations, Sicily and the Surrender of Italy,* Office of the Chief of Military History, Department of the Army, Washington, D.C.

sion, which was to his west, but because of severed communications both divisions had to go on their own without coordination. Meanwhile the parachutists had been busy organizing and preparing to meet the attack of the column coming through Niscemi toward the beaches.

The 1st Battalion of the 505th, commanded by Lieutenant Colonel Art ("Hardnose") Gorham, had the mission of landing on the high ground, north of the Y, so as to block the movement of any Axis forces southward, to control the Ponte Olivo airfield by fire, and to assist in reducing the Y if necessary. The best account of the action of that battalion was given immediately afterward by the Commander of A Company, 505th, Captain Edwin M. Sayre:

A Company took off at 2030 hours for the first check point at Malta. I do not know whether or not we saw Malta as I had never seen it before, but when we were to arrive there I thought I saw a light. In any event, we continued and about fifteen minutes before the scheduled jump time we could see flashes of gunfire through the door of the plane, on the left. This surprised me, because I had expected to see Sicily appear on the right. There was considerable firing, and the pilot turned to the right away from the island. We figured out later that we had hit the coast of Sicily somewhere between Noto and Siracusa.

We circled to the right, going out to sea, and came back in toward the southern coast. We followed along the shore until we saw the lake, which was a check point. The squadron then turned in toward the island. About one minute after the turn, we met with heavy ack-ack, apparently coming from the Ponte Olivo airdrome. The squadron turned to the right to avoid this fire and shortly thereafter the green light was given. It was about 0035.

Planes were under heavy machine-gun fire when we jumped, and there was a lot of firing on the ground. By 0230 I had assembled fifteen men from the company and contacted the battalion executive officer. Company A was to attack a point from which about four machine guns were firing. We first attacked at 0300. The point from which the machine guns were firing was a garrison surrounded by pillboxes and was pretty strong. The attack was held up until about 0530, at which time fifty more men had been assembled. The attack was resumed and the garrison was killed or captured by 0615. It was held by one hundred Italians, with German noncoms from the Hermann Goering Panzer Division. We could hear a lot of fire in the valley—up toward Niscemi and down toward the beach. At about 0630, Lieutenant Colonel Gorham, the battalion commander, arrived with about thirty troopers from headquarters.

Hardnose Gorham had about a hundred troopers under his control. He was in the valley astride the road from Niscemi down to the Y, and he decided to consolidate his position there for the time being. About 7:00 A.M. a German armored column was seen about 4000 yards away, coming from Niscemi. It was the Hermann Goering western column. It was preceded by a small advance guard of two motorcycles and a Volkswagen. The paratroopers kept concealed and let the advance guard get into their positions, where they killed or captured them. At that point the armored column stopped, having heard the firing on the advance guard. It was then about 3000 yards away. The Germans deployed their infantry, which looked to the troopers to be about two companies, approximately two hundred men. The troopers kept concealed and let the Germans approach to within 100 yards. They then pinned them down on open terrain. Most of the Germans were killed or captured. The German tanks came on, however, but two of them were knocked out by bazookas and two were damaged. The tanks then withdrew. Thus ended the first day's advance of the Hermann Goering Division's western column against the beaches.

After defeating the German force, Colonel Gorham reassessed the situation and decided that he should move on to his objective, Piano Lupo—which was the high ground off to his left—since it was terrain that controlled both the airfield and the road. Using about fifty prisoners, the troopers carried their wounded with them and moved on to the high ground and organized it for defense. Having accomplished that and remembering his mission, Colonel Gorham sent Captain Sayre with a small detachment, about a squad, to attack the Y.

As Sayre approached the fortification around the Y, heavy naval gunfire began to fall near the road about 100 yards north of the pillboxes. The pillboxes appeared to be sheltered in defilade. Sayre then directed one of the Italian prisoners to go to the pillboxes and demand their surrender. He ordered the prisoner to tell the occupants that if they did not surrender, the colonel would bring the naval gunfire right down on top of them. Actually, he didn't have any communications with the Navy, but the men in the pillboxes didn't know that. They surrendered, and the paratroopers occupied the pillboxes at about 10:45 A.M. A few minutes later four German tanks approached from Niscemi again. The paratroopers fired on them from the pillboxes and the tanks withdrew. At about 11:30 A.M. scouts from the 16th Infantry of the 1st U.S. Division contacted Captain Sayre at the Y. Colonel Gorham then attached all his troops to the 16th Infantry and advanced north with them. In a short while Captain Sayre, using 1st Infantry Division communications, was able to get in touch with General Ridgway and report, "All missions accomplished."

Actually, Colonel Gorham and his small group of troopers and the lieutenants from the 3rd Battalion, 504th, accomplished all the missions assigned to the entire regimental combat team. It was a remarkable performance, and I know of nothing like it that occurred at any time later in the war. Sadly, in the fighting the following morning, Colonel Gorham engaged a tank with a bazooka and he himself was killed. His death was a great loss to the division.

Due to Gorham's stand, Conrath's column, moving down the road from Niscemi, had had a difficult time of it on July 10 and had gotten not much farther than halfway toward the landing beaches. July 11, the same day of the attack on Biazza Ridge, was to be another story.

In response to verbal blistering from Kesselring, Conrath launched a vigorous attack early that day. The bulk of his tanks were sent far to the west of where the paratrooper stand had been made on July 10. They ranged far out over the flat land between Ponte Olivo airfield and Gela. By July 11 the U.S. 1st Infantry Division was well established ashore. Fortunately, it was a veteran division; otherwise, it surely would have broken under the weight and magnitude of the German attack. The German Panzers pushed through the parachutists on Piano Lupo. To the west they reached the outskirts of Gela. General Patton himself had come ashore and went up on the roof of a dwelling in Gela to observe the action. It was 9:30 A.M. when his boat touched shore. Not long thereafter he reached his observation post on the top of a building, and to him the horizon seemed filled with Panzers. Spotting a Navy ensign with a walkie-talkie, he yelled, "Hey, you with the radio."

"Can I help you, sir?" the ensign asked smartly.

"Sure as hell," Patton said. "If you can connect with your goddamned Navy, tell them for God's sake to drop some shellfire on the road." He pointed to the tanks approaching along the Ponte Olivo road.[4]

The Navy responded with a barrage of six-inch shells. The battle was still far from over, but slowly it turned in favor of the Big Red One and the paratroopers. That night General Terry Allen, Commanding General of the U.S. 1st Infantry Division, with characteristic courage

[4] Farago, op. cit.

ordered an attack. From then on Patton and the Seventh Army were not to be stopped until they seized Messina.

That same night, at Biazza Ridge, learning that the Germans had completely withdrawn from the action, I moved my Command Post from the top of the ridge back about a half mile under the olive trees. I deployed the troopers for the night, expecting an attack from the direction of Biscari to come into our right flank, probably at daylight.

It must have been about ten o'clock at night when all hell broke loose in the direction of the beaches. Antiaircraft fire was exploding like fireworks on the Fourth of July, tracers were whipping through the sky, and as we were observing the phenomena, the low, steady drone of airplanes could be heard. They seemed to be flying through the flak and coming in our direction. Everyone began to grasp their weapons to be ready to shoot at them. A few of us cautioned the troopers to take it easy until we understood what was going on. Suddenly at about 600 feet the silhouettes of American C-47s appeared against the sky—our own parachute transports! Some seemed to be burning, and they continued directly overhead in the direction of Gela. From the damaged planes some troopers jumped or fell, and at daylight we found some of them dead in front of our positions.

Later we learned that it was the 504th Parachute Infantry that was being flown to a drop zone near Gela to reinforce the 1st Infantry Division. General Ridgway had been there to meet them. Unfortunately, the Germans had sent in parachute reinforcements on the British front to the east the same night. In addition, there had been German air attacks on our Navy, so when the parachute transports showed up, our ships fired at them, and twenty-three were shot down and many damaged.

Soon the battlefield was quiet. I dug a foxhole and lay down. The next thing I knew, the bright warm sun was shining in my face and it was broad daylight. Everybody around me was sleeping soundly in their foxholes. We had been so exhausted by the experience we had been through since our landing that we were all physically out. I started to get up and found that my left leg was stiff and sore. My trouser leg was slightly torn, and my shinbone was red, swollen, and cut a bit. I must have been nipped by a mortar fragment the day before. I went to the nearest aid station; they put on some sulfa powder and I was as good as new. They said they would put me in for a Purple Heart. I said nothing about it—I had already learned that among twenty-four-hour veterans only goof-offs got Purple Hearts.

I then began to get the battalion organized for the move to our regimental objective near Gela. But the first order of business was to take care of our dead and wounded. We brought in fifty bodies and buried them near the top of the ridge. We tried to use German POWs to dig the graves, but they were not very helpful. The Regimental Chaplain made wooden crosses out of K-ration boxes, and we gave the troopers an appropriate burial. It had been a sad experience; many of them had had pieces of bazookas ground up in them by tanks as they were crushed. We had also lost more than one hundred wounded.

General Bradley, commanding II Corps, under whose command I now found myself, ordered me not to go beyond the Arcate River. I took a patrol and went to Ponte Dirillo, the span crossing the Arcate. The Arcate itself was bone-dry. The bridge was a new concrete slab, two lanes wide, stretching about two hundred yards across the riverbed and about eight feet above it. The riverbed was covered with tomato plants, and some of them were just beginning to ripen. After a couple of months in Africa on C rations and after the fighting we had been through, we found them very tasty. En route to the bridge, we encountered knocked-out German tanks, trucks, mortars, and abandoned enemy small arms. No Germans were in sight. I had heard rumors that Colonel Gorham and his battalion had been fighting near Gela and that Mark Alexander's battalion had been fighting near Vittoria.

Early in the morning of July 13 I made my way by jeep westward to the Y. I passed a knocked-out tank, still burning. The fortifications around the Y were impressive. I went up on the high ground that had been our objective. Quite a number of dead paratroopers were still about, badly bloated by the hot July sun, gas bubbles oozing from their wounds, and enshrouded by swarms of flies. It was a sickening sight. I went back to the road and on to Gela. As I drove up on the high ground overlooking the sea, there was General George Patton, ivory-handled pistols and all, standing overlooking the busy scene in the harbor. When I arrived in front of him, still gripping an M-1 rifle, he whipped out a huge silver flask. "Gavin, you look like you need a drink—have one." He exuded confidence and was very much in command. It was good to see him—first, because I liked him as a soldier, and second, because it was good to see an army commander in the midst of things. It was his first army command, and it was the start of a meteoric wartime career that ended, tragically, in a fatal automobile accident in Germany more than two years later. In the meantime he built a reputation for being the most colorful, aggressive, and venturesome general we had. But on July 13 he had special problems all his own, and in those problems were the seeds of troubles that would prolong the war by many months and cost many lives.

The battle for Sicily pitted Patton and his newborn U.S. Seventh Army against Montgomery and his veteran British Eighth Army. Having driven Rommel in defeat across North Africa, Montgomery enjoyed an extraordinary reputation. The senior officers, however, who had access to "Ultra," realized that Montgomery received copies of Rommel's communications to and from his higher headquarters daily. The question was: why hadn't Montgomery defeated Rommel at the outset, having enjoyed such an advantage? When it came time to plan Sicily, Montgomery insisted upon having his own way and relegating Patton to a secondary role. This rivalry was to continue until the end of the war. In time it would create bitter feelings toward Montgomery on the part of the senior American commanders. Montgomery, for his part, did little to alleviate it. In fact, he never seemed to realize the problems he was creating. But for the Americans, it all began in Sicily.

The morning of July 13 found Patton well established in Sicily. It had not been easy. The presence of the Hermann Goering Division had been a complete surprise to us; none of the pre-battle intelligence summaries of the higher headquarters reported the Goering Division as even being in Sicily. Not only had it been there, but it had been placed in exactly the right location to maximize its chances for throwing the amphibious forces back into the sea. Having defeated it, Patton at once began to drive his divisions forward. On July 16 Agrigento was seized, and on the following day the 82nd Airborne Division relieved the U.S. 3rd Infantry Division. Patton began to see the possibilities of an end run to Palermo. He flew back to La Marsa, Tunisia, to place before General Sir Harold Alexander his plan for such an attack on July 17. It began to appear to the staffs of Patton's army that unless his mission was changed, he would soon be relegated to the dull role of guarding the British Eighth Army's rear.

Major General John Porter Lucas had been visiting the Seventh Army, and after hearing the staff talk about it, he thought the situation was becoming rather dangerous, so he flew back to General Eisenhower's headquarters to discuss it with him. Eisenhower apparently had not known of the intensity of the feeling in the U.S. Seventh Army, and he told Lucas that Alexander should not be blamed for being cautious. Instead, said Eisenhower, Patton should be made to realize that he must stand up to Alexander or else Eisenhower would relieve Patton of his command! Alexander, it seemed, had been unaware of the strong feelings of the Americans about his role, so when Patton urged that he be allowed to seize Palermo, Alexander was in a receptive state of mind. Actually, the Americans had been making much more progress than Alexander was aware of. He gave Patton the green light, and on the following day, July 18, Patton organized a Provisional Corps consisting of the 2nd Armored Division, new to battle; the U.S. 82nd Airborne Division, and the 39th Regimental Combat Team from the U.S. 9th Infantry Division.

At 5:00 A.M. on July 19 the attack jumped off. According to the official report of the war, it was "little more than a road march," but it was a strange affair, unlike anything else I encountered during the war. True, it did seem like a road march, but suddenly a machine gun or antitank weapon would open up, and then the white flags would appear. A shot had been fired for "honor," but it was just as likely to cause casualties as a shot fired in anger. The 2nd Armored Division moved rapidly. It was a spectacular affair. Clouds of dust billowed into the sky for miles and at times obscured the sun. By late evening of July 22 Palermo was occupied.

The 505th Parachute Infantry, in an all-night march, arrived in the town of San Margherita late on July 22. The following morning, moving by truck, the 505th Parachute Combat Team swung west to the town of Trapani. The only hazards en route were the fruit and caramelos thrown by the Sicilians. Actually, the caramelos could sting if they hit you while you were in a fast-moving vehicle. As we reached the outskirts of Trapani, we encountered a roadblock and heavy artillery fire. The regiment deployed, swept into the town with no casualties, and accepted the surrender of the admiral in command. Thus ended the Sicilian campaign for the 82nd Airborne Division.

We at once began intensive training, using some knocked-out German armor for experiments to test their vulnerability to our antitank weapons. We also used some of the Sicilian pillboxes to train the troopers in fire and movement in reducing them. We all had been made tremendously aware of the need for a better means of knocking out tanks, and we acquired a new respect for the troopers who carried bazookas. Near Trapani are an old convent and monastery on the very high mountain of Erice. I arranged for the nuns there to embroider an insignia to be worn over the left breast pocket of the jumpsuit for the bazooka carriers. It consisted of crossed bazookas and a bolt of lightning in the regimental colors, red and blue. We issued them to all the bazooka men at the first regimental formation as soon as we got back to Africa a few weeks later. There was no authority in regulations for it, but it seemed like a good idea, and the bazooka men were proud to wear them.

On August 12 General Ridgway was called to General Patton's headquarters in Palermo. I accompanied him. There we met the Commander of the 52nd Troop Carrier Wing, which had flown us into Sicily. We had been brought together by General Patton to discuss a parachute landing along the north coast of the island. Patton's sweep around the west end of the island had been a dramatic example of the use of armor. However, as his forces advanced eastward toward Messina, they began to go through a narrow funnel as the rugged terrain moved closer to the sea. To avoid this difficulty, Patton proposed that parachute troops be dropped behind the German forces; this, combined with an amphibious linkup, would cut off the German delaying forces and bring an end to their increasingly successful tactics. I had some reservations about parachuting into such a confined area with inadequate antitank weapons, and our Troop Carrier friends liked the proposed mission even less. They were sure that they would suffer heavy casualties in dropping us at low altitudes over an area known to be heavily occupied by German troops.

We finally agreed that the terrain was too restrictive in its possibilities for paratroopers; nevertheless, General Patton launched two successful amphibious assaults. They had greater significance than we realized at the time. Winston Churchill, long an advocate of exploiting Allied sea power, was intrigued, and in referring to these amphibious coups, he wrote, "I had, of course, always been a partisan of the 'end run,' as the Americans call it, or 'cat-claw,' which was my term. I had never succeeded in getting this maneuver open to sea power included in any of our desert advances. In Sicily, however, General Patton had twice used the command of the sea flank as he advanced along the northern coast of the island with great effect."[5] The amphibious end runs

[5] Ibid.

worked, and Patton was in Messina on August 16, just before the British arrived from Catania. He was elated, as were most of the American senior staff officers. Patton's Seventh Army had been landed in an area without an adequate port, with a mission of guarding the flank of Montgomery's Eighth Army. At once he was attacked by a German Panzer Division, which took the Allied command completely by surprise. Overcoming these almost insurmountable odds, by drive and daring, Patton conquered most of the island, seized Palermo, and finally captured Messina itself—Montgomery's objective. When, in the future, the Supreme Command had to make decisions regarding the allocation of scarce supplies, such as gasoline and oil, Patton's supporters eagerly recalled the lessons of Sicily and Patton's generalship. And Sicily was only the beginning for Patton.

With the fall of Messina the battle for Sicily was over. The 82nd Airborne Division moved back to Africa to ready itself for the next campaign: Italy. Who would our opponents be—would the Italians fight once we landed on the mainland? We were especially concerned with German Panzers; there were rumors that many of them had escaped across the Strait of Messina. As we later learned, they had, and we were to fight them once again.

How did the bulk of the German and Italian forces manage to go scot-free? With the Allies enjoying complete superiority at sea and in the air, it seemed a simple matter to block the narrow Strait of Messina. The airmen were particularly confident that it could be done—but they had not learned the lesson of Dunkirk. Yet, beginning on August 11 and continuing until the occupation of Messina by Patton and Montgomery on August 16, the Germans moved 8000 men across the Strait daily. Forty thousand Germans and 62,000 Italians, together with 97 guns, 47 tanks, and 17,000 tons of ammunition, were moved across, most of it in the last few days in broad daylight. The airmen blamed the intensity of the antiaircraft fire, and the Navy blamed the heavy coastal guns emplaced on both sides of the Strait. Why, then, was an amphibious landing not made on the Calabrian side of the Strait to block their escape?

Writing of the affair after the war, Kesselring stated, "A secondary attack on Calabria would have enabled the Sicily landing to be developed into an overwhelming Allied victory." The latest Allied version of what transpired is recounted in Nigel Nicolson's biography of Field Marshal Alexander. It was published in 1973—when practically all the historical evidence was in. In it the author stresses that there was a more fundamental reason for a failure to block the Strait: "One reason that it did not happen was that the headquarters of the main commanders were far apart: Alexander was in Sicily, Tedder [Air] near Tunis, Cunningham [Navy] in Malta, and Eisenhower in Algiers. Another was that Eisenhower would take no initiative."[6] Eisenhower's insistence on commanding the battle and not turning it over to subordinates was entirely proper, but having assumed command, he had to place himself closer to the scene of action in order to maneuver the forces available to him in a decisive manner. Remoteness from the battle scene, when critical decisions had to be made, was to prove to be one facet of Eisenhower's type of generalship. For us the problem was to get on with the war and win the next battle, regardless of where it took place and what enemy we were to meet.

In the postwar years the combat of the Americans, and specifically that of the 82nd Airborne Division, was strangely downgraded by the British historians. Writing in 1967, a British military historian, W. G. F. Jackson, in *The Battle for Italy,* claimed that "The airborne operations were a fiasco in which carefully trained soldiers from both armies were literally thrown away by inexperienced and inadequately trained aircrews." Hardly. Certainly the aircrews were lacking in experience and training. That was one of the consequences of setting D-day for July 9, 1943. The author goes on to describe the actions of the Hermann Goering Division and reaches the conclusion that it withdrew because naval gunfire was so devastating east of Gela. Later Maurice Tugwell in a history of airborne warfare, *Airborne to Battle,* refers to the statement after Sicily of General Kurt Student in which he credited the airborne forces with blocking the Hermann Goering Division tanks from reaching the beachhead, going on to credit the Allied airborne troops with having delayed the Hermann Goering Division long enough to make the Allied landing a success. Tugwell says, "Research does not support General Student's generous statement." Most of Tugwell's account of the Sicilian action is devoted to a description of the actions of the British parachute and glider troops north of Catania. Also, writing for the magazine section of a London paper in 1972, Norman Lewis, who was with British Army Intelligence in Sicily during World War II, wrote an article entitled "Mafia Wins Sicily for the U.S. Army." Explaining the ease with which Patton's army went ashore, Lewis writes, "The Italo-German

[6] Nigel Nicolson, *Alex, the Life of Field Marshal Earl Alexander of Tunis.* London: Weidenfeld and Nicolson, 1973.

forces in the area had been intelligently pulled back some 30 miles from the American beachhead and had taken up defensive positions in the area of Monte Cammarata." This allegedly was accomplished through the offices of Lucky Luciano, then with the Mafia in Sicily. Either this must be totally untrue or the Hermann Goering Division and the Livorno Division did not get the word—an unlikely event. Both Guzzoni, the Sixth Army Commander, and Von Senger, his German adviser, were hell-bent on throwing the U.S. divisions into the sea and destroying the U.S. 1st and 45th Divisions, which were ashore.

Finally, in summing up the Sicilian affair in *The Battle for Italy,* the British author makes a gratuitous observation: "The American divisions had withstood the main weight of the Axis counterattack and in so doing had proved themselves to themselves, though not as yet to the 15th Army Group and the Eighth Army." Although written long after Sicily, the Americans sensed at the time this attitude on the part of the British. And after that bloody battle such a condescending attitude on the part of the higher British command was not particularly appreciated in the higher American headquarters or, for that matter, in the combat divisions. Unfortunately, it fired the flames of mistrust and misunderstanding among the U.S. planners and the U.S. commanders of the battles that were to follow.

The capture of Sicily placed the Allies in a much better position concerning the Axis powers. From Sicily they threatened Sardinia, Rome, and, much closer, Naples and Salerno. The distances from the air bases in Sicily were: Salerno, 175 miles; Naples, 190 miles. Further, the Allies captured a major port in Salerno, but, more important, the Americans and the British learned how to cooperate in planning, equipping, and launching a major amphibious assault. Clearly, they now posed a real threat to the Axis forces in all Italy within range of their fighter bomber cover. Hitler recognized this. He had already begun to change his troop dispositions so as to withdraw all German troops south of Rome. He further reinforced the Brenner Pass with an army group under the command of Field Marshal Rommel. He did this to be sure that, in the event it became necessary, he could safely withdraw troop formations from Italy. So the battle of Sicily was not only a military success; the military lessons learned were to prove invaluable to the Allies in the battles that were to come.

Most important were the lessons learned in how to organize and deliver our airborne troops. We at once set up a professional training unit at Biscari Airfield in Sicily. Its purpose was to develop specially trained pathfinder units, consisting of experienced pilots and reliable paratroopers who would land about twenty minutes before the main assault. A pathfinder team consisted of one officer and nine enlisted men, reinforced by enough protective troopers to insure the success of their mission. The team would be equipped with electronic gear on which the following troop carrier pilots would home. They would also be equipped with lights both to mark the drop zone and to help the landing paratroopers to reorganize.

In charge of the training at Biscari were Lieutenant Colonel Joel Crouch of the Air Corps and Captain John Norton of the 82nd Airborne Division. The program was very successful, and as the war went on, more and more pathfinder teams were trained to land ahead of resupply missions whenever they became necessary. We also learned to move on our objectives immediately on landing; we observed that the first minutes in a parachute operation, when the paratroopers have the initiative, are important to both their survival and the capturing of their objective. The airborne experience in Sicily proved valuable to us in our later battles and in helping train the green units and individuals coming from the United States.

Above: Troopers in jump training about to descend from the cargo door of an early version of the C-47. In that initial stage, parachuting was considered extremely hazardous, even though no weapons and not a single item of equipment were carried. (U.S. Army)

Below: A jump from an early-model C-47, in 1941, about the time of Gavin's own jump training. The Chattahoochee River is in the background. (U.S. Army)

Above: Winston Churchill on a visit in June 1942 to the training camp at Fort Jackson, South Carolina. He is accompanied by (left to right) General George C. Marshall, Field Marshal Sir John Dill, Secretary of War Henry L. Stimson, and General Robert L. Eichelberger. (U.S. Army)

Below: Foreign Secretary Anthony Eden and Gavin review the Honor Guard of the 505th Parachute Infantry shortly before the 505th left for Africa to participate in the battle of Sicily. (U.S. Army)

Above: In Sicily troopers used the native mode of transportation—donkeys—to carry equipment and weapons. (U.S. Army)

Below: Jack "Beaver" Thompson (left) of the *Chicago Tribune* with Gavin at the foot of Biazza Ridge shortly before the battle. (U.S. Army)

Above: A wounded trooper being cared for in Normandy after the crash of a glider. Many casualties occurred when most of the gliders were badly shot up or damaged on landing. (U.S. Army)

Below: Just after landing, the message center for the 82nd Airborne—code name CHAMPION, marked on a tree—was established. Gavin (center) meets with First Lieutenant Hugo Olson (facing camera) and Captain Arie Bestebreurtje (taller man, with back to camera). (U.S. Army)

General Gavin checks his equipment before boarding a plane for the airborne invasion of Holland on September 17, 1944. On his person are a knife and pistol, entrenching tool, grenades, first-aid packet, and some food. On the ground near his feet is his M-1 rifle with a muzzle protector. The musette bag contains a raincoat, rations, and extra ammunition. Under the helmet are the maps that will be used to check the route as the troops fly across the English Channel into Holland. (U.S. Army)

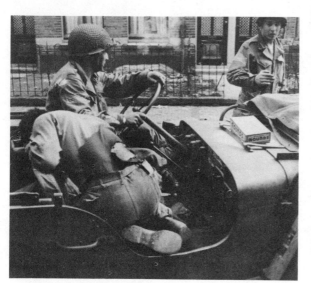

Above, left: Street scene in Nijmegen. A wounded soldier is being removed from the battle area. (U.S. Army)

Above, right: Lieutenant General "Boy" Browning, Commander of the British Airborne Corps, and Brigadier General Gavin near Grave, Holland, on September 19, 1944. The linkup with the British troops has just occurred. (U.S. Army)

Below: King George VI on a visit to the combat troops in Holland in October 1944. With the King are (left to right) General Brian Horrocks; General Gavin; Brigadier General Andy March, Commanding General of the 82nd Airborne Division Artillery; Colonel Roy E. Lindquist, 508th Parachute Infantry; Colonel Reuben Tucker, 504th Parachute Infantry; Colonel William E. Ekman, 505th Parachute Infantry, and Colonel Charles Billingslea, 325th Glider Infantry. (U.S. Army)

HOLLAND

Above: General Gavin in December 1944 visits the scene of a battle near Erria, Belgium, where a battalion of the 9th SS Panzers was "cut to ribbons"—according to the German account—by the 508th Parachute Infantry. (U.S. Army)

When the German thrust had subsided, the Allies, in deep snow and very cold weather, counterattacked through St.-Vith and to the Siegfried Line.

Below, left: General Gavin uses a field phone in the front lines to direct troops near Herresbach, Belgium. Nearby, the General recalls, was a wounded German, eagerly eating snow as a means of relief. (U.S. Army)

Below, right: Wounded soldiers being removed to safety in a "weasel"—the only means of rescue in rough, snowy weather. The light, efficient weasels, designed by the U.S. Army to travel over snow and rocky terrain, were able to carry tons of cargo. In February 1945, when heavy snowfall slowed progress, some major tactical decisions involved the availability of weasels. (U.S. Army Signal Corps)

An air drop. The white chute in the center is a reserve, released when the main chute did not open properly. (U.S. Army)

Italy

Sicily had been a sobering experience. For years we had been told that our weapons were superior to any we would encounter. After, all, we were soldiers from the most highly industrialized and the richest nation on earth. But that very preoccupation with our advanced technology caused many to assume that technology alone would win battles —more emphasis was placed on victory through air power than victory through better infantry. Yet this wasn't the only error. Our problems stemmed very often from the lack of imagination, if not lack of intelligence, of those responsible for developing infantry weapons. The small bazooka was a case in point. Its performance was based on a phenomenon first observed by a scientist working for the U.S. Navy, Dr. Charles E. Munroe. When an explosion was formed with a particular shape, the energy of the explosion upon detonation would focus into a very effective jet stream.

I looked into the situation after the war. One of the scientists advising the Ordnance Corps, Dr. Charles Lauritsen, Sr., of Cal Tech, had resigned because of the way in which the explosive was being made and out of the conviction that the weapon was too small. Nevertheless, we manufactured the weapon in large numbers and placed it in the hands of our troops for the Sicily battle. It could have been tested against German tanks captured in North Africa, but it evidently was not.

Ironically, after many lives were lost, in mid-August 1943 we received a War Department intelligence bulletin telling us that the bazooka would not penetrate the frontplate of the Tiger tank—as though we didn't know it already. More sadly, we still had not obtained a larger bazooka by the time General MacArthur sent the first troops to Korea seven years later to meet the Soviet T-34 tanks in the summer of

1950. The American infantry combat team there was overrun by Soviet armor.

As for the 82nd Airborne Division, it did not get adequate antitank weapons until it began to capture the first German panzerfausts. By the fall of '44 we had truckloads of them. We also captured German instructions for their use, made translations, and conducted our own training with them. They were the best hand-carried antitank weapon of the war, although the British had a large bazooka that was quite effective also. The American carbine in heavy combat was worthless. A scaled-down version of the M-1, it could be jammed with even a few grains of sand. Our artillery was good, and artillerymen made much progress between wars in learning how to mass fires, but we had nothing comparable to the German 88. Our antitank mine didn't compare with the far superior German antitank mine.

After Sicily our feeling was that we would have to start with the smallest building blocks and create a new force if we were ever going to cope effectively with the Wehrmacht. Fortunately, to deal with the tank problem, we had come across a British explosive, known as "plastic" or Explosive C. It had the appearance and consistency of putty and could be stuffed into anything from an old sock to a dispatch case; thrown against the side of a tank, it caused severe internal splintering. It could also be used against pillboxes and embrasures in buildings. We also learned of the British six-pounder, a 57 mm. antitank weapon that could be carried in by glider. Our idea of taking along essential items of personal convenience had been right, but we had not gone far enough. All comfort items—toilet articles, extra clothing, and blankets—had to be left behind and replacements captured after landing. As much ammunition and antitank mines as we could possibly carry had to be taken in, and they had to be carried on one's person. Scrambling about in the dark for bundles simply did not work.

To deal with the scattered drop problem, we at once began training a small pathfinder unit at Comiso Airfield in Sicily. As mentioned, the pathfinders, working with specially selected and trained Air Corps crews, were to land about twenty minutes before the main armada and thus help guide them in. Finally, we all learned that the few seconds that one had just before jumping were precious indeed, for they gave one a last look at the terrain and nearby villages, defenses, roads, and waterways.

The great confidence of the troopers in their own ability to do the job was not shared by everyone in higher headquarters. The War Department had observers in the headquarters in North Africa during the Sicilian operation, and they returned to Washington quite pessimistic. They doubted that the concept of an airborne division was valid. If a regiment could not be delivered more effectively than had occurred in Sicily, what chance would a division have? This, to me, was a peculiar astigmatism associated with those remote from the battle itself. Those of us in the foxholes knew what we could do. And if we believed that a single paratrooper was worth a squad of enemy and that a company of paratroopers could destroy a tank-reinforced battalion, now we had evidence to prove it. But Eisenhower's headquarters did not believe this. In a letter to General Marshall dated September 20, 1943, Eisenhower stated flatly, "I do not believe in the airborne division."[1] When I learned of this exchange of views, I was puzzled by the fact that no senior officers from higher headquarters were present at any of the airborne operations in Sicily. Their views therefore were based on impressions gained from Eisenhower's headquarters hundreds of miles away. However, in the United States, Army Ground Forces was of the view that the division should be continued in a forthcoming exercise involving the 11th Airborne Division in the United States. In a later study of this subject, both American and British Combined Staff planners saw nothing in the combat experience of the British or the Americans which indicated that the division was not a proper organization for airborne troops. "It had been a near thing for the airborne effort."[2]

Patton had great confidence in the paratroopers and at once wanted to use them on the north shore of Sicily. General Bradley had particularly high praise for their battle performance. When I talked to him not long after the Biazza affair, he told me about the many abandoned German tanks on the road between Biazza and Biscari. They all had been crippled by the fight with the 505th at Biazza. From then on he was an enthusiastic supporter of parachute operations. Indeed, by the time we began planning for Normandy, he told me he would not make the amphibious landings without being certain the parachute assault troops would go in first.

The British had a somewhat similar experience to that of the Americans, with many of their troopers badly scattered. Added to their dis-

[1] U.S. Army in World War II, Mediterranean Theater of Operations, Sicily and the Surrender of Italy, Albert N. Garland and Howard McGaw Smyth, Office of the Chief of Military History, Department of the Army, Washington, D.C., 1965.
[2] Ibid.

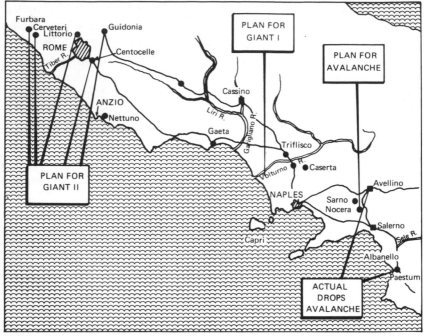

Fig. 5   Planned Landings in Italy

aster was the loss of a large number of gliders that had been cut adrift too far from the beaches and thus landed in the ocean.

But the highest praise came from the Germans. In an interview on October 19 General Student, who commanded the parachute-glider assault on Crete, said, "The Allied operation in Sicily was decisive despite widely scattered drops which must be expected in a night landing. It is my opinion that if it had not been for the Allied forces blocking the Hermann Goering Division from reaching the beaches, that division would have driven the initial seaborne forces back into the sea."

But now Italy loomed ahead, and after that there was a war to be won.

Immediately after the battle of Sicily the 82nd Airborne returned to North Africa, arriving there on August 20, 1943. It received reinforcements and equipped and prepared itself for the coming invasion of Italy. For the Division Commander, Major General Matthew Ridgway, and for the staffs of the division, this was an extremely busy period. Plans were made, and then there were changes, and more plans and changes. Yet all that was typical of what usually happens in the planning stages of an airborne operation.

The final plan for the amphibious invasion of Italy (*Fig. 5*) contained the following major elements: (1) the main assault by the U.S. Fifth Army with the mission of landing at Salerno and moving northwestward and capturing Naples; (2) two attacks by the British Eighth Army, one against Calabria and another against Taranto; (3) a naval diversionary attack in the Gulf of Gaeta. This was to be known as operation AVALANCHE: named, one can suppose, for the avalanche of combat troops soon to swarm onto the war-weary Italian Peninsula. But to some of the wags on the staff of the 82nd Airborne Division, the name was more indicative of the avalanche of airborne plans and papers that engulfed them in the days that followed.

To carry out its mission, the Fifth Army planned to invade Italy at the Gulf of Salerno, fight northwestward, capture Naples, and continue the fight northward until all Italy was overrun. The 82nd Airborne Division was made available to the Commander of the Fifth Army, General Mark Clark, for this operation. How best to make use of the division now became a problem of much speculation and concern.

The first mission presented to the 82nd called for the seizure by an airborne task force of the towns of Nocera and Sarno at the exits to the passes leading northwest from Salerno. The purpose was to cover the landing and debouchment of the Fifth Army from the Salerno area. All available transport planes and gliders, 318 of each, were to be used on the operation. The Division Commander gave missions to the regimental commanders at the Division Command Post at Trapani, Sicily, on August 2.

The staffs made hurried studies to select drop zones for the parachutists and landing zones for the gliders. Our airborne assault was to be supported by an amphibious assault by troops from the infantry division landing in the Amalfi-Maiori area on the Sorrento Peninsula. After considerable study in conjunction with the Air Force of the terrain, ack-ack, and possible flight routes, it was decided that the paratroopers of the 82nd would have to be dropped in Nocera Pass on the Sorrento Ridge at altitudes from 4500 to 6000 feet, in moonlight. The airborne operation was also planned at extreme fighter range, and this, coupled with the ground conditions, the ack-ack, and the possibilities of hostile fighter interception, as well as the real vulnerability of the C-47s to any kind of attack, ruled out anything but a night airborne drop. Fighter range and support are critical factors in any airborne plan.

It was decided, however, on August 12 to throw this whole plan out and use the 82nd Airborne farther inland. As I look back on it now, it seems to me that this first plan contemplated the use of our airborne units merely to gain a temporary tactical advantage. Their use according to this first plan would hardly have had a decisive bearing on the outcome of the operation as a whole. It was a good thing that the plan was dropped.

On August 18 General Ridgway was told that a new decision had been reached to conduct an airborne operation on the Volturno River, northwest of Naples and some forty miles from the nearest beach landings in Salerno. Initially, this new plan gave the 82nd Airborne Division the mission of destroying all crossings of the Volturno from Triflisco to the sea and of holding the Volturno itself against all enemy attempts to move south. The airborne force was to be given immediate support by an amphibious assault against beaches just to the south of the mouth of the Volturno, and contact between the 82nd and the nearest unit landing at Salerno, the British 46th Division, was to be expected, at the latest, in five days.

I was designated as the airborne task force commander. Staff planning for the new operation, known as GIANT I, was undertaken without delay at all staff levels concerned. But shortly the Navy announced that the beaches selected for the amphibious assault were unsuitable, so this phase was dropped from the plan. Without this landing of a force from the sea to back up our airborne task force, the problem of resupply for the airborne forces now became most critical. Our assault force was to be a task force of two regiments of parachute infantry, a battalion of parachute field artillery, two companies of parachute engineers, and two batteries of 57 mm. antitank guns, and medics, signal, and reconnaissance units to balance the force. To keep this force operating continuously, we would need supplies of 175 tons daily. This minimum of food and ammunition had to be delivered to us in one way or another, for an airborne force is, like any other, dependent on supplies. It cannot fall back toward a supply base. Obviously this would require a considerable airlift. And it would also require an almost incredible amount of good luck and good planning to deliver the needed supplies to each unit of the task force in the face of hostile interference and the many circumstances of combat that can cause the best of plans to go awry.

At the very least, the airborne task force would need regular supplies for a period of five days—until contact was made between our force and units of the British 46th Division, which would have landed at Salerno. There was some chance, as well, that the progress of these other forces would be slower than expected, and in that event we would need steady resupply for many days. In fact, if the operation had been carried out as planned, it is probable that we would have been on our own for a whole month. Any serious failure in the resupply of the 82nd Airborne task force could only mean its loss. This is true of any airborne force that drops into territory strongly held by an alert enemy. No surrounded force can hold out long without food, and when the ammunition is gone, the situation naturally becomes hopeless.

The planning for the airborne operation was carried through down to the smallest detail. General Ridgway emphatically presented the resupply problem to the Fifth Army staff. Approximately three groups of troop carrier transports, about 145 airplanes in all, would be needed to bring in our daily resupply by parachute. Because of the great likelihood of interception by hostile fighters, the supplies would have to be delivered at night, on a time schedule that was changed daily. Each day an observation airplane was to fly over our operation area on a prearranged schedule to confirm the daily delivery plan by panel and smoke signals.

One novel twist was given to the planning when it was realized that there were several thousand Allied prisoners of war in the area between Capua and Caserta. Resupply for these prisoners appeared to be a necessity, and just what we should do with them in the event of their liberation was a difficult problem. It was also of highest interest to the troopers of the 82nd that the rear echelons of the German 1st Parachute Division and the Hermann Goering Panzer Division were bivouacked near our proposed area of operations. Word was going around that if the Hermann Goering outfit had anything left after Sicily, it was about to lose it now. And every man was curious about the 1st Parachute Division and more than willing to meet it.

As task force commander I visited the Command Post of Major General J. L. Hawkesworth, commanding the British 46th Division, at Bizerte in late August. I arranged for delivery of American-type ammunition, for evacuation of our wounded, and for an exchange of information on day and night visual recognition signals, radio frequencies, and vehicular markings. General Hawkesworth estimated then that he could contact the airborne troops in from four to five days at the most. Concurrently with all this, the 82nd Airborne Division was directed to be prepared to drop a separate parachute battalion on either Battipaglia, Avellino, Nocera, or Sarno, for the purpose of blocking enemy movements to these localities. The 2nd Battalion, 509th Parachute Infantry, was attached to the division. This was the battalion that had jumped in North Africa after a 1500-mile flight from England in November 1942. Under the able leadership of Colonel Edson Raff, it had fought with great courage and effectiveness.

A final conference was held on August 31 in the headquarters of the Fifth Army at Mostaganem. All the senior officers taking part in AVALANCHE were present: General Eisenhower, Admiral Hall, Air Chief Marshal Tedder, General Clark, all British and American corps commanders, and a number of division commanders. General Ridgway was allowed three minutes to talk about the Volturno River plan. It immediately caused considerable discussion, after which it was decided by General Eisenhower that the Volturno plan should be canceled. For the time being, however, the part having to do with the seizure of Capua and the bridges was left in, and it was anticipated that they could be held with five days of supplies. This was a two-battalion mission, so General Ridgway decided to give it to the 504th. The 505th was kept on an alert status, and I was told that dock landing at Naples or an air landing at Rome was possible.

It became quite evident in the meeting that the high command believed that the Italians were definitely not going to fight. They had not fought a great deal in Sicily, and it was the Germans I was most concerned about. If German armored units had been positioned near the landing areas, we were still in for a very hard fight. But everyone at the conference seemed to exude confidence in a quick victory, and there was some loose talk about how long it would take to get to Rome. It made me quite uneasy after the battle shock of Sicily. I remember that General Clark commented that there would be adequate facilities for the press to get their stories out. He added, "There is no one more frustrated than a newspaperman with a story that he can't get out." Everyone chuckled sympathetically.

In preparation for AVALANCHE, an extensive bombing program

was already under way. The big bombers of the North African Air Corps were working over the boot of Italy from top to toe. The Air Corps had already carried out its costly long-distance raid on the Ploești oil field in Rumania from bases in Libya.

The airplanes of the Troop Carrier Command would be operating beyond fighter support, which certainly pointed to a heavy loss in transport planes to keep our task force going. Still in the minds of all the pilots was the recent interception of a German air transport column on the way to North Africa with badly needed supplies for the beleaguered troops of General Jürgen von Arnim. Seventy-five transports were shot down in not many more seconds. Air Chief Marshal Tedder and General Clark decided in the end that the possible gain from our Volturno mission would not be worth the probable losses. The mission was called off, and thus ended GIANT I.

Thirteen days remained until D-day. General Ridgway and the staff of the 82nd Airborne Division returned to the headquarters of the division at Kairouan in North Africa, where preparations were continuing for any type of airborne mission that might fall to the division's lot.

On the evening of September 2 the Division Commander and several staff officers were called to the Headquarters 15th Army Group at Siracusa, Sicily, to receive the first information of a new mission. It was to be the seizure of Rome, one of the most interesting airborne plans of the war, a plan that was extensively discussed and argued about many years after the war. This operation, known as GIANT II, called for placing the strongest airborne task force that the available aircraft could carry, on and near three airfields immediately east and northeast of Rome. Because of the distance of Rome from the proposed take-off airfields in Sicily, there was no possibility of fighter support. The date for GIANT II was the night of September 8–9. The mission was to secure Rome by operating in conjunction with the Italian forces in the Rome area. The airborne lift was to be repeated the next night and as directed thereafter until the mission of the 15th Army Group was accomplished. The airborne part of the operation was to be supported by a landing at the mouth of the Tiber River, also staged by troops of the 82nd Division.

At a meeting with General Bedell Smith, accompanied by General Kenneth Strong, in August in Spain, the Italians had agreed to cooperate fully once the operations were undertaken. However, we realized that the Germans might make it impossible for the Italians to be of much help to us. By the time of the Salerno landings, the Germans had taken away all but a small amount of ammunition and most of the Italians' gasoline, thus effectively immobilizing them. So, while the Italians were now going to be on our side, we could not completely rely on them.

The mission posed some new and extremely interesting airborne problems. Again, the operation was beyond friendly fighter range, and since enemy fighters were very active, the operation was limited to hours of darkness. The simplest method of delivering the troops was to air-land them on airfields with the cooperation of the Italians. But since our transports were not to enter the enemy fighter range until after dark and they had to clear by daylight, rigid limitations had to be placed on the time that could be spent on the Rome airfields. Parachute troops, of course, require no landing time whatever; a completely equipped fighting force is dropped while the airplanes remain in flight. Landing C-47 transports on a one-strip airfield with a control officer on the field from the landing troop-carrier unit can rarely be done at a faster rate than thirty-six transports an hour. That rate has been exceeded but not under combat conditions. This means that at best a battalion of infantry an hour per available airfield is all that could be landed. And for practical planning purposes this is a very optimistic expectation.

In the Rome area the forces that could be air-landed in a single night would be relatively small. The airfields were small ones without runways. Effective cooperation of the Italian ground forces was especially doubtful. We might well find units of the German Wehrmacht at or near the fields. There was no assurance of efficient handling of aircraft damaged in landing, and it was not clear how traffic in and over the fields was to be controlled.

The Rome area was beyond glider range from the take-off airfields in Sicily. It had to be accepted that the success of the mission was wholly contingent on such full cooperation from the Italian military forces. The Italians would have to neutralize the German antiaircraft defenses along the planned flight route, protect the landing fields or drop zones to be used, furnish essential supplies, and in addition provide for military cooperation of all Italian forces against German troops. This amounted to quite a bill of goods.

The agreement reached between Allied authorities and the Italians at Siracusa provided for all these things. There were, in fact, several pages of itemized needs, including such things as telephones, picks, shovels, wire, gasoline, and civilian laborers, all of which were to be furnished by the Italian commander to the airborne troops. The Italians had also agreed to clear the Tiber River so that there could be amphibious support for the airborne landings.

Nevertheless, the planning moved at a rapid pace, and the afternoon of September 8 found the troops of the 82nd busily checking orders and plans, loading the para-containers, and making a last check on rations, ammo, and weapons.

But I think the fact is that the Italians at Siracusa had simply promised everything—much more than they could possibly have delivered. And it became fully evident that there were no guarantees of the needed support at the airfields where the regiments of the 82nd were to land, so the plans were changed almost at the last minute.

The latest plan provided for the leading assault regiment, the 504th Parachute Infantry, to land on the Furbara and Cerveteri airfields near the seacoast. From there they were to push inland toward Rome. The regiment that was to jump on the second night was the 505th Parachute Infantry. It was to land on Guidonia, Littorio, and the Centocelle airfields, all of which are considerably nearer the center of the city of Rome.

Since the Sicily operation, we had paid a great deal of attention to pathfinders as a means of having parachute transports home on the proper drop zones. For the Rome attack pathfinder airplanes and men were to precede the main landings of the 82nd. The pathfinder planes and personnel were based on the field at Agrigento, Sicily. On the evening of September 8 these were fully loaded, engines running and ready to take off. But minutes before the take-off, word came from higher authority that the mission had been postponed for twenty-four hours.

Brigadier General Maxwell D. Taylor, Chief of Artillery of the 82nd Airborne Division, had been sent through to Rome twenty-four hours earlier to confer with the leading Italian authorities. He was to inform the Allied commander by code whether or not in his opinion the operation should be attempted. General Taylor was taken by a British PT boat to the island of Ustica, where he was transferred to an Italian corvette that landed him at Gaeta, the scene of much bitter fighting later in the war. He was quickly taken from Gaeta to Rome where he conferred with General G. Carboni, commanding the Italian troops in the Rome area, and the aging Marshal Pietro Badoglio. The Marshal and General Carboni agreed that in recent days the German forces in Italy had been greatly increased in strength. They said further that the

Italian troops had little or no gasoline and enough ammunition for only a few hours of fighting, that they could not guarantee that all the airfields would be in Italian hands, and that, anyway, our airborne landings would cause the Germans to take drastic steps against the Italians. Therefore the whole plan as proposed would be nothing less than disastrous.

General Taylor decided they were right. He radioed the prearranged code message, and the operation was called off. D-day came and H-hour struck, and despite the many plans and the days and nights of staff work, the airborne troops found themselves sitting and waiting on their take-off airdromes. Patience is an essential attribute of a good airborne trooper.

Since World War II there has been much discussion about the proposed parachute landings around Rome. Ambassador Robert Murphy in his excellent book *Diplomat Among Warriors* details the meeting-by-meeting diplomatic negotiations that took place.

Although I had not been aware of it at the time, General Ridgway had insisted that two of the diplomats who had taken part in the planning also take part in the operation. They were Harold Macmillan, later Prime Minister of Great Britain, and Robert Murphy. Murphy approached Eisenhower with the idea, and as he recounts it in his book, "Eisenhower looked at us for a moment, and then said dryly, 'Well, all right. There is nothing in regulations which says diplomats are not expendable.' " Murphy and Macmillan had made eager preparations to embark on the adventure, and they were convinced that it would offer the Allies incalculable political advantages, so they were, of course, disappointed when, in the judgment of Generals Taylor and Ridgway, the mission had to be scratched. Murphy finally concluded that the airborne commanders had set their minds against the operation from the start for standard military reasons and because nobody trusted the Italians.

Another participant in the events was Peter Tompkins, who was in Rome working for the OSS at the time the landings were planned. He gives a lengthy account in his valuable book, *Italy Betrayed*.[3] He was convinced that the operation would have succeeded and was greatly disappointed when it was abandoned.

In 1950 I was stationed in Naples as Chief of Staff of Allied Forces

[3] Peter Tompkins, *Italy Betrayed*. New York: Simon & Schuster, 1966.

Southern Europe. I visited the airfields we had planned to use and studied the terrain around Rome. There is no doubt in my mind that the decision to cancel was a proper one. The parachutists were to land the first night at Furbara, just north of the Tiber, near the seacoast. If the Italians had provided the needed trucks, which was doubtful, and if there had been no German opposition, a very dangerous assumption at least, they could have reached Rome by daylight. However, between the airfield and Rome are many miles of ridges crossing the main highway that had been used in military exercises designed to test the defenses of Rome from attacks from the sea. German armored units could have held up the parachute forces almost indefinitely. The other fields were on the average of twenty-five miles northeast of Rome. It was on these fields that I was to land the following night. In addition, there was heavy ack-ack along the Tiber and around many of the airfields. To me, it was totally unrealistic to believe that the parachutists could have survived all that en route by air and then prevail against any German armored force on the ground. And, although we did not know it at the time, Hitler had sent the man he considered his best general, General Rommel, to Italy to take charge in anticipation of an anti-German move by the Italian government and the possibility of internal disorder encouraged by the Allies.

As the battle of Sicily had come to an end, the German high command, OKW, had become increasingly concerned about the possibility of an Italian defection. Hitler saw no advantage in committing major forces to the southern portion of Italy: first, because the terrain could be made to do most of the defensive work, and, second, because there was a real danger of the Allies landing in the vicinity of Salerno, or farther north, and thus cutting off German formations farther south. OKW therefore came to a firm decision on two points. First, a major commitment would be made to northern Italy to disarm the Italians and protect the passes through the Alps. Second, all the forces in southern Italy would be regrouped just south of Rome. Furthermore, if the Italians quit the war, the troops assembled south of Rome were to move north and join Rommel. In carrying out these decisions, the following specific moves were made. In August Army Group B was established under Rommel's command with its headquarters at Lake Garda. It was to consist of three corps headquarters with five infantry divisions and two armored divisions—a force of respectable size. On August 8 the German Tenth Army was created. It was to be commanded by General

Heinrich von Vietinghoff. Vietinghoff's headquarters were to be in the vicinity of Rome. His two southernmost divisions, the 26th Panzer and the 29th Panzer, were ordered to withdraw, which they proceeded to do. The 16th Panzer was generally along the Gulf of Salerno and farther south. These dispositions were known in detail to the Allied high command. Thus Montgomery's landings in Calabria and Apulia, the southern tip of Italy, were unopposed.

In early September the 29th Panzer Division and the 26th Panzer Division continued their withdrawal, with the 29th in the van. There was a delay of a day or so because of a fuel shortage, but they continued to comply with their mission—to withdraw to an area just south of Rome.

On September 8 the U.S. Fifth Army under the command of Lieutenant General Mark Clark closed in on Salerno Bay. On the north, Lieutenant General Sir Richard L. McCreery's X Corps, consisting of the British 46th and 56th Divisions, was to land. On the south was the U.S. VI Corps under the command of Major General Ernest J. Dawley. It had for the assault one U.S. untried division, the 36th (Texas National Guard). The Army commander had part of the U.S. 45th Division, battle experienced in Sicily, in reserve. In addition, there were American Rangers and British Commandos.

A number of us wondered about the use of the untried 36th Infantry Division. We had assumed that the Fifth Army did not expect heavy opposition to the landings; hence the use of the 36th. With the advantage of "ultra-secret" information, we now know that the Fifth Army was given information on the locations of all the German divisions. Despite the presence of strong detachments of the German 16th Panzer Division, the 36th did exceptionally well. Driving inland, it seized the high hills at Altavilla, Albanella, and Rocca d'Aspide. After the first forty-eight hours there was considerable satisfaction in the higher command with the good work of the 36th, despite the fact that there was a gap almost ten miles wide between the U.S. divisions and the nearest British divisions to the north.

Vietinghoff was carrying out his mission, moving his Panzers toward Rome and well inland from the beaches, when news of the Salerno landings reached him. He asked Kesselring's permission to counterattack the Fifth Army. Kesselring did not reply, so on his own initiative Vietinghoff launched an attack. Based on information he received from his reconnaissance forces, which had successfully probed and discovered the gap between the British and the American corps, Vietinghoff attacked the northern flank of the U.S. 36th. Under the weight of the battle-experienced Panzers, the thinly held front of the 36th collapsed. The high ground and the villages on it were overrun. The Germans were ecstatic and reported that they were in pursuit of the retreating Americans and that they expected to drive them back into the sea. Indeed, General Clark told his Chief of Staff, General Alfred M. Gruenther, to talk to the Navy about withdrawal plans. Fortunately, the arrival of the 504th Parachute Infantry Regiment of the 82nd on the night of September 13 swung the tide of the battle back in favor of the Americans.

It is quite possible that Mark Clark's Fifth Army Headquarters and his staff had little confidence in "Ultra" intelligence. Author F. W. Winterbotham notes that when he first called on General Eisenhower and General Clark at Norfolk House in London to brief them on "Ultra" intelligence:

> Eisenhower excused himself from the meeting and Mark Clark was restless from the start. I explained not only what the source was, but in an endeavor to catch Mark Clark's interest, gave some pertinent examples of what it could do. I had intended to follow this with an explanation of how the information would reach him and the security regulations which accompanied its use. But Mark Clark didn't appear to believe the first part and after a quarter of an hour, he excused himself, and his officers, on the grounds that he had something else to do.[4]

On September 13, about 1:30 P.M., a tired, begrimed pilot from the Salerno beachhead landed at Licata Field in Sicily in a fighter plane. He had an urgent message for the Division Commander and refused to give it to anyone else. I talked to him on the field, but finally had the Chief of Staff radio General Ridgway, who had taken off for Termini. General Ridgway came back immediately.

The message was a personal letter from General Mark Clark, Fifth Army Commander. It contained an appeal for immediate help. Specifically, he wanted one regimental combat team dropped inside the beach-

[4] F. W. Winterbotham, *The Ultra Secret*. New York: Harper & Row, 1974, p. 90. In the opinion of the author of *The Ultra Secret,* if the Fifth Army convoys had held off their landings for forty-eight hours, and continued farther north, then turning back to Salerno, they probably could have landed unopposed and Vietinghoff's Panzers would have been north of Naples in continuation of the mission earlier assigned them. (Personal correspondence with F. W. Winterbotham, dated July 28, 1975.)

head south of the Sele River that night, another dropped on the mountain village of Avellino, far behind the German lines, on the night of September 14. (*Fig. 5.*)

The airborne and troop carrier staffs went into a hasty huddle. They reallocated the departure fields, reshuffled troops as necessary, and prepared flight plans. An immediate check was made to insure that our own ground troops and our Navy received clear warning of our routes and times, with descriptions of our flights. The messenger with General Clark's letter also delivered a plan for marking the drop zone prepared by a Fifth Army Airborne staff officer. The troops already in the area would use cans of sand soaked with gasoline, laid out in the form of a large letter "T." They would light them up upon the approach of the first flight of transports over the drop zone, and douse them out with dirt when the transports had gone.

In addition, special pathfinding homing equipment was to be dropped on the Sele River beachhead drop zone with the stick from the first airplane. This would then be used to assist the following airplanes to home accurately on the drop zone. All pilots and jumpmasters were carefully briefed on the plan. Such pathfinder refinements could not be used, of course, for the Avellino drop zone, which was well behind the German lines.

All plans were complete eight hours after the request for reinforcements came from General Clark, and the troops were loaded with their complete equipment, rations, and ammunition, and the C-47s were rolling down the runways on their way. By shortly after midnight the 504th Parachute Infantry, with Company C of the 307th Airborne Engineers attached, had made its landing and assembled near Paestum, and by daylight it was in the front lines, fresh, eager, and looking for a fight.

That same night the 509th Parachute Infantry landed at Avellino. The following night the 505th Parachute Infantry landed at Paestum.

I flew with the 505th. After the Sicilian experience we were all quite apprehensive. However, we were in such a rush to get our proper orders out and assemble the necessary arms, equipment, and ammunition that we had little time to think about what was going to happen to us. We took off on schedule. It was a beautiful, clear night with considerable moonlight. Soon after we left the northwest corner of Sicily, the Italian mainland came into view off to the east. We crossed a peninsula jutting out into the Tyrrhenian Sea. In the plane the red warning light came on to tell us that we were approximately four minutes out from the drop zone. We seemed to have been flying over the peninsula forever when a white beach and a river mouth appeared. The scene looked exactly like that in the photos of the correct drop zone. The green light flashed on. There was no burning T on the ground as we had been told there would be, but the area appeared to be correct in every way, so out we went.

The first parachutes had barely opened when the great T did light up directly under us. To the Germans who occupied the hills, the operation must have appeared bizarre. Units began to reorganize; they assembled without any interference. A combat team was in action by daylight.

The regiment that had jumped the first night, the 504th, had had little sustained combat in Sicily; it was commanded by a tough, superb combat leader, Colonel Reuben Tucker, probably the best regimental combat commander of the war. He seemed eager to get into combat, and as the troops prepared to load the airplanes, he drove by in a jeep, speaking to each planeload. His message was brief: "Men, it's open season on Krauts, you know what to do."[5]

The first mission assigned to the 504th was the seizure of the town of Altavilla and the high hill mass on which it was located. Two hills dominated the area, one 424 meters high, on which Altavilla was located, and the other close by, 415 meters. General Ridgway kept one battalion of the 504th as division reserve and committed Tucker to the seizure of the town, which was then well organized and held by the Germans. Tucker moved out in darkness and after a couple of hours' march reached the foot of the hills. One of the troopers in the regiment, writing about his experience after the war, described a scene involving Colonel Tucker:

> The little colonel was up to his ears in battle and seemed to be having a hell of a good time. Altavilla, where the enemy had heavy infantry and tank forces, lay under the hill and slightly to the rear. The little colonel turned to a Greek-American paratrooper named Perici.
>
> "Perici, take six men and go into Altavilla and find out how many Krautheads are in it."
>
> Resolutely Perici replied, "No, sir, I can't go into that town."
>
> The little colonel, gasping with rage, pulled out his .45. "Perici, why can't you go into Altavilla?"
>
> "Sir," rejoined Perici calmly, "I've been in this army for four years.

[5] Ross Carter, *Those Devils in Baggy Pants*. New York: Appleton-Century-Crofts, 1951.

I done learned that I can't go to town without a pass. The MP's would get me as shore as hell is red-hot."

With a tight smile on his lips, the colonel wrote out a pass for Sergeant Perici to enter the town with six men. Perici, satisfied, went into the town, where he and his patrol got shot up. They found out the krauthead strength, and, although wounded, Perici returned to report as follows to the colonel: "Sir, they's MP's in that damn town with tanks and half-tracks. A rough bunch, sir!"[6]

Tucker deployed his two battalions and moved out against the German positions during darkness. He completely overran the Germans, leaving a number of them in his rear. They reacted vigorously at dawn. Four successive counterattacks, well supported by artillery and tank fire, were made against Tucker's 504th, but it proved to be just as tough as its sister regiment, the 505th, at Biazza Ridge. It destroyed all the Germans and held on to its position.

They talked to me at some length after the battle. Evidently, upon landing, the 36th Division had seized the town. Because of its importance as an observation post, the Germans counterattacked vigorously and overran the 36th. When the 504th took over, the dead and wounded of the 36th were scattered about the streets and in the buildings. The 504th thought they were in very bad shape—not surprising, considering the fact that the 36th had never been in combat before. After forty-eight hours, knowing that very heavy fighting had been taking place and that Tucker had only two battalions, the Commanding General of the 82nd ordered him to withdraw. Colonel Tucker's reply was, "Hell, no! We've got this hill and we are going to keep it."[7] He also added, "Send me my other battalion." But the successful seizure and defense of Altavilla seemed to turn the tide, and shortly thereafter the Germans began a withdrawal.

The other unit that parachuted the same night as the 504th was the 509th Parachute Infantry. The 2nd Battalion of the 509th had been attached to the 82nd Airborne Division. It had participated in the landings in North Africa in the fall of '42. Since then, under the able leadership of Colonel Edson Raff, it had given a very good account of itself. It was now to drop on the small Italian town of Avellino.

Avellino is a typical Italian town nestled in a deep mountain pass about twenty miles from the Salerno beaches. It lies at the junction of

[6] Ibid., p. 54.
[7] Ibid., p. 64.

several important roads, to Salerno and Battipaglia to the north, and toward which German reserves were likely to come from farther south where hard-pressed German divisions were withdrawing under the pressure of the British Eighth Army. As a road center, Avellino was a stopping point for numerous transient units. There were, however, no suitable drop zones in the area; what few flat cleared areas the photographs showed were too small, and the mountains were so high that it was impossible to jump at proper low altitudes.

When the 2nd Battalion, 509th, flown by the 64th Troop Carrier Group, rolled down the runways at Licata Field, Sicily, early on the evening of September 13 and headed for Italy, it was undaunted and confident. But the small town of Avellino looked like many other small mountain towns, and the lower air was full of battle haze. From the high altitude at which the mission had to be flown, Avellino proved too hard to find. Few of the transport ships reached their proper drop zones.

The troopers were scattered over an area of more than a hundred square miles. Despite this first great handicap, individual troopers and small units gave a good account of themselves. They mined roads, blew up bridges, and destroyed German communications. They ambushed small enemy columns and shot isolated German messengers. The 509th caused a considerable number of German troops to be committed to antiparachute and searching work. Of the 640 troopers who jumped, approximately 510 eventually filtered back to the Allied lines. The experience of the battalion commander himself was typical of what happened to many who did not get back. He landed in the midst of a German tank park and immediately got into a small-arms fight. He was finally wounded and captured.

The battalion had accomplished what General Mark Clark had had in mind. It disrupted German communications and partly blocked the Germans' supplies and reserves. It also caused the Germans to keep units on antiparachute missions that otherwise could have been used at the point of their main effort at Salerno. In fact, the Germans used many more troops for corrective and preventive purposes against the airborne troops than were committed by the Allied high command.

Salerno had been a touch-and-go affair. It came very close to being a disaster. Higher headquarters believed that the fact that the 45th Infantry Division had done so well in Sicily indicated that the inexperienced 36th should be able to match its performance at Salerno. There were two big differences between these operations. First, in Sicily the paratroopers had landed in front of the 45th Division and intercepted enemy troops, knocked out pillboxes, cleared mines, until the 45th was well established ashore. In addition, the paratroopers had protected the left flank of the 45th Division from the attack of the Hermann Goering Division. The second difference was that in Italy German intelligence had discerned the Allied plans well, and German panzer troops were poised and waiting for the amphibious landing of the 36th Division.

In addition to the surprising strength of the German panzers and the rapidity of their counterattack, the Americans had a command problem. The American Corps commander, Major General Dawley, had not anticipated the intensity of the first days' fighting, and his command post was not organized and prepared to function when the fighting was at its bitterest point. General Clark personally took charge on the beachhead, and through his endeavors the situation was stabilized. With the arrival of the 82nd Airborne Division and then the linkup with the British Eighth Army, which was working its way up the boot, the battle for the landing had been won. I had reported to General Dawley as soon as I landed, and the 505th Parachute Infantry was his corps reserve. As a consequence, I stayed with him for several days. He seemed to be doing all a man could do in the circumstances. Much more had been expected of his command, and the weight of the German counterattack had been devastating. Shortly after the battle he was relieved of command and sent back to the United States, and Major General John Porter Lucas took his place.

The 82nd Airborne Division was moved to Amalfi, and the 505th Parachute Infantry moved up the mountain road from Amalfi to the top of the Sorrento Peninsula. There, near the small town of Agerola, where the Amalfi-Castellammare road goes through the tunnel at the top of the mountain, I established my command post. We were at one end of the tunnel and the Germans at the other. On September 28 I climbed to the top of the Sorrento Peninsula and there had my first view of Naples. Billowing black clouds of smoke covered the waterfront, and buildings were burning throughout the city. A pall of smoke and dust, so characteristic of a battlefield, hung over the area. I was told to attack and seize the town of Gragnano at the foot of the mountain the following morning. I had never fought in such terrain, and, looking back, I realize that if the plan I prepared had been carried out, it probably would have been a disaster. I had three separate columns moving down spurs of the mountains with the mission of making a combined attack on the hill overlooking Gragnano, about five miles away. Fortunately, at daylight on September 29, I learned that the Germans had withdrawn. I moved at once down the road into the town and then on to Castellammare. The following day we occupied Pompeii and Torre Annunziata. A battalion of the 36th Division had been attempting to make its way up the coastal road, with little success. It had been working closely with the British 23rd Mechanized Brigade commanded by Brigadier R. H. E. Arkwright. During the night of September 30 the 505th Parachute Infantry was attached to the British 23rd Mechanized Brigade and plans were made for an early jump-off in the direction of Naples.

I was sleeping on the floor of an Italian farmhouse when, just before daylight, I was awakened by a young British officer, reporting as a liaison officer from the 23rd Brigade. He was impeccable in appearance; his buttons shone with a high polish, and he looked as though he were ready to go on parade. From that moment on, I found my association with the British Army a most pleasant and delightful one. In many ways they took the whole war far less seriously than we, but, on the other hand, on matters of discipline and combat effectiveness they set very high standards.

The day began, as often happened during the early period of the battle for Italy, with the Germans completely out of sight, and our first attacks were blows into the air. The situation stiffened a bit; then late in the afternoon all resistance seemed to disappear. Soon there were throngs of people in the streets of the small villages along the main road to Naples. I wondered what would happen if the Germans were to counterattack. When we reached the city limits, we were ordered to halt while a unit of the 23rd Brigade made a reconnaissance into the city. The 505th had been attacking in two columns, the main column on the primary road and the right column, the 1st Battalion of the 505th, on a poor road up along the slopes of Mount Vesuvius. I was standing with the advance guard, discussing the situation, when the Regimental S-3, Major John Norton, approached. It was almost noon.

"Colonel," he said, "we are to wait until a triumphant entry is organized."

"A triumphant entry!" I exclaimed. "How in the world can we organize such a thing? It takes participation of the natives." I had never put anything like that together in my life, and visions crossed my mind of Napoleon's colorfully clad soldiers entering European capitals that had just capitulated, beautiful nubile women leaning over the balconies tossing flowers, much waving of handkerchiefs, and bands playing. And I recalled the entry of Allenby into Jerusalem—and here I was told to organize a triumphant entry.

Word came down that General Clark was going to come to the head of the column and that he would lead the triumphant march into the city. Then word arrived that we were to lead them into Garibaldi Square. I found it on the map; it was in front of the railroad station. But suppose instead of people tossing flowers there were Germans tossing grenades from the rooftops. And in any event, the masses of people milling around in the streets and throwing candy and offering bottles of wine to the troops all had to be dealt with.

There was also a certain amount of small-arms fire going on as the Neapolitans evened up old family scores, charging their enemies with being Fascists and German sympathizers. I finally decided that I would enter in a lead jeep, since I had to find my way through the streets, followed by a half-track in which General Clark would ride standing, with General Ridgway beside him, and that the 3rd Battalion of the 505th Parachute Infantry would be immediately behind them in trucks. The plan was to move directly into Garibaldi Square, and as General Clark's vehicle entered the square, the vehicles of the 3rd Battalion of the 505th would make a complete circle around the square and thus seal it off. The troopers would then jump from the trucks and clear all the people out of the square. Then, if General Clark wanted to make the customary conqueror's speech, he could do it from one of the trucks, or he might find some arrangement in the square more suitable. However, I was concerned about the likelihood of combat at any point along the way.

It was midafternoon before we were fully organized and Generals Clark and Ridgway took their place in the column. Finding my way in was not so difficult as I had anticipated, and the streets were ominously empty. The map took us right to Garibaldi Square, and as we pulled up into it, there was hardly a soul in sight. As General Clark described it in his book, *Calculated Risk,* "There was little that was triumphant about our journey. . . . I became aware that there was something besides the wreckage that impressed me. I felt that I was riding through ghostly streets in a city of ghosts. We didn't see a soul. . . . I made a quick survey of the area around Place Garibaldi and still saw almost no Italians, but I was becoming conscious of the eyes that peeked out on us from behind the closed shutters of every house and every building. It was still that way as we drove out of Naples."

Later I learned that thousands of people had massed at the Plaza Plebiscito about a mile away in another part of the city. It was here that the conquerors traditionally had been received, and the people had assumed that that was where the Allied generals would make their triumphant appearance.

The 82nd Airborne Division was at once committed to the task of cleaning up the city and restoring law and order. It was not easy, for there was a great deal of private fighting going on. The Germans had treated the Neapolitans severely, and anyone who was suspected of being a German sympathizer was at once the victim of retaliation. As darkness neared, I did not see how I could get the city under control, and General Ridgway was emphatic in his orders to me as he outlined my responsibilities. Occasionally a *carabinieri*, or city policeman, came by the command post, and while these men shrugged their shoulders and said the Neapolitans were difficult to control, they offered no help. Apprehensive about what would happen during the night, I told the Chief of Police just before darkness set in that any Italian, regardless of his sympathies, who possessed a weapon in the vicinity of where a weapon had been fired would be shot at once. He seemed startled and gulped a bit as we explained exactly what we meant; then off he went. A few minutes later a weapon was fired in a side street. I took a platoon of troopers and went right out to get anyone with a weapon. The men had orders to shoot. No one with a weapon could be found. Almost at once quiet descended over the city. The next morning the situation was well under control, and we began to clear up the debris, clear the port, get the utilities back in operation, and provide food.

The 505th Parachute Infantry continued to attack northward to the Volturno River. The fighting was not too costly, and the Germans were obviously withdrawing. They would usually make a stand by late morning, and after we drove them back and prepared for a heavy attack the following morning, we invariably found that they had withdrawn during the night. Just before we reached the Volturno, General Ridgway called me back to division headquarters and informed me that I was to be the Assistant Division Commander. I hated to leave the 505th, since I had been through so much combat with it, but it would still be in the division with me. On Sunday, October 10, I was promoted to Assistant Division

Commander and made a brigadier general. General Ridgway arranged for a brief star-pinning ceremony in front of the Questura, the city police station, which we had been using as a headquarters.

As Mark Clark's Fifth Army made its way from the Volturno northward and Montgomery's Eighth Army attacked northward on the other side of the boot, a gap slowly developed in the center. It was to fill this gap that Mark Clark asked General Ridgway for a parachute regiment. Ridgway chose the 504th. I made several visits to the 504th when it was in the mountains, in an unbelievable situation. The mountains were very high, totally rocky, and generally devoid of trees and cover. One hill they fought over was 1205 meters high. It was very cold at night, frequently rainy, and soon the first snow appeared. Unfortunately, most of the troopers were still wearing their summer jumpsuits. The fighting was extremely difficult, with frequent personal encounters and surprises for the unwary combatant. All supplies had to be brought up by mule. There was a chronic shortage of water, food, and ammunition, and, of course, the wounded had to be taken out by mule. But Colonel Tucker was a combat leader of extraordinary ability. Again, one of his troopers later described a situation that evolved about the defense of Hill 1205:

> About eleven o'clock the little colonel with one man as a bodyguard came down from 1205 wanting to know why in hell the attack had failed. The battalion medical officer who came with him brought one bottle of whiskey for the entire company! It was the best he could do and we appreciated his good will. Although every man thirsted for the whole bottle, no one more than touched it to his lips for fear the next man wouldn't get a taste. Some of the drinkingest men in the Army refused it entirely so that their buddies could get a drop.
>
> The little colonel took two men, walked to the pillbox, caught the Nazis cleaning the machine gun, and took eleven prisoners without firing a shot. He made us look silly.[8]

The 504th continued to fight in the mountains until well after Christmas. By the time it was taken out, the casualties had been heavy and the weather and terrain the worst in which it was ever to fight. From there, the 504th was brought back to the Naples area and readied for the Anzio landing.

By the time the 504th finished fighting in Anzio, it was beginning to discover that it had in its ranks quite a few troopers with a flare for the unusual. Among them was a youngster by the name of Bachenheimer.

[8] Ibid.

He had grown up in Germany and had come to the United States when he was twelve years old. He spoke English and German fluently. He had been captured by the Germans in Sicily but managed to escape. At Anzio he developed considerable facility in moving around among the German units. On one occasion he joined a chow line and, having finished a meal of wieners and potatoes, captured the German troops that had been eating with him and took them back to the 504th. When the 504th left Anzio after sixty-three days in combat, Bachenheimer knew most of the German command posts as well as their supply points and medical stations. According to the veterans of the 504th, he even knew the officers and their reputations among the German troops. His next combat after Anzio was to be in Holland, where he was to organize more than three hundred underground fighters, working behind the German lines. He was also to give his life.

The Anzio landing was made on January 22, 1944, by the U.S. VI Corps commanded by Major General John Porter Lucas. Tucker originally expected his regiment to remain in floating reserve and possibly not be committed to the battle at all. Very soon, however, his men were ordered over the side and went into the line on the right flank of the beachhead under the command of the U.S. 3rd Infantry Division. They were generally along the Mussolini Canal. The day of the landing was cold and wintry. Anzio itself was a small port from which the land stretched, flat and exposed, to a line of hills some distance away. The hills were never taken; they remained in the hands of the Germans and were used as observation posts. The troopers often talked to me about their Anzio fighting after the regiment joined the division in England. The mud, the cold, the constant harassment by artillery fire, and the heavy nighttime infantry attacks lingered in their memories.

Anzio remains one of the most controversial campaigns of World War II. Its launching was a consequence of a number of events that made it almost inevitable. By late November 1943 the German Winter Line in the mountains was well established and proving to be very effective. By mid-November General Clark was of the opinion that continuing frontal attacks would exhaust his divisions to a dangerous degree. In order to break the stalemate, on November 8 General Alexander had issued instructions to the Fifth Army to plan an amphibious landing to seize Anzio, thirty-five miles from Rome. General Clark, remembering the Salerno experience, was initially quite skeptical, believing the inadequate troops would be put ashore and that there would not be enough shipping available to support them. Nevertheless, he tried to carry out the wishes of General Alexander and began to plan for the operation. He insisted to Alexander that he could not do it without more assault shipping.

Alexander dealt with this by cabling Prime Minister Winston Churchill that fourteen more LSTs were required—they had sixty-eight. In late December Churchill, returning from the Cairo Conference, stopped in Tunis. He was in a very run-down physical condition, and his doctor decided that he had pneumonia. He remained in Tunis until he recovered and then went to Marrakech to recuperate. During this period he had frequent meetings with senior officers as he sought to convince them of the merits of the proposed Anzio landing. Churchill had always been a strong advocate of amphibious operations in the Mediterranean area, even going back to World War I and the ill-fated Dardanelles campaign. So the stalemate along the Winter Line, the availability of marginal amounts of shipping for a limited time, the availability of combat-experienced troops, and Churchill's enthusiasm for the "cat-claw" were brought together. But, when all was said and done, "It was essentially Churchill's decision."[9]

Obviously Winston Churchill expected an assault to be made in order to seize Rome not long after the landing. Alexander hoped that the troops would reach the Alban Hills, twenty miles inland, thus cutting a main north-south road to Kesselring's armies and seizing the high ground covering the beachhead. Clark continued to be skeptical, and his G-3—the staff officer responsible for all the planning and the conduct of army operations—cautioned Lucas against being too aggressive until he had the corps and beachhead in hand.

The landing on January 22 was virtually unopposed. The veteran divisions moved out to their initial battle lines, supplies and reinforcements were brought ashore, and the landings could only be described as having been successful. General Alexander, who had visited the beachhead on the first day, returned on January 25 and commented to General Lucas, "What a splendid piece of work."[10]

Churchill, however, continued to be very impatient. Kesselring had not stampeded. All the Allied efforts that were made to break through

[9] *U.S. Army in World War II, Mediterranean Theater of Operations, Salerno to Cassino,* Martin Blumenson, Office of the Chief of Military History, Department of the Army, Washington, D.C., p. 298.
[10] Ibid., p. 387.

the Winter Line came to naught, and Kesselring rapidly began to build up a force, initially made up of piecemeal detachments, to contain Lucas. In time the Germans were able to launch a major counterattack that they were confident would destroy Lucas's forces. In this they failed, but by now everyone was unhappy with Lucas's stalemate. He was visited by several high-ranking officers, among them General Jacob Loucks Devers and General Alexander. Alexander expressed doubts about Lucas's performance to Mark Clark. He also sent a telegram to Field Marshal Alan Brooke to consult Eisenhower. This, in turn, brought the matter to the attention of Churchill.[11] General Clark visited him on February 22, 1944, and told him that the pressures upon him, Clark, were so great that he was going to have to relieve General Lucas of his command. He did so at once.

The case of John Porter Lucas deserves some comment. Born on January 14, 1890, he was of the Class of 1911 out of the Military Academy at West Point. He was fifty-four at the time of the Anzio landings, senior in years to all the higher commanders then in the Mediterranean theater except Patton. A widely read man of unusual intelligence and sensitivity, he had been highly regarded in the peacetime Army. He was so well thought of that on December 17, 1943, Eisenhower, in writing to General George Marshall, had recommended that Lucas be given command of the Fifth Army, and Clark command of the theater when Eisenhower went to London to head the OVERLORD operation later in the year. In later years, in 1948, Lucas was Deputy Commander of the Fifth Army in Chicago, at which time I was Chief of Staff. We had numerous discussions about the Anzio affair. He was bitter about his relief. He told me that he had told General Clark and the Fifth Army staff that the troops were inadequate if he was to be expected to go to Rome or the Alban Hills. Nevertheless, Clark insisted that he either take the VI Corps in or be relieved of his command. Lucas, in turn, believed that Clark did not have the fortitude to stand up to Winston Churchill and General Alexander. As a consequence, Lucas was on the spot. As a career soldier, he could not refuse to carry out Clark's orders and thus be relieved of command. So the landing was made as planned and apparently was a successful one. Nevertheless,

---

[11] In *Triumph in the West,* a history of the war years based upon the diaries of Field Marshal Brooke, written in 1959, Arthur Bryant quotes Alexander as follows: "Field Marshal Alexander, in his Dispatches, written after the war, says that at the time he thought Lucas was wrong, yet, looking back, he feels he was right to wait and consolidate."

Lucas was relieved for not being more tigerish. Winston Churchill was to observe, "I expected to land a tiger and instead I have a stranded whale." With that observation, the blame had to be placed somewhere and someone had to go. It was Lucas.

In mid-November General Ridgway talked to me about the forthcoming landings in Normandy. They were to take place in the spring of 1944, and they would have a large parachute and glider contingent. In response to a request from General Eisenhower, he decided to send me to London to participate in the planning for OVERLORD, the code name for the Normandy landings. At the same time he told me that I would be returned to the division to participate in the battle—a most welcome assurance.

In Italy we continued to study our methods and the results we had achieved in our two airborne operations. North of Naples, along the ocean, there was an extensive area from which the inhabitants had been removed in anticipation of landings being made there by the Allies before Salerno. There were considerable barbed wire, pillboxes, and abandoned houses prepared for combat. All the troops were put through realistic training exercises in the area. We had been pleased with the Salerno landing, and it was obvious that the pathfinder teams had made a difference. It was difficult to miss a drop zone so well marked.

While we were in Italy, we continued to conduct experiments in both parachute landing and gliding landing in Sicily. In order to help our glider pilots we trained parachute pathfinders to jump with lights that were then used to mark a landing strip. The lights were placed in pairs about fifty yards apart, and about four pairs were placed the length of the landing strip. We found by experiment that they gave the glider pilots a sense of perspective, and we were quite confident, in view of our training experience, that we could successfully conduct large-scale glider landings at night. When we thought we had achieved a good state of efficiency, we invited a number of the senior officers to come to the troop carrier headquarters in Agrigento, Sicily, to see a night demonstration. Unknown to us, the troop carrier unit that was to provide the glider pilots had been changed and the pilots called upon to make the night landing were entirely inexperienced. The demonstration was a shambles, with gliders landing all over the place. Fortunately, only one pilot was hurt, and not too seriously. We were still convinced, however, that night landing of gliders was entirely feasible.

We changed our minds concerning one aspect of entry into combat.

Before Sicily, individuals and small groups were taught to attack the enemy at once, whenever encountered and regardless of the size of the force. With the Sicilian experience in mind, we decided that in some circumstances it would be better for individuals or small groups not to attack overwhelming numbers of enemy; that would result only in their death or capture. Instead, we now began to train troopers to avoid engagements with units they could not cope with and instead to make their way carefully to their objective area and there gain contact, if possible, with friendlier troops. This proved both realistic and helpful in the Normandy operation.

Normandy

Airborne combat in Sicily and Italy had been invaluable in preparation for the Normandy operation. We learned what could be done by parachute troops and troop carrier pilots, but, more important, we learned what they could not do. The airborne troops had more than held their own against German infantry, but meeting German armor in good tank country could be disastrous. The airborne-troop carrier team had to be thoroughly trained and honed to a keen edge. Small mistakes could lead to disaster, with airborne troops badly scattered and heavy troop carrier losses. On the other hand, with hard work and thorough training, the team could be made into an extremely effective battle force, a force that could tip the scales to victory in any future combat operation. And although we had made a number of mistakes and learned costly lessons in Sicily, that had been a comparatively small operation. For OVERLORD there would be three airborne divisions, more than 1300 transports, and 3300 gliders. It was to be a tremendous undertaking that would require a prodigious effort in troop and pilot training and in coordinating the endeavors of the many higher headquarters.

In the meantime changes in higher command positions were being made in anticipation of the needs of OVERLORD. They were to have considerable impact on the outcome of the battle. General Sir Alan Brooke had long aspired to the highest command, and he had been given some assurance by Winston Churchill that he would get it. Nevertheless, when the Prime Minister, accompanied by Brooke, went to Quebec in early August 1943 to confer with the Americans about the forthcoming battle, they found the Americans determined that the position should go to an American.

In anticipation of the conference in Quebec, Secretary of War

Stimson wrote a strongly worded memorandum to President Roosevelt, opening with the observation:

> First: We cannot now rationally hope to be able to cross the Channel and come to grips with our German enemy under a British commander. His Prime Minister and his Chief of the Imperial Staff are frankly at variance with such a proposal. The shadows of Passchendaele and Dunquerque still hang too heavily over the imagination of these leaders. . . .
>
> . . . I believe that the time has come when we must put our most commanding soldier in charge of this critical operation at this critical time. . . . General Marshall already has a towering eminence of reputation as a tried soldier and as a broad-minded and skillful administrator. . . . I believe that he is the man who most surely can now by his character and skill furnish the military leadership which is necessary. . . .[1]

The Prime Minister and General Brooke arrived in Canada on August 9, a few days before the Quebec meeting. Winston Churchill at once journeyed to Hyde Park to meet with President Roosevelt. He returned apparently convinced of the legitimacy of the American claim to the position. On August 15 he told Brooke of his judgment. It was a severe blow to Brooke, and he wrote in his diary: "I felt no longer necessarily tied to Winston and free to assume this Supreme Command which he had already promised me on three separate occasions. It was a crushing blow to hear from him that he was now handing over his appointment to the Americans, . . ."[2]

So General George Marshall was to be the Supreme Allied Commander. With the Quebec conference over, and as summer waned and the end of the year neared, President Roosevelt began to feel that Marshall was indispensable to the war effort in Washington. Therefore, at the conference in Cairo in early December 1943, President Roosevelt proposed that Eisenhower be substituted for Marshall. In this Winston Churchill concurred. Stopping off in Tunis on the way back from Cairo, President Roosevelt told Eisenhower of the decision. It was news to Eisenhower. It was also decided to move General Montgomery to London. There he would command the 21st Army Group, the highest land

[1] Arthur Bryant, *The Turn of the Tide*. London: William Collins Sons & Co. Ltd., 1957, pp. 700–701.
[2] Ibid., p. 707.

battle command in the Normandy invasion.[3] Thus Montgomery would command all the ground troops in the Normandy assault.

It was anticipated that Patton's Army would be committed to battle in July 1944, depending on how the battle developed. When Patton's Third Army was committed, General Courtney H. Hodges was to take command of the U.S. First Army and General Omar Bradley then would take command of the newly organized U.S. 12th Army Group. The 12th Army Group therefore would consist of the First and Third U.S. Armies; thus Montgomery and Bradley were to have equivalent command positions. Later Simpson's Ninth U.S. Army was to join Bradley's 12th Army Group.

It is important to note that Eisenhower was to have on his staff Admiral Bertram Ramsay as Naval Commander in Chief. He was British. And Air Chief Marshal Sir Trafford Leigh-Mallory, named Air Commander in Chief, also was British. There was to be no senior officer responsible for land affairs; Eisenhower himself was to have direct responsibility for the land battle. In time this arrangement was to be the source of much contention on the part of Montgomery, who believed that Eisenhower lacked any sense of strategy or command ability, although Montgomery conceded that Eisenhower had marked diplomatic ability in bringing Allied forces together. In these arrangements were the seeds of much trouble that plagued the command until the end of the war and well may have delayed it from the fall of '44 until the spring of '45.

En route to the United Kingdom, I left Pomigliano Airfield in Naples at 8:30 A.M. on November 16, stopped in Palermo for lunch with my friends in the Troop Carrier Command, and arrived in Algiers that evening. The delay in Palermo was important, since it gave me an opportunity to check on the progress of our pathfinder experiments. For the past month or so we had been experimenting with selected troopers and troop carrier pilots in developing pathfinder techniques. The experiments were quite successful, and we were to start training pathfinder crews and troopers as soon as we reached England.

Before leaving, I had a final brief meeting with General Ridgway. He cautioned me against the machinations and scheming of General F. M. Browning, who was the senior British airborne officer, and well he should have. For although the Americans had provided most of the

[3] To the Allies, it was to go down in history as "The Normandy Invasion," a term Eisenhower did not like. To the French, it has always been "The Embarkation."

troops and airlift, the British seemed determined to take command of the total Allied airborne effort. General Browning had not been in a command position so far but had been promoted to Lieutenant General; thus, because of his rank, he would automatically be given command of any combined British-American airborne force. I do not believe that he had any sinister design on our resources, but the British seemed to be convinced that they were better at planning and employing airborne troops than we were.

From Algiers I flew directly to Marrakech, arriving there at 4:30 in the afternoon of November 17. I left Marrakech that evening at 10:30 aboard a four-engine air-freight flight and flew well out over the Atlantic and turned north, staying beyond German interceptor range from France. During the night we stretched out on the floor of the plane, crowded in like sardines, and tried to sleep. We arrived at Prestwick, Scotland, at 11:30 the following morning. I flew directly from Prestwick to London, arriving about 4:00 that same afternoon. There I registered at Grosvenor House, where billets were provided by ETOUSA (European Theater of Operations United States Army).

On my first day in London I called on the American Deputy Chief of Staff of COSSAC (Chief of Staff Supreme Allied Command), Major General Ray Barker. COSSAC, which was located in Norfolk House on St. James's Square, had been established to do the initial planning for OVERLORD, the cross-Channel attack. General Barker took me in to meet the Chief of Staff of COSSAC, a British officer, Lieutenant General Frederick E. Morgan. General Morgan was a quiet, scholarly type of officer and an excellent chief of staff. He told me that I was to be the senior airborne adviser on the COSSAC staff. While I was in his office, General "Boy" Browning joined us. He made a rather unkind remark to me about General Ridgway's not having parachuted into Sicily. I told him that I thought General Ridgway had handled the division as it should have been handled, that he had had much more responsibility than just the parachute assault. When I left General Morgan's office, I stopped by the office of General Barker. I mentioned my brief meeting with General Browning, and he remarked, "Ah, yes, he is an empire builder." After the war I learned that a few weeks after this meeting General Browning had had a meeting with the commander of the U.S. Troop Carrier Force, General Lewis H. Brereton. General Brereton gave an account of it in his *Brereton Diaries,* published in 1946. The U.S. 9th Air Force, which in turn commanded all the U.S. Troop Carrier formations, was under General Brereton's command. The British depended on the Americans for most of their airlift. Neither the Americans nor the British had anywhere near enough lift for all our available forces. General Brereton's diary account follows:

> Stanmore, 9 December 1943. At a conference at AEAF headquarters on airborne operations, it was suggested by 21st Army Group (British) (General Montgomery's headquarters) and Lieut. Gen. Browning, British airborne commander, that all Troop Carrier Forces be under a single command. I agreed in principle provided the command is American. This was unacceptable to the British.

It was very strange indeed for a soldier to be recommending to the Air Force how to organize its troop carrier forces. I can only conclude that if he had been successful in persuading them to organize a single command, General Browning then would have pointed out the need for a comparable command for the airborne troops, of which he would then be the commanding general.

After visiting COSSAC, I went to the headquarters of General Omar Bradley in Bryanston Square. I had a good meeting with General Bradley, and I believe we were both glad to see each other. He was an enthusiastic supporter of airborne operations, and he insisted that the parachute troops be used. Some senior officers, particularly those in the R.A.F., believed that the airborne operation would be too costly. General Bradley and I discussed the then current COSSAC plan. We both realized, however, that it was likely to be changed when the Supreme Allied Commander had been appointed.

It was understood that when the Supreme Allied Commander was designated COSSAC would become the Supreme Allied Command. By mid-December the COSSAC staff had developed several plans, a number of them contingent on an anticipated early collapse of Germany. One of the plans anticipated a rapid movement by air of troops to Norway if there were indications of a German withdrawal; another, a quick seizure of the seaport at Le Havre and the nearby airfields. These plans were kept quite alive during the OVERLORD planning process, but the cross-Channel plan was by far the most important one. That plan envisioned the landing of three divisions, two British and one American, along the Normandy coast between the Orne and Vire rivers, with two more divisions as follow-up force. The two follow-up U.S. Airborne Divisions were to land close together, south of Bayeux, with the mission

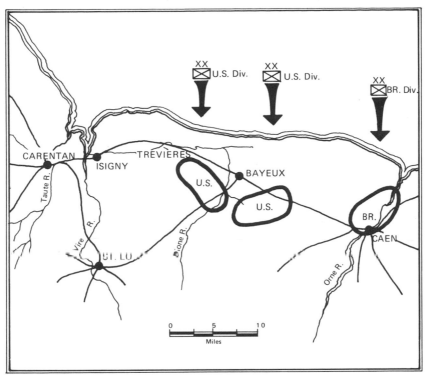

Fig. 6 First Airborne Plan, Normandy

of blocking German forces that might attack the amphibious landings. (*Fig. 6.*) It was a grossly inadequate force for the task and undoubtedly would have been an oversize Dieppe. General Bradley, in his book *A Soldier's Story,* written after the war, referred to it as "this miserly allocation of troops." Eisenhower first saw it in December when he was returning to the United States. He did not want to pass judgment on it, but it did strike him as being on too small a scale on too limited a front. General Montgomery first saw it when he visited Winston Churchill at Marrakech on December 31, 1943. He came to an identical conclusion: "the landing is on too narrow a front and is confined to too small an area." Fortunately, Montgomery arrived in London in January, and he at once began to make changes in the plan. Eisenhower, who was in the States, had asked Montgomery to represent him until he could arrive in mid-January. Both General Eisenhower and General Montgomery were convinced that the assault forces had to be larger than three divisions. Additional divisions were available but not the shipping. It was therefore decided that a proposed landing in southern France would be delayed until late in the summer. With the additional shipping, it was now possible to include an extensive portion of the Cherbourg peninsula in the landing.

On January 2 General Montgomery arrived in London. Crowds followed him about; by now he was a legend to the British people. Those who had fought beside him in Sicily had some misgivings. But he was a resourceful and thorough planner. The planning was moved from Norfolk House on St. James's Square in London to St. Paul's School in Hammersmith. There we got down to the realities of what had to be done.

Our planning had to begin with a determination of an objective for the amphibious assault. Early in our planning we were told that our first objective was to establish a firm lodgment from which we could not be driven by the German forces known to be nearby. Our next objective was to seize Cherbourg as rapidly as possible, and, finally, to achieve a build-up in the lodgment area and a breakout with a subsequent defeat of the major German commands opposing us. Searching for answers to the many questions these objectives posed was the first task of the planners. We had sufficient troops to establish a lodgment, provided we could cause the Germans to be misled and thus oppose us with much less than their total capability. This could be accomplished if we could select landing areas that would permit us to become well established ashore very quickly. And, of course, we had to be backed by adequate logistic support and reinforcement to meet any contingency.

With these points in mind, therefore, we undertook an exhaustive analysis of the German troop dispositions, man-made and natural obstacles to our landings, suitable port sites, and other circumstances. These points had been under study for several years, and there was a great deal of information available. Furthermore, daily air photographic runs were made by the R.A.F. and the USAF in the morning and in the evening when the shadows of objects were long. The amphibious forces, quite naturally, were intensely interested in the beach defenses, which were extensive, beginning with obstacles in the water that were mined, backed up by mortar and artillery positions on the high ground overlooking the beaches, and these, in turn, backed up by large-caliber artillery emplacements. They posed formidable obstacles to the amphibious landings. The airborne landing areas had to be selected so as to contribute directly to the success of the amphibious landings, both by blocking enemy troop movements toward the beaches and by helping open avenues of approach from the beaches to the interior. There was a great deal of information about the troop dispositions, both those along the beaches and farther to the rear. Further, the air photograph experts were skillful in identifying troop locations. For example, the French had practically no automobiles—they mostly used bicycles; however, all the German military formations had a number of vehicles that could invariably be identified near their command posts. The Germans had a practice of digging emplacements into the banks of the roads into which the vehicles would be driven to protect them from bombing attacks. Characteristically, these chevron-like excavations showed up at once when a command post of any size was opened. Usually, too, the Germans picked large, tree-surrounded châteaux for their headquarters. The digging would soon be followed by barbed wire surrounding the command post and, in turn, gun emplacements that could be located in relationship to the wire. There were other indications as well, and it was no problem to arrive at an accurate calculation of what German troops were present and the nature of their command: armor or infantry.

In looking at the possible port sites extending from Calais to Brittany, we found Calais obviously attractive, since a successful landing there would threaten all the German troops in Normandy and Brittany. On the other hand, Cherbourg would be a real prize if it could be seized quickly. But this would necessitate cutting the Cherbourg peninsula. Some thought was given to landing in Brittany, although the added distance made it less attractive. An airborne plan was made to seize the port of St. Malo with a reinforced parachute regiment. I followed that plan carefully, since I knew I might well be designated the commander. Nothing chastens a planner more than the knowledge that he will have to carry out the plan. The entire command was to land on the high ground overlooking the city. Two battalions were to defend against German counterattacks, and one battalion was to sweep through the town and seize the docks, where landings from ships would take place as soon as the dock area was cleared.

It would have been a very marginal performance, and I was pleased when it was discarded. There were very few beach defenses in Brittany, and the defenses at Calais were extremely heavy. The Normandy beaches, in between Calais and Brittany, although not lightly defended, seemed to offer the optimum choice. They led to open country that offered suitable landing areas for our parachute and glider troops. Most of the main German reserves were opposite Calais. It therefore appeared as though we could have sufficient time to permit the airborne forces to destroy what enemy was present and then organize a defense for the inevitable large-scale counterattack. By then the amphibious forces would have linked up with the airborne forces, and the battle for the port of Cherbourg would have begun.

It became obvious in our considerations that a cover plan would of necessity be a very important part of our work. The British had been giving considerable thought to this and had early decided that a plan was needed that would cause the Germans to believe that the actual landings were to take place at Calais, thus tying up their major armored reserves in the Calais area long enough to permit the actual landing to establish itself successfully ashore. Such a cover plan was developed in great detail.

Late in December General Bradley called me to his office to discuss the landing areas for the U.S. airborne divisions. He was beginning to think of landing the airborne divisions on the Cherbourg peninsula. We discussed the German troop dispositions and the layout of the land. He had some excellent photographs. One of the most reassuring things about them was that the Germans were beginning to flood the area—a clear indication that they did not intend to fight an offensive battle or to use large amounts of armor. We would be at our best under those conditions, where we would be engaging their infantry with little armor. Ideally, General Bradley would have preferred to use the airborne troops to sever the Cherbourg peninsula entirely, and then to have them fight a defensive battle while the remainder of the U.S. forces swung north to capture Cherbourg. Such an effort would have put the airborne troops too far beyond linkup with the amphibious assault and might have been unnecessarily risky.

Sometime later we went into the matter again and generally agreed on the feasibility of dropping the 82nd west of St.-Sauveur-le-Vicomte. (*Fig. 7.*) The other airborne division, the 101st, was to land farther south near Ste.-Marie-du-Mont and attack directly toward the causeways, opening them up for the amphibious troops. Bradley had a real feel for what could and what could not be done, and it was always reassuring to plan such operations with him.

In the meantime I began to realize that one of our most critical needs was to standardize the operating practices of our forces. Those of

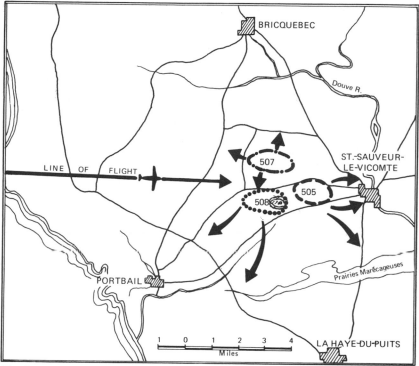

Fig. 7   Second Airborne Plan, Normandy

us who had fought in the Mediterranean theater had developed combat practices that we soon took for granted. The new formations in the United Kingdom obviously had a great deal to learn and were anxious to get started. Such simple things as plane loading, warning and jump signals, flight formations, and even simple terminology had to be agreed upon. For example, the British preferred to fly their transports in what they called "bomber stream" formations, which were no formations at all, simply individual planes flying in trail in a random manner. We preferred to fly in troop-carrier group formations of thirty-six to forty-five airplanes that flew in a V of V's with three aircraft in each V. We had always referred to the area where we would land as "the jump area." The British referred to it as "the drop zone," or simply "the DZ." After conferring with the staff of the 101st Airborne Division, all of whom were good friends of mine, I went to work on a document to standardize the American airborne practices, and I was able to publish the first memorandum on the subject, "Training Memorandum on the

Employment of Airborne Forces," late in 1943.

This was followed by the drafting of a document that would standardize the operating procedures for all the forces involved, British and American, R.A.F., and the Army Air Forces and both Navies. In the drafting of it, I was greatly aided by R.A.F. Wing Commander Dugald MacPherson. It turned out to be a very tedious task that involved frequent visits to all the higher headquarters. Everyone wanted to discuss, alter, criticize, and contribute to it, and it was terribly important that they all have an opportunity to do so, for when it was completed and everyone was properly trained, we would have achieved a state of complete flexibility in the employment of our forces. The British could fly in American transports; we could fly in British gliders, and so forth.

By early February I had accomplished about all I could in the way of standardizing our operational procedures and in developing an airborne plan. On February 6 I moved to Leicester, England, where the 82nd Airborne Division headquarters were located. By then the troops were en route from Northern Ireland to the Leicester-Nottingham area. It closed in the area about February 16. A few days later I had a scare when Supreme Headquarters asked General Ridgway to reassign me to my former airborne advisory role. Fortunately, he declined. From then on, I concentrated all my energies on planning, training the troops, and studying avidly the German defenses and the daily air photo coverage we were getting of our operational areas.

In February we were able to break up the mission assigned to the 82nd Airborne Division into separate regimental tasks. The 505th Parachute Infantry was to land just west of St.-Sauveur-le-Vicomte, seize the town and the bridges over the Douve River, and patrol aggressively well to the south to the Prairies Marécageuses. (*Fig. 7.*) The 508th Parachute Infantry was to land astride Hill 110 and, having consolidated its position, move aggressively to the south and west so as to intercept any German reinforcements coming into the peninsula. The 507th was to land north of the 508th and 505th by a mile or two, protect the northern flank of the division from German forces that might attempt to attack from that direction, and to patrol aggressively. As the regiments came to know their missions better and to understand them in detail, they began to pay more and more attention to the German operations, and there was much to pay attention to, for the Germans were energetically preparing to receive us.

Typical of the antiairborne measures we detected was the German preparation of Hill 110. This clear unwooded height rising 110 meters above the surrounding hedgerows was about five thousand yards west of St.-Sauveur-le-Vicomte. (*Fig. 7.*) From its higher points there was observation almost to the east coast on a clear day and to the west coast under any ordinary conditions of visibility. Seizing and holding it would undoubtedly have a decisive effect on the operations of the airborne troops destined to land in that vicinity.

The study of the day-by-day photo coverage of Hill 110 showed that its terrain was that of an average combat drop zone. Its slopes were too steep for gliders, but they were free of large boulders or timber that would deny the use of an area to paratroopers. Along its western slope, running for about a half mile, was a deep quarry about fifty yards wide. The hill itself was circular in shape and about a thousand yards in diameter. The regiment assigned to it had some reservations about it as a drop zone, but it was much better than many that paratroopers had landed on without excessive losses in Sicily and Italy. After a discussion of the probable losses, Hill 110 was designated as the drop zone for the 508th Parachute Infantry.

Then followed a careful and painstaking study of the enemy activity and disposition in and around the hill area. First, the hill had three windmills on it. Intelligence reports showed that these were now in use as radio towers. A small German caretaking detachment was always at these stations, but it was not large enough to be of any great concern to us. Next, the quarry began to show signs of occupation. From the air photos it appeared that weapons were emplaced in or near the quarry. These might be light ack-ack weapons. It was impossible to tell.

On the lower slopes of Hill 110, where it blended into the wooded hedgerows, parking bays for vehicles began to appear—a sure sign, as we learned later, of a command installation. At several points on the lower slopes of the hill the hedgerows were cleared away. We couldn't understand this, and although we watched each new photo very closely for weapons emplacements, none showed up. Finally, about three weeks before D-day, small black specks in a regular geometric pattern began to show up all over the hill. They continued to grow in number until the entire hill was covered with them. They were simply specks, apparently holes, for they didn't throw shadows on early-morning photos as objects above the ground do.

Some of us were sure now that the Germans knew of our landing plans and were taking some measures to counter them. We had already heard of *Rommelspargel,* but usually when these were installed one small field was completed at a time. *Rommelspargel* (Rommel's asparagus) were poles about six to twelve inches in diameter and eight to twelve feet long. They were sunk a foot or two into the ground and stood seventy-five to a hundred feet apart. They were obviously intended to deny the use of good landing zones to the Allied airborne troops.

Sure enough, after we spent several days of worry over Hill 110, the telltale shadows of the *Rommelspargel* began to appear. It was impossible to say whether or not they were connected by wires, or whether there were actual troop defense installations among or near them. But since the hill was not to be used by gliders, it was decided to drop the 508th on it anyway, despite the evident preparations being made for its reception. We had to have the hill, and if we didn't land on it, we would have to fight to get it. And it seemed likely that fighting for it would be most costly.

On Friday, February 18, General Ridgway told me to go to London without delay to attend a meeting at Bentley Priory, where there was to be a discussion with the British about the airborne plan. We met at the headquarters of Air Chief Marshal Sir Trafford Leigh-Mallory, who was assigned to the Allied Forces with the title of Air Commander in Chief. He had had considerable combat experience in the Battle of Britain, but he had had little experience in operations requiring close cooperation with ground troops. It was a fascinating conference. Leigh-Mallory began at once by explaining that the purpose of the meeting was to discuss what actually happens in parachute and glider operations. He seemed to be quite skeptical that we could do what we said we could. Further, he said that he was having a meeting with General Montgomery the following Monday, and he wanted to be well fortified with facts. He kept challenging our views.

Present was Major General William O. Butler, who was the senior U.S. Air Corps officer in Leigh-Mallory's headquarters. One of the things discussed was a plan sent over from Washington to land the parachute-glider forces in one huge airhead in what was known as the Orleans Gap. It was in the area of comparatively high ground between the headwaters of the Loire and Seine rivers. The Washington planners envisioned the Air Corps destroying the bridges over both rivers, thus denying their crossing to the German forces, then landing the airborne forces in the Gap between the headwaters of the rivers with the mission of blocking the movement of any German forces into the area between the rivers. The amphibious forces would then be free to move against those forces still between the rivers and thus destroy them.

Three aspects of the plan worried me. First, the airborne forces were quite incapable of dealing with any major armored units that might attempt to attack through the Gap. We had no antitank weapons worthy of the name. Washington did not seem to realize this. Next, our combat experience made it clear that there was no assurance that the German formations could not cross the rivers. Some of the bridges might remain intact despite all the bombing we could do, and at night the Germans would find ways to repair them and get across. Finally, the airborne forces would be dependent upon air resupply for an indefinite period.

We were told that General Marshall and General Henry Harley Arnold thought well of the plan and were hoping that the planners in London would see its merits.[4] It was a plan of great vision but totally unrealistic in terms of combat. Earlier I had attended a planning conference at 21st Army Group, where it had been suggested that the parachute troops might be used in small packets—platoon size, for example—to land on all the large gun sites on the bluffs overlooking the amphibious assault and engage the Germans at the water's edge. General Butler remarked, "This is like sending Michelangelo to paint a barn."

In principle, it would have been much better to place the airborne forces where they could seize key objectives and terrain that would permit them to block the movement of the major counterattacking forces. Psychologically, their being there would have stampeded many of the German defenders along the beaches, and some of the airborne formations could have been given the mission of attacking across the causeways against the defenders.

The talk with Leigh-Mallory went on for several hours with much give-and-take. I sensed in Leigh-Mallory a real lack of confidence in the American parachute-glider troops' ability to do the things they were confident they could do. I knew of no way to convince him of our ability to do our job in combat other than to point out what had been accomplished. But that, apparently, to him, particularly the Sicilian affair, was not at all reassuring. It was puzzling; he knew nothing about parachute combat, yet he was telling us that we would be ineffective. Apparently

[4] Forrest C. Pogue, in his biography, *George C. Marshall: Organizer of Victory, 1943–1945* (New York: The Viking Press, 1973), confirms this view but suggests another plan.

the British were all right; he did not question their ability to do their job. I was a bit afraid that he might recommend that we not be employed in an airborne role, which to us would have been catastrophic. The meeting wound up on a very uncertain note. Considering his high position in the military hierarchy, I was quite disturbed.

When our forces were moved to the take-off areas on May 30, 1944, Leigh-Mallory personally called on General Eisenhower to protest the use of the U.S. airborne forces, using the term, "the futile slaughter of two fine divisions." In Eisenhower's book, *Crusade in Europe,* he states: "[Leigh-Mallory] believed that the combination of unsuitable landing grounds and anticipated resistance was too great a hazard to overcome." Leigh-Mallory did not think that this was present in the British area, but he estimated that among the American outfits we would suffer some 70 per cent losses in glider strength and 50 per cent in parachute strength even before the airborne troops could land. Eisenhower reports that he went to his tent alone and sat down to think whether or not he should cancel the airborne operations. To do so would have meant canceling the assault on Utah Beach—the beaches along the Cotentin Peninsula. Bradley insisted on the use of the airborne troops. In fact, he told me that he would not make the amphibious assault without them in front of him. Finally Eisenhower telephoned Leigh-Mallory and told him that the attack would go as planned. Even today, more than thirty years later, I feel fury rise in me when I realize that Leigh-Mallory was going to have us left behind and that all our American airlift would have been given to the British.

About a week before our movement to the departure airfields, the drop zones of all elements of the 82nd Airborne Division were moved about ten miles east of St.-Sauveur-le-Vicomte. And so the drop on 110 was not made. I was so interested in it, however, that I made a thorough reconnaissance of it the very day it was captured, on D+11. It was the most thoroughly organized antiairborne defense area I had ever seen. The entire hill was covered with *Rommelspargel.* They were all wired together with barbed wire, some from top to top, others from top of one pole to the bottom of an opposite pole, and others from the bottom of one to the bottom of another. They were booby-trapped to artillery shells and some of them to mines. The whole perimeter of the hill was outlined with individual and crew-served weapons emplacements. All the emplacements were connected by narrow German-type trenches and also connected to dugouts where the troops apparently rested. There were concealed observation posts equipped with alarms along the perimeter of the hill. The quarry contained large troop shelters and numerous mortar positions with emplacements well camouflaged and with prepared concentrations covering the entire hill.

We studied intently the use of "asparagus" for a long time as a possible indication of the Germans' evaluation of each sector from the defensive viewpoint. We believed that there must be a reason for their being especially thorough in the preparation of one area and not of another. But, as one always finds, in the final analysis, human nature is still the most important factor to be dealt with in war. From interrogation of captured German commanders and French civilians, we soon found that the amount of asparagus in any one locality was more an indication of the efficiency and enthusiasm of the local German commander than anything else. Good landing areas were in some instances left untouched because the defense commander was just plain lazy. In other areas every square yard was covered because the defender had much enthusiasm for doing his job.

Meanwhile, throughout the tightly packed little island of England, preparations now accelerated at an intensive pace. Pre-drop bombings were laid on, and the smoke was planned to cover Hill 121 and Hill 131 during daylight landing hours—these were hills overlooking our landing areas. Flights were carefully coordinated with the amphibious fleet. And we anticipated and took care of the thousand and one details of orders, equipment, and organization. Finally, all seemed to be as ready as any airborne plan could be.

But the Germans were not spending their time idling. Across the breadth of northern France—and to some German commanders there must have seemed a great deal of it—the Germans were taking hurried, frantic measures with every means conceivable in their power to stop what was certain to be the greatest airborne invasion in the history of modern armies. According to what we later learned from General Student, the senior German airborne officer and commander of the German forces in Crete, the German army had been greatly impressed by the defensive measures taken by the British in 1940. The potential effectiveness of such devices was given heavy weight when the Germans decided to cancel their proposed invasion of England in the fall of that same year.

The Germans were particularly impressed by the posts, piles of rock, and wrecked cars used to obstruct all landing fields. They were taking similar measures in France as rapidly as circumstances would permit. General Student made an interesting statement in his postwar interrogation, to the effect that the Germans had prepared a counterairborne plan in great detail, including maps that showed all extensively mined and staked areas, and all areas that could readily be flooded. But all this was, according to Student, largely a work of imagination intended to fall into Allied hands and discourage airborne attempts. If such a map was prepared, I certainly never saw it. Student also said that he had tried to get Hitler's ear to gain approval of a plan to use the German paratroops against the ports of embarkation and thus break up the invasion before it got a good start. This was an interesting plan, and a plan of some merit. But, according to Student, Goering rejected it and wouldn't let the intuitive Fuehrer hear of it.

While all this high-level German talking was going on, local small-unit German commanders were improvising and making the best of every antiairborne means they could get their hands on. Asparagus was, of course, the favorite method. The extent to which asparagus was used in general, however, can be judged by Field Marshal Rommel's report after his inspection of the West Wall in the spring of 1944. Rommel said, "The construction of antiparatroop obstacles has made great progress in many divisions. For example, one division alone has erected almost 300,000 stakes, and one corps over 900,000." And Rommel further reported, "Erecting stakes alone does not make the obstacles complete; the stakes must be wired together, and shells and mines attached to them. The density must be about a thousand stakes per square kilometer. . . . It will still be possible for tethered cattle to pasture underneath these mined obstacles."

On April 15, 1944, the C in C West, Army Group D, published an excellent soldier's handbook entitled, "What Every Soldier Should Know About Airborne Troops." This was a printed booklet, well illustrated in color, which served its purpose well, judging from later prisoner-of-war interrogations. The German division with which the 82nd Airborne Division was closely opposed in its first fighting, the 243rd, published an excellent memorandum of May 1 about antiairborne obstacles. It followed this memo up with another on May 15 about the tactics the German units should employ in dealing with assaulting airborne troops.

Copies of both these memoranda were captured by the 82nd Division in the fighting that followed the invasion. All echelons of the Ger-

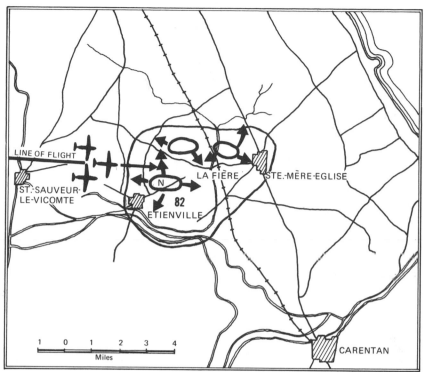

Fig. 8 Final Airborne Plan, Normandy

man 243rd Division had gone to work with imagination and vigor. They
established static sentinel posts and lookouts at critical points, and they
began regular antiairborne patrols. They held frequent antiairborne
training exercises and alerts and, as far as possible, took every step they
could think of to meet and destroy the threatening attack.

In mid-May 1944, however, the potential situation became so critical to the German high command that it was deemed necessary to move
still another infantry division into the Cotentin Peninsula. The Germans
sent in their 91st Infantry Division and, as well as we were able to
determine at the time, located it generally in the vicinity of St.-Sauveur-
le-Vicomte.

With that, the situation did not look promising for the U.S. 82nd.
Indeed, it looked so unpromising that it was decided to change our
landing areas. On May 26 we received new orders, moving the division
farther east. (*Fig. 8.*)

All plans had been completed for the 82nd Division to carry out its original mission. Field and administrative orders for our D-day operation had been published and distributed. And in a series of map maneuvers on a special large-scale map, regimental and battalion commanders of the division had outlined their plans in order that all commanders, down to those of the smallest units, could be made thoroughly aware of all plans of maneuver.

The seaborne echelons of the 82nd had already departed for the marshaling yards. They were scattered along the coast of Wales and southern England. It was just five days until Y-day (Ready Day).

The new lineup was as follows: The 82nd Airborne Division was to land on both sides of the Merderet River. It was then to seize, clear, and secure the general area of Neuville-au-Plain, Ste.-Mère-Eglise, Chef-du-Pont, Etienville, Amfreville. It was to destroy crossings over the Douve, and the 82nd Division was then to be prepared to advance to the west on Corps order. The mission of the 101st remained generally unchanged, except that responsibility for capturing the bridges over the Merderet was given the 82nd. The mission of the British 6th was also the same as before.

We received the new plan without a single regret. The 508th had never thought well of the Hill 110 mission. The 505th, although it was a veteran regiment with two combat jumps to its credit, had respect for the defending German forces around St.-Sauveur-le-Vicomte, the town it was to capture. The German activity around that town had been increasing steadily. According to the calculations made by the division intelligence officer, St.-Sauveur-le-Vicomte probably housed a division headquarters plus division special troops, and possibly an infantry regiment besides. The Germans were stocking gas and oil dumps near the railroad yards. They were clearing hedgerows around the town, and quite a few gun emplacements were coming into view day by day in the air reconnaissance photos.

We assigned regimental missions to conform to the new division mission merely by sliding the regimental drop zones the necessary number of miles to the east. We left unchanged the relative location of the drop zones. Consequently, no change had to be made in the assignment of units to take-off airfields and troop carrier units.

Despite the late change, all airborne troops were fully briefed and on their take-off airfields, ready to go on June 4. That was the night they had expected to take off. Then D-day was postponed one day. Nevertheless, calm and quiet prevailed, and the expected attacks by the German air force and V-bombs did not materialize.

The several dry runs of Y-day and D-day that had been held during the preceding month had taken the novelty out of the staging and sealing process. The cover plan for the D-day operation had apparently worked very well. Then D-day was finally announced as June 6.

Shortly after dark on the night of June 5, the pathfinder aircraft of the IX Troop Carrier Command roared down the runways of the airfield at North Witham, England. The airborne battle of Normandy, history's largest airborne assault, had gone into the decisive stage.

The weather was marginal. On the Continent the chief German meteorological officer had informed his high command that the weather was such that no invasion could take place. But, fortunately for the Germans, this information was not permitted to reach the troop commanders, and their state of readiness was not affected by the report. General Eisenhower had similar information, but after considering the whole situation carefully, he decided to go ahead.

The troop carrier flight plan was the most complex that had ever been attempted. It involved several thousand aircraft. It had to be carefully coordinated with the operations of the largest amphibious landing force in history. The work of friendly bombers and fighters, as well as the potential effect of German aircraft and flak, all had to be given the most careful consideration.

The flight plan in its final form is shown in *Fig. 9.* In general, each troop carrier unit marshaled over its home airfield and then moved on a time schedule to its place in the flight stream. All possible visual navigational aids were put to use in England so that the route was well marked until the planes reached the coast of France.

The first flights of the U.S. airborne divisions flew to the west of the amphibious forces on the English Channel and passed around the Normandy peninsula, carefully staying out of the range of the flak from the guns known to be on the islands to the west of the peninsula. They kept this course until they reached the coast.

Then the planes made a straight run to drop and landing areas. The aircraft then passed out of the east side of the peninsula, gaining altitude for the return trip. The British division flew to its drop landing area, staying to the east of the amphibious forces.

The first airborne men to touch French soil were the pathfinder personnel who landed between 0010 and 0020 hours on D-day. They

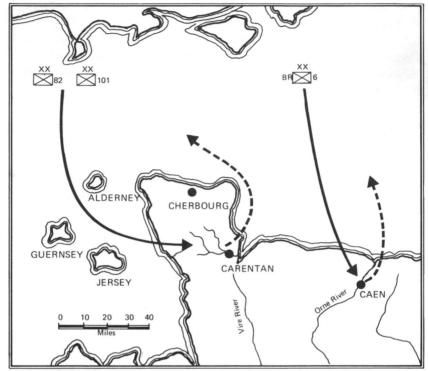

Fig. 9   Flight Plan, Normandy

encountered difficulties but marked their drop and landing zones as they had planned.

The pathfinder teams of our U.S. airborne forces preceded the main flights by thirty minutes. The team of the 101st Division was in the van. It was followed by the pathfinder team of the 82nd Airborne Division, which actually touched French soil at 0121 on the morning of D-day.

The 82nd Airborne Division had consolidated its three parachute regiments into a task force. It was Task Force A, and I was designated its commander. It consisted of the 505th, 507th, and 508th Parachute Infantry Regiments. To control the three parachute regiments, I had a radio operator, an aide, and an orderly, and one staff officer, Captain Willard E. Harrison. He had been recommended to me by Colonel Tucker of the 504th Parachute Infantry for having shown extraordinary courage in combat. He proved to be just as tough and courageous as Tucker had said he would be.

Our operation was launched by pathfinder teams followed by the 505th Parachute Infantry. It had the farthest to go and had the mission of seizing Ste.-Mère-Eglise. I flew in the lead plane of the 508th Parachute Infantry. The 507th Parachute Infantry followed the 508th. Altogether, it took 378 C-47 airplanes to lift the parachutists. These were to be followed by 375 gliders a day later. They were to bring in the 325th Glider Infantry. Fifty-two gliders carrying antitank weapons and heavy communications and other equipment were to land with the parachute echelon during darkness the first night. Major General Matthew B. Ridgway was in command of the division and landed with the parachute assault.

A night jump into combat is not as scary as it might seem. What apprehensions one experiences seem to go away once the commitment is made. When you hear the roar of the engines turning over and you move down the runway and become airborne, you realize at that moment there is no turning back. Then your total faculties are concerned with survival, and that means carrying out things you have been trained to do as well as you possibly can.

The spirit of this point of view was captured by a young artist with the 505th Parachute Infantry, William Linzee Prescott. He did a cartoon in color for the regimental paper of a young trooper taking jump training. The final stage was known as D-stage, and the trooper was preparing himself for his first jump. He was visibly shaken, already nauseated and trembling. Others were trying to light cigarettes, and there was obvious great apprehension and physical discomfort among them. The instructor was nonchalantly leaning on one elbow against the open door of the plane, quite unconcerned with his novice jumpers. With the same cartoon was another one of D-day. It was a scene of a planeload of troopers entering combat; the red light alerting them to leave the plane had already gone on. Most of them were sound asleep; boxes of demolitions were about; one of the troopers was reading "Superman"; and none showed any concern for the hazards of the moment.

While the cartoons overdid things a bit, the fact is that we were all so busy making certain that everything was done correctly that we did not have much time to think about what was going to happen in the next few minutes. The jumpmaster in particular must be totally absorbed in analyzing the terrain, learning and keeping track of precisely where he is, watching out for any enemy movement, observing where the heavy fires are coming from. Having done that, he must decide in what direction to move upon landing, listening and watching for any evidence of the plane's being hit, so he can get his troopers out in a hurry, and, of course, watching for the signal from the pilot to go.

In the Normandy landing, Lieutenant Colonel Vandervoort, for example, received a go signal long before he was over the drop zone. He simply told his crew chief to go back and tell the pilot to turn it off until he got to where he was supposed to go. The troopers then were experienced enough not to charge the door, as they did in Sicily on one occasion. As usually happens in combat, the planes flew at a much higher speed, which made the opening shock of the parachute quite violent. This was because the pilots' apprehension rose as the density of the flak increased and they could see other planes going down in flames around them. But with all these things to think about, there was little time to worry about the dangers of the undertaking. We long ago had disciplined ourselves to make a good exit at the right moment, and we knew we were quite prepared to meet any situation we found on the ground.

The exit was probably the moment of greatest danger. To begin with, the troopers were all heavily overloaded. Most of them carried an M-1 rifle loaded and ready to use, 156 rounds of rifle ammunition, a pistol with three clips of ammunition, an entrenching shovel, a knife, a water canteen, a first-aid packet, usually four grenades, reserve rations, some maps, and a raincoat. All this was secured, where necessary, with leather thongs to keep it from flying out from the body during the first few seconds of the jump. The Germans and the British wore smocks over all their equipment. We decided that such a garment would be a hindrance if combat took place immediately upon landing, so we designed a parachute suit with a number of large pockets. When a trooper jumped out of the door of the plane, it was important for him not to spin, thus fouling the parachute. If he made a proper exit, the static line would rip off the cover of the parachute and start its deployment. The prop blast of the airplane would then drive the parachute directly to the rear. If the speed of the plane was not greater than 100 knots, one might experience a deceleration equivalent to 5 or 6 times gravity and have a split-second blackout. In Normandy, however, some apprehensive pilots flew in excess of 150 knots, and many of the troopers there had some of their equipment ripped off their bodies. I was lucky that I lost only a wristwatch.

The rifle was a complicated affair. The Army had developed what the troopers called a "violin case," in which the rifle could be carried broken down into two parts. After Sicily all the survivors wanted to jump with the rifle right on their person and ready to use. We therefore put the rifle underneath the reserve parachute against the trooper's body and moved it into a vertical position to get out of the door. The muzzle was near his face and the butt of the rifle between his knees. Once the parachute opened and vertical descent began, he maneuvered the rifle into a horizontal position so it did not interfere with the landing. We knew that if the trooper survived the exit without undue difficulty, he was usually in pretty good shape for a landing, with a high probability of survival.

My flight took off from Cottesmore, England, and left exactly on schedule. Among those on board was Captain Hugo Olson, who was later wounded in Normandy and the Battle of the Bulge and who is now a very successful lawyer in Moorhead, Minnesota. Another man was given to me by Colonel Tucker of the 504th Parachute Infantry; Colonel Tucker insisted that I allow him to come along, saying that he was the toughest soldier he had in the regiment—and that was saying an awful lot. This man wore a gold earring in one ear and didn't do much talking, but he had a reputation for being a very rough character indeed. The tragedy is that I never saw him from the moment we went out the door. I suspect that he was worried about me and went looking for me and was killed. Also aboard was Corporal William Walton, who was a correspondent for *Time* magazine and who wanted to come along. He had never jumped, so I took him. He survived, and during the Kennedy Administration was prominent around Washington and was an adviser on matters of art at the White House. Lieutenant Thomas Graham and Captain Willard Harrison were picked for their combat experience and reputation for toughness and courage in combat.

I stood at the door of the airplane to check the navigational aids. By talking to the pilot through the crew chief, I was assured from time to time that all was well and that we were moving on schedule. As we left the coast of England, all was quiet below. We were flying quite low, down near 600 feet, the prescribed jump altitude. That altitude was selected to minimize casualties from enemy fire and at the same time to give us optimum time for the parachute to deploy and to enable the trooper to get set for the landing. We continued over the sea for what seemed an interminable time. Finally we began to approach the islands

off the coast of the Normandy peninsula. We had studied the antiaircraft
dispositions on these islands; we knew that they had heavy guns and that
if our flight plan had been properly selected they would not be able to
reach our planes. As we approached the islands, flak, both light and
heavy, came up, burst, and fell short. It was exactly what we had hoped
for when we had laid out the flight plan.

We continued on, and soon the French coast came into view. At that
time I had all the troopers stand up and hook up. It had been my
practice to have the troopers standing up once we crossed over into
hostile territory. If we had been hit, we would then have been able to
scramble out of the airplane with a minimum of delay. On the coast of
France the land was a reddish brown. The roads were visible in the
moonlight, and small clusters of houses stood out sharply. There was no
ground reaction, no firing, and all seemed extraordinarily quiet. We
could see a larger town off to the north; I assumed it to be Bricquebec.

Suddenly we entered a dense cloudbank. It was so thick that I could
not see the wing tips of our plane, and of course I could not see any
other planes. Since we had been flying in close formation, it was quite
dangerous. For a moment I thought we were in a smoke cloud put up by
the German defenders. In combat one always attributes the unexpected
to enemy guile and cleverness. As we continued to fly, the cloud proved
to be so extensive that smoke seemed to be out of the question. But my
plane was entirely on its own, and I could see no others, although a few
minutes earlier, when I had looked back, the entire air armada had
seemed to be visible. At the moment it had been a reassuring sight, but
now I began to worry and to check our time. Every jumpmaster had
been told to memorize his time from the moment of landfall. I knew that
my plane had to jump eight and a half minutes after passing the French
coast if we were to land on our drop zone, assuming that we were flying
on a correct heading. I knew also that the east coast of the Cherbourg
peninsula would come twelve minutes after we crossed the west coast.
After that, if we jumped, we would land in the English Channel. Unfortunately, some troopers did.

But my plane continued on into the fog, and with each passing
moment I felt increasingly disturbed and quite alone. About seven
minutes after we crossed the coast, the clouds began to clear. As they
did, I could see a great deal of heavy flak coming up off to the right of
our flight. I had studied the antiaircraft gun dispositions, and the only
town in that part of the peninsula that had heavy antiaircraft guns was

Etienville. That should be about where we were in terms of time. I quickly scanned the skies for other airplanes; none could be seen. Directly ahead of us in the distance I could see the moonlight reflecting off a wide river that made a sharp right-angle turn to the north. For a moment I thought we were south of the Douve River, but that did not check with Etienville and its flak. Very likely, therefore, we were farther north, farther to the left by a number of miles than we should have been.

We began to receive small-arms fire from the ground. It seemed harmless enough; it sounded like pebbles landing on a tin roof. I had experienced it before and knew what it was. So far none of us had been hit. Then, quite some distance away, another airplane or two could be seen. Directly ahead of us there was a tremendous amount of small-arms fire, and apparently buildings were burning. That almost certainly had to be Ste.-Mère-Eglise. The 505th by now should have landed and should be attacking the Germans in the town.

We were at about 600 feet, the green light went on, and I took one last precious look at the land below. We were about thirty seconds overtime. A wide river was just ahead of us, plainly visible in the moonlight. Small-arms fire was increasing. About three seconds after the green light went on, I yelled, "Let's go," and went out the door, with everyone following. I landed with what seemed to me a pretty loud thud in an orchard. Among the trees were some grazing cows which kept munching quite contentedly—entirely unconcerned about what to me was a most momentous occasion. My aide had landed near me, and together we began to assemble the troopers from our plane as per plan. I heard someone across a hedgerow, and we challenged each other at about the same time. It was Captain Carl M. Price of the Division Intelligence. He joined me. I moved quickly, and as I left the field, I came on a small, worn country road going to the right. I followed it and in about 400 yards came to a vast expanse of water.

By that time about fifteen troopers were with me. Bundles had landed in the water. It was important that we rescue them, because they contained our bazookas, radios, mines, everything critical to our survival. One man in our group, Lieutenant James H. Devine, at once took off all his clothing and waded out into the swamp to retrieve the bundles. I can see him now, pale white as a statue standing out against the swamp background; at the moment I was concerned that he would be a sure target if the Germans attacked. So far, they had not; we heard only an occasional shot some distance away. Along the marsh I found prepared foxholes. Evidently the Germans had prepared the bank for defense in the event of an attack coming from the other direction, from the English Channel.

A few minutes later a red light appeared on the far side of the swamp. It was soon followed by a green one. These were the assembly lights of the 507th and 508th Parachute Infantry regiments. They were far to the east of where they should have been. I directed my aide, Captain Hugo Olson, to cross the swamp, get in touch with those regiments, find out what they were doing, and, if possible, get some information on our exact whereabouts. In the meantime I kept trying to recover the equipment and get some order out of the confusion among the troopers around me. By then I must have had forty or fifty.

Captain Olson returned in about an hour and reported that, although the swamp water was shoulder-deep, he had been able to get to the far side. There he found a railroad. I checked my map; the railroad had to be the one along the east bank of the Merderet River, and we were probably about two miles north of La Fière. Olson had also learned from the 508th Parachute Infantry that they were moving south to seize the La Fière bridge over the Merderet. It had been one of the principal objectives given to the 505th Parachute Infantry. We had evidently overflown our drop zone by several miles, and I had no idea where the rest of the troopers were. However, they kept drifting in to join me. As daylight began to appear, I estimated that I had somewhere between 100 and 150 troopers. Some of them had been wounded, and a few had been injured as they landed. Our success in recovering bundles from the swamp had been just about zero. Not only was the water deep, but since the swamp had been recently flooded there was thick swamp grass, knee-high, sometimes almost waist-high. I was to learn more about that in an hour or two. The Merderet was about 1000 yards wide at this point.

With a hundred good troopers I should have been able to accomplish a lot. To my utter frustration, I found them completely disorganized, lacking unit organization and even unit leadership. They were mostly from the 507th and, although I should have discovered this in training, I didn't find out until that night that they had covered the insignia on their helmets. It had been the practice to do this in the Pacific theater, in fighting the Japanese, and somehow they had picked it up. In the veteran 505th we didn't do it, because we needed to know who the NCOs and officers were. With the amount of German fire increasing and the troopers milling about and seeking the protection of nearby hedgerows, it was impossible to get them organized in any rational way.

Shortly after daylight, I learned that a glider had landed about a quarter of a mile away. Since it probably contained an antitank gun that might be critical to our survival, I sent a patrol, led by Lieutenant Thomas Graham, a veteran of the 505th, to get it. The Germans knew it was there and increased their fire into the area. Lieutenant Graham came back to tell me that it would take an organized attack to get to the site of the glider, and that even when we got there, we probably couldn't get the gun out and drag it through the marsh and underbrush.

By this time I had managed to deploy most of the able paratroopers between 100 and 200 yards from the swamp in the form of a shallow bridgehead. I thought I would get a closer look at the glider myself, and I moved out along the line of our troopers. The Germans were firing into us quite heavily, and the 507th, being a green regiment, had not yet learned Lesson 1—to fire back and thus gain some freedom of movement. I went along the hedgerow, exposing myself to German fire to urge our troopers to get up and fire back. There was little response. They seemed more interested in survival. Suddenly what seemed like the taillight of a truck went by my face with a loud crack. I realized that it was a tracer bullet and that I was the target for their fire. I ducked, continued to move on, and kept trying to stir the troopers to react, with little success.

I made my way back to my original position on the edge of the marsh. There I talked the situation over with Captain Harrison. It was obvious that we could not organize a coordinated attack against the Germans. The ideal tactical movement would have been to move to our left down to the La Fière bridge, attack the Germans from the rear, and thus help seize the bridge, but that was out of the question with the disorganized group I had at my disposal. Besides, we did not know how bad the marshland and the terrain were and what Germans we would encounter. One thing was certain: they were steadily increasing their fire against us. I therefore reluctantly decided that I would have to withdraw across the swamp, leaving my wounded and injured for the Germans with the hope of recapturing them later. When I reached the other side, I would then be able to move down along the railroad, attack across the

La Fière bridge, and expand from that side, using the troops I knew were on the other side of the swamp. It was highly probable that the veteran 505th had already captured the bridge.

I got the word around to the troops to withdraw and follow me across the marsh. It was quite light then, and we started across, widely deployed. We must have covered an area several hundred yards across, with troopers 15 to 25 yards apart, holding their rifles and sometimes their equipment over their heads as they went into the marsh. Soon we were almost shoulder-deep and the going was exceedingly difficult. The grass wrapped itself around our legs and seemed to pull us down. By then the Germans had reached the bank and were firing at individuals. Occasionally troopers would be hit and go down, and occasionally there was a sickening whine as a bullet ricocheted nearby.

Finally we made the railroad embankment. It was about six feet high, firm and dry, and we crawled up on it. Evidently the Germans did not have weapons capable of reaching that far. We reorganized, helped those who were wounded, and started a column down the railroad track toward La Fière.

About a half mile from La Fière I came across the 1st Battalion of the 505th Parachute Infantry, organized, under control, and already launching an attack on the La Fière bridge. It was a most reassuring sight. I talked to the troopers; they were in great shape. They were lying on the side of the trail waiting for orders to move in to the attack. In the meantime the battalion commander, Major Frederick Kellam, was attacking the bridge with the leading company. I learned shortly thereafter that he had been killed in the attack and that the battalion had been taken over by the Executive, Major James McGinity. I left the 505th, took a group of the 507th, which by then had reorganized itself, and started down the railroad track to see if I could find another crossing site. In about three or four miles we came to a small track going off to the right toward the river, and some buildings could be seen. I had hoped that if we could find anything that would float, even a barn door to use as a raft, we could ferry our forces across and then move back against the La Fière bridge. Not a boat, not a raft, not a piece of usable timber could be found. Apparently the Germans had cleverly removed everything that would be of any assistance. I knew that there were a road and a causeway farther down the river, near the town of Chef-du-Pont, so I took my small force, which had been augmented by a few more troopers, and Lieutenant Colonel Edwin J. Ostberg of the 507th.

We continued down the track. As we reached the outskirts of the town, a train began to move from the railroad station. There were German troops aboard, and they fired at us and then scattered. We quickly overran the train. To my surprise, the train consisted of half a dozen box cars filled with empty bottles. In the middle was an antiaircraft car with antiaircraft guns mounted to protect the train. There was also a cargo of Normandy cheese aboard. None of the German troops were to be found.

In the middle of the town we turned back toward the Merderet River. Again we came under fire, and the troops were driven into the buildings for cover. A causeway about a mile long crossed the Merderet at this point. Halfway across was a small island with dwellings on it, and from it we were receiving fire. I left Ostberg with the 507th to organize an attack across the river whenever it would be feasible, probably after it got dark, and with two or three troopers and Captain Olson I started back to La Fière. It was midafternoon. I arrived at La Fière before darkness and learned that Major McGinity had been killed. The 505th had managed to drive the Germans back across the Merderet, but they had not been able to cross the causeway. Normally, the Merderet River at this point is not more than ten yards across. There is a small stone bridge over it with a causeway approaching from the higher ground. Because of the flooding, all that could be seen was the causeway, and the river was more than five hundred yards wide. The causeway itself was vulnerable and exposed.

As darkness descended, I moved up to see what the situation looked like. The 1st Battalion of the 505th had taken heavy casualties. It was well organized and had the situation in hand, but the German defenses on the causeway seemed quite strong and there was no way to force a crossing of the causeway that night. From the causeway a road went directly back to the east, to our rear, to the town of Ste.-Mère-Eglise about five miles away. I went back to where the road crossed the railroad and decided that I would establish my Command Post there. In that way I could control the situation at the causeway and stay in touch with the 507th at Chef-du-Pont. I established radio contact with division headquarters.

General Ridgway was back near Ste.-Mère-Eglise and knew where we were and what we were doing. There was still a great deal to be done in sorting things out. I had one officer who spoke German, Captain Miller, and one jeep that I had obtained from division headquarters. It helped me to keep in touch with the various fragments of my command. We established radio communication with Lieutenant Colonel Thomas J. B. Shanley's battalion of the 508th, which was across the Merderet River and about three miles from the La Fière bridge, well behind the German lines. They were under fire but intact.

I decided to get some rest. June nights in Normandy can be very cold. I looked around for something to cover me; all I could find was a dead paratrooper with his parachute over him. He must have been killed in descent and some trooper had covered him with his own parachute. Although I was shivering with cold, I did not have the heart to take it away from him. I finally found, of all things, a camouflage net that had arrived in the battle area. I chose a place against a hedgerow, so as to be protected from artillery fire, which was coming in spasmodically during the night, and I rolled up in the camouflage net. It was surprisingly warm.

I had hardly fallen asleep when someone shook me and told me General Ridgway wanted to see me. This was unlike General Ridgway; he always went forward to see his officers in combat rather than take them away from their tactical commands. I checked again; there was no question about the accuracy of the message. I had not been back that way, but his Command Post should have been near the road to Ste.-Mère-Eglise. I took Captain Olson with me, and we started along the road. It was as light as day in the full moonlight, and we walked in the shadows, one on each side of the road. We did not realize it at the time, but during the night a German infantry battalion had passed between my Command Post and that of General Ridgway. We learned about it several days later from Captain Miller, who suddenly found himself in the midst of a German column. They captured him, and two days later they locked him in a barn for safekeeping. He escaped and rejoined me. So it was just as well that we moved along the road with care. I felt bone weary, having been up for two nights and a day. In addition to the physical exhaustion, combat itself, with its tension and excitement, takes a great deal out of you.

After several miles of walking, I came on the Command Post off to the left of the road. I went to the Operations Center, which was in a tent, and asked for General Ridgway. They pointed out that he was asleep in a small ditch off to the side. I went over and shook his shoulder and woke him up. He didn't seem too happy about it and said he had nothing for me and didn't need me. No doubt a zealous staff officer, thinking it might be a good idea to get a firsthand report on the situation along the Merderet River, had sent the message in the name of General Ridgway, and by the time I arrived, the message had been forgotten or the staff officer who sent it was fast asleep.

I was surprised to read in General Ridgway's memoirs, written many years later, the comment:

> Just before midnight, tottering on my feet as many another soldier who had fought there on that day, I rolled up in a cargo chute and lay down for the first sleep I'd had in forty-eight hours. . . . Far in the night, I was roused by someone shaking me. It was a messenger from one of the battalions fighting toward the river crossing. The Germans, he said, were counterattacking in strength across the causeway. I couldn't see what in the hell I could do about that, single-handed. So I sent back word that the battalion was to hold if it could. If this was impossible, then it could pull back. Then I turned over and went back to sleep.[5]

I went back to my Command Post. Shortly after daylight General Ridgway joined me where the Ste.-Mère-Eglise road crossed the railroad. Already troopers were speculating that the amphibious landing had not taken place. We had been fighting for a full day and a night, and so far, as near as we knew, we were on our own. General Ridgway and I talked it over and decided that if the amphibious landing for some reason had been called off, we would continue to fight on our present objectives.

By daylight, D+1, June 7, the 82nd Airborne Division occupied an area roughly triangular in shape, five or six miles on a side, on the English Channel side of the Merderet River. (*Fig. 10.*) To the east it occupied the town of Ste.-Mère-Eglise. A number of the troopers had jumped into the town and had been killed by the German occupying forces. One trooper had dangled from one of the spires on the church and saved himself by feigning death. Shortly before daylight the 3rd Battalion of the 505th, commanded by Lieutenant Colonel Edward Krause, drove the Germans from the town and took over complete occupation. The 2nd Battalion of the 505th, commanded by Lieutenant Colonel Ben Vandervoort, had the mission of occupying Neuville-au-Plain, about five miles north of Ste.-Mère-Eglise, and in that position blocking any attempts of the Germans to move southward.

[5] *Soldier: The Memoirs of Matthew B. Ridgway,* edited by Harold H. Martin. New York: Harper & Brothers, 1956, pp. 10–11.

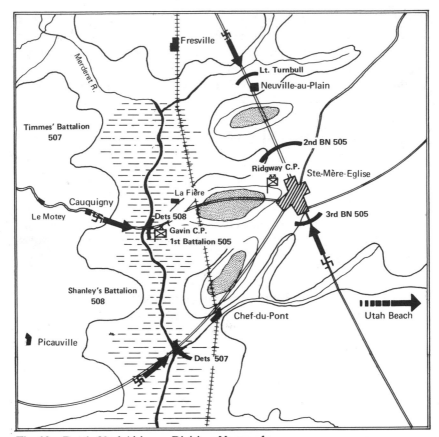

Fig. 10   D +1, 82nd Airborne Division, Normandy

At daylight Colonel Vandervoort and the 2nd Battalion moved out to accomplish their mission. A counterattack against the 3rd Battalion in Ste.-Mère-Eglise, however, made it necessary for General Ridgway to stop him. Vandervoort then made one of the best tactical decisions in the battle of Normandy. He, on his own, sent a reinforced platoon, Lieutenant Turner B. Turnbull and forty-four men, to do the best they could to accomplish the mission originally assigned to the battalion. Turnbull rooted out the few Germans who were in Neuville-au-Plain and moved to the high ground to the north, where he organized a defense. Not long after daylight, to their amazement, a German column appeared as though on peacetime maneuver, coming down the road from the north. It was the 1058th Infantry Regiment reinforced. They came in close formation, walking along both sides of the road with vehicles interspersed through the column. Turnbull's platoon allowed them to walk practically up to their positions before he and his men opened fire on them, killing and wounding many and scattering the remainder. From then on, a hard engagement was fought, but Turnbull managed to hold them, although greatly outnumbered, until darkness. It had been a gallant engagement, and the cost had been heavy. Only sixteen troopers of forty-four survived to withdraw. The next day the Germans continued their attack south of Neuville-au-Plain. Finally, with the aid of armor that had landed with the amphibious forces, Vandervoort, with his 2nd Battalion, counterattacked, destroyed the German force, and retook Neuville-au-Plain. From then on, the German situation continued to deteriorate until the fall of Cherbourg.

The third point of the triangle was the bridge over the Merderet River at La Fière, about five miles west of Ste.-Mère-Eglise. Company A of the 1st Battalion of the 505th was the lead unit that first encountered Germans near the bridge. They organized a defensive position along the slightly higher ground looking across the causeway. It was more a causeway than a bridge, and at that point the flooded area was about five hundred yards across. As soon as the 505th drove the Germans across the bridge, a group of the 508th Parachute Infantry crossed to the other side. Their drop zones had been planned for the west side of the river, and many troopers were known to be cut off over there. However, they had hardly reached the far side when they were attacked by a German force, and they withdrew into the position held by the 505th. From then on the German forces attacked aggressively and increased in strength. It was the reinforced 1057th regiment. Practically all the American defenders at the south end of the bridge were killed or wounded in the first day's fighting. One survivor more responsible than anyone else for holding the Germans back was Sergeant William D. Owens. His account follows:

I had the 1st squad. We placed our antitank mines right on the top of the road where the Germans could see them, but could not miss them with their tanks. We placed our two bazooka teams where they had a good field of fire. There were two men to a team. As I recall, it was about 8:00 a.m. when we first heard armored vehicles coming from across the river. We let them come on. It was an armored column with trucks of infantry. When the lead tank got approximately forty feet from the mines, the tank stopped. Then our bazooka teams let loose and both got direct hits, disabling the first tank (they were old French Renault tanks with comparatively thin armor). This blocked the road, and as there were deep ditches and water, the other tanks could only retreat. Then they tried to get the infantry through to knock us out. All we had was small arms and some 60 mm. mortars, but we succeeded in driving them back. The Germans pulled back on the other side, and in about a half hour or so, they began throwing 88s and 120 mm. mortars at us. They really clobbered us. All our communications were knocked out. And the fellow, Private Ross, with our walkie-talkie, took a direct hit with an 88, so from then on, as far as we were concerned, we were a lost platoon. Then they sent the infantry again, and again we drove them back. Our platoon leader, Lieutenant Oakley, was badly wounded (he died a few hours later). After he left, I began crawling around, getting all the ammunition and grenades from the dead and wounded, for I knew we would need every round we could get our hands on. I took stock of what weapons we had, and it turned out to be a good thing, for right after that the Germans hit us again. They must have received reinforcements, for the artillery shells and mortars were coming in like machine-gun fire. I don't know how it was possible to live through it. Then the infantry came again and we gave them everything we had. The machine gun I had was so hot it quit firing. I took Private McClatchy's BAR, he had been wounded earlier, and I fired it until I ran out of ammunition. I then took a machine gun that belonged to a couple of men who took a very near hit. They were killed. The gun had no tripod, so I rested it across a pile of dirt and used it. With this and one other machine gun and a 60 mm. mortar, we stopped them, but they had gotten to within twenty-five yards of us. I really thought we'd had it, but then they threw up a Red Cross flag and stopped firing. I quickly stood up and stopped my men. I sent a man back to see if he could find some help for us. I moved to where I could get a good view of the causeway. I estimated that I could see at least two hundred dead or wounded Germans scattered about. I don't know how many were in the river. It took them about two hours to get their wounded out, then they started shelling us again but not as bad as before. About two in the morning I heard a tank on the causeway and thought here we go again. Then I heard them trying to push the disabled tank out of the way and I knew if they succeeded we would be through, so I took a couple of gammon grenades (plastic C) and crawled to approximately thirty or forty yards from them. It was quite dark. The first grenade I threw missed and hit the disabled tank instead of the one that was trying to move it. The Germans didn't take any more chances, they put the tank into reverse and moved back. They continued shelling us all day long, but it was only spora-

dic. They never tried to get the infantry across again after they raised
the Red Cross flag.[6]

Sergeant Owens' unit was relieved by the 508th Parachute Infantry
the night after the second day of fighting. All but a few of the officers in
the battalion had been killed or wounded, but they had kept the Germans from crossing the bridge. The tactical situation confronting us now
was how to get across the bridge ourselves and establish ourselves on the
far bank. We already were in touch with one battalion of the 508th
Parachute Infantry, which was about three miles from the bridge to the
south of it. Approximately one battalion of the 507th, commanded by
Lieutenant Colonel Charles J. Timmes, was about three miles from the
bridge to the northwest of it, both behind the German lines. There were
individual pockets of paratroopers here and there scattered about on
the far side with whom we had not been able to establish contact.

The 325th Glider Infantry, which had landed on D+2, was given
the mission of forcing a crossing. The regimental commander decided
that the best way to cross the Merderet was to move north of the La
Fière bridge a couple of hundred yards where the map showed there was
a ford. It had disappeared at high water, but clearly the crossing was
there. Colonel Harry L. Lewis, commanding the regiment, decided to
send the 1st Battalion of the 325th, under the command of Lieutenant
Colonel Terry Sanford, across during darkness. Once established on the
far side, it would move southward to attack the Germans defending the
bridge. It was to be joined by Lieutenant Colonel Timmes' 2nd Battalion of the 507th with any other scattered paratroopers it could find. It
was a great deal to ask of a battalion that had not been in combat, but
the attempt was made.

By daylight the command was almost completely across and moving
on its mission with sporadic resistance. Then the Germans counterattacked violently and by sheer numbers overwhelmed the inexperienced
glidermen. One of their members, Charles N. DeGlopper, Private First
Class, Co. C, 325th Glider Infantry, stood up in plain sight, firing a

[6] Based on personal correspondence with Sergeant William D. Owens. A vivid
account of this action by Sergeant Owens is also in *Night Drop,* written by S. L. A.
Marshall and published by Little Brown & Co. in 1962. This account, in turn, was
based on notes made in after-combat interviews by S. L. A. Marshall, who was the
Chief Historian of the European Theater of Operations.

BAR into the German forces until he was gunned down and killed. His actions saved the lives of many who were able to withdraw. He was awarded the Congressional Medal of Honor.

I got the details of the failure of this attack at daylight, and by that time the situation at the bridge was becoming desperate. We could not lose a moment in forcing our way across and rescuing troops on the other side, and the German strength was obviously building steadily. General Ridgway made available to me the 3rd Battalion of the 325th and instructed me to seize the bridge and drive the Germans back on the far side. The artillery of the U.S. 90th Division was ashore then, and the 155 mm.'s were available to support us. I was also given about a dozen medium tanks.

I took the 90th Division's artillery commander, Brigadier General John M. Devine, as close to the bridge as we could get, about seventy-five yards from it. Just short of the bridge and off to the right there was a hollowed-out area. We crawled through it and up to a rise, where we had a direct view of the causeway and the buildings on the far side. There were a number of old stone dwellings, houses and barns, that were occupied by the Germans. No Germans were in sight. I pointed out the areas where we assumed the Germans to be and from which we had been receiving fire. I set the hour of 10:45 for the attack to be launched by our infantry and asked for all the artillery support he could give me beginning at 10:30. I then had Captain Hugo Olson, my aide, line up the tanks about ten yards apart, a couple of hundred yards behind us. They had the mission of opening direct fire on the Germans beginning with the artillery concentration at 10:30.

By then, it was between 9:00 and 9:30, and the 3rd Battalion of the 325th Glider Infantry was approaching. I asked the battalion commander to come forward to get his orders, and at that moment he declined to go into the attack, saying that he did not feel well. He was relieved of command and another officer put in charge of the battalion. I was quite apprehensive about the ability of the 325th to make the crossing, since they, too, had not been in battle before. With all the fire power that I could put on the German positions, I was quite confident that enough men could make the crossing to establish a bridgehead if they had the courage and tactical skill to seize that brief opportunity between the lifting of our fires and the closing with the Germans. I had one company of paratroopers commanded by Captain R. D. Rae. I talked the situation over with him and told him that I wanted every weapon he had to fire in support of the 325th, once the crossing began. I told him also that I was a little afraid that the 325th might break in the fury of the battle. I said that if they did and any of them started drifting back across the causeway, I would signal to him and he was to lead the paratroopers in a charge across the causeway into the German positions. I figured that the momentum of this action would take the 325th along with it.

At 10:30 everything we had opened up with a tremendous explosion. Dust and smoke and flames seemed to cover the far shore. Soon Germans in a bad state of shock, their faces covered with dust, and blood trickling from their mouths, began coming across the causeway with their hands up. Up to now the Germans had been opposed only by rifle, machine-gun, and small mortar fire. The enormous artillery concentration and tank fire came as a shock to them. In the midst of it General Ridgway came down and looked at the knocked-out tank, trying to figure how to get it off the bridge, I assume, so that we could clear the bridge for our own armor. At the moment for the 325th to go—they had all been instructed to run as fast as they could across the causeway—I gave them the signal, and from their positions, crouching along the side of the road, they began to run. At once many of them were hit and fell on the causeway, but some made it all the way across. After a few minutes of this, the first signs of a break occurred as we had expected. The overwhelming fire power of the Germans was just too much. I signaled Captain Rae. He, in turn, alerted all his troops. They jumped from their foxholes, yelling and following Captain Rae across the causeway into the German positions. From then on the battle was decided. Rae took command of the forces on the far side and continued for several miles before finally digging in.

It had been a costly affair, and many 325th men were stretched head to foot along the causeway; one had to move with care in running across to avoid stepping on them. The disabled tank was pulled off the bridge, the 325th dead and wounded were removed, and we then got our first armor across within minutes. When I had gone across, I knew I had not realized the extent of the German strength on the far side. In a field a hundred yards from the bridge were a dozen mortars dug in in huge square holes in the earth. There was a great deal of artillery, half-tracks, self-propelled guns. Much of their artillery was horse-drawn, and horses killed and wounded were still in harness.

I started down the road to the left toward Colonel Shanley's position. All along the road were litter, dead Germans, and abandoned vehicles. One of our armored cars had just driven down ahead of me. I came on a German 81 mm. mortar squad. They were all killed or wounded, lying in a ditch, head to foot, having toppled as they were walking when they were surprised by the armored car. The lieutenant at the head of the column had fallen face down, and in his hands was a map he had been carrying. Hoping that the map would contain information about the German dispositions, I took it from him. He was still limp. The map was of the La Fière area. It showed no troop dispositions whatsoever. I turned it over; on the other side was a map of England. It was of the very area that we had come from and had, no doubt, been prepared for the planned German invasion of England more than two years before. I took the lieutenant's wristwatch—my own had been lost in the opening shock the night I jumped.

As I continued down the road toward Shanley's position, I came across an abandoned German Command Post. Nearby was a paratrooper in his harness hanging from an apple tree. He was dead, having been shot rather than taken prisoner. We continued to tidy up the bridgehead, and we established physical contact with Colonel Shanley's battalion. I went back to La Fière to check the situation there and then back to Division Command Post to talk things over with General Ridgway and to learn how the division as a whole was doing. At about 6:00 P.M. I received word that the bridgehead was breaking and the troops were withdrawing across the causeway. Taking Captain Harrison and Lieutenant Colonel Arthur A. Maloney, the Executive Officer of the 507th, with me, I went to the causeway as quickly as I could. It was true: the situation was deteriorating badly. The regimental executive of the 325th was in the stone farmhouse, and his command group was beginning to withdraw. The regimental commander had been hospitalized earlier. The regimental executive said that the Germans were attacking and that he could not hold.

After what we had been through for three days, we simply could not give up the causeway. I told the regimental executive of the 325th that we were going to counterattack with every resource we had, including himself, regimental clerks, headquarters people, anyone we could get our hands on with a weapon. He blanched a bit, seemed rather startled, but accepted the order. I then posted Colonel Maloney and Captain Harrison at the causeway with instructions to stop anybody who attempted to recross it. Maloney was an impressive sight—a tough, burly trooper, wearing three days' red beard streaked with dry blood from being hit earlier in the day. No one was going to get by him.

I sent an armored car off to the left toward Shanley's position with instructions to tell any troopers that we were going to counterattack and that we were not withdrawing. I then went forward in the direction of the small town of Le Motey. Le Motey was a key crossroads and a logical counterattack objective. When I encountered troopers, I told them of the plan.

The German fire was fierce. I was walking bent over in a grain field when I suddenly noticed the stalks being cut as though by a giant invisible scythe. I had not realized that the fire was quite that intense, and I got down on all fours. I reached Captain Rae and told him what I wanted him to do, and he went ahead with the attack and occupied Le Motey. On the way back I encountered an 81 mm. mortar squad in the process of withdrawing. I turned them around and ordered them to report to Captain Rae, telling them where he was. It took about two hours to get the situation back under control, but we did succeed.

It was anticipated that the newly arrived U.S. 90th Division would pass through our bridgehead that night and launch an attack against the German positions in the morning. Fresh from the boats, just at dusk they marched from Ste.-Mère-Eglise toward the causeway, getting more apprehensive with each kilometer. The signs of the battle—the dead, knocked-out vehicles, and scattered equipment—were everywhere. As they made the last turn approaching the causeway, a column of German prisoners unfortunately emerged from the stone buildings on the other side and started across the causeway. The 90th opened up with everything they had. But their jitteriness soon disappeared, and they went on to relieve Captain Rae and the small band of parachute troops who had accomplished so much that day.

Unfortunately, the 90th had a difficult time and the 82nd went back into the attack in another twenty-four hours. By then, however, the initiative had slipped entirely from the Germans and they were fighting a delaying action. By D+11 we had reached Hill 110. The U.S. 9th Division, a veteran division from Africa, passed through us and severed the Cherbourg peninsula, and Cherbourg was doomed. It was liberated on June 26, 1944, and a major objective of Operation OVERLORD had been realized.

The final attack of the 82nd Airborne Division was launched on July 3. Attacking were three parachute regiments abreast and the 325th

Glider Infantry; the division swung south through Etienville, across the Douve River and the Prairies Marécageuses for several miles, then turned to the southeast, finally capturing the high ground overlooking the town of La Haye-du-Puits. There it remained in a defensive role until it was relieved and withdrawn into Army reserve on July 11, 1944. It was to be its last battle in Normandy. Shortly thereafter it was withdrawn to the United Kingdom to its old billets. Memories of them seemed old and faraway. A lifetime of combat experience had been acquired since D-day, and, of course, many of our troopers did not come back with us. The Division Commander made a report to the Supreme Commander on July 25, the leading paragraph of which read:

> Landing during darkness, beginning at H-4 hours on D-day, this division participated in the initial operations of the invasion of WESTERN EUROPE for thirty-three continuous days without relief and without replacements. It accomplished every assigned mission on or ahead of the time ordered. No ground gained was ever relinquished and no advance ever halted except on the order of Corps or ARMY. It sustained an aggregate loss of 46 per cent in killed, missing, and evacuated wounded. Prior to launching its final offensive, its infantry had sustained a loss of 45 per cent. At the conclusion of its operation it went into ARMY reserve, with fighting spirit as high as the day it entered action.

It might also have been added that we had gone into the battle with four regimental and sixteen battalion commanders, as well as several replacements if they were to be needed. They were. In the course of the Normandy combat, fifteen of these commanders had been killed, wounded, or captured—a striking indication of the leadership given to our parachute commands. A number of those wounded continued in command; for example, Vandervoort and Krause.

The troopers had been splendid; resourceful and courageous in the attack, resolute in the defense, they fought superbly. The attack had been costly, particularly to the infantry. Unfortunately, many casualties had resulted from the widespread landings, some of them miles from their planned drop zones. A surprising number of troopers were drowned in the flooded Merderet and Douve rivers. One of the lessons we learned was that troopers who landed in isolated areas must show more care in working their way back to their units than we had believed advisable in our prior battles. In Sicily the troopers had been instructed to attack the enemy, regardless of the size of the opposition, wherever they met him. I had numerous conversations with troopers who had landed miles from the proper drop zones in Normandy, and the survivors all told stories about moving at night, holing up during the day, and avoiding large enemy groups.

Actually, Cherbourg was doomed and the outcome of the battle of Normandy was decided with the severance of the Cotentin Peninsula. On June 10 the Chief of Staff of the German Seventh Army opposing our landing summarized the situation for higher German headquarters in a brief message entitled "Representation of the Events."

> The superior navy and air force have given the enemy advantages which cannot be compensated for, even through strong fortifications. The operation of the "new weapon," the airborne troops, behind the coastal fortifications, on one hand, and their massive attack on our own counterattacking troops, on the other hand, have contributed significantly to the initial success of the enemy.

For us the battle of Normandy was over. I left France almost convinced that Germany was through and that the war would end in '44. But many in the division felt more cautious, since the fighting at times had proved to be far more difficult and costly than we had anticipated.

The few days of fighting between the Merderet and Douve rivers, and the capture of St.-Sauveur-le-Vicomte on the Douve had been surprisingly difficult. This was because of the hedgerows. Although there had been some talk in the U.K. before D-day about the hedgerows, none of us had really appreciated how difficult they would turn out to be. All the *bocage* country of Normandy is cut up into small fields that have been handed down for centuries from family to family, and for centuries trees have grown up in the hedges between the fields. The hedges themselves were three to four feet thick and three to five feet high. Rocks, old tree roots, and the roots of living trees and dirt entwined into an impenetrable mass. In each field a small opening occurred, to permit a man, or, in some cases, vehicle, to enter. These openings were invariably covered by machine-gun fire, and thus each field was a small fortress in itself.

In addition, in some areas where they had anticipated an attack, the Germans had put in a prodigious amount of labor and had burrowed through the lower portions of the hedgerows where machine guns would be placed to sweep at ground level the adjoining fields. In some cases they had succeeded in digging standing slit trenches down into the hedgerows. Fortunately, an ingenious American, Sergeant Culin, early in combat developed a steel blade to attach to the front of the tanks that enabled them to cut their way through sections of the hedgerows as they fired against their opponents. But the hedgerows played a far more significant tactical role than either the Americans or the British had anticipated. Thus, from D-day on, the Allied attacking forces lagged behind the objectives planned in London. There was a man who would change that, and he was reposing in London, angry and frustrated. He was General George Patton.

Since General Patton had been brought from the Mediterranean theater to the United Kingdom early in 1944, German intelligence had kept track of him as closely as they could, and frequent references to "Armeegruppe Patton" showed up in their intelligence summaries. He was the only general besides Eisenhower they seemed concerned about. Patton, who was to command the U.S. Third Army, remained passive during the many months of planning. However, the Supreme Allied Commander made clever use of his presence. As the Allies planned to land in Normandy, they prepared a cover plan that suggested that an entire field army was poised in southern England ready to cross the Channel and land in the Calais area.

This was part of an elaborate deception plan intended to mislead the Germans into believing that an Army Group commanded by General Patton was prepared to attack Calais. One of its armies was across from Calais and one in northern England and Scotland. Complete communications networks were deployed and kept active. Part of the plan was for Patton to show himself about London and other areas, where his presence would be obvious and news of it would reach the Germans. On the night of the landings shredded tinfoil was dropped to mislead the Germans as to where the landings might take place and to clutter up the German radar. Several drops of miniature parachute dummies were also made. (The French called them "mannequins," the Germans "dolls.") They were so successful that in some situations the Germans reacted tardily to the actual landings, believing them to be "dolls."

It all made good sense, for a lodgment in Calais would permit the Allies to make a deep and rapid thrust into Germany, thus cutting off the Germans in Normandy and Brittany from the homeland. It was the shortest route across the Channel and the closest landing site to Germany itself.

A complete field army communications network was laid out across from Calais and regular communications traffic set up to cause the Germans to believe that the army was, in fact, there. So successful was the hoax that the Germans tied up a complete field army in Calais during the entire Normandy operation, and even eleven days after the landing in Normandy Hitler refused to release the army in anticipation of a crossing being made by "Armeegruppe Patton" at Calais. Patton, however, was kept in reserve and indeed did not leave the U.K. for France until early July.

Patton was kept informed of the Normandy planning, and from the outset he was apprehensive about its goals. The purpose of OVERLORD was "to seize and secure a lodgment area in continental France from which further operations could be developed." Phase I was the "assault and capture of an initial beachhead, including the development of airfield sites around Caen, and the capture of Cherbourg." Phase II was to be an enlargement of the area seized in Phase I to include all the Brittany peninsula and the area between the Loire and Seine rivers. It was the "seize and secure a lodgment area" that troubled Patton. It smacked too much of the tidy set piece that Montgomery liked so much. If the Germans reacted carefully, the Allies might well end up stuck in a lodgment area and so well boxed in that they might not get out. Speaking to General Bradley about it in the spring of '44, Patton said, "I still don't think the British have their heart in OVERLORD, and the planning, which is their handiwork, shows it . . . the plan as it now stands was made for Monty . . . he is not a man for fast and bold action. He is a master of the set battle, more concerned with not losing the battle than with winning one. . . . Monty is supposed to take Caen on D-day . . . well, Brad, he won't take it. He'll take his time, and in the meantime the Germans will get ready for the counterattack."[7]

General Patton continued to follow the operations after the landings. The progress ashore was painfully slow. On June 13 General Montgomery wrote to the Chief of the Imperial General Staff, "I am satisfied with the progress of operations," and two days later he wrote, "We are in a very reasonable position in the British Second Army," then, for no apparent reason, he added, "The American situation is not so good." At

[7] Farago, op. cit.

that time Montgomery had not yet seized Caen, his D-day objective. But if Montgomery was satisfied, the Americans were not—neither General Marshall, General Eisenhower, nor the Americans back home.

"The trouble started with Montgomery," Forrest C. Pogue was to note in his comprehensive biography of Marshall written after the war.[8] "Conceited . . . and unwilling to attack until he had everything in sight," was the way Eisenhower had described Montgomery to Marshall. Furthermore, the British Press, "MONTGOMERY'S TROOPS DRIVE ON CHERBOURG," and "MONTGOMERY'S FORCES ATTACK ST. LO," did not go down well with many Americans, who knew that neither Montgomery nor British troops were within miles of either place. And as the battle of Normandy went on, with Montgomery stopped at Caen and the Americans making steady but not spectacular progress through the difficult *bocage* country, the American casualties continued to mount. "By late July there were mutterings in Washington that Marshall could not ignore."[9] Fourteen thousand Americans had died in June out of a total of 21,000 Allied dead. The same ratio prevailed among the wounded; two-thirds of the 100,000 Allied wounded were Americans. Eisenhower visited the battle front on July 25 and 26 and in a meeting with Montgomery mentioned the disparity in casualties. Later he lunched with Winston Churchill, after which Churchill discussed the meeting with the Chief of the Imperial Staff, General Sir Alan Brooke. Afterward Brooke noted in his diary, "July 26, at 4:00 P.M., I was sent for by Winston and kept for an hour. Eisenhower had been lunching with him and had again run down Montgomery and described his stickiness and the reaction of the American papers . . . in the end I was asked to dine tomorrow night to meet Eisenhower and Bedell Smith."[10] The dinner was held as planned with the Prime Minister and Eisenhower and Bedell Smith present. Brooke thought that "it did a lot of good," and he so wrote in his diary the next day. He then went on to observe that "Ike is all out to do all that he can to maintain the best of relations between the British and the Americans," adding, "It is equally clear that Ike knows nothing about strategy." The following

[8] Pogue, op. cit.
[9] Ibid.
[10] Arthur Bryant, *Triumph in the West*. London: William Collins Sons & Co., Ltd., 1959.

morning he wrote of the dinner in a letter to Montgomery in which he observed, "Ike has the very vaguest conception of war."[11]

Referring to the meetings of July 25 and 26, Montgomery wrote in his memoirs after the war, "The troubles which began in this way in Normandy were to grow and to develop into storms which at times threatened to wreck the Allied ship."[12] This incident passed, but there were to be others.

As a great admirer of Montgomery both as a soldier and as a person, I do not believe that he ever understood how he was seen by the Americans. His name may have been "a household word" to the British, as Churchill expressed it, but to the Americans he was a man of colossal ego who always insisted upon getting the bulk of the resources before commencing a battle and then fighting a very conservative set battle, phase line by phase line, after it began. And in comparison with Patton, Montgomery did not come off well. Again, I do not believe that it ever entered Montgomery's mind that his behavior did not go down well with the Americans. Furthermore, he persisted in being appointed to the role of over-all ground commander; Ike was to be relegated to the position of Chairman of the Board, as it were. Such was the troublesome state of higher-command relations as the Allied Armies prepared for the final stage of the battle of Normandy, the breakout of the lodgment area, and, it was hoped, the complete destruction of two German field armies.

All through June Patton languished in London, hoping for an opportunity to participate in the battle with his Third Army. He knew intimately the area in which it would be fought; having been a military student in France, he had reconnoitered all the area from Cherbourg to Samur in 1913, and again in World War I when he was training his tank corps. The more he followed the tightening up of the situation in front of Caen and the drawing in of the U.S. First Army to support Montgomery, Patton was struck by the analogy of the situation with one that confronted the Germans in World War I. At the outset of that war the famous Schlieffen plan called for a pivot of all the German armies about Alsace. If the right flank had been adequately reinforced and the operation carried out as planned, it would have swept around and engulfed Paris and brought a decisive end to the war in 1914. What Patton began

[11] *The Memoirs of Field-Marshal Montgomery,* Cleveland and New York: The World Publishing Co., 1958.
[12] Ibid.

to see was the possibility of pivoting on Caen and launching his Third Army on the right for a wide sweep through Brittany and toward the Seine that would eventually engulf the German armies confronting them. In anticipation of this, he developed a plan he referred to as "Opus No. 1." In the meantime, in anticipation of a possible breakout, General Bradley had launched Operation COBRA. This was a tremendously powerful drive preceded by all-out carpet bombing that was intended to make a breakthrough that would set up conditions for a breakout by Patton's army. It was launched in late July with great success.

In the meantime, on July 6, Patton had been brought to France, where he established his headquarters in Normandy. July was to be a bad month for him. Time and again he begged Bradley to allow him to bring the Third Army into action. In late July Bradley put him in charge of "supervising" the VIII Corps as it attacked south out of the Cotentin Peninsula to Avranches.

Finally, on August 1, Patton's Third Army was turned loose. He at once pushed his armored divisions through the infantry divisions, and in what was unquestionably the most spectacular campaign of the war, he moved rapidly into Brittany. By August 3 his troops were threatening St. Malo; they had overrun Rennes and moved to the west, reaching Brest and Lorient on August 7. Sweeping south and east, they occupied one town after another, driving the Germans fleeing ahead of them. In the initial stages of the breakout, Patton's 4th Armored Division passed within a couple of hundred yards of the German Seventh Army Command Post. The Germans ran for their lives and managed to make their way to the east. Only Field Marshal Gunther von Kluge sensed the significance of the rapidly moving armored thrusts. He radioed Hitler, "as a result of the breakthrough of the enemy's western spearheads, the whole western front has been ripped open."

Patton's divisions and corps went on, finally reaching the crossings over the Loire River. Patton ordered his divisions to sweep east and north so as to engulf the German 5th Panzer Army and Seventh Army, which were opposing the British and Canadians and the U.S. First Army. I remember following his movements in the war room of the 82nd Airborne Division in Leicester, England, and to one with combat experience, it was an amazing display of audacity. I asked about the danger of Germans moving up from the south and learned that he had planned to have the Air Corps bomb the crossings over the Loire River and then disregard all Germans to the south. Years later, when I was in the Paris Embassy, I made it a point to visit all the crossing sites just to find out how audacious George had been. He certainly had been audacious; the river is wide but not too deep, and with proper engineering support, the bridges could have been rebuilt overnight. But such was the daring and vision of this great cavalry general that he was able to ignore such threats and continue his sweeping operation.

Early in August, at a conference held by the Americans and the British, they talked about the possibilities of a linkup somewhere around Argentan. Lieutenant General Miles C. Dempsey, commanding the British Second Army, said that he expected to be in Argentan before Patton. As it turned out, Patton's leading columns reached Argentan the night of August 12, less than two weeks after the breakout at Avranches. Montgomery was then struggling to reach Falaise twelve miles north of Argentan. Patton's performance had been amazing. His aide, Colonel Charles Codman, described him:

> The old man has been like one possessed . . . the spearheading armored divisions, following the motorized infantry, have been moving bumper to bumper . . . pushing, pulling, exhorting, cajoling, raising merry hell, he is having the time of his life. I have never seen or heard of another ETO commander who can even remotely compare with General Patton in respect to his uncanny gift for sweeping men into doing things which they do not believe they are capable of doing, do not really want to do, which, in fact, they would not do, unless directly exposed to the personality, the genius—call it what you will— of this unique soldier. . . .

Meanwhile the Germans were far from despairing. Actually, the Commander in Chief West, Field Marshal von Kluge, looked with some optimism on the growing evidence that a landing was not to be made in Calais. The number of air units as well as ground formations that began to appear under Patton suggested clearly that the long-anticipated Calais landing was off. The Germans had lived in some fear of such a landing because, if it had been successful, it would have placed German forces in Normandy and Brittany in clear danger of being cut off from the homeland. Rommel had suggested that the Allied tactic would probably be to attempt a breakout of the Normandy beachhead at the same time that the landings at Calais took place. As they slowly began to realize that the total Allied resources were now committed and that they were in

Normandy and Brittany, the Commander in Chief West felt considerable relief. He had little time to philosophize about the latest turn of events, however, for at 7:00 A.M. on August 3 he received an order from Hitler directing him to attack the narrow corridor through which the Third Army had passed at Avranches, to seize Avranches and cut off the Third Army. This mission was given to the XLVII Panzer Corps. Three divisions were to be employed: the 2nd SS, the 2nd Infantry, and the 116th Infantry. In addition the Corps was given eighty Mark IV tanks and other combat support reinforcements.

The attack was launched in the early hours of August 7 and met with limited success. The U.S. 30th Infantry Division, reinforced, fought an extremely effective defensive battle. Hitler was convinced, however, that the attack could succeed if given added weight, and the 10th SS and the 21st SS Panzer Divisions were to arrive in the Seventh Army sector on August 8. They were both added to the attack. On August 9 Hitler renewed his attack order; he reserved for himself the designation of H-hour; such was the degree of control that he sought to employ over even the smallest formations.

By this time five and a half of the seven Panzer divisions in the pocket were committed against the Americans, with one and a half remaining against the British and Canadian armies. Hitler could not have played into the hands of the Allies more completely if the Allies had planned it, for there was no question about the troops at Avranches holding. They were more than capable of doing so, and the Allies had complete air superiority. This was devastating to the Germans, and they were constantly handicapped in daylight by Allied air. Ultimately, practically all the roads in the pocket were littered with German vehicles, artillery pieces, and the dead. Not until the very last moment did Hitler realize the disaster that was about to befall his forces. At that time he directed an attack against the left flank of General Wade Hampton Haislip's U.S. XV Corps, which had reached the outskirts of Argentan. (*Fig. 11.*)

Up to now it had been Sicily all over again, with Montgomery making very little progress and Patton making an enormous enveloping movement; the destruction of two German armies was in their grasp. To the military professionals, it was to be a Cannae. If they could have been successful in realizing that objective, it would have saved many Allied lives and almost certainly have ended the war in 1944. But Patton had been ordered to go no farther than Argentan. As mentioned,

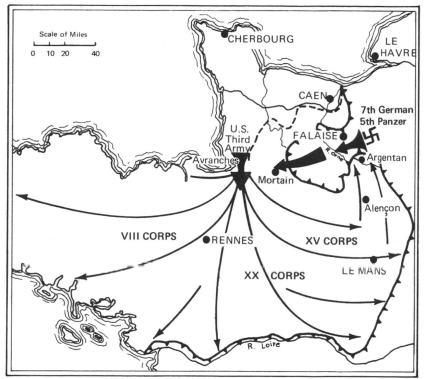

Fig. 11   Situation on August 13, 1944

Argentan had been a British objective, and General Miles Dempsey had expected to be there before the Americans. When Patton learned, near midnight on Saturday, August 12, that his advance elements were at Argentan, he called Bradley. "We have got elements in Argentan . . . let me go on to Falaise and we will drive the British back into the sea for another Dunkirk." "Nothing doing," Bradley replied. "You are not to go beyond Argentan. Just stop where you are and build up that shoulder." Patton was then in his Advance Command Post just north of Le Mans, and he couldn't believe the order. He checked with General Bradley's Chief of Staff, Major General Lev Allen, and Allen confirmed it.

All day on August 13 Patton tried to get authority to move north and thus link up with the British and Canadians and cut off the Germans. But by the end of that Sunday afternoon, it was quite definite that he was not to be allowed to go north and close the gap. Instead, his leading corps was instructed to assemble and prepare for further operations in another direction. Thus, incredibly, was lost one of the great tactical opportunities of the war. German General Walter Warlimont, who was in Hitler's headquarters, noted that the Operations Staff War Diary recorded that "a good half of the troops thus encircled fought their way out," characterizing the escape as "one of the great feats of arms of this campaign." How could this possibly have happened?

The failure to close the gap between Argentan and Falaise was partially attributable to the command structure and to the degree of misunderstanding that may have existed about who was responsible to whom. To begin with, when the Normandy landings took place, General Montgomery commanded the 21st Army Group and was in charge of one British Army, one Canadian Army, and the U.S. First Army, commanded by Bradley. The U.S. buildup was expected to be quite rapid, and as soon as Patton's Third Army became active, Bradley was expected to take over the U.S. 12th Army Group, commanding both the U.S. First Army and the U.S. Third Army, and thus be in a position comparable to that of Montgomery. Up to that moment Montgomery had directed the land battle. Eisenhower was supposed to be in charge of both Army Groups once the U.S. 12th was brought into being. Montgomery, however, continued to give directions to Bradley even after Bradley had assumed command of the 12th Army Group. Thus, Bradley cleared the dispositions of Patton's Third Army with Montgomery before Patton was allowed to go ahead. If there was need for over-all guidance, it should have come from the Supreme Commander, General Eisenhower.

When General Wade Hampton Haislip's XV Corps reached Argentan, Patton had no recourse but to go to Bradley. He was turned down in his request to continue the advance. The next day, when he tried to reach Bradley, he had to deal through his Chief of Staff, for General Bradley was at General Eisenhower's headquarters at SHELLBURST in Normandy. Captain Harry C. Butcher, General Eisenhower's aide, described General Bradley as "playing bridge as calmly and peacefully as if he had just come off the golf course on a Sunday afternoon. He stayed for dinner." General Eisenhower, in his book, *Crusade in Europe,* states, "I was in Bradley's headquarters when messages began to arrive from commanders of the advancing American columns, complaining that the limits placed upon them by their orders were allowing Germans to escape. I completely supported Bradley in his decision." On the other hand, Patton, in his book, *War as I Knew It,* claims that he had reconnaissance troops in Falaise on August 13; thus he had already crossed the gap. In the official U.S. Army history of the war, Bradley is quoted as saying, "If Monty's tactics mystified me, they dismayed Eisenhower even more and . . . a shocked Third Army looked on helplessly while its quarry fled and while Patton raged at Montgomery's blunder." And long after the event General Eisenhower implied that "the gap might have been closed," which "might have won us a complete battle of annihilation."

It is difficult to understand how a tactical blunder of this magnitude could have occurred. Surely General Bradley should have gone forward at least to Patton's headquarters to discuss the situation with him on August 13. The place for a general is where the critical action occurs and decisions must be made. It would have been better for him to have gone forward to the XV Corps headquarters, but by removing themselves from the scene of action and at the same time tying Patton's hands, Eisenhower and Bradley allowed at least half of two German armies to escape. Actually, they were counting on Montgomery to close the gap, but if there was any doubt, one of them should have been there. Bradley could justify not going north because Montgomery had assured him that he would close the gap, and indeed Argentan was one of the objectives of Montgomery's attack. But from D-day on, Montgomery was usually late in reaching his objectives. In these circumstances the man who ultimately had to take the responsibility for failing to order the gap closed was the Supreme Commander, General Eisenhower. It was he who commanded both Army Groups, and it was he who had the ultimate responsibility for how they conducted the battle.

So the battle of Normandy ended on a very bad note. What could have been a battle of annihilation had been a battle that allowed many Germans to escape and fight again. As they went reeling across France to their homeland, using horses, bicycles, broken-down vehicles, and any other form of transport they could get their hands on, many French, Belgian, and Dutch people who saw them making their way through the occupied countries were convinced that the war was over.

Normandy saw our first airborne operation of a division size. The problems posed by the need for prompt reorganization after landing and quick seizure of initial objectives were many times more difficult than those of the smaller-type operations we had been in before. Nevertheless, the lessons that we had learned in the Mediterranean were very valuable to us.

I had a meeting of all the surviving battalion and regimental commanders in mid-August to discuss our experience. All agreed that the pathfinder aids were excellent. We were also happy with the training and the physical condition of our troops. With very few exceptions, there were complaints about our Troop Carrier colleagues. When they began to fly into heavy flak, some of them climbed as high as 2000 feet and stepped up their speeds to 150 miles an hour, which is 50 per cent more than the customary jump speed. This resulted in severe opening shocks and the loss of equipment on the part of a number of jumpers. And, of course, jumpers complained about the length of time it took them to descend and their vulnerability during that period.

We were still plagued with the lack of antitank weapons. In Normandy, for the first time, we came across a small German rocket based on the same principle as our bazooka. It was called "faustpetrone." It was a shaped charge warhead slightly larger than the bazooka. When I first found these weapons in German positions that we overran, I did not know what they were, but we soon found out when we fired them. They were quite effective.

Holland

When we surveyed the wreckage of Normandy and added this to the experience of Sicily, several things became clear. First, Montgomery was a very conservative soldier, one who demanded tremendous resources before he would be willing to commit his armies to battle. Next, Patton was an impulsive, daring commander, impatient with his subordinates, aggressive and determined to win tactical victories regardless of risks. He was forever "seeking that bubble reputation, even in the cannon's mouth."[1] He gave one the impression that he considered World War II, so far, to be Patton versus the Wehrmacht. Next, Patton's envelopment of the German Seventh Army and the German Fifth Panzer Army, and the very serious losses inflicted upon them by Allied air power, caused an unanticipated deterioration of the German position and, as a consequence, a rapid Allied advance eastward. This, in turn, put the advancing Allied armies well beyond where the logisticians had anticipated they would be. Critical supply problems were in the offing. Finally, the employment of airborne troops in Normandy had been very effective, despite their widespread drops. The 101st Airborne Division had assisted in opening the causeways. The 82nd Airborne Division had blocked the movement of German forces from Cherbourg and from the western part of the peninsula, thus giving the amphibious forces time to consolidate and take the offensive. The 82nd played a major role in that offensive.

Montgomery's problem was complex. He had a very high opinion of himself as a soldier and believed that he alone should control the land battle. He demanded tremendous resources without great concern for their availability, and most of them had to come from the Americans. Finally, he seemed insensitive to the political burdens that Eisenhower

[1] Shakespeare, *As You Like It,* II, vii, 139.

had to bear in his responsibility to General Marshall and the American people. Despite the understanding before the Normandy landing that Bradley would be given an Army Group and thus would be on a command level with Montgomery, both reporting to Eisenhower after Patton's army went ashore, Montgomery was reluctant to give up command of the land battle. As his Chief of Staff, General Francis de Guingand, put it, "Montgomery . . . never, I believe, thought that the day would come so soon."[2] Not only had George Patton's Third Army been committed to battle, but by the end of August the Americans had twenty combat divisions on the Continent and six American divisions, including three airborne, in the United Kingdom, compared to twelve British divisions, three Canadian divisions, one French division, and one Polish division on the Continent. There were no more British divisions available.

To add to the difficulty that Montgomery was unwittingly getting himself into in Europe, the impression that he was making in America was far from favorable. Aware of Patton's spectacular breakout and overrunning of Brittany, the Americans were at last beginning to see Montgomery as the "do-nothing" general. They were beginning to tire of the publicity he was receiving for battles fought and won by the Americans. American wounded were returning in large numbers. They had won spectacular battles from Normandy on, but their casualties had been very high. There was growing public concern, and General Marshall was beginning to receive questions from members of Congress.

The problem of public opinion in America seemed to escape Montgomery entirely. At one time in late August he recommended to Eisenhower that Patton be brought to a full stop and that he, Montgomery, be given all the resources to go ahead and win the war. "The American public would never stand for stopping Patton in full cry, and public opinion wins wars," Eisenhower told him. "Nonsense," Montgomery shot back angrily. "Victories win wars. Give people victory and they won't care who won it."[3]

As the month of August ran out and the British Second Army surged through Belgium to the Dutch frontier, Montgomery was convinced that he, and he alone, should lead the decisive battle all the way to Berlin and that to do this he should be given priority on all supplies and troops.

[2] Major General Francis de Guingand, *Generals at War*. London: Hodder & Stoughton, Ltd., 1964.
[3] Farago, op. cit.

It was true that he was on the northern flank, close to the Channel ports where, in theory at least, he could be better supplied. In late August he proposed to General Eisenhower a plan to end the war. As Eisenhower described it in his memoirs, "Montgomery suddenly presented the proposition that, if we would support his Twenty-first Army Group with all supply facilities available, he could rush right on into Berlin and, he said, end the war."

While this had been going on, the British press had become aroused because Montgomery had been relieved of over-all command of the ground forces and Bradley's Army Group given command of the American armies. To soften the blow, on September 1, he was made a Field Marshal and thus became senior in grade to all other Allied officers in Europe.

On September 10, in response to Montgomery's request for a meeting, Ike flew to Brussels. He had sprained his knee several days earlier and so remained aboard his plane for the meeting. Montgomery brought along his administrative and supply officer, Lieutenant General Miles Graham. Montgomery insisted, however, that Eisenhower's Assistant Chief of Staff for Administration, Lieutenant General Sir Humphrey Gale, not be permitted to attend. Ike concurred. This was a strange command relationship. Here was the Supreme Commander deeply worried about his rapidly deteriorating logistics situation—he desperately needed the port of Antwerp opened. So far, Montgomery had captured the docks and port facilities only, leaving the fifty-four-mile estuary under German control. So Montgomery, who insisted on all available supplies, brought along his own staff expert, insisting that Eisenhower's not be present.[4]

Montgomery began, as was expected, by denouncing Ike's "broad front" strategy. He wanted absolute priority and demanded a decision on whether he or Patton was to get priority. Later Eisenhower was to recall saying at the meeting: "What you're proposing is this—if I give you all of the supplies you want, you could go straight to Berlin—right straight to Berlin? Monty, you're nuts. You can't do it."[5] Montgomery pointed out the seriousness of the newly established V-2 launching sites in Holland from which the Germans had already begun bombarding

[4] Chester Wilmot, a distinguished British historian, who wrote *The Struggle for Europe* and who was consistently pro-Montgomery, observed, "This request was hardly tactful. . . ."
[5] Interview with General Eisenhower by Cornelius Ryan, reported in his book *A Bridge Too Far.*

London. He then made a very bold proposal. He recommended that the First Allied Airborne Army be used to penetrate deeply, sixty-four miles, into Holland, seizing five bridges over major waterways and numerous smaller objectives that were essential to the success of the battle. He would follow with the British Second Army, using paratroopers and glidermen as a "carpet."

Ike was intrigued. He had been under considerable pressure from both General Marshall and General Arnold to be much bolder and more imaginative in his employment of the new and fledgling arm. Marshall had pointed out to him that this new force was analogous to the tank forces of World War I. In the earlier war, tanks were used in small packets to assist ground formations in short tactical gains. Only when they were used en masse, as in World War II, was their full potential realized. So he urged Ike to be more daring.

The proposed operation, later dubbed Operation MARKET-GARDEN, seemed to fill the bill. Eisenhower concurred in Montgomery's proposal, even though it meant delaying the opening of the port of Antwerp and slowing down, if not stopping, Patton. Shortly thereafter, in reply to a query by Montgomery, General Browning estimated that the assault could be launched by September 15 or 16. Characteristically, Montgomery then pressed for additional supplies, threatening to delay the attack, possibly until September 26, unless the supplies were received. General Bedell Smith, Eisenhower's Chief of Staff, went to call on Montgomery and to assure him of additional supplies and transport. He also promised him that Patton's drive in the south would be held up. Montgomery was pleased.

Far south of Montgomery's Army Group was Patton on the right of Bradley's U.S. 12th Army Group. During August Patton had once again proved himself to be a great cavalry commander in the battle of Normandy. He was willing to take great risks, and he had the ability to drive men to the limit of their endurance in order to achieve his goals. He was brilliant in exploitation, and the battle of Europe was about to enter the exploitation phase. Breakout and pursuit were ending, and now the final decisive battle was in the offing.

Patton was the man to lead it and he knew it, and many Americans believed that he should lead it. But by late August he was beginning to worry. Indications were that the flow of supplies might be slowing down and Montgomery might be favored. Hearing that Major General Harold Bull, Eisenhower's G-3, would be in Chartres on August 30, Patton flew there to plead his cause. Pointing out the weakened condition of the Wehrmacht, and the most recent performance of his fine Army, he saw no problem that he could not handle, including a penetration of the Siegfried Line in a few days. All he needed was the signal to go—and the necessary supplies, especially gasoline.

The unanticipated successes of the Allied armies were the very cause of their difficulties. They were far ahead of goals set in London before crossing the Channel, and they were still being supplied over the Normandy beaches. And by late August it was a three-hundred-mile trip from the Normandy beaches to the nearest Army supply dumps. The situation was made more critical by the needs of the essential services for the cities and towns that had been overrun. Paris, for example. Despite these problems, on August 31, two of Patton's divisions, the 7th Armored and the 9th Infantry, established a bridgehead over the Meuse at Verdun. On that date Patton did not receive a single drop of gasoline. This caused a shocking awakening to the realities of the logistics situation. A corps in Patton's army needed 200,000 to 300,000 gallons of gasoline in a movement that averaged about fifty miles. In addition, thousands of tons of ammunition, medical supplies, blankets, and food were needed. So Patton's Army was stopped.

It is ironic that at about the same time the Germans, too, were deeply preoccupied with Patton. They considered him their most dangerous opponent and pitted their best troops against him. So both sides were doing their damnedest to stop Patton. To be true, for entirely different reasons—but they were. And so when Patton's staff learned that Montgomery was to be given the First Allied Army, including two American airborne divisions, first priority on supplies, and truck companies from the U.S. First and Third Armies to help move Montgomery's supplies, it was Sicily all over again, only worse. And word had gotten to Ike that Patton's staff was saying that Eisenhower was the best general the British had.

Meanwhile, the Germans were far from supine, awaiting the final, fatal blow. On September 4 Hitler recalled General Karl von Rundstedt and placed him in charge of the German armies in the West. Von Rundstedt had been relieved of the same command on July 1. When the battle of Normandy was most intense, Hitler's Chief of Staff, Field Marshal Wilhelm Keitel, asked Von Rundstedt the obvious question, "What shall we do?" Without hesitation, Von Rundstedt replied, "End the war, you fools. What else can you do?"

Subordinate to Von Rundstedt was Field Marshal Walter Model, who commanded Army Group B. Model had Germany's northwest frontier, including the responsibility for a seventy-five-mile-wide gap that had been torn open by the Allied surge into Belgium. He desperately sought to screen out all the German refugees and stragglers and funnel them into new formations if not their old outfits. He selected for a Command Post a modest hotel in the town of Oosterbeek. It was several miles west of the bridge over the Rhine River at the town of Arnhem in Holland.

The same day that Von Rundstedt journeyed to his new command near Coblenz, Colonel General Kurt Student received a call from Hitler's Chief of Operations, Colonel General Alfred Jodl; he told Student that he was to organize and take charge of the "First Parachute Army." The "Army" was to be used to block the gap that had been torn open by Montgomery's Army Group in its plunge through Belgium to the Holland border. To Student, it was a paper army and a sad commentary on his own career, for he had pioneered the use of parachute and glider troops in Holland in the opening days of World War II and in the seizure of Crete. In Crete he had used about 22,000 troops, and they had suffered one-third casualties—too high a casualty rate for Hitler's stomach. They were not used again, even though several promising operations arose, such as the possible seizure of Malta.

So, with patience and hope, Student set himself to the task of gathering all the parachute troops wherever they could be found to organize an army. He did have one hard-core unit, the 6th Parachute Regiment, with another battalion totaling approximately 3000 men. Also in the area were the remnants of the 9th and 10th SS Panzer Divisions. They were under the command of Lieutenant General William Bittrich. They were directed to move into the area in early September, and they chose as their bivouacs forest and park areas that would provide good cover. They were in the suburbs of Arnhem. Although they had been badly mauled in earlier fighting, they immediately began gathering replacements and re-equipping.

In the meantime Von Rundstedt sought to divine the intentions of the Allies. Some of the best German divisions were in front of Patton because they feared him most. For some time Von Rundstedt believed that if a final great battle was to be waged, Patton would play a major role in it, so he watched Patton warily. On the other hand, he sensed that the Allies were having serious logistical problems; otherwise, why would they have stopped in late August, just when victory was in their grasp? He knew also that Montgomery was a very methodical soldier, who would not move until all supplies were on hand and all troops carefully placed. In the midst of these serious pressures his attention became focused on Antwerp. If the Allies were having logistics problems because of their overextended supply line, why then did they not clear the port of Antwerp?

At the end of August, the British Second Army, under the leadership of General Dempsey, sent its leading division, the British 11th Armored Division, 250 miles in five days to capture Antwerp with complete surprise. Assisted by the Belgian Underground, they had taken over the entire harbor intact on September 4. Meanwhile, on September 3, the British Guards Armored had seized Brussels. Both actions made clear that the German situation in Belgium was catastrophic and that they were rapidly withdrawing into Holland.

The seizure of Antwerp, however, was not sufficient to make the port operational, for it was at the end of the fifty-four-mile estuary that was held by the Germans on both sides all the way to the sea. After the war there was much discussion about this oversight, "the blunder at Antwerp," as it was described. There is no doubt that the British 11th Armored was completely exhausted when it reached Antwerp, but even after a day or so of rest it could have gone on. Liddell Hart, in his *History of the Second World War,* attributes it to a "multiple lapse—by four commanders from Montgomery downward." And Charles B. MacDonald in his book *The Mighty Endeavor* called the failure "One of the greatest tactical mistakes of the war." I cannot understand how a historian can avoid placing the responsibility on Eisenhower. He, more than anyone else, had a keen awareness of the critical nature of the logistics situation in his armies. The commander of the British 30 Corps, General Horrocks, in a characteristically self-effacing remark said that his "eyes were fixed entirely on the Rhine," and added, "Napoleon would, no doubt, have realized these things, but Horrocks didn't."[6]

The holdup at Antwerp began to suggest to Von Rundstedt an extraordinary possibility. When the Allies had landed in Normandy, the German Fifteenth Army had been poised near Calais. It had been there to repel what the Germans considered to be the real crossing of the English Channel that was expected to be directed toward Calais. By the

[6] Sir Brian Horrocks, *A Full Life.* Toronto: William Collins Sons & Co., Canada, Ltd., 1960.

end of August it had been under some attack, but it still had 80,000 troops, and although cut off from Germany by land, it could possibly be returned by sea. Of course, the Allies had complete control of the sea, and by merely keeping the shoreline under surveillance day and night, they could have anticipated any move of General Gustav von Zangen's army to escape. When Montgomery did not move to clear the estuary, Von Rundstedt decided that there was a chance of extricating the German Fifteenth Army and thus augmenting the thin forces he had in Holland. It was a tricky move. The troops had to be ferried along the shore and across the three-mile mouth of the Schelde. It obviously could be undertaken only at night. But Von Rundstedt believed that it was worth trying, and he set the operation in motion.

It succeeded beyond his highest expectations. The Fifteenth Army, with approximately 65,000 troops and accompanying artillery, trucks, wagons, was moved to Holland without the Allies' realizing that the move had been made. In retrospect, admittedly, one wonders why the actions of the Allied Naval forces were not coordinated with those of Field Marshal Montgomery's Army Group so as to keep the German Fifteenth Army under surveillance. Perhaps it was because the Supreme Commander was remote from the battle itself, as had happened in Sicily. But the fact is that the move was successfully accomplished in the face of overwhelming Allied air, land, and sea power. It was to have a decisive bearing on the battle that followed.

By mid-September the Allies were poised and ready for the final battle. The Allies had been surprised by the ease with which they had driven the German Seventh Army out of France and Belgium, in the final stages as chaff before the wind. Now they were due to be surprised again by the extent to which the Germans had recovered.

The major problems of the Allies as the summer of '44 came to an end were those of logistics and decision-making. Eisenhower was later to remark, "No relocation of our present resources would be adequate to sustain a thrust to Berlin." His problem was therefore one of taking from others to sustain Montgomery's decisive battle. At the same time, the decision did not seem to be as critical as it later turned out to be, and there was much optimism that Germany had already been beaten.

Optimism was pervasive in the highest headquarters. As early as August 11 Major General Kenneth W. D. Strong, Eisenhower's Chief of Intelligence, thought that the war would be over in three months. Most astounding, post-exchange officials distributed a memorandum saying that they were arranging to return Christmas presents—already in the mail—to the United States.[7] According to Captain Butcher, General Eisenhower's aide, Major General Bedell Smith, Eisenhower's Chief of Staff, told members of the press in early September, "Militarily the war is won." Those of us who saw the war at the foxhole level were not quite so optimistic. Not that we had not beaten the Germans badly in Normandy; we had and we were supremely confident that we could take care of their infantry again. But we had great respect for their tanks and antitank weapons, and we believed them to be superior to our own. I suppose it is fair to describe our mood at that time, since we did not know the big picture, as being hopeful but still quite apprehensive about our next encounter, wherever it would be.

By the third week of July the 82nd Airborne Division was back in its old billets in mid-England. Division headquarters and three infantry regiments were near Leicester, and other divisional troops were in Nottingham and Market Harborough. Immediately following their return from Normandy, all the troopers were given short furloughs. On their return we settled down to dealing urgently with the problems of taking in new volunteers and giving them parachute training, welcoming back our wounded, re-equipping—and finally intensive training. Our casualties had been heavy; some infantry companies lost more than 50 per cent killed, wounded, or missing. Offsetting those losses was the extensive battle experience gained by the survivors. Now the problem was to transmit this experience to the new young troopers who were joining us.

Division headquarters in Leicester was established at Braunston Park, just outside the town, in Nissen huts, and a War Room was set up and kept posted around the clock. The battle on the Continent was followed very carefully, and we tried to anticipate possible airborne missions that might suddenly be thrust on us. On August 11 a Division Review was held for General Eisenhower and General Brereton. Although we had long since ceased paying much attention to close-order drill, the troops marched with great élan. Individual and unit pride seemed to take over, and the troopers were superb.

After the review General Eisenhower stopped at General Ridgway's home, the Glebe Mount House in Leicester, for tea. Some of the staff were surprised when his chauffeur, Kay Summersby, joined us. Chauffeurs do not normally join their generals for tea. She was an

[7] Pogue, op. cit., p. 430.

attractive woman, and she seemed to be a very nice person. I was struck once again, as I always was in my association with the British people, by how their women pitched in and supported the war effort as chauffeurs, clerks, staff officers; wherever they could contribute, they made an effort, and it was impressive. There was considerable gossip about Kay Summersby. It must have been troublesome to General Eisenhower—if he was aware of it. I once asked John "Beaver" Thompson of the *Chicago Tribune* if it wasn't just gossip. "Well," he replied, "I have never before seen a chauffeur get out of a car and kiss the General good morning when he comes from his office."

Miss Summersby wrote a book immediately after the war, *Eisenhower Was My Boss*.[8] It was a straightforward, businesslike account of the role she filled as a co-worker with the General and as she became an American citizen and advanced to the grade of captain in the Women's Army Corps. Many years later, and just before she died of cancer, she wrote another book, far more intimate, about her relationship with the General. It was entitled *Past Forgetting, My Love Affair with Dwight D. Eisenhower*. I found it rather poignant and very sad. In reading it, I was startled to learn that after General Eisenhower's visit to the airborne troops, before they took off for Normandy on the night of June 5, he chose to spend the night in a caravan with Miss Summersby. In describing the difficulty of waiting for the first news from the battle front, she wrote:

> All you can do is be there—and bite your tongue. It meant a lot to me that I was the person he chose to be with in those crucial hours. If Ike had wished, he could have been surrounded by top brass, by Churchill and De Gaulle, by any of the important personages who were gathered just a few miles away in Portsmouth. But he preferred to wait in solitude.[9]

Immediately following the review, we went back to work, and there was much work to be done. In early August arrangements were being made for General Ridgway to assume command of the XVIII Airborne Corps, and I was pleased to learn that I was to be given command of the 82nd Airborne Division. On August 16 he formally relinquished com-

[8] Kathleen Summersby, *Eisenhower Was My Boss,* ed. by Michael Kearns. New York: Prentice-Hall, Inc., 1948.
[9] Kay Summersby Morgan, *Past Forgetting, My Love Affair with Dwight D. Eisenhower.* New York: Simon & Schuster, Inc. 1976, p. 217.

mand, and I was designated Division Commander. General Ridgway had given the division attributes that would serve it well for the remainder of the war. His great courage, integrity, and aggressiveness in combat all made a lasting impression on everyone in the division and on all commands.

My first task was to bring together a division staff, since most of the old staff had transferred to the newly formed XVIII Corps. I picked Colonel Robert Wienecke, former Division G-3, as Chief of Staff. G-1, in charge of personnel affairs, was to be Lieutenant Colonel Al Ireland; G-2, intelligence, Lieutenant Colonel Walter Winton; G-3, plans and operations, Lieutenant Colonel John Norton; and G-4, logistics, Lieutenant Colonel Albert Marin. It was unquestionably the youngest division staff in the European Theater of Operations. It was also a very able, dedicated, hard-working staff. At once we entered into discussions about how we might be used to assist the Allied Armies in advance.

In late August we began to receive a series of alerts to ready ourselves for an airborne landing. The British Second Army was making rapid progress, and the Wehrmacht was in a precipitate retreat. On September 1 we were given an outline plan for landings near Tournai, Belgium. The landings were canceled and the objective was changed to Liège. Troopers were dispersed to take-off airfields. This mission was canceled at the last moment. But the experience was useful in training our new troopers and junior officers to cope with the problems of pre-drop preparation; ammunition, food, maps, and air photos all had to be distributed, all commands had to be prepared, and every conceivable operational detail anticipated and covered.

On Sunday afternoon, September 10, I was in London visiting some friends when I received a phone call from General Brereton's headquarters in Sunningdale about an hour's drive west of London. I was told to be at his headquarters for a meeting as promptly as I could get there. There was to be another airborne operation, and they considered it to be imminent. It was 6:00 P.M. when I arrived at the meeting; it had already been under way for a few minutes. General Browning had just flown over from the Continent, from Montgomery's headquarters, and he was holding forth. In addition to General Brereton there were present General Maxwell D. Taylor of the U.S. 101st Airborne, General Robert F. Urquhart of the British 1st Airborne, and all the senior troop carrier commanders, British and American. General Browning continued to outline the plan for the proposed operation. It envisioned

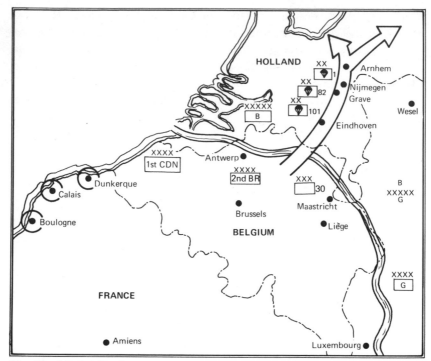

Fig. 12   Market-Garden

seizing bridges over five major waterways, as well as a number of other tactical objectives extending from the present front of the British Second Army along the Albert Canal, sixty-four miles into Holland, to the farthest bridge, over the lower Rhine in the town of Arnhem. (*Fig. 12.*)

After a brief discussion about who would take what mission, it became apparent that the present locations of the divisions in the U.K. would determine what objectives would be assigned to each division. As they were located, the British 1st Airborne Division was best positioned for the Arnhem drop, the 82nd Airborne Division for the operation between Nijmegen and Grave, and the U.S. 101st Airborne Division for all the southern bridges. The next decision had to do with the allocation of airlift and the bringing together of the appropriate parachute-glider troops with the proper troop-carrying units. Since the airborne divisions had not had an opportunity to analyze their tactical plans in any detail, it was decided that the troop-carrying role would be determined later, preferably early the following morning. In the meantime I had to get information about the German dispositions, and obtain air photo coverage of the entire area, so as to be able to select drop zones and landing zones, and then begin the process of determining what troops would be assigned to what specific objectives.

General Brereton was pressing for an early decision on D-day, and he sought for a commitment of an operation on Thursday, September 14, just four days away. It soon became apparent that this was most unlikely, since we would not be able to get the troops briefed before the following day and we still had ahead of us the issuance of maps, ammunition, and the allocation of artillery and supporting arms. Finally, moving all the troops and their equipment to the appropriate airfields posed a major time problem. After some discussion we all agreed that we probably could make the date of Sunday, September 17, without great difficulty, but not an earlier date. It was also decided to conduct the operation in daylight. This was an unprecedented decision, since all prior airborne operations had been conducted during darkness. It was believed, however, that the Luftwaffe's capability to interfere was very limited, and with the fighter-bomber support that the R.A.F. and the U.S. Air Force could give us, we would probably carry out the operation with a minimum of losses. In addition, for the first time in the Allied experience hundreds of gliders were to be used in the assault. There were also a number of green pilots who had not had the Normandy experience. Carrying out the operation in daylight would be much easier for them, and we all agreed that this was the way we wanted to go about it. The optimistic mood of the higher headquarters had reached the First Allied Airborne Army, and there seemed to be little concern about any substantial German resistance.

Since August the Luftwaffe and Wehrmacht had been on the defensive and retreating behind the frontier of Germany, so we were inclined to go about our planning with more preoccupation with our own plans than any concerns for the enemy, since his resistance was expected to be negligible. Nevertheless, as soon as the meeting broke up about 9:00 P.M., I went directly to the headquarters of the British 1st Airborne Division and the British Airborne Corps, which was nearby at Moor Park. Immediately after the meeting several British officers had spoken to me about my mission, since they had been planning an operation in

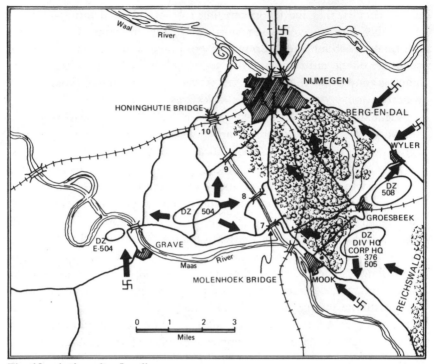

Fig. 13   Action after Landing

the vicinity of Nijmegen for some time and they believed they had available all the information that the Allies had about the German situation in that area.

The mission assigned to the 82nd Airborne Division was to seize the long bridge over the Maas River at Grave, to seize and hold the high ground in the vicinity of Groesbeek, to seize at least one of the four bridges over the Maas-Waal Canal, and finally to seize the big bridge over the Waal at the city of Nijmegen. (*Fig. 13.*)

The U.S. 101st Airborne Division had the mission of seizing the bridges of several canals and rivers south of Grave. Finally, the British 1st Airborne Division was to seize the bridge over the lower Rhine at the town of Arnhem. General Taylor expressed some reservations about the way his division would be scattered in penny packets, as it were, along a string of bridges from the front of the British Second Army northward. For my part, I was concerned about the very widespread dispersal that would take place in the initial landing. Inevitably, there would be huge gaps in the perimeter that I was to seize and defend, and some very difficult decisions had to be made concerning where the landings were to take place. We had learned, from the very beginning in Sicily, that it is better to land near an objective and take heavy landing losses rather than to have to fight on the ground to get it. On the other hand, we had so many objectives over such an extensive area—approximately twenty-five miles—that a complete loss of control of the division might take place the very moment the landings occurred if careful judgment was not exercised in allocating troops to particular objectives. But first I had to learn more about the German dispositions in and around Grave-Nijmegen.

The British had been gathering information about the Nijmegen area for some time. One of the first persons I met was a Dutch officer, Captain Arie Bestebreurtje. The British referred to him as Captain Harry, and we quickly picked up the name. He was an extraordinary officer. Thoroughly trained, he had already participated in several behind-the-line parachute jumps as an agent. He was very courageous and a man of great intelligence. As a native of Nijmegen, of course he knew the area well.

The British were greatly preoccupied with the Reichswald, a very heavily wooded area of approximately twenty-four square miles, just inside the German border. It provided excellent cover, and the British were convinced that considerable German armor was in the forest. Directly in front of the Reichswald, in the direction of Nijmegen, was a high hill mass crowned by the small town of Groesbeek. This, in turn, was backed by a heavily wooded area, and beyond this began the outskirts of Nijmegen. Several miles to the northeast of Groesbeek was the small German town of Wyler, just inside the German border. Several miles to the southwest was the town of Mook. Hence, the critical terrain was a triangle, with the Wyler-Groesbeek-Mook road as a base and the two legs, each approximately five miles long, the Wyler-Nijmegen road and the Mook-Nijmegen road. Nijmegen was the apex. (*See Fig. 14a.*) The wooded high ground within the triangle was considered a favorite vacation spot by many of the Dutch, and newlyweds frequently spent their honeymoon in the several hotels along the high ground overlooking the Wyler-Nijmegen road. One of these, the De Groot Hotel in Berg-en-Dal, halfway between Wyler and Nijmegen, was occupied by a large contingent of German officers on September 17, 1944. As the wooded slopes of the high ground reaches the Wyler-Nijmegen

Fig. 14a   Principal Features Around Nijmegen, Groesbeek, and Grave

road, the terrain becomes as flat as a billiard table. Interspersed here and there by dirt roads and ditches and small pear and apple orchards, the flatland extends for five miles away to the Waal River. At that point the river sweeps in a huge curve eastward to cross under the bridge at Nijmegen. The retention and control of the high ground would mean control of the flatlands and the glider landing areas, and would prove to be the key to the success of the over-all Grave-Nijmegen operation.

In addition to the Panzers in the Reichswald, there was supposed to be approximately a regiment of SS troops in the barracks in the city. Around the entire Nijmegen area were deployed twenty-nine heavy antiaircraft weapons and eighty-eight light antiaircraft weapons. It was assumed that the crews would be prepared to fight as infantry, an assumption that we later learned the Germans had made also. But the antiaircraft crews were to prove to be no match for the incoming parachute infantry.

The Nijmegen bridge itself was an enormous affair compared to anything that we had had to cope with in the past. It was many stories high and more than 1800 feet long. Later we learned that, when it had been built, cavities for demolitions had been constructed into the bridge and demolitions put in place. We assumed that the bridge was prepared for demolitions and that one of the critical actions would be to cut the wires to the demolitions wherever they could be found and in any circumstances that would permit us to get to them.

My memory of the next three days is a blur of checking troop units, re-examining the details of our tactical plans, flying a light plane to various units to check their planning, and then every evening poring over the aerial photographs of the areas in which we were to land and fight, searching for signs of enemy weapons or enemy activity. In addition, I thoroughly studied the intelligence reports coming from the Continent, the R.A.F., and the U.S. Air Corps headquarters in the U.K.

On Thursday morning, September 14, the Division Commanders, each with one or two staff officers, met at General Browning's headquarters at Moor Park. There he outlined for us the over-all situation and then asked each of us, beginning with General Taylor, to outline the details of his plan to carry out his mission. Taylor had managed to get approval to use three major landing zones rather than to drop in many small packets as had been originally planned. His plan was very good and was acceptable. I then outlined my plan, and in response General Browning particularly directed me not to attempt the seizure of the Nijmegen bridge until all other missions had been successfully accomplished and the Groesbeek/Berg-en-Dal high ground was firmly in our hands. I could not have agreed with him more, but I was deeply troubled by the possibility of failing to accomplish some of my objectives. The perimeter of our endeavors would extend beyond twenty five miles with the great likelihood of major battles being fought at several different points simultaneously. I knew that I had to hold the high ground if for no other reason than to bring in the reinforcements so essential to continuing the battle, for that was where the drop and landing zones were. On the other hand, if I could possibly spare a battalion, I knew I had to commit it to the Nijmegen bridge as quickly as I could send it in that direction.

I was followed by Major General Urquhart, commanding the British 1st Airborne Division, whose objective was to seize and hold the bridge over the lower Rhine River at Arnhem. As he outlined his plan and told us that he had selected drop and landing zones six to eight miles to the west of Arnhem bridge, I couldn't believe my ears. It seemed to be contrary to all that we had learned so far. I turned to Colonel John Norton, my G-3, and said, "My God, he can't mean it," and Norton replied, "He does, and he is going to try to do it."

I had the highest regard for British generalship and British troops, and I was well aware that they had had a lot more combat experience in World War II than we had. As General Urquhart began to explain his dispositions, it became clear that the R.A.F. was reluctant to fly close to the heavy ack-ack near the bridge; thus they would not make a drop there. Furthermore, they wanted to avoid flying over Deelen Airfield several miles north of Arnhem, which was also surrounded by heavy ack-ack. That meant that the closest they would go to Arnhem itself was where General Urquhart had placed his troops, but I felt very apprehensive about his prospects, since he would have to move on foot through the city of Arnhem and its suburbs where even a few German infantrymen could impose an indefinite delay upon him. If he had dropped some troops below the river, possibly at night, and they moved through open country, they might have captured the bridge quickly, but I knew that he had considered this and that there was some concern about the nature of the ground south of the river. He had planned on three lifts over as many days, the last being the Polish Parachute Brigade, commanded by Major General Stanislaw Sosabowski. General Sosabowski was sitting to my right rear in the next row. As the meeting seemed to be coming to an end, he sounded out quite loudly, "But the Germans, how about the Germans, what about *them*?" I too was very much concerned about the Germans and the British 1st Airborne Plan. It seemed more like a peacetime exercise than war, and this is what his outburst was about. There was no answer. Later Sosabowski was to serve under me in the 82nd. He was a tough, determined fighting man, emotional and very dedicated to fighting the Germans. He had an excellent brigade.

On Friday, September 15, all troops were moved to take-off airdromes. They were sealed in by darkness Friday night; thus, they had one full day to ready themselves finally for the battle. In the meantime I assembled all the battalion commanders in one room and went over once again the detailed plans of each battalion.

All our commanders were reminded of the basic techniques in attacking bridges. First of all, cut all wires leading to a bridge, whether they were obviously connected to demolitions or not, and even though they might be communication lines; then remove the demolitions. Next, wherever possible, bridges must be attacked at both ends simultaneously. While a movement to reach the far end of any bridge might be costly, it very likely would be nowhere near so costly as piling up casualties at one end of the bridge where all the enemy fire power could be brought to bear in a small area, after which the enemy would blow the bridge.

The big Nijmegen bridge posed a serious problem. Seizing it with overwhelming strength at the outset would have been meaningless if I did not get at least two other bridges: the big bridge at Grave and at least one of the four over the Canal. Further, even if I captured it, if I had lost all the high ground that controlled the entire sector, as well as the resupply and glider landing zones, I would be in a serious predicament. Everything depended upon the weight and direction of the enemy reaction, and this could not be determined until we were on the ground. The problem was how much could be spared how soon for employment against the bridge.

I began discussions about this with Colonel Roy E. Lindquist at about this time, and they continued, whenever we had a chance to meet, up to take-off. I told him that if, in his opinion, the situation along the Groesbeek high ground was quiet in the late afternoon of the day of our landing, he was to send a battalion against the Nijmegen bridge that night. I further cautioned him to send it off over the flat ground under the cover of darkness and not through the city. A few well-placed automatic weapons could hold up a battalion indefinitely in narrow city streets. With those final discussions, we seemed to have gotten ourselves as ready for the battle as possible, since we did not know much about the German dispositions or how they would react.

The day of September 16 was a busy one—preparing weapons, distributing ammunition, poring over maps and aerial photographs, and checking out the fine details of every unit down to squads and patrols.

From time to time during the past week the thought had crossed my mind that we were asking a great deal of the survivors of the preceding three combat jumps. They had been through many difficult battles, and many of them had been wounded, some several times. I knew practically all the survivors personally, and I knew what went on in their minds. They were well aware of our heavy losses in the past, and to ask them once again to jump into combat more than fifty miles behind the German lines in broad daylight was asking a great deal. I remembered Lord Moran's *The Anatomy of Courage*. His book was based on World War I experience, and from it he concluded that courage, for every man, is like a bank account—it can be overdrawn. The parachute veterans, although quite fatalistic, believed that the odds went up significantly with further exposure to combat, no matter how experienced or how careful you were. So whenever I met a veteran during those last few days, I talked to him about our plans, assured him that we had an abundance of air power and that we could make the jump in daylight without heavy losses. Finally, I assured him that we had adequate troops and weapons to deal with the Germans on the ground.

Sunday, September 17, was a beautiful day. The sky was clear, and it was sunny and moderately warm. Everyone was up before daylight, busily trucking bundles of weapons and supplies to airplanes and taking care of final personal preparations. Because of our experiences in Normandy, the troopers loaded themselves with all the ammunition and antitank mines they could carry. Having checked personal loads of all the troopers in each regiment, we decided that about 700 individuals could each carry an antitank mine apiece. This would bring our total up to 2000 antitank mines the first day. In addition, troopers carried overloads of ammunition, and by Holland every trooper who could get his hands on a pistol carried one as well as a rifle. So overloaded were they that one or two troopers stood beside the steps of the C-47s and helped boost the others up the steps and into the planes.

Finally all the gliders, parachute planes, and towplanes were marshaled, and from all over England they began to take off and converge on the cross-Channel flying routes. The London *Daily Express* reported the following morning:

> Thousands of people on England's east coast yesterday saw the great glider armada streaming out to sea toward Holland.
> For an hour and a half, from 11:00 a.m. to 12:30 p.m., the fleet filled the skies.
> So great was the roar that no one on the coast could use the telephone until the planes had passed.

So the die was cast. We were uncertain about the German opposition we would encounter, but we believed it to be minimal. Weather, very likely, would control our reinforcements by air, and there were many uncertainties in the vast unknown that now confronted us. But we were confident that the troopers, with their traditional courage and ability to improvise, would prevail.

The first planes of the 82nd were off the ground at 11:09. I flew in the lead plane of my group with the Division G-3, Colonel John Norton, and an aide, Captain Hugo Olson, as well as a dozen or so troopers. Olson had recovered from his Normandy wounds. The airplanes marshaled as planned and started on their long route out over the English Channel. As far as one could see, the sky was filled with planes and gliders, and as we neared the coast of Europe, we could see the fighter-bombers flying back and forth over the land beneath us, looking for antiaircraft guns and enemy weapons to knock out. We seemed to be flying at about 1500 feet. As soon as we crossed the coast, I had all the troopers stand up and hook up so we would be ready for a quick exit if we were hit by ack-ack. As I followed the flight on the ground, all the small Dutch villages looked alike. The land was very green, dotted here and there with clusters of red tile roofs in small villages.

About a half hour after we crossed the coastline, down beneath us a flight of C-47s came into view, flying across our path. Suddenly parachutes began to blossom from them. I knew of no planned flight of this character, and I was disturbed about it. I mentioned it to Norton. None of the terrain looked like the drop zones we were to jump on, and we were quite high. I decided that it must be the 101st that was to jump farther south. As it turned out, it was the 101st. I was becoming concerned because I did not recognize the terrain when suddenly ahead the Grave bridge came clearly into sight. Some ack-ack was coming up from it. We went on and in seconds I could see the Groesbeek high ground just ahead of us. Along the woods, as we approached, could be seen a newly dug trench system that extended for quite some distance. Small-arms fire was coming up from it. As the ground rose, it seemed to be very close to us, and everything that I had memorized was coming into sight. The triangular patch of woods near where I was to jump appeared under us just as the jump light went on. Although we seemed quite close to the ground, we went out without a second's delay, and we seemed to hit the ground almost at once. Heavily laden with ammunition, weapons, grenades, I had a hard landing while the parachute was still oscillating.

At once we were under small-arms fire coming from a nearby woods. I took my .45 caliber pistol out of its holster and laid it on the ground beside my hand. I quickly began to take my rifle out from under the reserve chute, and I got out of the parachute harness while I lay on the ground. The moment I had my equipment off and my rifle ready to use, I replaced my pistol in the holster and ran over toward the woods.

One of the first men I met was Captain William H. Johnson of the Engineer Battalion, who told me that he had just killed two Germans in the woods and that there were quite a few more there. My immediate problem was to take my headquarters group to the site we had selected for our Division Command Post. It was in the woods about a mile away, but the simplest and surest way to get to it was to follow a dirt road to the outskirts of Groesbeek and then turn back on a paved road that would bring us right to the Command Post. The Command Post was to be at a point where a road crossed a paved road and a railroad and where it could easily be identified by any messenger or runner looking for me. The only "infantry" I had with me were the Engineers, so I told one of their officers to send out a point and start down the dirt road to Groesbeek without delay. They were exceedingly timid because of the firing that had taken place, and it was obvious that we would not get to the Command Post at that rate for a long time, if ever.

Captain Arie Bestebreurtje was with me, and I told him that he and I would take up the point—that he was to walk on the left side of the road and that I would follow about five yards behind him on the right side of the road and that the Engineers would follow us and that we would move as fast as we could go. If the Germans shot at us, we would give them the first shot and then take care of the situation.

With his past battle experience, he was just the man for that role, and we started down the road at a very fast clip. It was a sunken road through a heavy pine forest. The banks on both sides of the road were seven or eight feet high, just a foot or two above our heads. We had gone only about five or ten minutes when suddenly a machine gun fired from just over my head on the right; apparently they were shooting at Bestebreurtje. A small notchlike drainage ditch had been cut into the shoulder of the road, and they apparently had fired down it. The moment the weapon fired, I scrambled up the bank, pushing my rifle ahead of me to engage the Germans. As I stuck my head over the top, I saw a German darting between the trees and running away. I raised my rifle to shoot at him, but I probably would have ricocheted shots off the trees and wounded some of my own people if they were in the vicinity. In the meantime a German machine gun was in position about ten yards ahead of me, pointing at the road. The gunner had been hit in the forehead and was obviously dead, sprawled over the gun. There were no other Germans in sight.

I quickly came back to the road and asked Bestebreurtje how he'd gotten off such a good shot. He said that when he had been fired upon he had swung to the right and at once had seen the white forehead of the gunner between the top of the machine gun and his steel helmet. He had fired from the hip, killing the German instantly. He was quite excited, and we were both a bit elated to have escaped such a close call, so we resumed our fast pace, moving toward Groesbeek.

In a short time we came to the outskirts and Bestebreurtje went into a house and got on the telephone. Through a code he was able to communicate to Nijmegen and Arnhem with the Dutch Underground. They told him that the Arnhem landings had taken place and that all seemed to be going well. Without further delay we swung back to the left on the paved road and in another half hour reached the Division Command Post site. I at once went to work with the staff, getting in touch with the parachute regiments and the other troops. All seemed to be going well. Later we learned from the Groesbeek police that there had been several thousand Germans in the wooded area outside the town. It had been used as a training area, and it also was the site of an ammunition storage dump. When Nijmegen had been bombed earlier in the day, many of the Germans had fled toward Germany, fearing a ground attack. It is well that they did; otherwise, we would have had to fight even to get to the Command Post.

Early indications were that the drop had been unusually successful. Unit after unit reported in on schedule, and with few exceptions all were in their pre-planned locations.

One of the first units to land was E Company of the 504th Parachute Infantry. It had the mission of landing south of the bridge over the Maas River, not far from Grave. After landing it was to seize the southern end of the bridge, put up a roadblock to block any approaches to it, and take over the town of Grave. The platoon leader who captured the bridge was Lieutenant John S. Thompson. As his flight approached, he recognized the bridge at once, from a distance, and within seconds they got the signal and went out the door. They could see the bridge as they descended. Some fire was coming from the vicinity of Grave. Lieutenant Thompson quickly assembled a platoon and their equipment and started moving in the direction of what appeared to be large flak towers guarding the south end of the bridge. They used the various canals for cover, and, wading up to their necks in water, holding their weapons over their heads, they slowly worked their way to the flak towers. The fire was increasing steadily. As they neared the bridge, they noticed German soldiers running from what appeared to be a power plant at the southern end of the bridge. Assuming that the Germans might have been carrying explosives, they raked the ground between them and the bridge with machine-gun fire. Later they found four dead Germans and one wounded. Very soon they noticed that the fire from the flak towers was passing over their heads. The flak towers were wooden towers topped by sandbagged walls about shoulder high, from which the occupants were prepared to engage aircraft with 22 mm. antiaircraft weapons. They were not able to fire at ground troops within a hundred yards or so of the tower.

About the moment the troopers figured this out, two large trucks came up the highway from the south toward the bridge. One of the troopers fired, killing the driver of the leading truck, and the truck careened off the highway with German soldiers scrambling to get out. The second truck stopped, and the German soldiers jumped out and deployed themselves across the highway. It was evident that the Germans were trying to get away; they succeeded in doing so by moving under cover. The troopers returned their attention to the flak tower; a bazooka man worked his way to within twenty feet of the tower and fired three rounds, two going through the gun slits at the top of the tower. The gun ceased firing, and the troopers scrambled up the tower and there found two Germans killed and one wounded. They took over the antiaircraft weapon and at once engaged the German weapons in the flak tower at the other end of the bridge.

At the same time, Thompson had his men break up into two teams, working their way around the end of the bridge, cutting all wires leading to the bridge and across it. In a matter of minutes he was contacted by elements from his battalion which had landed on the other side of the bridge, and with the cooperation of Thompson's platoon they captured the flak towers at the northern end of the bridge. They, too, cut all wires, and the first bridge was captured intact. To us this was the most important bridge of all, since it assured us of a linkup with the British 30 Corps, provided, of course, that General Taylor captured his bridges.

More than 1100 feet long, spanning the wide flowing Maas (Meuse) River, its capture was essential to the division's survival.

As Thompson was consolidating his position, he was surprised to see two automobiles tearing up the highway at high speed. As the leading vehicle neared the bridge, a trooper fired at it, killing the driver. The second man tried to escape by running over the embankment to cover but got only part way before being shot. The second vehicle tried to turn around but did not make it. Three Germans in it were killed.

In the meantime fire continued to come from the south, so part of Thompson's company moved to a point about 1000 yards south of the bridge to establish a roadblock. D Company of the 504th came over the bridge and moved on to capture the town of Grave. On their approach they ran into heavy machine-gun and mortar fire, but they overran the town and captured it and secured it by dark. The troopers told me later how the Dutch celebrated all night long, drinking and singing "Tipperary."

One unfortunate incident occurred at the roadblock just after the last mines were placed and the men were digging in for the night. A large camouflaged tank approached from the south. A few men on the roadblock, thinking that it was the British armor that was to contact us later, shouted "British tank." Some men immediately moved toward the tank which, in turn, opened fire, killing three troopers and wounding eleven—a tragic incident. That ended the fighting around the Grave bridge, since the Germans did not approach it again in force.

The 504th Parachute Infantry Regiment, commanded by Colonel Reuben Tucker, landed exactly as planned between the Grave bridge and the Maas-Waal Canal. Colonel Tucker immediately sent patrols to the main Grave-Nijmegen road. The patrols had no contact with the Germans. Colonel Tucker also sent strong patrols to seize the bridges over the Maas-Waal Canal.

Before leaving England we had given a code number to all the principal bridges. The south bridge at Molenhoek was number 7. The next bridge farther north near Malden was number 8. Several miles north was the Hatert bridge, number 9, and finally the largest of the canal bridges that was both rail and road was the Honinghutie bridge, number 10. Naming them this way permitted us to talk in the clear about where we were and what we were doing for the first forty-eight hours before the Germans could begin to understand our simple code. Tucker's force, going for bridge number 7, approached it late in the afternoon and drove the German defenders to a small island in the middle of the canal. They cut all the wires they could find. They kept the Germans pinned down and did not permit them to move about. In the midst of this the 505th sent a patrol which attacked the bridge from the other side, and together both forces overcame the German garrison at six o'clock in the evening, thus capturing the bridge intact. Now we had our second bridge, making it possible for armor to get to Groesbeek and Nijmegen when the 30 Corps arrived.

Bridge number 8 was blown up in their faces as troopers from Tucker's regiment approached it. The same thing happened at bridge number 9. Bridge number 10 was substantially larger than any of the others and was on the direct route between Grave and Nijmegen. A railroad bridge crossed the canal beside the highway bridge. Seizure intact was of the utmost importance to us. It was the one bridge between Grave and Nijmegen that I was sure could support the weight of armored vehicles. The Germans seemed to be aware of this also, for, as we soon learned, they had organized a highly effective defense of entrenchments, pillboxes, and barbed wire. These were, in turn, protected by minefields.

The first troopers to attack it were from Lindquist's 508th Parachute Infantry Regiment. It was a platoon of twenty-five men commanded by Lieutenant Lloyd Polette. Polette was a very courageous young officer who won a Distinguished Service Cross for extraordinary heroism in action. Unfortunately, later he was killed in action. He moved out with his platoon at 3:30 on the morning of September 18. He was able to move quite close because of the early-morning darkness, and later the early-morning sunlight shone into the eyes of the defenders, making it possible for Polette's men to work their way closely up into the German position. When they had advanced within 150 yards of the German pillboxes, they came under a tremendous amount of small-arms, machine-gun, and mortar fire. Polette's platoon was pinned down and was suffering heavy losses. He had been in touch with Lieutenant Tomlinson of the same regiment, who had attempted to seize bridge number 9 earlier. He called on Tomlinson for help, and Tomlinson joined him.

During the fire fight they noticed Germans moving about the bridge, whenever they could move, and they attempted to stop them, assuming that they were placing explosives. About 10:30 German demolitions were fired, destroying the railroad bridge. Although Polette did not know it at the time, they also seriously damaged the highway bridge. About 11:00 A.M. Polette and Tomlinson resumed the attack with 81 mm. mortar support and overran the German positions. The Germans fled across the bridge to the southwest.

That morning I was in touch with Lindquist and learned of the difficult time Polette was having, and I urged Tucker to send a patrol to the other end of the bridge without delay. The 504th troopers arrived on the bridge just as Polette swept across it. After our linkup with the British 30 Corps, it was decided that the bridge was not safe for British armor, so bridge number 7 at Molenhoek was priceless to us. It was the only bridge that could get armor to us and to the British at Arnhem. I was well aware of this, and its retention proved to be the center of a dramatic confrontation with the German 6th Parachute Division several days later.

Reports coming to the Division Command Post late in the afternoon of September 17 continued to be favorable. Units seemed to have landed as planned with minor exceptions. Both glider troops and parachute troopers landing behind the Germans were, in most cases, able to fight their way back with little difficulty.

One of the problems we had worried about was the antiaircraft batteries. It was well that we had anticipated the danger from them. As we learned a few days after we landed, the Germans had issued an order four days before the landing to all antiaircraft units, directing them to be prepared to defend their positions against ground attack. Entitled "The Threatening Danger," the order began with the statement that "the war situation now demands that Luftwaffe units [antiaircraft units were members of the Luftwaffe] prepare to be used as ground defenses in the West." It then went on to direct such specific measures as training units to fight as infantry and preparing defenses around antiaircraft batteries. Fortunately for the troopers, their mere arrival caused most of the Germans manning the antiaircraft batteries to scatter and disperse in the interest of survival. Remembering an experience in Ste.-Mère-Eglise where German antiaircraft guns were shooting descending troopers, a number of the troopers from the 505th began firing their pistols at antiaircraft gunners the moment their parachutes opened and they began to descend. Troopers talking about it later recalled it as being pretty silly because they were just as likely to shoot themselves as the Germans. In retrospect, it also seemed foolish to have engaged a big antiaircraft gun with .45 caliber pistols, but they did, and most of the

Germans broke and ran. One lieutenant recalled seeing a young German soldier throw away his rifle and run toward Germany. He didn't have it in him to shoot at a young, unarmed boy running for home. In another case a platoon of the 508th deployed and attacked an antiaircraft battery that was continuing to fire at the air transports. It overran the guns and took the Germans prisoners. But we were all pleased with the ability of the troopers to jump in daylight on antiaircraft positions and destroy them. After Sicily we were told time and again that parachute operations might succeed at night and under conditions where antiaircraft could not engage the air transports, but if they ever dared to fly over German antiaircraft guns in any numbers, they would be totally blown from the skies.

As the shadows grew longer on D-day, and darkness threatened, I decided to visit some of the units. The reports coming in continued to be favorable, and so far German reaction, except for antiaircraft fire and the fighting around the bridges, seemed to be at a minimum.

I had a jeep by late afternoon, and I drove toward Groesbeek and beyond. The first unit I encountered was the 376th Field Artillery. The battalion commander, Lieutenant Colonel Wilbur Griffith, had broken his ankle and was being moved about in a wheelbarrow. As he saw me approach, he laughed, saluted, and said, "General, the 376th Field Artillery is in position with all guns ready to fire." Bringing in the 376th Field Artillery had been an experiment. We had reasoned that the first units the Germans would commit against us would be make-up formations of soldiers on furlough and local home guards, and that good, accurate field-artillery fire would keep them deployed and far from our infantry for some time. It turned out to be a correct assessment of what was to follow. The 376th fired 315 rounds in the first twenty-four hours and was most effective in keeping large German formations at some distance. In addition to fighting as artillerymen, it captured four hundred German enlisted men and eight German officers. Nevertheless, with darkness the 508th became heavily preoccupied with Germans emerging from the German frontier between Wyler and Beek. I drove from Groesbeek toward Nijmegen, encountered a few troopers on patrol, and arrived back at the Command Post after dark.

Reports continued to come in from the widely dispersed parachute battalions. All were getting on with the tasks assigned to them. Sometime during the night I heard the plaintive wail of a locomotive whistle. I first heard it some distance away, and it very quickly came near the

Command Post. I had been stretched out on the ground under some pine trees to get some sleep, and I awakened. I had slept rather fitfully. I was very much concerned about what our combat units would be doing during the night and what the tactical situation would be like at first light. I tried to get up, but my back was giving me considerable difficulty. I held on to a nearby pine tree and pulled myself to my feet. Many years later I learned that I had fractured two vertebrae in the landing. Having pulled myself to my feet, I went to the operations center. I asked a member of the staff to call the 505th outpost in Groesbeek.

They told us that the train came right through the town and went on toward Nijmegen. They hadn't anticipated it and had not attempted to stop it. When another train tried to run through the division area an hour or so later, the locomotive was hit by a bazooka round, which stopped it. Germans came boiling off the train in all directions, and we were rounding them up most of the next day.

During the night all three parachute regiments reported that they had the situation well in hand. Colonel Tucker with the 504th had captured the big Grave bridge and helped capture bridge number 7 at Molenhoek. He was patrolling aggressively toward the West, expecting a major German reaction from that direction. Colonel William E. Ekman in the 505th, with two battalions, was organizing a defensive position from Mook through Horst, swinging back toward the town of Kamp, approximately a mile out of Groesbeek. Patrols had been sent to the Reichswald. The 2nd Battalion, 505th, under Colonel Ben Vandervoort, was in division reserve on high ground about a half mile from the Division Command Post. Colonel Lindquist's 508th organized a defense from Kamp to Wyler, established several roadblocks along the south of the high ground at Berg-en-Dal. The principal one was at Wyler, where no German reaction had been anticipated. Although we did not realize it when we were in the U.K., the town of Wyler actually was in Germany, so the Germans reacted violently to every attempt to occupy and hold it. It was puzzling for a while, since it did not appear to be of great tactical significance, until we realized that we were among the first Allied troops to enter Germany in World War II.

Colonel Lindquist had the most difficult regimental mission of all. First of all, he encountered German resistance at once because several of the roadblocks he attempted to establish were in Germany. Next, his mission was a bit ambiguous, since he had authorization to take a battalion from the Groesbeek-Wyler front, where the glider landings were to take place the next day, if, in his opinion, the situation was quiet enough to permit it. That battalion was then to be committed to the seizure of the Nijmegen bridge. When we looked back on the situation years later, we realized that it should have been obvious that Tucker's 504th was much better prepared to spare a battalion to go to the Nijmegen bridge that night. However, there was no way to determine this on the night of September 17, 1944.

The 1st Battalion of the 508th Parachute Infantry, commanded by Major Jonathan E. Adams, landed as planned and immediately moved out to organize defensive positions. About 6:00 P.M. he was ordered to move to the Nijmegen bridge area. Darkness fell in the midst of the regrouping for the new mission, and there was some delay in getting started. About 10:00 P.M. it was decided to send the first company, Company A, on the mission; the others would follow when they could be assembled. It was a pitch-black night. The Company Commander was introduced to a man supposedly of the Dutch Underground who was going to lead them to the bridge and also to the control station for blowing the bridge. They moved out shortly after 10:00 P.M., checked several houses along the way where the Dutchman said German soldiers might be, but found no one. Upon reaching a critical crossroads short of the bridge, the Underground man left, telling them that he would be back. He was never seen again.

After waiting for some time, the company moved on toward the traffic circle just short of the bridge. They came under heavy fire. Fortunately, B Company of the battalion was able to join them at that time. The leading Company Commander had orders to hold up when he reached the traffic circle. This he did, unfortunately giving the Germans more time to build up at the south end of the bridge. The Company Commander was then told to take a combat patrol to the building they assumed was the control station for the bridge demolitions and to destroy it. He and one of his lieutenants with a platoon leader proceeded to the building. There were quite a few Germans in it, but nothing in their opinion that seemed to indicate that it was the control station. Nevertheless, they set it afire and destroyed it. In the action one man had been killed and two wounded.

They then returned in the direction of the traffic circle and found it heavily organized for defense by German troops. The Germans were well equipped with armored vehicles, 88s, machine guns, and small arms. Major Adams withdrew in the face of heavy fire, losing two men wounded. He remained cut off from the remainder of the division for two days.

In anticipation of the need for more troops in seizing the bridge, Colonel Lindquist had told the commanding officer of the 3rd Battalion, Lieutenant Colonel Louis G. Mendez, to be prepared to move against the bridge from the south side. Mendez had the platoon that was manning the roadblock from Wyler to Beek to the south of the Berg-en-Dal high ground. Figuring that he would be given the mission, he therefore sent a platoon of his G Company commanded by First Lieutenant Howard A. Greenawalt to make a reconnaissance in the direction of the bridge. His platoon had already been in a position at the roadblock about halfway between Beek and the bridge. He moved his platoon out not long after darkness, finally reaching high ground south and east of the city and a few miles from the bridge, and he organized a defensive position, awaiting further word from his Company Commander, Captain Wilde. Captain Wilde had decided to move the remainder of his company off to the right in the direction of the bridge. They soon came under sniper fire, and as they neared the bridge, they came upon a German roadblock which they attacked and overran, killing seven Germans who were working on it. They continued to advance, reaching the eastern side of the traffic circle, where they came under very heavy mortar and 88 mm. fire. Lieutenant Greenawalt lost five men in the action. By daylight they were engaged with the Germans at the southern end of the bridge and not making any further progress.

This encounter with 88s, heavy mortars, and stout German resistance at the southern end of the Nijmegen bridge was the first indication to us that something had been amiss in the intelligence briefings given us before we left England. This was not a broken German army in full retreat. The Panzer Grenadiers we killed fought hard and were well equipped. Those we captured were tough and confident. The Germans were in far better condition to fight than we had realized.

Field Marshal Model had been put in command of all the Holland area. Under his command he had the rapidly forming First Parachute Army under General Kurt Student. He also had under his command General von Zangen's Fifteenth Army, which, without Allied knowledge, had escaped from Calais and was now confronting us. In addition, as chance would have it, two Panzer divisions were in the process of being refitted. They were bivouacked north and east of Arnhem under the Corps command of General Bittrich. The two divisions were the

Hohenstaufen Division under Lieutenant Colonel Walter Harzer and the Frundsberg Division under General Heinz Harmel. As soon as Bittrich made his first evaluation of the Allied landing, he directed Harzer to send his reconnaissance troops south to the Nijmegen bridge. He began to sense that the bridge was the key to the operation. The reconnaissance troops made up the 9th SS Reconnaissance Battalion, which was under the command of Captain Paul Graebner. Graebner moved promptly and was able to cross the Arnhem bridge, moving south toward Nijmegen, before the British arrived at the Arnhem bridge. As soon as they crossed the Waal River bridge at Nijmegen, they had a small-arms encounter, but nothing more serious. He continued to move his forces south and left a few antitank guns and heavy mortars at the southern end of the bridge. Graebner placed the detachment at the south end of the bridge under Captain Fritz Euling. He then turned northward with the remainder of his force, finally positioning his men near the town of Elst midway between Arnhem and Nijmegen. His troops had established themselves south of the bridge by 9:00 P.M.

In the meantime Bittrich directed the Frundsberg Division to cross the Rhine River several miles to the east of Arnhem, where there was an old ferry site. By building and improvising a ferry, the Germans were able to get troops moving across the river and southward. By September 19, five hundred Germans had crossed or moved southward to defend the Nijmegen bridge. To Bittrich, that bridge was now definitely the key to the whole operation. He was determined that if he could not hold it, he would destroy it so the Allies could not use it.

As early as the afternoon of the second day, September 18, Bittrich was arguing with Field Marshal Model about the bridge. He argued that it *was* the key to the entire operation. Further, if they were to "destroy it then the Allied attack would be stopped in its tracks and Arnhem cut off and destroyed. 'Herr Field Marshal, we should demolish the Waal crossing before it is too late,' Bittrich said. Model was adamant. 'No!' he said. 'The answer is no!' Not only did Model insist that the bridge could be defended; he demanded that Student's army and the Frundsberg Division halt the Anglo-Americans before they ever reached it."[10]

The Frundsberg Division continued to build up in the Nijmegen area. By nightfall of September 19 they had increased the troops on the southern end of the bridge to five hundred men, increased the number of

[10] Cornelius Ryan, *A Bridge Too Far*. New York: Simon & Schuster, Inc., 1974.

mortars and 88s, and had sufficient 88s to dig in two on the northern end of the bridge.

We were unaware of all this as the crescendo of the battle neared and as the decisive day and hour approached. As we had seized all our other bridges in the division area, the key to the success of the battle was now the Nijmegen bridge. It absolutely had to be seized and its destruction prevented as well.

During the first night, September 17, the staff, with some concern, watched Lindquist make significant troop commitments against the big bridge. There were high hopes that he would get the bridge quickly. On the other hand, as he increased his efforts, he depleted his troops protecting the landing zone on the east side of the airhead. As daylight neared on September 18, the front of the 508th facing the Reichswald was almost devoid of all troops. Thus the Germans could penetrate deeply into the woods toward the Command Post and the location of division reserves. The first report of success of the 508th came in the form of a brief message at 6:55 A.M. They reported that they had a patrol on the Nijmegen bridge. Another message shortly thereafter confirmed this. Both reports, unfortunately, were in error.

At daylight on September 18, when I went to the 508th Command Post, the report was grim. My heart sank. They had failed to get the bridge. The situation of the 1st Battalion was confusing. No one knew what had happened to it. They had not moved out over the open ground; instead, following the man presumed to be of the Dutch Underground, they had been led into the city and there were heavily engaged, so they had failed to capture the big Nijmegen bridge the first night and had left the area from Kamp to Wyler to Beek almost wide open to the Germans.

I had to get troops back to clear the glider landing zone without delay. I therefore instructed Colonel Lindquist to disengage the 3rd Battalion and move it back to clear the glider landing zone of Germans. It was a big order, for already Germans were in the woods between Bergen-Dal and Wyler, and attacking. The 3rd Battalion had been moving and fighting most of the night, and now they had to march six or seven miles back to Wyler, attack and destroy Germans in the woods, and travel on to clear the drop zone beyond.

After talking to Lindquist, I followed the main road into Nijmegen. Near Marienboom I came on Captain Arie Bestebreurtje with about six hundred Dutchmen. It was a main road intersection, and the men were milling about in the streets, on a nearby lawn, and in a café on the corner. Many of them were wearing orange armbands. Bestebreurtje told me that they had volunteered to fight with us, and all they wanted were weapons from our dead and wounded. I pointed out to them the dangers of fighting in civilian clothes and the fact that if they were captured they would be killed. I did not tell them that I had no idea how the battle would come out and when and if linkup with the British would occur. I told them that there was only one mission I wanted them to carry out and that it absolutely had to be accomplished: they had to save the Nijmegen bridge from German demolition. I urged, therefore, that they be posted in houses and under cover on both sides of the river, their function being to deny any Germans access to the bridge. They were to cut any wires leading to the bridge, and no Germans were to be allowed on or near the bridge. I did not realize until after we had captured the bridge that the demolitions had been placed years before and painted over to give the appearance of being part of the bridge structure. They agreed to do their best. Their attitude was most reassuring, and after a year and a half of war, they proved to be among the bravest and most patriotic people we had liberated.

After meeting with the Dutch, I went to the headquarters of the 1st Battalion of the 508th. The Battalion Commander knew no more about his battalion than was known at his regimental headquarters. The troops apparently had met devastating artillery and mortar fire as they neared the traffic circle. In the fire fight they had become scattered in the labyrinth of buildings and narrow streets and were under intense small-arms fire. The German build-up near the traffic circle was increasing, and more 88s, armored vehicles, and mortars were being added to the forces already there. It is highly likely that the battalion would have been destroyed and overrun even if it had reached the bridge, since it had no weapons capable of successfully engaging German armor in large numbers. But the failure of the 508th to capture the bridge that first night and my realization that we had wide gaps in our dispositions on the Groesbeek side of the division area worried me.

Once I was satisfied that I had done all I could with the 508th, I hurried back to Groesbeek to check that front. The 505th took me to an observation post in the upper story of a building on the outskirts of Groesbeek. German infantry could be seen deployed and advancing. The 505th with the support of the 376th Field Artillery was delaying them and felt confident that it could hold them. Fortunately, no German armor had yet appeared, despite the stories we had heard about the German armor in the Reichswald. With two battalions, the 505th was attempting to hold from Mook on its right to Kamp on its left a front of six or seven miles. It did this by establishing strong roadblocks at key road intersections and small villages where the Germans would be expected to appear. The gaps were kept under surveillance by patrols. The technique was to reinforce a unit once it was attacked, but with only sufficient force to beat back the Germans. If a major attack developed, a major commitment would be made. This was to occur at Mook two days later.

If the Germans had been aware of how thin the dispositions were, they could have moved quite readily through the huge gaps in the 505th front, but they did not probe deeply and the 505th was able to hold its positions. It reminded me once again of Biazza Ridge in Sicily. If the Germans had moved around either flank of the small force I had, they could have easily overrun us. Instead, once the battle was joined, they continued to build up the initial commitment. Historically, this is characteristic of what so often occurs. Even Gettysburg in our Civil War was the accidental outcome of a meeting engagement of a Confederate force seeking to find shoes in Gettysburg for Lee's army.

The 505th at Groesbeek was having a busy time of it but seemed to have the situation under control. Heavy firing increasing in volume could be heard in the direction of Kamp-Wyler. I hurried back to the Division Command Post to check on the over-all situation. The glider reinforcements were due to land in early afternoon. I therefore took the immediately available reserves of two Engineer companies and moved them through Groesbeek and toward Kamp. The battalion commander, Captain Johnson, was in command of the two companies, and I accompanied him for several miles through broken country. I ordered him to clear the landing zones of Germans and to watch out for the 3rd Battalion of the 508th, which was due to come in on his left. It was imperative that we get the Germans off the glider landing zone before the gliders arrived; otherwise the casualties among the glidermen would be devastating.

Late in the morning I went back to the Division Command Post to find out if we had any information from the British Second Army or 30 Corps. By then we should have had radio or patrol contact. There was no information whatever in division headquarters. Shortly after noon I returned to Groesbeek. We had not entirely succeeded in clearing the landing zones. Considerable firing was taking place all along the front of the 505th and the 508th. As I watched, I wished there were some way I could get word to the gliders so that they would not be surprised by the German fire immediately upon landing. Four hundred and fifty gliders were expected to land, and there was no way to communicate with them, since they were already en route.

Shortly before 2:00 P.M. the great air armada could be seen approaching from England, 900 aircraft in all: 450 gliders and 450 C-47 tugs. The drone of the engines reached a roar as they came directly over the landing zones. I experienced a terrible feeling of helplessness. I wanted to tell them that they were landing right on the German infantry. Soon they were overhead, and the gliders began to cut loose and start their encircling descent. As they landed, they raised tremendous clouds of dust, and the weapons fire increased over the area. Some spun on one wing, others ended up on their noses or tipped over as they dug the glider nose into the earth in their desire to bring them to a quick stop. Glidermen could be seen running from the gliders and engaging the Germans. Others were attempting to extricate their artillery and jeeps.

It seemed almost a miracle when the battle was over and a count was taken of the men and equipment. The 319th Glider Field Artillery Battalion recovered twelve of its twelve howitzers and twenty-six of its thirty-four jeeps; the 320th Glider Field Artillery Battalion recovered eight of its twelve howitzers and twenty-nine of its thirty-nine jeeps. The 456th Parachute Field Artillery Battalion recovered ten of its twelve howitzers and twenty-three of its thirty-three jeeps. Some of the glider units landed far behind the drop zones in Germany, but most of them fought their way back. In addition, the medical battalion brought in twenty-six jeeps. The 307th Engineers Battalion had 100 per cent recovery, five out of five jeeps; the Signal Company eight out of ten jeeps. And finally, most important of all, eight of eight 57 mm. antitank guns and eight of nine jeeps were recovered by Battery D of the 80th Airborne Antiaircraft Battalion. A highly creditable performance and one that I never would have thought possible as I watched them approach the landing zone. The landings had begun at 2:00 P.M., and the last glider had landed by 2:30.

About ten minutes after the glider landing, the parachute resupply mission arrived. It consisted of 135 B-24s. About 80 per cent of the supplies were recovered, much of it after dark since they had landed in no-man's land.

Throughout the afternoon and evening the battle front from Nijmegen to Beek and Wyler and Groesbeek continued to flame. Only in the 504th area were things reasonably quiet. There was still no word from the British, who were expected to arrive from the south at any time. During the night I received a message that the Guards Armored Division was expected to reach the Grave bridge at 8:30 the morning of September 19. After checking our Groesbeek front, I went to the Grave bridge, and there, with General Browning, I met the first elements of the Guards Armored. It is difficult to describe my feeling of elation at that moment. So far, we had been spared a major German armored attack, but now, with the availability of British armor, we felt equal to anything that could happen, so we wanted to get armor into our area as fast as it could be poured over the bridge and moved northward.

Despite the thinness of our infantry on the Groesbeek-Wyler front, I now felt that I could spare the division reserve, Ben Vandervoort's 2nd Battalion of the 505th. I discussed it with General Browning and an officer of the Guards Armored Division. Vandervoort was attached to the Grenadier Guards and was at once committed to the battle for the southern end of the Nijmegen bridge. To replace Vandervoort in division reserve, a battalion of the Coldstream Guards was attached to the 82nd. I directed that they be moved to the general vicinity of where Vandervoort had been. It was most reassuring to have the linkup occur. Not only did it permit me to commit Vandervoort to the capture of the southern end of the Nijmegen bridge; it now freed the 504th for further use.

We were still very short of infantry, but we expected the 325th Glider Infantry to land the following day, September 20. It took an hour or so to get everything arranged; then I moved once again to the 508th sector in which combat was the most intense in the division area. The pressures continued to mount all through the wooded area from Beek to Wyler and from Wyler to Groesbeek. I went down through the woods, following the Berg-en-Dal-Wyler Road. Close to the outskirts of Wyler, the German dead were all about, testifying to the violence of the fighting. In front of Groesbeek itself, where we had good fields of fire, the fighting seemed to have eased off. Still, no German armor from the Reichswald.

Late in the afternoon of September 19 I learned from the Airborne Corps Commander that the Commanding General of the British 30 Corps, General Horrocks, had established an advance Command Post in a schoolhouse in the small town of Malden. It was several miles north of Mook. So far, the 508th had been unable to do anything with the southern end of the Nijmegen bridge, and it was fully preoccupied with the Beek-Wyler front. I had great confidence in Vandervoort's battalion, probably one of the best in the division, and the Grenadier Guards, but it was evident that they would not be able to launch a full-scale coordinated attack until early the following morning, September 20. Even then, the German 88s firing down the streets of Nijmegen would hold up the armor for some period of time.

It seemed to me that the hour was becoming desperate. Urquhart had now been cut off for three days, and I still did not have the big Nijmegen bridge. If I did nothing more than pour infantry and British armor into the battle at our end of the bridge, we could be fighting there for days and Urquhart would be lost. And the Germans, in control of the other end of the bridge, would blow it up as they withdrew. I decided therefore that I somehow had to get across the river with our infantry and attack the northern end of the bridge and cut off the Germans at the southern end. The question was how. There were no boats around Nijmegen; they had long ago been removed by the Germans. Further, except for the contact with the Germans at the end of the bridge, we were still several miles from the riverbank all along the front. That did not trouble me, however, because I was sure that, once released, Tucker's 504th could clear all the Germans up to the riverbank with little difficulty.

General Horrocks, commanding British 30 Corps, General Browning, commanding the Airborne Corps, and General Allan Adair, commanding the Guards Armored Division, and I had a meeting near the sidewalk in front of the Malden schoolhouse late in the afternoon of September 19. Earlier Browning had warned me, "The Nijmegen bridge must be taken today. At the latest tomorrow." The capture of the Nijmegen bridge was squarely on my shoulders. This I knew. But most important to me were the lives of General Urquhart and the British First Airborne.

As we discussed what might be done, I remember General Horrocks's saying to me wistfully, "Jim, never try to fight an entire Corps off one road." As General Horrocks tried to force the 30 Corps armored vehicles and trucks bumper to bumper and track to track up the two-lane road, he found himself under harassing attacks time and again. We did not know it at the time, but the German general opposing us, General Student, had in his hands a complete copy of our attack order within an hour of the landings on D-day. It had been taken from a wrecked glider. It told him exactly what roads we were to use and what troops were given what specific missions. He at once organized counterattacks that cut the road at several places. So, not only was Horrocks frustrated by the overwhelming logistics problem that he had on his hands, but in addition he had to fight a series of battles at several points along the tenuous, threadlike route that led from Belgium up to Nijmegen, and the initiative was now with the Germans.

In the American army a corps acting in an independent role, such as 30 Corps in the Holland situation, would have an engineer battalion or regiment attached to it, and that would include a company of boats. As we stood talking, I asked General Horrocks about it, and he said he thought they had some boats well down the road in the train somewhere. The discussion on this point quickly spread among the staff. They finally agreed that they should have about twenty-eight folding canvas boats in trucks somewhere farther to the rear. American boats, with which I was familiar, were plywood, but at that moment boats were boats and I had to have them.

I told General Horrocks that if he could get the boats to me, I would move the 504th Parachute Infantry to the riverbank and make a crossing as rapidly as possible, and thus we would be in a position to attack the far end of the bridge. He accepted the plan, and I immediately began preparations for the river crossing. I was uneasy about when the boats would arrive, but he could not assure me beyond the point made by his staff: that they had the boats and that they would get them up as quickly as they could. I asked the staff if they thought they would have them up by daylight. They were of the opinion that they would.

It was then getting dark, and I returned to the Division Command Post to put together a plan that would force the crossing. At that time I thought we could make the crossing at about 8:00 the following morning. There was, of course, no opportunity to make a reconnaissance of the riverbank and the launching site, since it was occupied by the Germans. Ideally, I would have preferred to have waited twenty-four hours and to have crossed during darkness the following night, but I doubted that Urquhart and the British Airborne Division at Arnhem would have survived that much longer a delay.

Back at Division Headquarters, we pored over the maps. I finally decided that the best place to make the launchings was where the Maas-

Waal Canal entered the lower Waal. Thus, by loading the boats in the canal, the troopers would have an opportunity to familiarize themselves with them before moving out into the open river. The plan was to move down the canal toward the river and at a given signal make a break for the far shore. In the meantime, every artillery piece, every tank gun, and every weapon we had would pour fire into the German positions on the far side. This would include as much smoke as we could get our hands on to cover the crossing. It was a risky tactic, but something had to be done. I could not conceive of sitting on the southern bank with a regiment of infantry and the Guards Armored Division while Urquhart was destroyed eleven miles away.

At 11:00 P.M. the regimental executive officer of the 504th came to the Division Command Post, and the situation was outlined and the order given to him for Colonel Tucker. It was obviously a very iffy situation. If the boats arrived, and if the Germans were cleared as far as the riverbank, and if everything could be organized—all this during darkness—we could get off shortly after daybreak. During the night I got a few hours' sleep, and at daybreak I was at Tucker's Command Post, which had moved quite far forward. No boats were in sight or to be found; they were somewhere down the road.

Taking Captain Olson and Sergeant Walker E. Wood with me, I moved by jeep up some side roads to the east of Nijmegen toward the launching site. I was most anxious to see what it looked like and to modify the assault orders if necessary. About a mile or two from the river where it was open countryside, we encountered a line of German infantry deployed and advancing toward us. The driver quickly turned the jeep around. Sergeant Wood, Captain Olson, and I jumped out, and from around the corner of a red brick building we engaged the German infantry which was between 300 and 400 yards away. I quickly fired from man to man, since I wanted to impress them with the amount of fire that was coming from us. They all hit the ground at once.

We jumped in our jeep, and I went back to Tucker's Command Post and reported the situation to him. He then made plans to sweep his infantry through the area, and he assured me that he would let me know when he reached the riverbank. In the meantime the crossing was tentatively postponed until 11:00 A.M., and then 1:30 P.M. I went back to the other areas of the division. The fighting was building up with great intensity at Beek and near Mook. Time seemed to fly, and it was nearly

noon before I got word from Tucker that they were just about in control
of the southern bank of the river.

In the meantime Vandervoort's battalion and the Grenadier Guards
had been attacking toward the railroad bridge and the highway bridge.
Actually, they had been able to join forces the preceding afternoon,
September 19. They had moved in two columns, one against each
bridge, and had begun to make slow progress. The tanks of the
Grenadier Guards were very vulnerable in the city streets to the German
88s. Vandervoort's troops had to fight their way from building to building. The Germans had been reinforcing during the night, and by daylight
on September 20 they were well dug in and organized. The left column
fighting toward the railroad bridge was having just as great difficulty as
the right column. I had ordered the seizure of the railroad bridge because we had learned in our fighting in Sicily that such a bridge could
quickly be converted to a jeep bridge and to a tank bridge if captured
intact. In any event, it would be able to take infantry that could cross
during darkness.

The fighting for the railroad bridge was hard, and we lost one of our
best lieutenants, Waverly W. Wray, who had been with us all the way
from North Africa. He was killed near the bridge. At daylight on
September 20 the battle increased in intensity as both columns pressed
the Germans back against the railway bridge and the highway bridge.
It was a new experience for the troopers, but they soon discovered that
the best technique was to fight from rooftop to rooftop; thus they were
always on the high ground. Where necessary, they blew holes in the
upper floors of adjoining buildings so as to make their way forward and
still be on top of the Germans.

I went forward to see the battalion at one point in the battle, but
there was little to be seen, since most of the fighting was taking place in
the buildings and on the rooftops. Later the veteran troopers told me
about the experience. What they wanted to do, they said, was to get as
close to the traffic circle as they could so as to fire down into the gun
positions of the 88s and the foxholes of the Germans. This they eventually did. They did not realize the strength of the German forces at the
time. Since September 17 the Germans had been building up. When
Vandervoort's troopers attacked on September 20, there were 500
Panzer Grenadiers at the southern end of the bridge, well equipped with
machine guns, heavy mortars, and 88 mm's. So the 505th fought its way

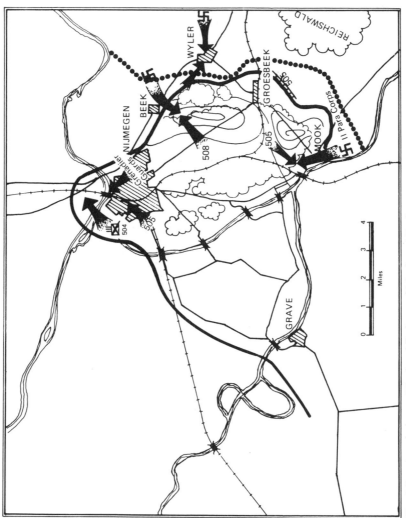

Fig. 14b   Attack Across Waal and Defense of Mook and Beek

forward from building to building. As a British officer of the Grenadier Guards later described it, "A jolly sight to see those paratroopers hopping from rooftop to rooftop." By late afternoon the 2nd Battalion of the 505th was steadily making its way forward with fire support from the Grenadier Guard tanks.

About 1:30 in the afternoon I went up to the area where the Maas-Waal Canal meets the river. Near the junction there was a huge power plant. No one else had arrived, so I parked my jeep behind the power plant, awaiting the arrival of the troops. I had been there about a half hour when I received a frantic call from Division Headquarters. The Chief of Staff told me that both Mook and Beek had been overrun and that the Germans were making their way into our positions there. If I wanted to save both areas from German take-over with all its disastrous consequences, I had to get back and make some decisions about the use of the reserves.

I had to make a difficult decision right then. Since the river crossing was going to be extremely difficult, I should have stayed; on the other hand, Tucker was a very competent battle commander and I knew there was a real likelihood of losing Mook and the only bridge over the Maas-Waal Canal at Molenhoek and also losing Beek and the high ground at Berg-en-Dal. There seemed to be no question that my proper place was back where the decisive fighting was then taking place. I had my jeep driver take me as fast as he could to the Division Command Post; to my surprise, I met Major General Matthew Ridgway, Commanding General of the U.S. XVIII Corps. I told him that I had a very difficult situation on my hands and that I would have to move on. He seemed to understand, although I sensed that he was quite unhappy with the fact that both his divisions were now under British Airborne Corps. I left at once for Mook, which seemed to be the more dangerous situation.

Driving southeast out of Molenhoek, in about half a mile we came to a railroad overpass just north of the town of Mook. A two-lane macadamized highway passed under the railroad and into the town. Beyond the underpass to the right was a high dike between fifteen and twenty feet high, erected to hold back the high water of the Maas River. There the dike swung to the south and east, following the river.

As I arrived, just short of the railroad overpass, a tremendous amount of small-arms fire passed overhead. About twenty-five yards from the railroad overpass a paratrooper was in a foxhole with a bazooka. He seemed a bit shaken, and he was all alone. Just ahead of him mines were laid across the highway under the railroad. They resembled a string of large beads; they were uniformly placed and on top of the road. Beyond them a British tank was in position. Just after I arrived the tank apparently decided to withdraw, since German infantry was coming quite close and the tank was all alone. As it attempted to turn around, a track hit one of the American mines and it was blown from the tank, thus disabling the tank. The crew jumped out and took off to my rear. As I watched the scene, a cow slowly climbed up the dike. As it reached the top, it visibly shook under the impact of the bullets that hit it. It went down and rolled over. By then the town was overrun and the Germans were upon us. I had Captain Olson and Sergeant Wood climb up on the railroad bank and engage any German infantry they could see coming through the town. I then sent the jeep driver back for the Coldstream Guards, with an order for them to double-time to where I was. (*Fig. 14b.*)

What had happened was that a German battle group from the 6th Parachute Division had overrun part of the town. The troopers took to the buildings and cellars, fighting them building by building. Slowly Colonel Ekman, commanding the 505th, brought together enough troops to mount a counterattack. The 505th retook Mook at about the time the Coldstream Guards arrived.

Just then an American paratrooper brought a German paratrooper prisoner through the underpass, and I had a chance to interrogate the German. He was a young, apple-cheeked, very healthy-looking young man; he couldn't have been older than eighteen. He was part of a combat team that had the mission of driving through Mook, Molenhoek, capturing the bridge over the canal, and joining up with an attack that was coming through Beek, four or five miles to the north. At about this time I received assurances from Colonel Ekman that he had the Mook situation in hand. I went at once to Berg-en-Dal. In the meantime I learned that the 3rd Battalion of the 504th had started to cross the river to the north.

As I neared Berg-en-Dal, the fire was intense. The Germans were halfway up the hill between Berg-en-Dal and Beek. Evidently they had used armor and half-tracks, and one half-track was knocked out on a sharp curve in the road up the hill. Other German armor could not get around it.

I wanted to talk to some of the infantrymen and see for myself how bad the situation was. To get across the ridge, I had to get on my stomach and wiggle across the macadam road. Fire coming up the hill from the Germans was intense, but it was passing overhead. About fifty yards over the top of the ridge, I encountered 508th troopers digging in, a bit shaken and very weary. They told me that the Germans had half-tracks firing 20 mm. antiaircraft weapons as ground weapons. They were nasty to deal with, since the 20 mm. round exploded in the air and inflicted severe casualties. The Germans also had tanks. The division log showed that eight half-tracks and eight tanks had been reported just beyond Beek at 6:35 P.M. There were others in the town along the road up the hill to Berg-en-Dal. Colonel Louis Mendez, commander of the 3rd Battalion of the 508th, told me that he had been able to hold the Germans by shifting a platoon here and there whenever a threat was most serious. He did not know how long he could keep it up. He had been driven out of Beek, and he was now digging in near the top of the ridge. I assured him that we would give him all the artillery support we could and that, if needed, I might have more infantry to help him the following day. So far the 325th Glider Infantry had been grounded by weather in England.

By now it was beginning to get dark and we were hopeful that the Germans, as they often did, would stop their attack at darkness. They did, and afterward I returned to the Division Command Post to check on the situation in the other areas. I remembered that during the night I had to decide whether or not to concentrate our artillery fire on the town of Beek. What troubled us was that some of our troopers might still be in the town. I decided to go ahead in preparation for a 508th counter-attack that was due to jump off before daylight. It went off as planned and overran Beek quickly. Since we had the momentum, and in order to provide greater protection for the Nijmegen bridge, I ordered the regiment to continue the attack out on the flatlands. In two days they had driven the Germans several miles back to the Rhine River, near the town of Erlecom. We then were able to base our left flank on the Rhine River, and the front extended from the river to Wyler and then on through Groesbeek. September 20 had been a day unprecedented in the division's combat history. Each of the three regiments had fought a critical battle in its own area and had won over heavy odds, but the most brilliant and spectacular battle of all was that of the 504th to get across the Waal River.

The paratroopers of the 504th Parachute Infantry, commanded by Colonel Reuben Tucker, moved up to the crossing site shortly after I left at 1:30 P.M. The assault crossing was to be made by the 3rd Battalion under the command of a twenty-seven-year-old West Pointer, Major Julian Cook. It was a tough, experienced battalion; its last fighting had been in the Anzio beachhead. If it had been able to make the crossing shortly after daylight, as originally planned, it would have had reasonably good prospects for success, but as the day dragged on the Germans must have realized that something was in the offing. Cook paced the riverbank, asking where the boats were. H-hour was set ahead to 2:00 P.M., then postponed until 3:00 P.M. In the meantime tactical air support in the form of a strafing mission on the German positions across the river was laid on for 2:30. It was expected that the strafing mission would be followed by supporting fire by artillery and tanks.

The Irish Guards, under Lieutenant Colonel J.O.E. (Joe) Vandeleur, were to support the crossing. Vandeleur planned to use about thirty tanks. They were brought forward to the river embankment, track to track, prepared for direct firing into the German positions. This was to be reinforced by the artillery of the 82nd Airborne Division and the 504th mortars; approximately one hundred guns would support the crossing, and as much smoke was to be delivered on the German positions as the artillery could get their hands on.

Two-thirty came, and the fighters came in on schedule, machine-gunning and rocketing the far shore. Finally the boats arrived. To the paratroopers they were flimsy-looking affairs—folding canvas with the sides held erect by wooden slats. Each craft weighed about two hundred pounds, and it was expected that each would carry thirteen paratroopers and a crew of three engineers to row them across. That may have been someone's idea of how the crossing was to be made, but in effect every paratrooper tried to row, using the butt of his rifle for a paddle when necessary. The width of the river startled, if not shocked, those who saw it for the first time. As the boats were prepared for the crossing, there was little reaction from the German side. As soon as they were put together, paratroopers loaded their gear on board and got ready to dash to the water's edge. Now a deafening barrage of artillery and mortar fire lashed the far shore.

Twenty-six boats were assembled, someone yelled, "Go," and there was a rush for the water's edge. The troopers had a hard time getting the boats into deep water while they climbed over the sides with their weapons. To add to their difficulties, German small-arms fire began to intercept the fragile flotilla. Never having rowed together, the troopers sometimes worked against each other, and boats were spinning in the river. The German firing steadily increased, heavy artillery fire joining the machine-gun and mortar fire. A young lieutenant, Mulloy of the 504th, recalled that "it was worse than anything we took at Anzio."

Actually, on the far shore, about two hundred yards from the water's edge, a road on top of an embankment was being used by the Germans for protection while they fired at the badly chopped-up armada. Nevertheless, as we expected, the 504th kept battling its way across the bloody river. There were many individual acts of courage, many casualties, and later the troopers told me of stuffing handkerchiefs in the bullet holes to keep the water from pouring into the boats, and using their helmets to bail out water, while all around them men were being killed and wounded. Huge gaps began to appear in the smokescreen, and the protection we'd thought it would give almost disappeared. At the same time the German resistance was far greater than anything we had expected.

To those watching the crossing, it seemed forever before the first boats touched down on the northern bank. Men struggled out of the boats, waded and made their way through the mud, running forward. Some of them said later that they were so glad to be alive that they had only one thought: to kill the Germans along the embankment who had been making the crossing so difficult. As reported by Cornelius Ryan in *A Bridge Too Far,* Lieutenant Colonel Giles Vandeleur, who was watching the landings, later said, " 'I saw one or two boats hit the beach, followed immediately by three or four others. Nobody paused. Men got out and began running toward the embankment. My God, what a courageous sight it was! They just moved steadily across that open ground. I never saw a single man lie down until he was hit.' Then, to Vandeleur's amazement, 'the boats turned around and started back for the second wave.' Turning to Horrocks, General Browning said, 'I have never seen a more gallant action.' "

The troopers charged forward with grenades and bayonets, digging the Germans out of the foxholes on the other side of the embankment. They continued on to an old fortification, Fort Hof Van Holland. One of the sergeants swam the stinking water-filled moat to get near the opening of the fortress. He took the enemy guarding the entrance by surprise and then waved over the other troopers. They took the fort in short order.

By now the 3rd Battalion was badly disorganized and badly shot up.

Two of the captains, Captain Thomas M. Burriss, commanding I Company, and Captain Carl W. Kappel of H Company, taking all the troopers they could round up, moved as fast as they could go for the bridges. As they closed in on the Germans, fighting their way through orchards, around houses, and across fields, the Germans began to crack. To the amazement of the troopers, the Germans retreated across the railroad bridge into the guns of Vandervoort's battalion and the Grenadier Guards. By five o'clock, two hours after the start of the assault, they had gotten control of the northern end of the bridge, and the Germans were fleeing across it. The German losses on the bridge were heavy; many of them were killed in the girders, and others jumped into the river below. By now Colonel Tucker had crossed by boat and had gone ahead to coordinate the hard fighting on the northern shore. He directed the troopers to push on beyond the railroad bridge to seize the big bridge. In the meantime Colonel Vandervoort's battalion and the Grenadier Guards were pressing the Germans heavily at the south end of the highway bridge.

By 6:00 P.M. Vandervoort and the Grenadier Guards were closing in on the last of the German foxholes. The fighting was heavy, but the 505th troopers moved forward from rooftop to rooftop, supported by the Grenadier Guards' tanks. In the final all-out assault they overran all the German positions. Of the five hundred Germans Captain Euling had south of the river as a bridgehead, only sixty survived.

The Division Log for this date shows that the 504th sent a message at 4:45 saying that the regiment was across the river and advancing against the Germans. It was close to 7:00 P.M. when they reached the northern end of the highway bridge, and they waved to the British and Americans who were on the Nijmegen side. Tradition has it that they waved an American flag, but this does not seem to be substantiated by the facts.[11] In any event, the Grenadier Guards' tanks started across the bridge. Would the bridge blow up with them on it?

In anticipation of this very moment German General Heinz Harmel had gone forward to a point where he could keep the bridge under observation. He had with him an engineer with a detonator box connected by wires to demolitions on the bridge. The afternoon had been confusing for Harmel. Earlier in the day the Germans had seemed to

---

[11] Chester Wilmot in his excellent book, *The Struggle for Europe,* writes, "They secured the northern end of the railway bridge, and there they raised the American flag." New York: Harper and Brothers, 1952; Toronto: William Collins Sons & Co., Canada, 1952.

have the situation under complete control. The heavy artillery fire and air attacks down the river a mile or two had caused them some uneasiness, but General Harmel could not believe that anyone would attempt to cross the Rhine River by boat at that point. From the time of Julius Caesar a "crossing of the Rhine" was considered a major military feat, to be attempted only after thorough preparation. Yet he had heard that boats were being launched into the river; he did not know how many.

As the afternoon waned, he sensed a German defeat. Finally the British tanks approached the big highway bridge. Using his binoculars, he surveyed the scene carefully. He decided to wait until the tanks were halfway across. At that moment, as described in *A Bridge Too Far* by Cornelius Ryan:

> He shouted, "Let it blow!" The engineer jammed the plunger down. Nothing happened. The British tanks continued to advance. Harmel yelled, "Again!" Once more the engineer slammed down the detonator handle, but again the huge explosions that Harmel had expected failed to occur. "I was waiting to see the bridge collapse and the tanks plunge into the river," he recalled. "Instead, they moved forward relentlessly, getting bigger and bigger, closer and closer." He yelled to his anxious staff, "My God, they'll be here in two minutes!" Rapping out orders to his officers, Harmel told them "to block the roads between Elst and Lent with every available antitank gun and artillery piece because if we don't, they'll roll straight through to Arnhem."

The tanks of the Grenadier Guards engaged the two 88s dug in on the northern shore, destroyed them, and continued across the bridge. The first people to greet them were the paratroopers of the 504th. So enthusiastic were they that one of them actually kissed the leading British tank.

Tucker continued to round up his fighting troopers. He organized a bridgehead and a defensive position to protect the costly won bridge. I joined him at daylight in a small Dutch farmhouse about three-quarters of a mile beyond the bridge. Even as I made my way to his Command Post, Germans were coming out of the woods and nearby fields offering to surrender.

Tucker was livid. I had never seen him so angry. He had expected that when he seized his end of the bridge, the British armor would race on to Arnhem and link up with Urquhart. His first question to me was, "What in the hell are they doing? We have been in this position for over twelve hours, and all they seem to be doing is brewing tea. Why in hell don't they get to Arnhem?" I did not have an answer for him. I congratulated him and his regiment on the extraordinary feat. He was now assessing his casualties and building up the defenses on his bridgehead. I left and went back to look into the reasons for the delay.

Although we did not know it, on Wednesday evening, September 20, one of the most courageous actions of the battle was being fought by a handful of British troopers at the northern end of the Arnhem bridge. When General Urquhart's British Airborne Division was landed eight miles to the west of the Arnhem bridge, three battalions were dispatched at once by three separate routes with the mission of converging on the bridge. Two of them quickly ran into heavy German resistance and were stopped. The third, the 2nd Battalion of the 1st Parachute Brigade, under the command of Lieutenant Colonel John Frost, moved by a secondary road along the northern bank of the Rhine River. He occasionally encountered German resistance, and it was quickly overcome. Nevertheless, it took him seven hours to reach the northern end of the bridge. Already the Germans had crossed the bridge and held the southern end. He at once deployed his battalion around the northern end, occupying buildings in a small bridgehead. He arrived in that position shortly after 8:00 P.M. His battle began that night and continued relentlessly through Wednesday evening. By that time, he was badly wounded and had more than two hundred casualties that he was trying to save in the cellars of buildings. Finally the buildings were set afire, and when burning timbers began to fall and it was obvious that the troopers would be roasted alive, he sent out a Red Cross flag and asked for a truce. It was a tragedy that help was so near but did not reach him.

We did not realize it then, but September 20 had been the day of decision in the mind of Field Marshal Model. He had organized an all-out attack from Zon to Arnhem with the intention of destroying the airborne forces. The road in the 101st area was cut, and we in the 82nd area had received the brunt of his attack at Mook and Beek. On this day, also, the last of the troopers at the Arnhem bridge had been overrun and Colonel Frost seriously wounded. Therefore 30 Corps decided not to advance until the situation was better in hand.

I was back with Tucker the following morning and for the first time the British armor began to move to the north. In the meantime the Polish Parachute Brigade had been south of the lower Rhine River, about five miles to the west of Arnhem. The remains of Urquhart's command had been compressed into a small pocket around the town of Oosterbeek, two and a half miles west of the Arnhem bridge. Finally on the night of September 25–26 more than 2000 survivors of Urquhart's command of 9500 men were ferried across the river. We brought them to Nijmegen, where we provided them with blankets, shelter, and food. They had fought an extraordinarily gallant action and a desperate battle for survival in their small bridgehead. We in the 82nd had a lasting regret that we had not reached them. They were brave men and they had done all that human flesh and human spirit could accomplish. Thus, the great gamble to end the war in the fall of '44 came to an end.

The days that followed were comparatively quiet; anything would have been after September 20. Hitler announced that the Nijmegen bridge was to be destroyed by the Luftwaffe. To accomplish its certain destruction, he committed his newest planes; they were jets, and we had not seen them before. They were very noisy and very erratic. They made quite a few bombing runs at the bridge the first few days, and the bombs were just as liable to strike a mile from the bridge as not. Furthermore, when one heard the scream of the jet in its dive, it was almost too late to see it, since it had already left the target area. A number of our troop carrier friends came up to have lunch with me and to see what these new propless airplanes looked like. We were having lunch in a tent that had a sandbag wall around it when we heard a jet starting a bombing run. Most of the troop carrier men ran outside the tent to see it, and one of the airborne officers, who didn't bother to go out, joked to his commanding officer, "They all look like that, Colonel." Finally, a demolitions team floated down the river a contrivance that they were able to tip up under the bridge and with it blow a small opening across the floor. The British were able to repair it promptly. "Scratched up a bit, it was," said General Horrocks.

Several days after the capture of the bridge, General Browning took me aside and told me that Field Marshal Montgomery was coming up for a visit. Montgomery was going to ask me to resume the offensive and attack to the north. I told General Browning that I believed I was not in a position to agree to such a thing without clearing with General Ridgway. General Browning seemed to understand. Field Marshal Montgomery arrived the following day. It was my first personal meeting with him, although I had seen him in staff meetings in London before Normandy. He was impressive, a perceptive, quick-minded man, incisive in his judgments. I could understand why he had been so popular with the Eighth Army in North Africa. I took a liking to him that has not diminished with the years. Naturally, there were questions in my mind about the battle we had just been through. Why hadn't it been better planned? Why was Montgomery not given adequate troop and logistic support—at least one more division? Why had higher headquarters so seriously underestimated the German strength and attitude? I had no idea at that time that the German Fifteenth Army had managed to escape and to oppose us.

When the 504th was relieved north of the bridge, it was withdrawn and committed to the front between the 508th and the 505th. The 82nd then had its left flank resting on the Rhine River, extending directly across the flatland to Wyler. Here the 504th took up the front and held it until it was near Groesbeek, where it was taken up by the 505th. The right flank of the 505th was on a small hill mass close to the Reichswald at Reithorst. A small detachment of A Company was in a pivotal position at Reithorst, and I had heard that they were uneasy about the possibility of being cut off. They were a couple of miles beyond the town of Mook. Taking Sergeant Wood with me, I walked out the road from Mook to Reithorst shortly after daylight after the new dispositions had been made. The troopers were a bit nervous and were troubled by the Germans who were dug in on the edge of the Reichswald, very close by. I assured the troopers that we would give them all the support they needed to hold their positions.

I had started back on the road toward Mook when I was challenged by a guttural "Halt," coming from what must have been a German patrol in the flatlands between the road and the Maas River. It was no place for a division commander to be caught by a German patrol, so I scrambled up a hillside through the trees and made my way back to the Division Command Post.

The 325th Glider Infantry Regiment finally landed in the old 504th drop zone area on Saturday, September 23, six days after our first landing—five days late. I had been asked by General Horrocks to clear a bridgehead over the Maas River in the vicinity of Mook. The British intent was to bring another corps into that sector on the right of Horrocks's 30 Corps. To establish the bridgehead, the 325th attacked on the right of the 505th. With good support from the Sherwood Ranger Yeomanry Tank Battalion, it finally occupied a front from Reithorst to the Maas River. This put the division in a defensive position extending from the Rhine River on its left approximately twelve miles to the Maas River on its right.

At about this time I had my first visit from the commanding general of the British Second Army, Sir Miles Dempsey. By then I had moved my Command Post into a small woods on the south side of Nijmegen. He greeted me warmly with the statement, "I'm proud to meet the Commanding General of the finest division in the world today." I accepted it with reservations, believing that he was being too kind. However, an alert staff officer overheard the comment, and it became part of the division's history.

Immediately on his arrival, General Dempsey went into the situation with me in great detail. We began talking about a mutual acquaintance, and he observed that "he is a decently shy sort of man." This, in fact, was a good description of General Dempsey himself. He was reticent, almost shy, and yet a very hard, demanding taskmaster as an army commander. I was to serve under him on the Elbe River later, and I know that when a job had to be done, he never hestitated to ask, no matter how demanding the circumstances. As he gazed about my sylvan setting, I could see him look with wonder. Actually, I used what the Americans call a small wall tent for a shelter. It could quickly be taken down and moved. I had a foxhole just outside the tent that I could roll into during the night if we came under attack. I had to use the foxhole only once, when several tents were struck by artillery shrapnel. As a paratrooper I always made it a practice to sleep on the ground. Immediately following a parachute landing one could end up with a few troopers, or sometimes a larger number, and one had to live off the land. Parachute officers had to set an example and learn to live like other troopers. In any event, it would have been unwise to succumb to the physical comforts of a bed and a permanent shelter.

Later, when the winter war arrived, I slept fully clothed on the floor of German farmhouses, with a field telephone near my head so that I could be alerted quickly if the need arose. General Dempsey, before he departed, again commented on the fighting qualities of the division and took a last look at our rather spartan setting. A day later a handsome van arrived with his compliments. It was well equipped with a bunk, toilet facilities, a place for battle maps on the wall—typical of the vans then in use by all the senior officers. I couldn't think of using it. Obviously, it never could be parachuted into combat. I thanked him for it and told the staff that they could use it for whatever purpose it might serve. The only time I was in it was on the occasion of a small party the staff gave when my promotion to Major General came through in October.

I visited Tucker to see how he was getting along in his defensive role. He and his regiment were in fine form. They had captured a truckload of panzerfausts with training instructions in German which they had translated. They were the best antitank weapons we had for the remainder of the war. I asked him why he continued to feed his troops K rations when better rations were available. He said that not to do so would cause some of them to want to build fires for cooking, and they were happy with K rations. It was beginning to be quite cold, and I commented about the troopers' continuing to wear nothing more than their jumpsuits. He said that they had noticed that the Germans wore long overcoats, so the troopers all agreed they would wear their jumpsuits, and during night patrol actions, of which there were many every night, everyone wearing an overcoat would automatically be shot. It seemed to be a very effective way of keeping the Germans under control. One might think that these small hardships would have been demoralizing, but the morale of the 504th could not have been better. It was a fine regiment.

Toward the end of September the first British newspapers began to arrive. Although we had not realized it, BBC had had reporters with the British 1st Airborne Division at Arnhem. Beginning on D+1, the British press had been full of Arnhem stories. The *Daily Express* had a daily story filed by Alan Wood. All the reports were about the British 1st Airborne; there was no mention of any fighting by the 101st and 82nd Airborne Divisions. The only mention of Americans occurred in a story in the *Daily Telegram* on September 22: "British tanks yesterday drove across the Rhine at Nijmegen and thrust toward Arnhem. The drive to Arnhem followed a brilliant maneuver in which American paratroops forced a crossing of the Rhine at Nijmegen."

We began to receive the newspapers regularly, and day after day they published glowing accounts of the British fighting at Arnhem, with no mention of either of the American divisions. Finally, on September 29, the *Daily Express* quoted from three American papers: The *New York Sun*: "The stand at Arnhem will be recorded as among the greatest dramas of the war." The *Washington Post*: "Arnhem hereafter will be a prouder name in British memories than Agincourt or Waterloo, or even

Trafalgar." And *The New York Times*: "There will be no prouder men in years to come than those qualified to wear the Arnhem badge or ribbon." No mention of the costly victory at Nijmegen or by the 101st farther south.

Members of the staff at first were puzzled by the total omission of any word about the 82nd Airborne Division or the 101st Airborne. It could not have been for reasons of security, for the Germans knew very well that we were fighting in Holland. The more the staff thought about it, the more they decided that Field Marshal Montgomery's headquarters had to present Arnhem as a great victory. A defeat at Arnhem after his efforts to launch the battle that would have won the war would have been too much. The way to make it appear to be a victory was to report no fighting by any other divisions and show that Operation MARKET-GARDEN had been entirely successful by advancing British troops as far as the city of Arnhem itself. Hence no stories about the 82nd or 101st were to be released. This may have been presumptuous thinking in the division, but there seemed to be no other rational reason for completely excluding the 82nd and 101st from the news.[12]

The crowning blow came in a column in a London paper that reported news from America. It quoted an American as saying how gallant the British had been at Arnhem and what a shame it was that some people in America were trying to take some of the credit for the fighting by saying that American paratroopers had fought in Holland also. Thus, Arnhem seemed to take on the semblance of a great victory. Years later, when new cadet barracks were built at the United States Military Academy at West Point, American victories in World War II

[12] After the publication of *A Bridge Too Far*, Mrs. Cornelius Ryan received a letter from William F. Boni, who was a war correspondent for the Associated Press. He landed near Nijmegen. He, with Cyril Ray, a British correspondent, had been assigned to the 82nd Airborne Division. Since the British Airborne Corps had landed at Nijmegen, they sought to file their outgoing dispatches through that headquarters. (There were ten correspondents with the British 1st Airborne at Arnhem.) Not long after the landing, he checked in at the British Airborne Corps headquarters. He was told that they could file fifty or one hundred words that the Corps would get to Associated Press in London. Two or three days later they stopped by Corps headquarters again and there encountered the staff man they had met earlier. "Oh, I say, you chaps, I'd quite forgotten about your dispatches—I still have them here," and he patted the pocket of his battle jacket. Boni and his colleagues were not able to get anything out of Nijmegen. After the linkup occurred, they were told that with ground-bound correspondents in the area, their accreditations had run out. They proceeded to Brussels, thoroughly frustrated. There, they "got their first bath, a good meal, and proceeded to get very thoroughly drunk."

were commemorated by having granite sallyports through the barracks named after them. The name of the battle was etched above the passageway. Strangely, Arnhem was one of those selected, thus perpetuating the myth that Arnhem was a great victory, but this time an American victory.

The troopers did not like not being given credit in the press for what they thought had been their best fighting of the war. It troubled me, too, and it was potentially damaging to troop morale, for soldiers like to believe that the people back home learn about what they are doing, and when they do well, they want their families to know it. Finally, nothing pleased them more, from time to time during the war, than to get a press clipping from back home in which their outfit was praised for gallantry in action.

On October 8 the 82nd Airborne Division was transferred to Horrocks's 30 Corps from Browning's Airborne Corps. Shortly after the transfer General Horrocks told me that he wanted to visit the battalions of the division with me. We arrived at the Division Command Post in a jeep with an aide and a wicker lunch hamper, then started out. We visited every battalion Command Post and some Company Posts in the division. In some localities General Horrocks was exposed to considerable danger, but as he explained to me, "The only place you can get the real smell of battle in your nostrils and know what is going on is at the battalion command posts." He was quite right. At noontime we stopped behind a haystack and had lunch. After that day of activity he asked me if he could meet with every battalion when it came out of the line so he could talk to the troopers assembled.

He was very good with troops, and one can understand why he was so popular. He asked the 82nd troopers if there was anything they wanted, and, to my embarrassment, they replied, "Yes, we want more to eat." The problem was that they were on British rations and they didn't like them. He promptly doubled the ration. As the days got colder, he frequently asked me if I would want to issue a rum ration to the troops. I turned him down because our company commanders complained that most of the troopers were too young and did not drink rum, except for a few, and they invariably would collect the rations from the others and get drunk. I am sure that General Horrocks did not understand why we declined the offer, for on the last night with his Corps, he sent me a note saying, "You will issue a rum ration tonight."

In the midst of the fighting earlier, on September 21, the G-4 of the Division came to me and told me that he had found a liquor warehouse belonging to the Wehrmacht. I told him that he should keep it locked, and when the division was withdrawn we would take its contents with us to distribute to the division. Horrocks's logistics people came upon it, however, and all I saw of it was a single quart of whiskey, which was sent to me with the compliments of the Corps Commander. I asked about it and learned that it was customary in his corps to confiscate all liquor and then to distribute a proper share of it to everybody in the corps. I spoke about it to Lieutenant Colonel Vandeleur of the Irish Guards, and he said that was no problem; they were going to send a reconnaissance patrol off some twenty miles the next day, and if I liked, I could send a reconnaissance squad with it, and anything we captured we could keep. We went along, but it was a fruitless quest. Later the Irish Guards invited me to tea. I do not believe that I have ever seen such a lavish spread of food, even in peacetime. The Guards lived very well in combat, but they fought well, too. General Horrocks was quite a character and a great soldier. I learned a great deal from serving under him.

Shortly after being assigned to 30 Corps, I was told that King George VI would visit the corps and that I was to bring my regimental commanders and the artillery commander to be presented to him. The thought crossed my mind that they had better do something about the appearance of the Guards Armored officers before the King arrived. They customarily wore old corduroy trousers and chukka boots. Frequently they wore gay-colored scarves. Vandeleur and all his officers in the Irish Guards always wore bright green scarves. The only items of uniform they wore were a battle jacket and their headgear. However, under their battle jackets many of them wore colorful sweaters that hung six or eight inches below the jackets. As we assembled at Corps headquarters, one of the senior British officers appeared wearing a robin's-egg-blue sweater. It seemed to extend halfway from his waist to his knees. He was sent back. After the war a British writer observed, "At the time the British Army was at its best, its uniform discipline was at its worst." But the King did not seem to be disturbed by the personal touch given to the uniforms. He spoke to each of the regimental commanders of the 82nd and to the division artillery commander. He seemed to be a gentle, kind, intelligent man.

Five days after meeting with the King, I was directed to fly to Rheims, France, to look at billets that were proposed for the 82nd Airborne Division. They were old French army cantonments that had been used by the Germans. They were at Sissonne and Suippes, both about twenty miles from Rheims. They did not offer much in the way of comfort, but they were far better than foxholes in the fall and winter in Holland. On November 13 I turned over our sector facing the Reichswald to the 3rd Canadian Infantry Division, and the 82nd moved back to France to its new billets. There it was to get replacements and, of course, train them. One of the first things I had ordered done was the distribution of ammunition and rations down to the companies so that we could move back into combat promptly if necessary.

In the meantime one of the most effective airborne operations of the war had taken place in southern France. It consisted of a force under the command of Major General Robert Frederick. In it was the 1st Special Service Force, the British 2nd Independent Parachute Brigade, the U.S. 517th Parachute Infantry Regiment, the 551st and 509th Parachute Infantry Battalions, as well as a glider infantry battalion and three artillery battalions. Actually, it was a composite division, and it was officially titled "The Provisional Airborne Division." The assault had been carried out in mid-August under the command of Lieutenant General Lucian K. Truscott, Jr. General Jacob Devers, who commanded the VI Army Group, and who had over-all responsibility for the entire operation, judged it to be "the most successful airborne operation of the whole war." A number of the airborne participants were to join the 82nd later in the war, and they were most welcome, particularly the 517th Parachute Infantry Regiment, which fought with us in the winter war that was to follow.

After the war, and as the memories of the battle of Nijmegen lingered in our minds, there was much talk about it among the veterans. There has been a lasting discontent over the historical record of the Americans in MARKET-GARDEN. From the viewpoint of the 82nd Airborne Division, it was its most difficult battle in extremely difficult circumstances, a battle in which the division was frequently outnumbered and yet won every tactical engagement. People who know their history comment on the fact that the 82nd captured the Grave bridge intact, captured two of the canal bridges, and captured the big bridge at Nijmegen. And while capturing these objectives, the 82nd had to be capable of beating off any attacks the Germans might launch against it.[13]

We knew that the risks were great, but we believed that the battle we were about to fight would lead to the battle that would bring the war to an end. And by the fall of '44 we were becoming aware of the proliferating number of concentration camps in Germany itself. As the battle developed, thanks particularly to the skill of the individual troopers, the NCOs, and junior officers, we were able to beat off major German counterattacks by patrolling actively the huge gaps around our perimeter and building up before each German counteroffensive began to take shape. And after each German attack we counterattacked and destroyed them.

After the war I received a letter from one of our opponents, General von der Heydte, who enclosed a letter from a German general officer who had opposed us at Molenhoek. He commented that "in forest fighting and night fighting the members of the 82nd Airborne Division proved superior to the Germans." Finally, in a desperate effort to reach our comrades at Arnhem, the 504th Parachute Infantry made a gallant crossing of the Rhine River, and the huge Nijmegen bridge was ours. Although our losses were heavy, they were about the same as those sustained by the 505th Parachute Infantry in the defensive actions in Sicily against the Hermann Goering Division. We never could have fought and won the battle of Nijmegen without all the combat experience from the battles of Sicily, Italy, and Normandy.

And when it was over, every trooper was proud of what had been accomplished. It is the one battle they still talk about years later. I believe that they all sensed the risks we were taking and knew how marginal each tactical engagement was until the outcome of the battle was finally resolved five days after we landed. That portion of the Netherlands that we liberated was never retaken by the Germans, and it proved to be a launching area from which the final offensives were made in the following spring, thus bringing Germany to defeat.

What had been a dream in 1941 had now become a reality. We had the First Allied Airborne Army. Solutions to our problems, from that of

[13] In a personal account of the battle of MARKET-GARDEN, written in 1977, Sir Brian Horrocks, who commanded the British 30 Corps in the battle, said, "The key to the whole operation was the Dutch town of Nijmegen." Sir Brian Horrocks with Eversley Belfield and Major General H. Essame, *Corps Commander*. London: Sidgwick and Jackson, 1977.

individual training to the massing of thousands of transports, gliders, and fighter-bombers, had been found. Equipment, weapons, and standardized operating procedures had all been developed. Now we could move and strike with an army by air, not only against Germany but later against Japan.

Above: Lieutenant General Kurt von Tippelskirch, right, leaving the Command Post of the 82nd Airborne at the castle in Ludwigslust after the surrender of his army. (U.S. Army)

Below: Russian and American commanders meet and lay out a buffer zone between their troops. At left is Major General Dzinet, who never spoke. The short officer next to him is General Smirnow. General Gavin is in the center, General Ridgway is at the extreme right, and the officer beneath the painting is General Ralph Eaton. (U.S. Army)

Above: May 1945. The German army and its followers as they traveled through the lines of the 82nd Airborne. The Germans, using horse-drawn wagons and bicycles, with thousands traveling on foot, were fleeing from Russian troops, who swept all remaining troops from their path as they advanced across Germany to meet the U.S. troops traveling east. (U.S. Army)

Below: May 1945, Wobelein Concentration Camp. The dead and the near dead. The troops discovered inmates piled together before the camp was abandoned, and separated the living from the dead. (U.S. Army)

Opposite, above: German citizens, carrying shovels, after they had been required to dig the graves of dead inmates of the Wobelein Concentration Camp. Attendance of the entire population was mandatory at the funeral service in the town square, at which Protestant, Catholic, and Jewish chaplains officiated. (U.S. Army)

Opposite, below: Surviving inmates of the Wobelein Concentration Camp. The thirteen-year-old boy at the right had been in concentration camps for three years. Four times he had been to the gas chambers, four times withdrawn. (U.S. Army)

Below: At Epinal, France, in July 1945, General Gavin talks to the assembled 82nd Airborne Division about the forthcoming occupation of Berlin. (U.S. Army)

Opposite, above: General Eisenhower attends a review on Tempelhof airfield, given in his honor by the 82nd Airborne Division in September 1945. The review was followed by the drop of a parachute battalion and the landing of a dozen gliders. General Eisenhower recommended that Marshal Zhukov receive a similar review, and it was given the following weekend. Left to right: General Bedell Smith, General Eisenhower, General Gavin. (U.S. Army)

Opposite, below: Marshal Zhukov receives a review of the 82nd Airborne given in his honor on Tempelhof airfield. An interpreter stands between Zhukov and General Gavin. (U.S. Army)

Above: In Berlin, August 1945, General George C. Patton, shown here with General Gavin, visits the 82nd Airborne Division. (Time-Life photograph)

Below: American, British, and Russian officers, gathered for a conference in Ludwigslust, Germany, salute passing troops. Front row, left to right: Lieutenant General Crishin, Commanding General, 49th Russian Army; Lieutenant General Sir Miles C. Dempsey, Commanding General, British Second Army; and Major General Matthew B. Ridgway, Commanding General, XVIII Airborne Corps. At the left, in the second row, is Major General Gavin. (U.S. Army)

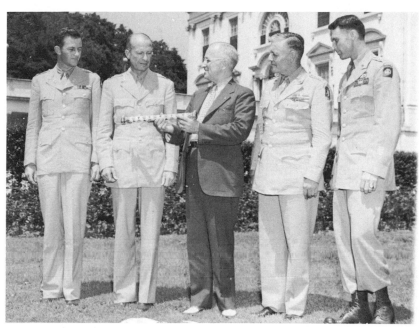

Above: President Harry Truman being shown, during the summer of 1945, the special baton that belonged to Hermann Goering. The baton is now in the museum at West Point. Left to right: an aide-de-camp; Lieutenant General Alexander McCarrell Patch, Commanding General of the Seventh Army; President Truman; Lieutenant General Lucian K. Truscott, Commanding General of the Fifth Army; and General Gavin. (Press Association, Inc.)

Below: On the reviewing stand as the troops march up Fifth Avenue in the Victory Parade. Left to right: General Jonathan M. Wainwright, General Gavin, Mayor William O'Dwyer, Governor Thomas E. Dewey. (Press Association, Inc.)

Great moment in the Victory Parade. Troops of the 82nd Airborne march through the Arch in Washington Square and up Fifth Avenue.

The Winter War

We were glad to leave the cold, damp foxholes of Holland. At the same time our mood was one of disappointment and frustration. Our hopes of seeing the war end in '44 had reached a low ebb. The fighting in Holland had been costly; at one time we had more than six hundred troopers crowding the wards and lining the halls of a Nijmegen hospital; we left more than a thousand buried in a cow pasture between Molenhoek and the Maas-Waal Canal. The division had fought hard to achieve its objectives. When the battle was done, we possessed a hundred square miles of war-torn, bloody land to show for it, and the war was no nearer an end. To be sure, a deep narrow salient intruded into the back door of Germany, but whether or not something could be made of this remained to be seen.

Immediately after the battle there was much talk about why MARKET-GARDEN had been a failure. Among the troopers in the 82nd there was complete agreement that the British 1st Airborne landing zones and dropping zones had been too far from the Arnhem bridge. Long before, we had learned to take losses and land on an objective rather than try to fight overland for it. If the division had landed in the flatland south of the bridge, on the edge of the flak, it could have seized and held the bridge with one brigade and then committed the remainder of the division to securing the corridor to Nijmegen. If necessary, it could have assisted in capturing the Nijmegen bridge. In the midst of the battle Horrocks had told me that he intended to go right through to Apeldoorn and the Zuider Zee. If he had succeeded the Allies would then have been in a position to enter northern Germany on a decisive scale. The Allies had lost a great opportunity. Among the higher staffs, Army and Army Group, there was much talk about other aspects of the campaign, of which we were unaware at the time—lack of adequate logistic support for Montgomery's main effort, lack of troops, failure to open the port of Antwerp, why Montgomery was given responsibility for the main effort in the first place. The lost opportunity became the great argument.

Confronting the Supreme Commander in early September was one of the most difficult dilemmas that a general commanding coalition armies must face. It was made up of part national pride, part doubts about the actual ability of a senior commander, strong personalities that were in conflict, and the whole compounded by a seriously deteriorating logistics situation. A decision could have been made that would have brought the war to an end before the end of 1944, but if it had been made then, some Armies would have had to be stopped and held in defensive positions, while others would have been given maximum support and orders for an all-out offensive. Geography and the realities of harbors, docks, roads, railways, and distances all favored Montgomery's making the main offensive. But equally real as the logistics constraints were the political and military pressures on Eisenhower to allow Patton to continue to attack even if it meant holding Montgomery back.

The Americans did not trust Montgomery, and their memories of Africa, Sicily, and Normandy were all too vivid. To many Americans, Montgomery's manner was imperious, his demand for supplies insatiable, and his addiction to the set-piece battle incurable. He gave many Americans the impression that he was teaching the former colonials how to fight a war, and at the same time he was quite willing to use their lives as well as their supplies and transport while doing so. It did not go down well. Yet those of us who fought under his command formed a high opinion of him. He was pragmatic, intelligent, and a dedicated soldier. His relations with his subordinates were warm and sensitive. One can understand the impact of his leadership on the British Eighth Army in North Africa. Not only was he an able commander; the troops under his command performed well for him. I had a high opinion of British troops, particularly the infantry, with whom I was frequently in close association. In defense they were probably as good as any in the world. But Montgomery's idiosyncrasies and his so-called flair irritated many Americans. It was almost embarrassing at times to hear what was being said about him in some of the higher American commands. Yet he was, in his own way, trying to support Eisenhower in the manner he thought best to win the war quickly.

For example, he had recommended that he be put in over-all charge of the land battle. After all, there was a Naval Commander in Chief, Admiral Sir Bertram Ramsay, and an Air Commander in Chief, Air Chief Marshal Sir T. L. Leigh-Mallory, so why not an Army Commander in Chief, Field Marshal Bernard Law Montgomery? But the political pressures on Eisenhower emanating from Washington, the War Department, and Congress simply would not allow the placement of Montgomery in that position. Yet so convinced was Montgomery that this was a sound proposal that he suggested that, if he was not acceptable, Bradley be placed in charge of the over-all land battle, in which case Montgomery would be happy to serve under him. However, the British would never have accepted Bradley's being placed in a position above Montgomery. So Eisenhower had on his hands one of the most difficult decisions of the war. In solving it, he denied Montgomery's recommendation and retained direct command of the three Army Groups. He then gave Montgomery the First Allied Airborne Army and authority to launch Operation MARKET-GARDEN. At the same time, he allowed Patton, under Bradley's command, to continue the attack.

Patton posed a particularly difficult problem. He simply would not accept orders to slow down his attack. He used what he referred to in his memoirs as the "rock soup" method. He described it in a story about a tramp "who went to a house and asked for some boiling water to make rock soup. The lady was interested and gave him the water, in which he placed two polished white stones. He then asked if he might have some potatoes to put in the soup to flavor it a little, and finally ended up with some meat. In other words, in order to attack we first had to pretend to reconnoiter, then reinforce the reconnaissance, and finally put on an attack—all depending on what gasoline and ammunition we could secure."[1]

Again, for example, on the day that MARKET-GARDEN was launched, General Patton wrote in his memoirs, "Bradley called to say that Monty wanted all the American troops to stop so that he, Monty, could make a 'dagger thrust with the Twenty-first Army Group at the heart of Germany.' Bradley said he thought it would be more like a 'butter-knife thrust.' In order to avoid such an eventuality, it was evident that the Third Army should get deeply involved at once, so I asked Bradley not to call me until after dark on the nineteenth."[2]

[1] General George S. Patton, Jr., *War as I Knew It*. Cambridge, Mass.: The Riverside Press, 1947, pp. 125, 133, 136.
[2] Ibid.

When Eisenhower finally ordered Bradley to put Patton in a defensive position, Patton noted that "we also selected successive points along this [defensive] front on which we would attack on the 'rock soup' plan, ostensibly for the purpose of securing a jump-off line—actually hoping for a breakthrough."[3]

So, early in September Patton's cries for greater logistics support were rewarded. The long gasoline drought in the Third Army began to end. According to the official U.S. Army history, *U.S. Army in World War II,* by September 12 "adequate stocks of gasoline were available and all fuel tanks and auxiliary tanks were full." On the same date 3554 long tons of portable Bailey bridging were moved all the way from Normandy to the front to support his offensive. The week of September 10 he launched an assault in Lorraine employing eight divisions.

In the meantime Montgomery was given the First Allied Airborne Army and authority to launch a major offensive. The plan was risky, but the prize was worth the risk—entry into northern Germany and an end to the war. Yet so critical was the supply situation that "on the first two days of MARKET-GARDEN Dempsey was able to employ offensively only three of nine British divisions available, and, as already recorded, the actual attack was made by two battalions advancing on one narrow road. This was the direct result of Eisenhower's policy. If he had kept Patton halted on the Meuse, and given full logistic support to Hodges and Dempsey after the capture of Brussels, the operation in Holland could have been an overwhelming triumph." [4]

On September 22, five days after launching MARKET-GARDEN, General Eisenhower called a meeting at his new headquarters in Versailles. It was to be the most important conference since the Allies had landed in Normandy on June 6. Twenty-three generals, air marshals, and admirals, including all the senior Allied advisers to Eisenhower, attended. Instead of attending, Montgomery sent his well-liked Chief of Staff, General Francis de Guingand. Bradley was somewhat incensed and in his memoirs recalled that "Monty's absence was viewed by the other commanders as an affront to the Allied chief" (Eisenhower) and, later, "I was annoyed myself two days later when Ike instructed me to visit Monty and review the decisions we had agreed to at Versailles.

3 Ibid.
4 Wilmot, op. cit.

During a bad weather flight to Monty's headquarters, we lost our way and almost flew into the enemy's lines as the result of a radio failure."[5] Montgomery did not explain his absence. Chester Wilmot defends it with the words, ". . . he would have to appear as an advocate, almost a suppliant—a role for which he knew he was ill cast."[6]

After this Montgomery and Bradley appeared in the role of adversaries; this came out quickly in the meeting as Bradley sought to obtain approval for his Army Group to make a double envelopment of the Ruhr, urging at the same time that Montgomery clear the Schelde so that Antwerp could be operational. He was of the view that this had to be of top priority, a view shared by everyone by this time. Montgomery, however, wanted Eisenhower to give absolute priority to the British Second Army while Patton was stopped. The British Second Army would then sweep out of its present positions facing the Reichswald and on across the Rhine to the seizure of the Ruhr. Eisenhower gave his support to the Montgomery plan; thereafter Montgomery was to get full support while Patton was to be stopped. In addition, two American divisions, the 104th Infantry Division and the 9th Armored Division, were to be attached to the British Second Army. It was a decision that came at least a month too late.

During October the Canadians and British began clearing the estuary of the Schelde. It was a difficult task. One of the largest islands, Walcheren, is shaped like an enormous saucer. Almost the entire interior is below sea level. It is surrounded by dikes that have been built up through the centuries. They are formidable. One, for example, the Westkapelle Dike, is 330 feet wide at its base. The Canadians used R.A.F. bombers to open gaps in the dikes, thus flooding the island. The bombing combined with amphibious assaults finally enabled them to overcome all German resistance by November 9. It took two more weeks to clear the estuary of mines. In the meantime Montgomery was building up his forces in the Nijmegen area for a major offensive through the Reichswald in the direction of the Ruhr. Although continuing to probe the German defenses, Patton seemed content to remain on the defensive. Captain Butcher, Eisenhower's aide, reports in a conversation of October 29 that Patton approved Montgomery's use of the First

[5] Omar N. Bradley, *A Soldier's Story*. New York: Henry Holt & Co., 1951, pp. 422–423.
[6] Wilmot, op. cit., pp. 533–534.

Allied Airborne Army. He further added that "he didn't expect to need the paratroopers to cross the Rhine." Instead, he would use "heavy bombers to pulverize the opposite shore and then let his men row across."[7]

The pressures on Eisenhower to regroup his forces, moving the bulk of them to the north, continued. On December 7, in response to a suggestion from Montgomery, Eisenhower, Montgomery, Tedder, and Bradley met at Maastricht. The purpose of the meeting was to review the situation from early September and to arrive at some understanding of how they would employ their forces in the future. Eisenhower does not mention the meeting in his *Crusade in Europe,* which is strange, since it was of considerable importance. Montgomery covers the meeting quite thoroughly and carefully in his memoirs, pointing out that he and Eisenhower "differed, not slightly, but widely and on fundamental issues." Montgomery pleaded to be given authority to take charge of all the forces north of the Ardennes area, and with those forces he would make a major offensive. Bradley would take charge of the forces south of the Ardennes, and he would also be put on the offensive. Evidently nothing came from the meeting, but it did leave a residue that was to result in some bad words in a few weeks.

So the high hopes of the late summer of '44 faded with the first chill of an early winter. Never were the problems of coalition warfare more in evidence. National interests, national pride, and public opinion seemed to prevail in Allied councils. This, despite the dedication to objectivity and to common victory by the Allied generals, and Eisenhower in particular.

War was being waged in many dimensions in the summer and fall of '44. The summer saw the climax of an electronics war: a war of communications interception and deception, spies and counterspies, on a grand scale. Thanks to the information gained through these unusual means, and the deceptions perpetrated upon the Germans, the Allied armies had gained a decisive victory in Western Europe in August 1944.

We sometimes wondered what it must have been like at the time in Germany and in the councils of the German high command (OKW). The Wehrmacht itself seemed to be regaining strength, and it was becoming increasingly formidable. To those in the foxholes, winter loomed

---

[7] Captain Harry C. Butcher, U.S.N.R., *My Three Years with Eisenhower.* New York: Simon & Schuster, Inc., 1946, pp. 693–694.

as a grim prospect. Actually, the situation in Germany was far from good. The German military establishment, including Hitler, was inescapably caught in the tentacles of a new form of warfare. It was a war between the British Secret Service, the Allies—and the Abwehr, the highest German intelligence agency.

Rear Admiral Wilhelm Franz Canaris headed the Abwehr. It was on this organization that Hitler and his Supreme Command (OKW) depended for its worldwide intelligence and counterintelligence support. Canaris, who was a dedicated military man, had reservations about Hitler's ambitious goals for Germany. He sought and obtained Hitler's approval, but it was approval he did not reciprocate. The "Bavarian corporal" was too ambitious and ruthless for Canaris's liking. At the outset of the war Canaris summed up his views to his staff, "A defeat for Germany in this war might be disastrous, but a victory for Hitler would be catastrophic."[8] An unusual and dangerous statement for the head of German intelligence to make, but Canaris was determined to thwart Hitler in every way possible.

The war was scarcely six hours old when Canaris established contact with the British diplomatic Mission in Berlin, just before it was to leave for London. Canaris was to maintain contact with London through those who had been on the Mission as well as through other agents. Canaris arranged for one, Dr. Josef Mueller, a Catholic lawyer in Munich, to open contact with London through the Vatican. He also established contact through Spain and Switzerland. He tried in every way to thwart Hitler's aims. For example, on the eve of the German invasion of Poland, Canaris sent a delegation of officers to London to appeal to the British to make a demonstration in the Baltic in order to dissuade Hitler, to no avail. Admiral Canaris also approved of a resistance movement that was growing among the German officer corps, the Schwarze Kapelle. The Schwarze Kapelle from the outset had the sympathetic approval of and at times the active support of General Ludwig Beck, Chief of the German General Staff. The activity of the Schwarze Kapelle stepped up when Hitler's ventures were unsuccessful, and it declined with his successes. Nevertheless, by the summer of 1944 it had among its supporters Field Marshal Rommel, Field Marshal Gunther von Kluge, General Beck, General Hans Speidel, General Carl-Heinrich

[8] Anthony Cave Brown, *Bodyguard of Lies*. New York: Harper & Row, 1975, p. 139.

von Stuelpnagel. The failure of the July 20 attempt on Hitler's life was to cost most of them their lives.[9]

Opposing Canaris in the war of espionage and deception was General Sir Stewart Menzies, Chief of the British Secret Intelligence Service. Working closely with the British Secret Service was the American Office of Strategic Services. Throughout the war General Menzies continued to receive information from the Schwarze Kapelle. In addition, he had Ultra, which provided for the interception and decryptment and translation of secret German wireless communications between Hitler and his field commanders. Thus he was at all times in a position to check one against the other—the information from the Schwarze Kapelle against the actual transmissions to the field commands.

In addition to the Schwarze Kapelle and Ultra, the British intercepted and picked up many agents sent to England. Most of them were converted to British agents, although in most cases the Germans continued to assume that they were working for them. This was done under the so-called XX system. The British also had contacts through Czechoslovakia. In that country, the head of the Czechoslovakian Secret Service, General Frantisek Moravec, had a number of contacts in Germany, the most useful being simply designated as "A-54." The exact position of A-54 in the German military hierarchy was never accurately identified, but he proved to be the most useful agent of all. For this he was to give his life late in the war. When Czechoslovakia was overrun, General Moravec fled to London, where he continued to communicate with A-54.[10]

As the volume of communications coming out of Germany continued to increase, the British listened and sometimes used the information—they did not always trust it—used the contacts the Germans had established, encouraged the Germans to oppose Hitler, but never overtly moved to help the dissidents. This pattern was repeated time and again,

[9] General Hans Speidel was the only one of this group to survive. I have discussed his survival with him, and recently he has confirmed by letter the circumstances:

"In September of 1944 I was confronted with the cousin of Colonel Graf von Stauffenberg, already sentenced to death, Lieutenant-Colonel, Ret., Dr. Caesar von Hofacker. At that time I was under arrest in the basement of the Gestapo headquarters in Berlin. Caesar von Hofacker had—perhaps under the influence of drugs and tortures—denounced me. I pointed out to him that his testimony did not conform with the facts. I was able to communicate with him through my eyes. He recalled the statement, which had been a mistake, and stood up for me in a very noble way."

[10] *Master of Spies—the Memoirs of General Frantisek Moravec.* New York: Doubleday & Company, Inc., 1975.

sometimes with nations as well as with individuals. They were encouraged to take action against Hitler at very great risk, but never did the British intervene. As a high official in the British Foreign Office was to write, "If we could trick the generals into action against the supreme war lord, I was going to have no regrets. A coup by the generals, whether successful or not, even so much as a suspicion of an anti-Hitler conspiracy among them, would all help to hasten Hitler's defeat. I am sorry that the generals ended their lives on Hitler's meat hooks, but I cannot say I have any compunction for having raised false hopes in them."[11] Albion was never more perfidious.

So by mid-November 1944 the German army in Western Europe had taken a very severe mauling. The internal affairs in Germany appeared to be no better, and the Allied high command was well aware of it. The situation suggested that the time had come to maximize the Allied military effort against a decaying German establishment and thus bring a quick end to the war.

Since World War II the most discussed aspect of the war in Europe has been why Eisenhower did not bring the war to an end in the fall of 1944. Obviously the Germans had been badly beaten and were in a rout, scrambling in desperation back to the Fatherland. We also know now that the internal situation in Germany was critical, to say the least. Numerous senior officers wanted to get rid of Hitler and bring the war to an end. And many believed that an accommodation should be sought with the West before Germany was further overrun by the Soviets.

Any plan to defeat the Germans after the summer of 1944 would have had to accomplish the following:

The port of Antwerp had to be opened. Troops should have been allocated to the task as quickly as possible.

The German Fifteenth Army had to be contained at Calais. Montgomery had the troops to accomplish this task, and the Navy should have been directed to cooperate with him.

Next, a decision had to be made whether or not to give first priority to Patton or to Montgomery, both for logistic support and for troop reinforcements. Of the two, Patton was much more feared by the Germans. On the other hand, Montgomery would be methodical and slow and least likely to penetrate deeply and quickly into Germany. In either event the final thrust was certain to draw heavy German reaction on its flanks.

[11] Brown, op. cit.

Finally, General Eisenhower's command of his armies would, of necessity, have to be very active. It was a situation that desperately called for a "hands on" policy. His remote form of generalship, made evident at Messina and Falaise, would not be adequate in this final decisive battle. He would have to take very close control of the Army groups and the Armies.

Obviously, these problems were manageable with the resources Eisenhower had at his disposal. The choice, therefore, had to be between Montgomery and Patton for the final offensive. It seems to me to be overwhelmingly clear that Patton should have been given the task. With it he should have been given priority on troop reinforcements and logistics support. At the same time, Montgomery should have been directed to open the port of Antwerp and to contain Von Zangen's Fifteenth Army at Calais. Montgomery also should have been directed to maintain an aggressive posture against the Germans on his front so as to keep them as heavily involved as his troop strength would allow. Patton should have been directed to penetrate deeply into Germany, the final objective depending on how the battle went. While the capture of Berlin was of great importance, it was not overriding. The destruction of the German armed forces and the surrender of Germany were paramount.[12]

There has been much discussion about Eisenhower's logistic situation in the fall of '44. The expenditures on MARKET-GARDEN alone made it clear that he was not too bad off. The problem was one of distribution and control. There is evidence that the ratio of ammunition to gas and oil delivered to the combat units during the battle of Normandy was continued on into the summer. Thus, when the heavy fighting stopped, the armies left vast dumps of ammunition in their wake when they were running short of gasoline. In any event, by curtailing Montgomery's movement and putting highest priorities on Bradley's Army Group and Patton's Army, the final test of the German capacity to resist further could have been made and, undoubtedly, Germany would have been defeated. Instead, a "broad front" strategy was continued, and a stalemate ensued. Winter was arriving, and snow mixed

12 Correspondence with General Sir Brian Horrocks in 1975 revealed that he was of the opinion that if the above plan had been followed, the time would have come when Patton would have drawn on himself most of the German formations. At that time, Montgomery should have been allowed to make the final thrust to Berlin. It is somewhat analogous to the battle of Normandy when Montgomery drew on himself the major formations and thus permitted Patton to break out into Brittany.

with freezing rain came to the bloody Huertgen Forest, and snow and overcast skies to the high Ardennes.

So far in the war the Allies had been immeasurably aided by the British Secret Service and the OSS. If they continued to receive their help, the Allies would continue to enjoy a tremendous advantage. However, Hitler began to suspect that the Allies had been intercepting his wireless communications. He decided at the end of the summer to discontinue the use of wireless in communicating with the larger formations. This came as a surprise, and a very costly one, to the Allies.

During this time the 82nd Airborne Division was settling into its billets at Suippes and Sissonne. All the troopers who could be spared were given short furloughs, and most of them were off to Paris. They made a good impression. General J. C. H. Lee later told me of a brief conversation he had overheard at SHAEF. One staff officer commented to another, "Those paratroopers are the smartest, most alert-looking soldiers I have seen." The other replied, "Hell, man, they ought to be, you are looking at the survivors." Soon we began to receive replacements, and we opened a parachute jump school. General Ridgway's XVIII Airborne Corps established itself not far away in the town of Epernay. My own headquarters was in an old French barracks at Sissonne. We had assumed in the 82nd that if SHAEF was successful in mounting a large-scale offensive we would probably be used to seize bridgeheads over the Rhine, and if the German situation deteriorated fast enough, we might even be used in the capture of Berlin.

On December 16, 1944, the first indication of trouble in the Ardennes was received with the news of a small penetration along that front. I was concerned because some of the troops in the Ardennes were quite green, and all were spread very thinly. Indeed, they were placed there because they were green, in order to allow them to get some battle experience without their becoming too heavily involved. Later Bradley described it as a "calculated risk."

Early on the evening of December 17, as I was dressing for dinner, I listened to the evening news on the radio. It sounded ominous. Serious German penetrations had been made in the Ardennes area. Knowing our thinness in that area and the paucity of reserves, I was quite concerned. A few moments later, as I was at dinner with the staff at our house in Sissonne, I received a phone call from the Chief of Staff of the XVIII Corps. He was Colonel Ralph Eaton, formerly Chief of Staff of the 82nd

Airborne Division, and we were good friends. He told me that I was the Corps Commander, that General Ridgway was in England. It was news to me. Further, that the XVIII Corps was the SHAEF reserve. Of course, I had to make decisions and move the Corps at once if this was what SHAEF ordered. But I was troubled that I had not been told earlier, and, to the best of my knowledge, we had no existing plans for the movement of the Corps.

Finally, also to my surprise, I learned that Major General Maxwell Taylor was on leave of absence in Washington, D.C. Colonel Eaton then went on to tell me that SHAEF considered the situation on the Ardennes front critical. Further, the 82nd and 101st Airborne Divisions were to be prepared to move twenty-four hours after daylight on the following day. He said that so far he had been unable to get in touch with General Ridgway. I told him to issue orders at once to the Commanding General of the 101st Division, Brigadier General Anthony McAuliffe, to prepare immediately for a movement in accordance with SHAEF's wishes.

I returned to the dinner table, and we continued with small conversation. Once the movement of the Corps began, the staff around me would get very little sleep for the next few days and nights, and we had no idea how the battle would develop in the Ardennes, so I decided not to trouble them during dinner. As soon as dinner was finished, I had the staff assemble in the War Room, where the situation map was posted with the latest information. Fortunately, the division was ready to move, since we had already issued ammunition and food for four days to each of the regiments.

We began the meeting about 8:00 P.M. As well as we could determine, the main German thrusts seemed to be in the direction of St.-Vith, which was still in our hands. At 9:30 P.M. I had another call from the Corps Chief of Staff, who told me that the Corps had orders to move without delay in the direction of Bastogne, where further orders would be issued to them. As Corps Commander, I was to report to General Courtney Hodges, commanding the U.S. First Army, without delay. He was in Spa, Belgium.

We began to prepare our movement orders. Troopers had to be recalled. It appeared that the best time to move would be just after daylight. It would minimize the confusion, and we would arrive in the battle area, it was hoped, before dark. The 82nd was farther from Bastogne than the 101st, but it was in a high state of readiness for the move, and it definitely would be rolling at daylight. The decision seemed unimportant at that time, but it later had considerable significance. I decided therefore to move the 82nd, although it would pass near the area occupied by the 101st, and then to follow it with the 101st. Destination, Bastogne. With the issuance of these orders I had accomplished about all I could at Corps and Division Headquarters.

I left at 11:30 P.M. for Spa. I took with me the Division G-1, Lieutenant Colonel Al Ireland, and an aide, Captain Hugo Olson. Olson had been wounded in Normandy, but he had fully recovered. He was a smart and dependable combat soldier. I had no idea what I was getting into. In fact, it seemed possible that I might encounter German troops before I got to Spa, so we made the trip in an open jeep, prepared for any eventuality. It was a wickedly miserable night. There was a steady light rain, considerable fog, and quite a few bridges were out. I arrived at Spa not long after daylight and reported to General Hodges in person about 9:00 A.M.

We went directly to the War Room, where the Chief of Staff, Major General William Kean, and the G-3, Brigadier "Tubby" Thorsen, were present with General Hodges, the Army Commander. I thought General Hodges seemed a bit weary—he had been through a trying forty-eight hours. General Kean was very much on top of the situation. I had served under Hodges earlier in the Philippine Islands in the 1930s. He was a fine soldier with a distinguished record in World War I, quiet in manner and thoughtful and considerate in his relations with his subordinates. He was highly regarded in the peacetime army.

General Hodges's First Army rested its left flank on the city of Aachen, approximately twenty miles to the north. He had three corps in the line—the VII on the left, the V in the center, and the VIII on the right a frontage of about one hundred miles. The situation on the left was quite stable, although the troops were heavily engaged. The situation on the right appeared to be wide open, how wide open we did not know. We began our discussion with General Kean talking about two regiments of the 106th Division that had been cut off by the German attack. They were in a heavily forested, mountainous area. General Kean discussed the possibility of delivering supplies to them by parachute. Considering the densely forested terrain, the impossible flying weather, and the uncertainty about the exact location of the troops, it seemed to be impractical.

We then went on to discuss the possible employment of the XVIII

Corps. Kean ran his finger over the map, looking for a logical blocking position. He first settled on Bastogne. Many roads radiated from Bastogne, and its possession by the Germans would seem to be essential to the furtherance of their offensive. With the concurrence of General Hodges, he ordered that one division be placed there and that it be under the command of VIII Corps, which had headquarters at Bastogne at that moment. We then examined the map, looking for a suitable position on the northern shoulder of the German offensive, as we understood it at that time. We agreed on the dominating hill mass around the small town of Werbomont, twelve miles southeast of Spa. Since the 82nd was in the lead from Sissonne and Suippes, I ordered it to continue on to Werbomont. The 101st, which was following, was ordered into Bastogne.

In the midst of this discussion, a staff officer walked in and handed a field message to the Chief of Staff. It was one of those small yellow slips of paper used by NCOs to send a message to a platoon leader or a company commander. I was struck at once by how unusual it was to have the Army Commander receive such a message. It was from a noncommissioned officer at an outpost in Stavelot, eight miles away, and it reported that a German armored unit had arrived across the Salm River, engaged his unit by fire, and then demolished the bridge. I thought it was a very important bit of information since it suggested that the unit undoubtedly was a reconnaissance force that had the mission of covering the advance westward of a major formation. Otherwise, it would not have destroyed the bridge; it would have saved it to facilitate the advance northward.

I thought the message was reassuring, but it was neither reassuring nor accurate. The false message was one of the many minor mysteries in the early stages of the Battle of the Bulge. The Germans had sent through the rear areas a number of jeeploads of specially trained English-speaking German soldiers in American uniforms. The uniforms were complete in every detail, including identification tags taken from prisoners and from the dead. These soldiers interrupted communications, cut wires, sent false messages, changed directional road signs, and generally made a nuisance of themselves. M.P.s at key crossroads were soon stopping jeeps and asking soldiers such questions as "Who was the winning pitcher in the final game of the last World Series?" It was all quite baffling to the British.

The bridge at Stavelot had not been blown and, in fact, would not be blown for another thirty-six hours. Furthermore, between Stavelot and Spa was a huge Army supply dump, containing, among other things, more than two million gallons of gasoline. In the meantime, the 1st SS Panzer Division would pass through Stavelot in the direction of Werbomont. It was almost as close to Werbomont as I was at the time and much closer than the 82nd Airborne Division, which was rolling across Belgium in trucks on what was essentially an administrative move. In our state of mind at the moment, it was difficult for us to conceive of the Wehrmacht, having been so badly beaten and having lost all its tanks, trucks, and other equipment a few months before, now being capable of mounting a major offensive, especially in view of the fact that we now had complete control of the air. No factory and no industry could escape the overwhelming effectiveness of our air power, many believed, but the German military establishment survived—indeed was in far better shape than any of us realized—and the 82nd was once again engaged with the Wehrmacht, this time under heavy odds and difficult circumstances.

It all began a day before we parachuted into Holland, September 17, 1944. The location was the Wolf's Lair, Hitler's East Prussian headquarters. The Fuehrer was conducting a daily conference, and Field Marshal Alfred Jodl was ticking off the depressing statistics: shortages of ammunition, shortages of tanks, German troops withdrawing from southern France. Suddenly Hitler interrupted. "I have just made a momentous decision. I shall go over to the counterattack, that is to say—" He pointed to the map unrolled on the desk before him. "Here, out of the Ardennes, with the objective—Antwerp."[13]

His decision came from a deep-seated frustration—a frustration of which every German with military background was becoming increasingly aware. The Germans could not win a military decision as long as they continued to fight a war on two fronts. Stalin was aware of this, and he feared that the Germans might make a deal with the Allies, freeing Germany of the responsibility of waging a war in the West, thus permitting her to throw her total resources against the Russians. To be assured on this point was one of the reasons he constantly urged the Allies to establish a second front.

As the disastrous defeats of the summer of 1944 became clearly

---

[13] *U.S. Army in World War II, European Theater of Operations, The Ardennes: Battle of the Bulge*, Hugh M. Cole, Office of the Chief of Military History, Department of the Army, Washington, D.C., 1965, p. 2.

apparent, the Germans knew that they had to seek a political solution. It was too late to defeat the Russians decisively as Hindenburg had done at Tannenberg in World War I. The Russians in the summer of 1944 had 555 divisions. There was nothing further the Germans could do on the eastern front except to hold as long as possible. A counteroffensive against the Allies, however, might bring about conditions that would cause the Allies to end the bloodletting and accept a solution short of total victory; thus the desperate gamble that Hitler was about to make. When it was all over, senior Allied officers thought it had been utter folly for Hitler to have attempted such a counteroffensive stroke, but it was a gamble that had to be taken. Associated with the gamble, too, was Hitler's hope for new miracle weapons. So the decision was made.

Already desperate measures had been initiated to find the necessary manpower. On August 24 Reich Minister Joseph Goebbels had announced a new mobilization scheme:

> schools and theaters were to be closed down, a 60-hour week to be introduced and holidays temporarily abolished, most types of publications to be suspended, small shops of many types to be closed, the staffs of governmental bureaus to be denuded, and similar belt tightening. By 1 September this drastic comb-out was in full swing and accompanied within the uniformed forces by measures designed to reduce the headquarters staffs and shake loose the "rear area swine," in the Fuehrer's contemptuous phrase.[14]

As for airplanes, tanks, weapons, and ammunition, the Germans were far better off than the Allies had reason to suspect. The United States Strategic Bombing Survey conducted after the war showed that German production of essential war material increased in direct relationship to the Allied bombing tonnage, or even faster. During 1944 more than 40,000 aircraft were produced, three times the production of 1942. Tank production between April and December 1944 was five times the production of 1942, with a peak of 598 tanks in December alone.

Immediately after Hitler's decision, planning was under way. Initially, Hitler kept the planning group very small, so as to protect the secrecy of the operation. The Allies called the operation the Von Rundstedt Offensive. Even today the Belgians, in referring to the battle, speak of time in terms of "before Von Rundstedt" or "after Von

14 Ibid., p. 8.

Rundstedt." Referring to it in his testimony at Nürnberg, Von Rundstedt said, "My entire general staff training revolted against an operation of this sort. If old Von Moltke thought that I had planned this offensive, he would turn in his grave." His attitude had been so gauged by both Eisenhower and Bradley. They assumed that since Von Rundstedt, being the conservative soldier that he was, was in command, an offensive such as that planned by Hitler would not take place.

The German staff estimated that the attack could be launched between November 20 and 30. However, the task of organizing, refitting, re-equipping, and placing the assault forces in position posed some complex and difficult challenges. Nevertheless, the German staff officers went about their work with characteristic thoroughness. As planning moved ahead, Hitler and Jodl estimated that about thirty divisions could be made available, of which twelve would be armored. Most of the professional military people estimated that the best they could hope for would be bridgeheads over the Meuse River. Hitler insisted, however, on the capture of the port of Antwerp. Thus, he would drive a deep wedge between the British forces and the Americans. No specific missions were assigned to the force after the seizure of Antwerp. It was assumed that a political solution to the war might then be sought by the Allies.

As the planning moved along, Hitler insisted that D-day be established at a time when the Allied Air Force would be grounded by weather. Also, at that time of the year daylight was very short. For example, on December 16 in the Ardennes area sunrise was at 8:29, and sunset was at 4:45.

Finally, by December 16, all was in readiness, and bad flying weather was predicted for at least forty-eight hours. The attack jumped off at 5:30 A.M., three hours before daylight, with three German armies abreast on a frontage of about seventy miles. The Sixth Panzer Army was on the north, the Fifth Army in the center, and the Seventh Army on the south. Opposing them were three U.S. divisions: the 99th, which had just arrived on the Continent in November; the 106th, which was considered essentially a green division; the U.S. 28th Division, which had been badly mauled in the Huertgen Forest and was refitting and resting; and a thin cavalry screen manned by the 14th Cavalry Regiment.

The German effort was to be made by the Sixth Panzer Army, commanded by Lieutenant General Sepp Dietrich, a political crony of Hitler's. It consisted of the 1st Panzer Corps and the 2nd Panzer Corps.

It was to attack on a twenty-mile front with the 1st Panzer Corps in the assault, followed in column by the 2nd Panzer Corps. The assault corps, the 1st, consisted of the 1st SS Panzer Division; the 12th SS Panzer Division; and three infantry divisions: the 3rd Parachute, the 12th Volksgrenadier, and the 277th Volksgrenadier. The following corps, the 2nd, had but two divisions, the 2nd Panzer and the 9th SS Panzer. It was a very powerful force attacking on a narrow front. It was equipped with about 500 tanks and armored assault guns, including 90 Tiger tanks. It was like a monstrous steamroller with five divisions, including two Panzers, in the huge front roller, and two Panzer divisions in the smaller rear roller. There had been some discussion in the German General Staff about the old problem of whether to lead the assault with the Panzer formations or to use the infantry divisions for the breakout and then turn the Panzers loose into open country. Field Marshal Model ruled in favor of the latter.

The most inexperienced U.S. division of all, the 99th, received the full weight of the Sixth Panzer Army. Part of it flowed over onto the northern shoulder of the 106th Division. Considering the extent to which they were surprised, the Americans fought well and kept fighting delaying actions as they fell back or were surrounded and killed or captured. Hitler had figured on a complete breakthrough for the armor in the first twenty-four hours, followed by a race to the crossings over the Meuse River which were to be reached on the third day. From the outset, however, serious delays were encountered.

The 1st SS Panzer Division, the Leibstandarte Adolph Hitler (Hitler's Bodyguard), was picked for the key assault role. Its leading battle group was commanded by a twenty-eight-year-old colonel, Jochen Peiper, a tough, ruthless, daring commander who had made quite a reputation for himself on the eastern front. Sepp Dietrich, who commanded the German main effort, hand-picked Peiper for the decisive role. To get an accurate measure of the performance that could be expected of his tanks, Peiper had rehearsed a night drive of fifty miles well behind the German lines. He was fanatically dedicated to the accomplishment of any task and obviously intended to brook no obstacles in accomplishing this one. His division had been badly depleted in mid-October, but by the time of the Ardennes attack it had been built up to 250 tanks. He had been given first pick of reinforcements and new tanks. His division was poised and eager behind the 12th Volksgrenadier Division, which made the initial infantry assault. As the American green troops fought valiantly, Peiper's impatience rose in direct relationship to the delay imposed on the Volksgrenadiers. Earlier, as an indication of his impatience with any delay, he had passed on information to his officers that "no time was to be wasted with prisoners."

He fretted as D-day wore on and the Americans did not collapse. By two o'clock in the afternoon of D-day he could delay no longer, and he went forward to see what could be done. The roads were clogged with traffic, and a key bridge was out. He decided to switch routes and move over behind the 3rd Parachute Division, which seemed to be making progress. At best this is very difficult to do. Behind every combat infantry division in an attack, the roads are clogged with ambulances taking wounded back, ammunition and supply vehicles going forward, artillery being displaced forward, command vehicles. Nevertheless, Peiper forced his tanks through the traffic, and by midnight of D-day he was pressing the 3rd Parachute Division to get on with the advance. Impatiently he went forward and asked a young SS Panzer colonel the cause of the delay. He was told that there were about 1000 American defenders in front. Not having received satisfactory answers to his further questions, Peiper demanded a battalion of troops and said he would lead the breakthrough. As he explained it later, "I lost my temper and demanded that the parachute regiment give me a battalion and I would lead the breakthrough." He did; with half the parachute infantry riding his tanks and the others proceeding along the sides of the roads, he moved ahead aggressively. He moved ahead without opposition, was now well into the rear area, and reached the outskirts of Honsfeld just before dawn without having fired a shot. Honsfeld had been a rest area for the 99th Division, and the only combat group there was one troop from the U.S. 14th Cavalry. Within a short time Peiper had captured fifty reconnaissance vehicles, including half-tracks, quite a number of trucks, and antitank guns from the troops in the town. He had a map showing a large supply dump in the town of Büllingen off to the north; he seized the dump and then, to the amazement of American forces, who witnessed his approach and who expected to receive the full weight of his armored attack, he swung back south. By midmorning of December 17 he believed that he had achieved a complete breakthrough.

Sometime just after noon his leading tanks ran into an American truck convoy moving to the south just across his advance. It was part of the U.S. 7th Armored Division which General Hodges had ordered to St.-

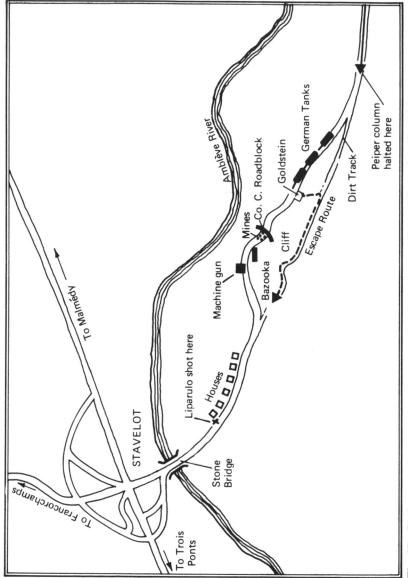

Fig. 15   Engineers at Stavelot (Company C Roadblock at Stavelot Night of December 17, 1944)

Vith. The sudden appearance of the German Panzers took the truck convoy completely by surprise. It was Battery B of the 285th Field Artillery Observation Battalion. The leading Panzers shot up the convoy and then went on, leaving the Americans to be taken care of by the Germans who were following. It took about two hours for the Germans to round up and assemble the wounded and dazed survivors in a snow-covered field. At a given signal the Germans fired machine-gun and pistol fire into the Americans until they were satisfied they had killed them all. Those who appeared to be only wounded or made sounds were sought out and shot through the head. It was an outright massacre. A few escaped by feigning death; at least eighty-six Americans had been killed.

Later, irrefutable evidence established the fact that Peiper's column had shot down nineteen unarmed Americans in Honsfeld and fifty in Büllingen. His Panzers murdered unarmed Belgian civilians also, and as his Panzer columns went forward he left in his wake a bloody trail of horror unmatched in a war that had seen just about everything. (Peiper was later tried as a war criminal.) By dusk he reached the high ground overlooking Stavelot.

Peiper's arrival immediately south of Stavelot brought him, for the first time, up against a force that was to prove to be as effective as a good combat division. They were the Engineer troops of the U.S. First Army, specifically the 296th, the 291st, and the 51st Engineers. B Company of the 291st Engineers had established a roadblock south of Malmédy. Although Peiper had avoided Malmédy in his eagerness to move to the west, several of the survivors had crawled into the outpost, and word of the massacre quickly spread. Most of the Engineers had been based near Trois Ponts.

On December 17 an Engineer squad from the 291st was detailed to establish a roadblock at Stavelot. The traffic on the road between the two towns was heavy, and they had difficulty making their way. They arrived at Stavelot about 6:30 P.M., well after dark. They crossed the bridge and ascended the hill on the far side. The squad was under the command of Sergeant Charles Hensel. They came to a point near the top of the hill where the road made a sharp turn to the right around a rock cliff. Sergeant Hensel decided that that would be a good place for a roadblock. (*Fig. 15.*) They strung their mines across the road. He sent Private Bernard Goldstein ahead to give the alarm on the approach of the Germans. Behind the mines, as a covering force, he deployed a bazooka team and a .30-caliber machine gun.

It was now nearing 7:30 P.M. Goldstein partially concealed himself behind a cement building when he heard the approach of the tanks. They were moving very slowly, and he could hear the German soldiers talking. Sergeant Hensel was approaching Goldstein with another man when, to his disbelief, he heard Goldstein, in good GI fashion, challenge the tanks with a loud, commanding "Halt." The Germans reacted instantly, spraying the area with small-arms fire and firing their tank guns in the direction of the challenge. Incredibly, Goldstein escaped and finally made his way back to his squad, which by then had assembled near the bridge, close to 9:00 P.M. There was considerable confusion about the bridge, and no one was exactly sure who was responsible for what happened. Explosives had been placed, but the bridge was not blown. Among the Engineers at the bridge site was a Company from the 202nd Engineers. Janice Holt Giles, in her superb book, *The Damned Engineers,* upon which this account of the Engineers has been based, tells a story about the bridge:

> When the war ended, the 202nd Engineers Combat Battalion was guarding prisoners at Le Havre. One day Sergeant Josephs and a companion were walking past the POW cage and a prisoner called out to them in good English, "What outfit are you with?"
> "202nd Engineers."
> The prisoner laughed. "You were at Stavelot. I can tell you why that bridge wouldn't blow the night of December 17. We fixed it so it wouldn't."[15]

This well could have happened, for there were quite a few Germans wandering around in American uniforms, making a nuisance of themselves during those fateful days. At daylight Peiper descended to the bridge over the Amblève, crossed it, and entered Stavelot. Before doing so, however, he sent one Panzer company in the direction of Trois Ponts along a very poor road on the south side of the Amblève River. Considerable firing took place in Stavelot, and it was heard clearly at Trois Ponts, where the Engineers were busily preparing the bridge for demolition.

Trois Ponts is located where the Salm River pours into the Amblève. From there the Amblève meanders northward through a deeply forested

15 Janice Holt Giles, *The Damned Engineers.* Boston: Houghton Mifflin Co., 1970.

canyon. During the night of December 17 a 57 mm. antitank gun, towed by a half-track, belonging to the 526th Armored Infantry, had slithered off the road near Trois Ponts when the half-track became disabled. The Engineers took over the gun, since it was the only antitank weapon they had, other than bazookas. A 57 mm. antitank gun, known as a six-pounder to the British, since it throws a six-pound projectile, is not very effective against the frontplate of a Panther. Its best hope is to hit a track or in some way get a side shot. Nevertheless, the crew went into position to cover the approaches to the bridges in Trois Ponts. At 10:45 Peiper's column was sighted rapidly approaching from Stavelot. The 57 mm. opened up and disabled the first Peiper tracked vehicle. It was a Panther tank. The next Panther opened fire, knocked out the gun, and killed all four members of the gun crew. Within seconds the Engineers blew the first bridge, the bridge over the Amblève.

Peiper had no choice but to turn up the gorge of the Amblève River toward the small town of La Gleize. There was a small stone bridge over the Amblève at Cheneux. If he could get to that and cross there, he still could get to Werbomont. The bridge was unprepared and undefended. There remained one other bridge, and that was over Lienne Creek in the valley below Werbomont. In the meantime the separate Panzer company they sent along the south bank of the Amblève made it to Trois Ponts. It was seen approaching the crossings over the Salm by the Engineers, and they blew the first bridge at 1:00 P.M. in the face of the Panzers and then blew the second a short distance down the Salm River at 2:00 P.M. In the case of the second bridge, an Engineer waited until the Germans were actually on the bridge. There was a scramble for the Engineers to get out of the area and away from the German fire, which was heavy. Nevertheless, the Engineer in charge managed to get together a group of Engineers, whom he at once dispatched to Habiemont to block again, if they could, the advance of Peiper. The work of the Engineers had been superb. They were courageous and resourceful. Little wonder that ". . . Peiper could only sit with leaden heart and face the fact that time and his luck had entirely run out on him. . . . And he could only sit helplessly, pound his knee and swear bitterly, 'The damned engineers! The damned engineers!' "[16]

To add to his difficulties, the weather cleared a bit and his long tank columns were spotted by a light observation plane from the First Army. For the first time in the battle they brought in Air Force fighter-

[16] Ibid., frontispiece.

bombers. They inflicted considerable damage and delay on his column. Nevertheless, he crossed the bridge at Cheneux and raced on toward Werbomont, which was very close.

In the meantime I was just leaving the First Army headquarters in Spa. I, too, was hurrying to Werbomont, to place the 82nd in a blocking position as soon as it arrived.

Immediately following the conference with General Hodges and his staff, I left Spa by jeep and drove to Werbomont. I arrived at Werbomont by midafternoon and immediately made a reconnaissance of the entire area. It offered excellent defense possibilities. In the course of my reconnnaissance I went down to the foot of the hill to the town of Habiemont. There I met a lieutenant with a detachment of Engineers. They had prepared the heavy masonry bridge over Lienne Creek for demolition. Quite a few civilians carrying bundles of clothing and bedding were coming down the hill from the direction of Trois Ponts. They were excited, and all stated that the Germans had passed Trois Ponts and that they were coming this way. I drove along Lienne Creek in the direction of the Amblève River and encountered no signs of the enemy. However, I did find a small bridge intact near the town of Forges. It was about a quarter of a mile from the main bridge at Habiemont. It did not appear to be strong enough to take heavy tanks. Nevertheless, when I returned to Habiemont, I asked the lieutenant about it. He said that he needed all the explosives he had to blow the Habiemont bridge and that he could not divert any explosives to the bridge I had found; further, that he did not think it was an important bridge. Satisfied that I had accomplished about all I could before the troops were due to arrive later that evening, I decided to drive south to Bastogne and there issue General McAuliffe his orders in person. Besides, I wanted to find out more about what was actually happening from the VIII Corps.

It took about an hour to drive to Bastogne. As I approached Corps headquarters, there was considerable confusion. Vehicles were being loaded, and members of the staff seemed to be hurrying away. Corps headquarters was in a schoolhouse. I met General Troy Middleton, the Corps Commander, and had a short conversation with him. I also talked to members of his staff. They had no solid information except that the situation was quite fluid and that they were leaving. The 28th Division evidently had been overrun, and they were uncertain about what had happened to it. I talked to some of the 28th Division officers, who were quite depressed and disturbed, not knowing the whereabouts of their division.

At about this time General McAuliffe arrived. I gave him his orders to put the 101st Airborne Division in Bastogne and to organize the city for all-around defense and to stay there until he got further orders, reporting to the Commander of the XVIII Corps. Having gotten about all the information I could from Corps headquarters, which was very little, and having given McAuliffe his orders that I had received from the Commanding General of the First Army, I left, driving north through Houffalize shortly after dark. I understood from other people who drove the same road that I just missed the spearhead of some German columns passing through Houffalize, moving to the west. I arrived at Werbomont at about 8:00 P.M., just about the time the first vehicles of the 82nd began to arrive.

While I was in Bastogne, Peiper's Panzer column had moved across the bridge over the Amblève River at Cheneux. It was well after sundown when he went through the small town of Rahier, halfway to Habiemont. If he could get the bridge at Habiemont, he would then be clearly in the open for a fast run to the Meuse during the night. The Engineers, however, had put together a demolition team commanded by Lieutenant Alvin Edelstein. They hastily prepared the bridge with explosives. They then located the detonator a short distance away, where the man in charge, Corporal Fred R. Chapin, would be able to see the signal from Lieutenant Edelstein if he was to blow the bridge. It was important that the bridge be saved for our own purposes if the Germans did not approach it. So the Engineers watched carefully in the early dusk for the approaching Panzers.

Finally, the form of a long, slow-moving column of tanks began to take shape. As it got nearer, the Panzers fired an 88 as a warning to those near the bridge to leave. The psychological experience of being on the receiving end of an 88 is devastating. The projectile has an extremely high velocity, and on impact fragments fly in all directions. Corporal Chapin ducked and stayed, watching for the signal from the lieutenant. Finally the lieutenant frantically signaled for him to blow the bridge. He depressed the plunger and then saw a streak of blue lights and a heaving blast of dust and debris. The bridge was blown. The Germans opened up with all their weapons from the far side, but by then it was too late. They turned back in the direction of Rahier.

Following this encounter, an infantry battalion of the 30th Division deployed along Lienne Creek to secure the Werbomont area for the arrival of the 82nd Airborne Division. Its deployment was generally toward the north toward the Amblève River, where the remainder of the 30th Division was slowly closing in on Peiper's column. They left a platoon at the site of the Habiemont bridge. The platoon leader put several men in foxholes near the road, covering the bridge site. The remainder of the platoon went to the upper story of a nearby house. In the middle of the night they heard the sound of tracks and the approaching German Panzers. Evidently, although the main bridge at Habiemont had been destroyed, the Germans had found that they could cross the smaller bridge farther to the north with light vehicles. They now moved cautiously toward the main road to Werbomont.

As they neared the roadblock, a soldier from the upper story of the house saw them and fired a bazooka into the lead vehicle. I talked to him about it later. Evidently the back blast of the bazooka was a tremendous shock to those in the room from which he was firing. Nevertheless, the combination of the fire from above and the small-arms fire from the road caused the Germans to make a hasty withdrawal, abandoning their vehicles. However, they did take some of the Americans with them as prisoners, probably for identification purposes.

When I arrived in Werbomont earlier in the evening, I established a Command Post in a farmhouse a few hundred yards off the main road. As the 82nd troopers arrived, they were deployed around Werbomont into combat positions. Trucks continued to arrive all during the night, the last before daylight on December 19. In the meantime, having been up for two nights and two days, I fell asleep on the floor of the farmhouse sometime around midnight. It was a restless night. I knew that combat was imminent and that the troops were moving into position under cover of darkness; I hoped they were properly disposed for whatever daylight would bring. I knew that I had to get some sleep if I was to be effective the following day—a day that might prove to be critical. After a few hours' sleep I awakened and checked on the situation with Colonel John Norton, the G-3, and members of the staff. They told me of the action that had taken place near the Habiemont bridge during the night. Other than that, the 82nd had had no contact with the Germans. As soon as it was light enough to see, I drove down to the Habiemont bridge.

About a half mile from the bridge I passed the last 82nd trooper in a foxhole, so I parked the jeep beside the road and went ahead on foot.

There was absolute quiet. The trooper thought that there might have been Germans ahead, but he was not certain. As I moved along, I felt as though I were in no-man's land. There is a peculiar stillness and lack of activity beyond one's own front lines until you encounter the enemy. Combat veterans sense this condition quickly as they become intensely cautious and listen, seemingly with every pore of their bodies.

I came on five knocked-out German armored vehicles, including armored cars and self-propelled guns, with several German dead lying along the road. There were no dead Americans anywhere in sight. This was the scene of the action during the night. I returned to the 82nd Command Post and then visited the deployed regiments.

The arena (*Fig. 16*) in which the 82nd was to join the 1st SS in battle, and the German 9th SS, the German 2nd SS, and the 62nd Volksgrenadier Division in turn, is a huge square of approximately ten miles on a side. It begins with Werbomont in the northwest corner. From Werbomont moving to the east the mountains fall off sharply to the small town of Habiemont, which is on Lienne Creek, three miles away. The creek is about 273 yards above sea level at this point, and the mountainous terrain throughout the area varies from this elevation to well over 547 yards, changing unexpectedly and precipitately as one moves across country. From Habiemont a good paved road moves over a high mountain to the key town of Trois Ponts about seven miles away. From Trois Ponts to La Gleize the Amblève River meanders through high forested hills northward. From Trois Ponts southward flows the Salm River, all the way to Vielsalm, a key city diagonally across the 100-square-mile area from Werbomont. One and a third miles to the southwest of Vielsalm is a dominating terrain feature, Thier Dumont. This mountain dominates the area for many miles. Along its southern side was a paved road all the way to the western end of the division's area of responsibility, and the towns of Fraiture and Manhay. This was an excellent position for defense. Between four and five miles south of Werbomont, moving eastward, one encounters a uniform hill mass dominated by heavy pine growth, with few trails throughout.

The snow began to fall a few days after we moved into the locality. This made these mountain areas almost impassable, although the infantry fought through them throughout the battle. The southern slopes of this hill mass, extending from Tri-la-Cheslaing to Bra and then to Fosse and Bergeval, was a superb position. From that area there is a clear view of the valley extending to Lierneux and on to Vielsalm. In the

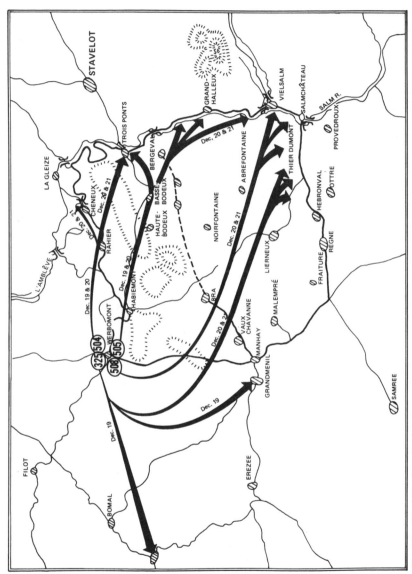

Fig. 16   82nd Deploys in Belgium

eastern part of the valley, massive hills again rise just north of Abrefontaine. An analysis of the terrain made it clear that the key defensive position had to be the dominating terrain from Fraiture to Salmchâteau. To support those positions, the artillery and supporting services had to be in the valley to the north and in the wooded hills beyond. The loss of Malempré or of Vielsalm, followed by a penetration of the valley toward Lierneux by the Germans, would make the southern position of the 100-square-mile area untenable. In turn the occupation of the foothills extending from Bra through Fosse and including Abrefontaine afforded another good defensive position. Supporting artillery could be placed behind the hill mass several miles to the north. The next good defensive position extended from Werbomont to the very high hill mass on the northern banks of the Amblève River. There were a few key north and south roads in the area. The Habiemont-Lierneux highway provided access to and from the battle area for all artillery and service vehicles. The Werbomont-Manhay-Fraiture road provided access to all the rear areas to any enemy who could advance up that highway. The heavily forested hills on one hand offered excellent cover for defenders; on the other hand they required considerable troop density to defend because of the cover they afforded an attacking enemy.

The entire area began to go under snow just before Christmas, and by the time the battle for control of the area ended early in January, the high hills were waist-deep in snow. It was an extremely challenging prospect, from a tactical point of view, for the division to be pitted against the best of the German divisions leading the main effort toward the Meuse in this snow-blanketed and difficult terrain. But this is an after-the-battle analysis of the terrain; on December 19, full of confidence, we were advancing rapidly to attack.

The XVIII Airborne Corps opened its headquarters just north of the 82nd headquarters in Werbomont on December 19. We immediately came under the command of that Corps. I was delighted to see General Matthew Ridgway and his Corps back in action. He was a fine man to serve under in combat, undoubtedly the best combat corps commander in the American Army in World War II. He was very demanding of his subordinates, but he made a point of knowing what was going on by getting out and spending time with the combat troops. Among his first orders to the 82nd was to get troops deployed well out from Werbomont.

Ridgway's orders were for the 82nd to deploy in the direction of

Trois Ponts, Vielsalm, and to open communications through Vielsalm with St.-Vith and the U.S. 7th Armored Division, whose headquarters was in St.-Vith. Detachments of the 325th were also sent well to the west. Because I wanted to make the most of the short period of daylight, I assembled all the battalion commanders, as well as the regimental commanders, at the Division Command Post for the issuance of orders. The 504th would be deployed from Cheneux near the Amblève River to Trois Ponts. There the 505th was to take up a front south to Grand-Halleux. The 508th was to pick up at Vielsalm, occupy Thier Dumont, and protect its flank to the west. The remains of the 325th were kept in division reserve. The regiments moved rapidly out of their defensive positions around Werbomont during darkness. There was so much uncertainty and so many rumors about the Germans, however, that they did not reach their final objectives until the next day.

I began to realize during the day that some of our troops had not arrived at Werbomont during the night; in fact, it was several days before the entire division was rounded up. In the meantime, on December 19, the 325th Glider Infantry sent troops to Barvaux, approximately thirteen miles to the west, and also to Grandmenil and Manhay, ten miles to the south. The 505th sent troops to Habiemont and then on to Basse-Bodeux and Trois Ponts. The 504th moved in the direction of Rahier. The 325th Glider Infantry, minus a battalion, was kept near Werbomont in division reserve. There were still a great number of unknowns in the situation on December 19. We were aware that a Panzer column seemed to be bottled up in La Gleize, and that the U.S. 7th Armored had been fighting a brilliant delaying action around St.-Vith, nine miles beyond Vielsalm. The moves made on December 19 were prudent and designed to get information and gain contact with the enemy, all under such conditions that we kept the initiative and maintained control of all the division, even though it was being scattered over 100 square miles of terrain.

Shortly after daylight on December 20 I met Colonel Reuben Tucker, commanding the 504th, in the small town of Rahier. He told me that he had learned from civilians that approximately 125 vehicles, including 30 tanks, had moved through the town the afternoon before, going in the direction of Cheneux. It was an interesting bit of information. Obviously, this was one of the armored columns of the 1st SS that had attempted to cross at Lienne Creek at Habiemont and then had turned back. I discussed the situation with Tucker; he was anxious to go after them without delay. Any ordinary infantry regiment would want at least a battalion of tanks in support before it attacked, but Tucker's idea was to attack the Germans and take their armor away from them. He figured he would then have his own. Besides, he had been carrying with him about a truckload of panzerfausts he had captured from the Germans in Holland, and they were to prove to be the paratroops' best antitank weapon.

(One of the disturbing aspects of this was that the U.S. troops in Sicily had used the 2.36-inch bazooka, and many of them had been killed because they were not effective against German armor. The Germans captured a number of them and immediately applied the principle on which they were based to the development of their own weapons. In Normandy I first came across weapons labeled "faustpetrone." It was a small warhead of approximately 3 inches, made like the bazooka round, but it was on a wooden stem. By the time we got to Holland, the Germans had developed a 6-inch warhead on a wooden stem that could be fired from a pipe about 3 inches in diameter. Only the stem was inserted in the pipe. It could penetrate the frontplate of any known tank and was an extremely effective weapon for many uses. Even as late as 1950, at the time of the beginning of the Korean War, the U.S. Army had not placed into the hands of its troops a weapon any better than those that had failed them in Sicily.)

So, with his German panzerfausts and his superb infantry, Tucker moved at once to attack the Panzer forces in Cheneux. We particularly wanted to capture the bridge over the Amblève. Initial contact with the Germans was made at the western exit of Cheneux by a patrol which had been sent from Rahier by the 1st Battalion of the 504th. They fired on a German motorcyclist who was accompanied by a small foot patrol. This, in turn, was followed by approximately a company of Germans moving along both sides of the road. Heavy fighting took place, lasting all day long. I was present during the attack, and the German fire power was impressive. They were using a great many 20 mm. flak weapons that infantry find most uncomfortable to be exposed to. Colonel Tucker had deployed the 1st Battalion of the 504th against the Germans trying to exit from Cheneux. It was a hard fight, and as darkness descended on the battlefield, Companies B and C were under tremendous fire from the village. Not to be daunted, Colonel Tucker ordered the Battalion Commander, Lieutenant Colonel Willard E. Harrison, to make a night attack. Harrison had parachuted with me in Normandy, and he was a very courageous soldier. They now had two tank destroyers, which made them feel equal to just about anything they would meet. As they pushed toward Cheneux, they came across well-organized defenses surrounded by barbed wire. The force opposing them turned out to be the 2nd SS Panzer Grenadier Regiment heavily reinforced by mobile flak pieces, mortars, machine guns, and assault artillery.

> To breast this heavy fire and rush the four hundred yards of open terrain, the two companies attacked in four waves at intervals of about fifty yards. The moment the leading American assault waves could be discerned through the darkness the enemy opened an intense, accurate fire. Twice the attackers were driven back, both times with gaping ranks. The first two waves were almost completely shot down. Company C ran into the wire and, having no wire cutters available, was stalled momentarily. Finally the two tank destroyers worked their way to the front and began to shell the German guns. With their support a third assault was thrown at the village. This time a few men lived to reach the outlying houses. In a brief engagement at close quarters the Americans silenced some of the flak and machine guns, then set up a defense to guard this slight toehold until reinforcements could arrive.[17]

The battalion commander set up his Command Post in a house on the edge of the town. During the night Tucker decided to make a wide envelopment of the town, using his 3rd Battalion, commanded by Lieutenant Colonel Julian Cook, the battalion that had made the daylight crossing over the Rhine River in folding canvas boats three months before. They made a wide flanking movement over very rough ground; the move took six hours, but by late afternoon they were overlooking the bridge across the Amblève. They cut off Germans in the town and completely destroyed their command. It had been costly. Tucker had lost 225 dead and wounded, mostly from the two assault companies. Company B had eighteen men left and no officers. Company C had thirty-eight men and three officers. Few Germans were captured. The rear guard fought to the end, but most of the Cheneux garrison still living escaped during the night.

Tucker captured fourteen flak wagons and a battery of 105 howitzers as well as many vehicles. The 504th was proud of the battle. The troopers had actually jumped aboard the flak wagons and in hand-

---

[17] *U.S. Army in World War II, European Theater of Operations,* op. cit., p. 352.

to-hand combat had taken them over. When I went over the battlefield with them the next day, they pointed out that they were now the 504th Parachute Armored Regiment. It had been costly; the Germans were well equipped and gave us a good fight.

Farther to the east the 505th Parachute Infantry, to their amazement, found Engineers still in occupation of Trois Ponts. They quickly established themselves on the bank of the Salm River, extending their right flank as far south as Grand-Halleux.

The battalion assigned to the Trois Ponts sector was Lieutenant Colonel Ben Vandervoort's 2nd Battalion of the 505th Parachute Infantry. It was the battalion that had destroyed the German Kampfgruppe that attempted to move from Cherbourg to Ste.-Mère-Eglise in Normandy. It was also the battalion that, attacking from rooftop to rooftop, destroyed the German bridgehead holding the southern end of the Nijmegen bridge. It was an aggressive, tough, battle-seasoned battalion.

The Engineers were still occupying the west bank of the Salm River, harassing the Germans on the far side, when Vandervoort was ordered up. Vandervoort had been called to the Regimental Command Post of the 505th to receive his orders. There he met the Assistant Division Commander of the 82nd, Brigadier General Ira Swift. He was instructed as follows: (*Fig. 17.*)

No one knows what is in Trois Ponts. The 2nd Battalion 505 is to move east on the Trois Ponts road and, if possible, enter Trois Ponts. If the battalion occupies the town, it should then try to seize positions overlooking the riverbank; they should then try to establish a bridge-head on the high ground on the other side, but not to commit more than one company to the task. The remainder of the battalion is to be deployed so as to prevent the enemy from crossing the river—if he was not already on our side.

Very "iffy" orders, but the situation was just as vague to the 505th at that moment. Vandervoort's battalion moved out with troops in columns on each side of the paved road, crossing over the mountain and down into the town where, to their surprise, they met the Engineers. It was early afternoon, December 20. Except for a few women and children the town was deserted. At that point the Salm River was no more than a dozen yards wide, easily fordable, but the steep banks made it a formidable obstacle for vehicles. Near the railroad station they found a

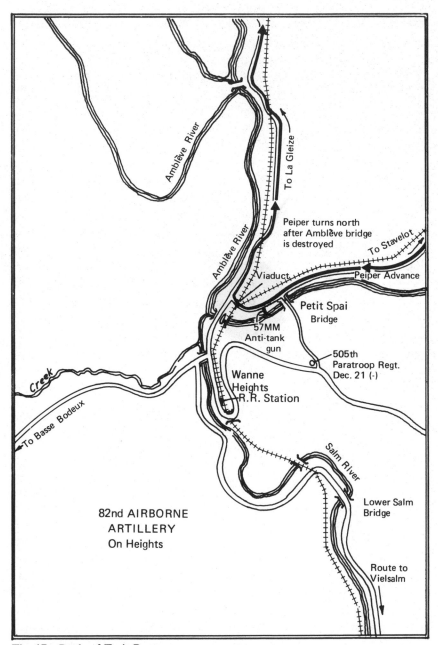

Fig. 17   Battle of Trois Ponts

bridge intact, and D Company was sent across to the far side. It occupied a high hill that overlooked Trois Ponts to its rear. Ahead there was a large open field where they could see the Stavelot road. D Company dug in at once, placing its six bazookas on the right flank where there was a road and good tank country. Beyond the main line of resistance were placed some antitank mines. By darkness they were dug in and ready for whatever the night would bring.

At about 3:00 A.M. a German armored reconnaissance vehicle approached the right flank. It was knocked out by the bazookas. Troopers then moved the minefield to the other side of the knocked-out German vehicle. Less than an hour later a second German armored car came up and was blown up on the mines. At daylight the 1st SS Panzer Infantry hit their position with a rather mild, feeling attack which was driven back by fire. Vandervoort could see the German troops and armor, and he was amazed by what he saw. He reported to Regiment that he was confronted by the 1st SS Panzer Division; the identification had been made on the bodies of the Panzers they had killed during the night. In midmorning a German infantry attack supported by four or five tanks was launched against D Company. As he told me later, "The attack culminated with some very young German soldiers dead among the D Company foxholes and others taken prisoner. The battalion intelligence officer, who spoke German fluently, asked the prisoners why they had come straight across the open ground—shouting and yelling. They replied that that was what they had been doing since the start of their offensive, and up to now everybody had run away or surrendered."

When Vandervoort reported to Regimental Headquarters that he was confronted by the 1st SS Panzer Division, Regiment was skeptical. Vandervoort's holding of this key corner position was of the utmost importance to General Hodges and the First U.S. Army. As long as Vandervoort held, they were confident that they could destroy Colonel Peiper's Kampfgruppe, and having done that, they could then turn all their power against the remainder of the 1st SS Panzer Division. The 1st SS was given top priority before the German offensive began and it was the best-equipped division in the German Army. Skepticism about Vandervoort's ability to hold it was well founded, but Vandervoort was certain that it could be held, thanks to the very difficult terrain that the Panzers were up against, as well as the paratroopers of his veteran battalion.

By now a massive attack was being mounted by the Germans. Vandervoort moved across the river to D Company to get the situation firsthand. He asked for permission to pull back D Company or to take the remainder of his battalion across to help them. Without orders to do so, he had F Company cross the river well below the position of D Company for the purpose of attacking the German troops on the flank, thus spoiling their planned attack against D Company. F Company's mission was to withdraw across the river once it had accomplished its purpose.

The weight of the German attack, however, was on such a scale that F Company harassment didn't deter the Germans one bit. It was obvious that D Company would be surrounded and cut off in very short order, so Vandervoort issued the classic tactical order, "Let's get the hell out of here." He would have much preferred to wait until darkness to withdraw D Company, but the weight of the German attack made clear that they would be wiped out, surrounded, and captured by that time. There were just too many Panzers on top of them. The withdrawal was a scramble down the bluff and across the river; many not killed or wounded made it. They did lose the one 57 mm. that they had taken over. From then on, the 2nd Battalion 505 was satisfied to hold the riverbank and deny several vigorous efforts by the Germans to force a crossing. The Germans did not make it.

I had heard of the action and went to Vandervoort's Command Post at once. He laughed as I walked in; he knew that I had made it a practice to visit battalions that were in trouble, and he reasoned that I had decided that the 2nd Battalion was having a hard time of it. There was considerably more to it than this. General Hodges, commanding the First Army, had asked General Ridgway of the XVIII Corps if the 1st SS Panzer Division could be kept from linking up with Peiper, who was in a cul-de-sac at Stoumont-la-Gleize. Ridgway, in turn, had asked me if I could hold them off. I assured him that we could do so. I decided that it might be necessary to move troops from other parts of the 82nd area to fight the 1st SS at Trois Ponts, but they could be stopped. It was with this in mind that I went to the Command Post to talk to Vandervoort. He described the situation on the far bank, emphasizing the numerous tanks and flak vehicles that they had encountered. Nevertheless, with the river between them and the Germans, he assured me that they would not get across. Knowing him from our extensive combat experience together, I felt there was no question but that he would hold it, and I so reported to Ridgway. Colonel Ekman's 505th was positioned southward along the Salm River and soon linked up with patrols from the 7th Armored Division that were aggressively patrolling along the east bank of the Salm.

The 508th Parachute Infantry moved in the direction of Vielsalm and Salmchâteau, occupying the high ground at Thier Dumont. On December 21 I visited the Command Post of the U.S. 106th Infantry Division at Renceveaux, a small town just west of Vielsalm. General Alan W. Jones was the division commander, and as I entered his Command Post, he was the picture of dejection. I felt very sorry for him. Outside his Command Post, which was in a schoolhouse with a large parking area nearby, were dozens of trucks, trailers, and other divisional vehicles. I was impressed and a bit envious at how new the equipment looked. There were two huge trailers containing doughnut-making machines and all kinds of vans and administrative vehicles. I could not recall when I had seen such fine-looking new equipment before. It was understandable, since the division had recently come from the United States. General Jones was depressed by the loss of two of his infantry regiments. They had been overrun several days before. He was uncertain of what he had remaining, but in any event he had placed his command under the leadership of the Commanding General of the 7th Armored, Bob Hasbrouck.

I crossed the river into Vielsalm and there went to the Command Post of the 7th Armored. The division had been fighting a tremendous action day and night for the past four or five days. The integrity of its defenses was intact, and it was beating back several German divisions that were beginning to flow around its flanks in their efforts to move west. Obviously it could not maintain its present position much longer without reinforcements. Hasbrouck had been able to get a staff officer through to First Army on the morning of December 20. With him he sent a letter outlining his situation and telling them that he needed reinforcements. The linkup with the 82nd reassured him for the first time that he could either be reinforced or, if the First Army decided, withdrawn through the 82nd gateway at Vielsalm.

So far the 82nd was in good shape, with the regiments in line, beginning with the 504th on the left. It opposed Colonel Peiper's 1st SS, which was across the Amblève River heavily engaged by the 30th Infantry Division. The 505th was extended from Trois Ponts to Grand-Halleux. It was opposing the remainder of the 1st SS Panzer Division, which wanted desperately to link up with Peiper. The 508th extended our front from Grand-Halleux to Salmchâteau and there occupied Thier Dumont. Part of the 325th was on the right of the 508th and part kept in reserve. By the evening of December 21 only the 504th and 505th had been heavily engaged. The Division Reconnaissance Platoon had sent patrols to the south and there established contact with some German Panzers moving west.

On December 21 I discussed the situation with General Ridgway. He expressed the view that the St.-Vith forces would probably be withdrawn through the 82nd. He then instructed me to make a reconnaissance of the divisional area with the view to withdrawing to a good defensive position after the extrication of the St.-Vith forces. Since there was no pressure on us around Vielsalm, Salmchâteau, or Thier Dumont, it seemed to me that we should not give up the Thier Dumont line until we were forced to do so. It was an excellent defensive position, but I was quite concerned about my right flank. That would be unsettled until I could get in touch with the 3rd Armored Division on my right. I made the reconnaissance as General Ridgway had directed, and it was quite clear that a new line from Trois Ponts-Basse-Bodeux-Bra to Manhay offered us an excellent defensive position.

Because of the threat to the 82nd Airborne Division right flank and the importance of controlling the main highway from Fraiture to Manhay, I went to call on Major General Maurice Rose, commanding the 3rd Armored Division, at his Command Post at Manhay. General Rose sought to assure me that he would cover our right flank, but he was somewhat preoccupied with his mission that would extend his division far to the west in a covering role. He wasn't quite certain how demanding it would be. He told me that he would let me know if there were any changes in his dispositions. I returned to the division and ordered the 325th to extend its right flank and seize and hold the small town of Regne.

On the afternoon of December 22 we had our first contact with the Germans coming from the south. A force of approximately one hundred vehicles, preceded by about twenty-five tanks, advanced north through Ottre. The tanks entered the town of Joubieval, and the column closed up. All the artillery we could bring together was brought down on the column. It inflicted tremendous damage, scattering the Germans through the woods on both sides of the road. It was later identified as a portion of the Fuehrer Begleit Brigade. Despite the effectiveness of the artillery fire, an outpost of the 325th was forced to withdraw. An examination of the map and terrain made it quite clear that the Germans would have to use a small road over a bridge near the town of Petite-Langlir in the middle of the sector of the 325th if they were going to use armor against the 325th. It was the only suitable passage between Salmchâteau and the Fraiture crossroads for armor. The possibility of blowing the one key bridge on the Petite-Langlir road was obvious.

During the night of December 22–23 an Engineer team, led by Major J. C. H. Lee, Jr., made its way behind the enemy lines, carrying large quantities of explosives. It detonated the bridge while it was being used by the German vehicles. The patrol returned safely. During the following twenty-four hours, the enemy pressure on the southern front built up significantly. It was obvious that the 325th was going to be outflanked if no more troops were added to its right. I therefore released the last division reserve, a battalion of the 325th, to the regimental commander, who deployed it in an extension of his right flank toward Fraiture crossroads. The reinforcement arrived just in time, for the enemy soon overran the town of Regne with infantry and armor. The 325th was ordered to counterattack and retake the town, which it did. In the midst of the fighting the regimental Adjutant of a German SS Panzer Division Regiment drove into the 325th lines in a motorcycle sidecar. He assumed that the Germans still held Regne. He was captured, and on his person were the march orders for the 2nd SS for the following day. It was to pass through Werbomont en route to Liège. The orders were sent back to Corps and Army headquarters without delay.

So far we had held the Germans, but now the volume of fire and movement made clear that they were going to seize the Fraiture crossroads. If they succeeded, they would have an unopposed march to Manhay and thus completely turn the division's right flank. I therefore ordered Colonel Charles Billingslea of the 325th to send one rifle company to the Fraiture crossroads to hold it until relieved. He sent Company F. In the meantime I decided to take a battalion from the 504th and bring it all the way across the division's area to back up the right flank. It was a difficult decision to make because in doing so I would surely uncover the crossings of the Amblève and thus possibly permit some of Peiper's forces to escape. When I weighed the alternatives, it seemed clear to me that the integrity of our own defensive position, now extending to more than twenty-five miles, was most important. Major

Edward Wellems' 2nd Battalion of the 504th Parachute Infantry was ordered to move to a wooded area several miles to the northeast of the Fraiture crossroads.

In the meantime the 508th at Vielsalm-Salmchâteau-Thier Dumont came under heavy attack from the 9th SS Panzer Division.

December 23 was an unbelievably busy day in the division area. This was the day that the 7th Armored Division, Combat Command B of the 9th Armored Division, the 112th Infantry Regiment, which was from the U.S. 28th Infantry Division, and what was left of the 106th Infantry Division all moved through the Vielsalm-Salmchâteau gateway to the rear. They had performed with great gallantry for five days, holding off two to three times their numbers of Germans in a series of delaying actions. As Field Marshal Montgomery expressed it when he authorized their withdrawal: "They can come back with all honor. They come back to the more secure positions. They put up a wonderful show." As the official Army history expresses it, "Montgomery showed the ability to honor the fighting men which had endeared him to the hearts of the Desert Rats in North Africa."[18]

General Bob Hasbrouck's handling of the 7th Armored Division was one of the great actions in the Battle of the Bulge. Yet, strangely, because of his evaluation of the division's predicament and its need to be reinforced or withdrawn, he was relieved of command by his Corps Commander early in the morning of December 22. More interesting, however, is the fact that when the situation became clearer to Corps he was restored late in the afternoon of the same day. The order relieving him of command was dated 0625 December 22, and that reinstating him was 1853 hours of the same day.[19] The commander of the 106th Infantry Division, however, Major General Alan W. Jones, fared far worse. He was relieved of command of his division.

Once again I was struck by the manner in which the system treats senior officers in combat. I have a haunting memory that does not diminish with the passage of time of how unfairly and thoughtlessly we treated some of our senior officers. And I use the word "system" because that is what it is. It is not a personal matter. It is simply something that one has come to expect of senior officers in our Army. In this case, one is particularly impressed by the manner in which Montgomery congratulated all those who fought at St.-Vith for the fine job they did. We

18 Ibid., p. 413.
19 Wilmot, op. cit., p. 596.

relieved the two senior commanders, although one was restored. In the situation at Arnhem, in our earlier battle in Holland, the British general lost three-quarters of his command and a battle. He returned home a hero and was personally decorated by the King.

There is no doubt that in our system he would have been summarily relieved and sent home in disgrace. In the case of General Jones and his 106th Division, higher command knew no more about the German plans than he did. Higher command also knew of his dispositions and approved them. His leading green regiments were overwhelmed before they could offer much resistance, and there is little that he—or anyone else, for that matter—could have done about it. Summarily relieving senior officers, it seems to me, makes others pusillanimous and indeed discourages other potential combat leaders from seeking high command. Again, it is not individuals acting against other individuals—it is not a personal matter—it is the way the system works and is expected to work. It must be changed. The shift from peacetime to war footing and then to battle has a tremendous psychological impact on individuals. Summarily relieving those who do not appear to measure up in the first shock of battle is not only a luxury that we cannot afford—it is very damaging to the Army as a whole. We have much to learn from the British about senior command relationships.

As the afternoon of December 23 waned, I became increasingly concerned about the Fraiture crossroads. At that time Billingslea's regiment was deployed with riflemen 100 to 200 yards apart, very little antitank defense, and a serious threat was developing near the crossroads. I went to the town of Fraiture and proceeded from there toward the crossroads. I encountered such a tremendous volume of fire that it was suicide to go any farther. Small-arms fire was ricocheting in all directions. Interspersed with this was artillery, mortar, and tank fire. F Company was under the command of Captain Junior R. Woodruff, and from time to time he was reinforced by Sherman tanks that came down the Manhay road. When he first moved into position on December 22, he was confronted by the 560th Volksgrenadier Division. That division was simply holding a covering position for the 2nd SS Panzer Division, which was having difficulty closing up to the jump-off line.

The 2nd SS launched an attack just before dawn on December 23, employing the 4th Panzer Grenadier Regiment reinforced by a battalion of artillery and some tanks. The attack was driven back after a bitter fight with the troopers. Surprised by the setback, the Germans settled

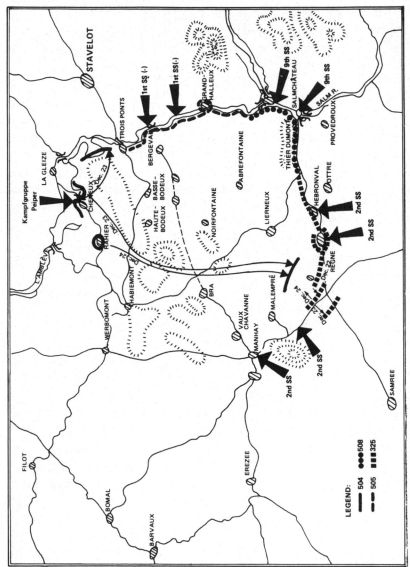

Fig. 18 December 23, 1944

down to pounding the small garrison into submission with mortar, artillery, and tank fire. They were finally overwhelmed by the sheer weight of tanks and men. As reported in the official history of the battle:

> But at the crossroads time was running out. Shortly after 1600 the German artillery really got to work, for twenty minutes pummeling the area around the crossroads. Then, preceded by two Panzer companies (perhaps the final assault had waited upon their appearance), the entire rifle strength of the 4th Panzer Grenadier Regiment closed upon the Americans. Outlined against the new-fallen snow, the line of defense was clearly visible to the Panzers, and the Shermans had no maneuver room in which to back up the line. The fight was brief, moving to a foregone conclusion.[20]

The company stood its ground until Colonel Billingslea gave it permission to come out. Ultimately, 44 of the 116 who had gone to the crossroads returned to their own lines.

By darkness Major Wellems' 2nd Battalion of the 504th had moved across the rear area of the division and was getting into a position to protect its right flank. (*Fig. 18.*) He had already gotten in touch with Captain Woodruff and the survivors of the stand made at the crossroads. He told me that he had never seen men who were withdrawing with such high morale. They claimed that they had inflicted tremendous casualties on the Germans before withdrawing. I put Wellems in position to cover the flank and went directly to Manhay to the Command Post of the 3rd Armored Division, where I found the town completely abandoned. There was one MP on duty at the crossroads. I went at once to Corps Headquarters to explain the situation to them and to obtain some assistance in holding the main highway from Fraiture to Manhay. Although it was out of my sector, its retention was essential if the 82nd was to survive in its present deployment. To my amazement, the Corps Chief of Staff showed no reaction whatever. I asked him what I should do, and he told me that it was up to me. I asked him if he could commit more troops, particularly armor, in the area, and he said that they had none.

I left the Corps Command Post and got into my jeep, with a profound feeling of foreboding. I had followed the battle closely. A major German attack was certain to come up the main highway through Manhay. It should come during the night or at first light. The 3rd

[20] *U.S. Army in World War II, European Theater of Operations,* op. cit., p. 391.

Armored Division, which should have been protecting my right flank, had disappeared into thin air. Corps gave up all responsibility for the right flank of the division, and we had already extended it about five miles, the division covering an over-all front of about twenty-five miles. We were engaged with the 1st SS, the 9th SS, and now the 2nd SS. If the right flank of the division was turned, the front from Grand-Halleux—to Thier Dumont—to Fraiture—all would be placed in considerable jeopardy. I could get no more information from Corps, and apparently no more troops. I could bring the rest of the 504th from Cheneux, as I had already brought the 2nd Battalion, but that would uncover Peiper's 1st SS and thus jeopardize the left of the division's front. As for the division headquarters itself, it had been well forward in the town of Lierneux and had just withdrawn a couple of days ago to Bra, where it was in an old château. I was reluctant to move it farther to the rear and thus create some nervousness in the subordinate commands.

All these thoughts crowded my mind as I made my way by jeep back to Bra by way of Habiemont. One thing was certain: if the division was truly on its own, I would have to withdraw to a new defensive position extending from Bergeval to Manhay, backed up against high forested mountains. If the main direction of the withdrawal movement of the U.S. First Army was back to Liège, it was in that direction that I would have to fight the division in a retrograde action. If somehow I could get my hands on some armor, we would be in pretty good shape for some time, since we never had trouble with the German infantry. But there seemed to be little prospect of this.

I arrived at the Division Command Post in Bra. About 10:00 P.M. I got Colonel Tucker on the telephone and ordered him to be prepared to move the 504th Regimental Headquarters and one battalion to the right flank of the division and to be prepared to engage the Germans there during the night. In the meantime I located two tank destroyers, which were moved southwest of the Command Post to give it some protection from the direction of Manhay. About this time I received a message from Corps headquarters telling me that Manhay had just fallen to the Germans. This information was given to all our troop units, and orders were transmitted to them to be prepared for an all-out defensive battle at daylight the following morning. We were now engaged with three Panzer divisions and part of a fourth; the decisive battle would be fought on the right, provided the 2nd SS could get up enough troops to make a fight of it. It may have been prudent to have executed a withdrawal during darkness the night of December 23. By darkness the last of the St.-Vith forces had passed through the 82nd, and except for a few abandoned and damaged vehicles and artillery pieces in our area, there was no evidence of their transit. But a withdrawal is never a pretty sight. Intuitively, I felt that I did not want to start a withdrawal of my own in the wake of what we had just seen. In addition, our fighting had been turbulent during the day, and it seemed to me it would be prudent to spend one more night in our present positions. Also, I did not have authority to withdraw, although I could have asked for it.

Throughout all this the ubiquitous British field officer and a phantom jeep and radio stayed in close touch with us. Field Marshal Montgomery had a policy of stationing a young field officer at every division headquarters. His mission there was to keep Montgomery's headquarters informed at once of everything that was taking place. I thought that the system was excellent, since all too frequently information does not get to an army headquarters or higher for hours, until it is too late.

During the night I was told that I would be assigned Combat Command B of the 9th Armored Division under the command of Brigadier General William M. Hoge. Evidently this was in response to my visit to Corps headquarters earlier. Combat Command B had been part of the forces in St.-Vith and had fought a hard fight along with the 7th Armored. General Hoge reported to me about 7:00 A.M. In the meantime Colonel Tucker was ordered to leave the smallest possible force to cover the 1st SS in the northern sector and to move to the vicinity of the Division Command Post without delay. The 505th was ordered to regroup one battalion, Vandervoort's 2nd Battalion, and to have it prepared to move on division orders without delay.

I discussed the situation with General Hoge. He told me that his troops were absolutely exhausted and not capable of any kind of sustained combat. Despite this, I told him that we had to clear Malempré of any Germans, and we had to have armor on our right. In the meantime I learned that the 7th Armored, having just gotten out of St.-Vith, was ordered by the Corps to attack down the road to Manhay. I therefore put Combat Command B of the 9th Armored between Tucker, who was now on my right, and the 7th Armored. By noon General Hoge was in position. In the meantime I had withdrawn the Division Command Post from Bra to Habiemont.

By midmorning on December 24, except for sporadic firing across the Salm River, the situation was quiet on the 505th front. During the night of December 23–24, the Germans had attempted to resupply the beleaguered Colonel Peiper by parachute. Most of the containers landed in the 504th and 505th areas, thus causing a flurry of rumors about German parachutists having landed. We soon recovered a number of the containers, and we found them quite interesting. Metal cylinders about eighteen inches in diameter and about six feet long, they were equipped with a large metal button that, on impact with the ground, opened the container automatically. Of course, in the Ardennes most of them landed by having their chutes snag the tall trees and thus they didn't open. They must have been great for resupply of the Afrika Korps in North Africa.

At 1:15 P.M. General Hoge reported to me that he was holding Malempré. The situation in this sector was somewhat confused by the presence of German troops wearing American uniforms and using American tanks. Earlier they had attacked up the Manhay road and destroyed quite a few American tanks whose crews were taken by surprise by what appeared to them to be another American force. Between Malempré and Fraiture the 2nd Battalion of the 504th was engaged with part of the 2nd SS. The battalion was commanded by Major Wellems, a veteran of extensive combat experience. He had heavy fighting on his hands but was absolutely confident he would be able to hold his position. During the day Colonel Tucker brought up the remainder of his regiment less one battalion, which he left at Cheneux. So the right flank now seemed to be stabilized.

Earlier I had received a warning order from the Corps Commander to be prepared to withdraw. Orders were then issued to all unit commanders early on December 24, assigning them defensive sectors on the new line and ordering them to undertake reconnaissance of the area. At 1:30 P.M. Corps Headquarters issued the formal orders for the withdrawal of the division. The division, in turn, issued orders during the afternoon for withdrawal that was planned to start after dark. There has been much discussion about the division's objection to withdrawing. Obviously, in the tactical situation confronting the XVIII Corps, a withdrawal was very much in order. It shortened the sector allocated to the 82nd by about 50 per cent, thus enabling us to do much better on the defensive. The new defensive position was far superior in terms of fields of fire and cover for the defenders than the old position. Finally, we would be in a much better position to launch a counterattack when the moment for that came, and we knew it was inevitable.

While these are all valid tactical considerations, morale is just as important. The fact is that the troopers did not like to withdraw in front of the Germans. The memories of all the older veterans went back to North Africa and Sicily. Stories too numerous to mention came to them from troopers, who were wounded, captured, and who later escaped, about how badly they were treated by the Germans. We know that troopers in their parachute harnesses had been shot while hanging from branches of trees in Normandy instead of being taken prisoner. I saw at least one of those myself. Even in the winter fighting a few days before our withdrawal, we had an incident in which a trooper was captured, disarmed, and then badly beaten. He managed to escape and return to his own outfit. Rather than withdraw, if the troopers had had their way, they would have much preferred to attack. Besides, they knew they had beaten the Germans in every tactical engagement so far, and they did not see why they could not resume the offensive. Finally, after the battle of Normandy, the division very proudly published a report that concluded with the comment, "No ground gained was ever relinquished." Obviously, this might be considered tactical stupidity, but from the viewpoint of morale, it had great meaning. Even though the withdrawal was planned and carried out successfully, it did not make any of us feel one mite better.

The withdrawal was planned for Christmas Eve. It was a very cold, bright moonlight night. The snow was packed on the few hard-surfaced roads, and it crunched when one walked on it. I was out most of the night with the troops during the withdrawal. It started after dark. Covering forces were to be left in place until 4:00 A.M., when they would be withdrawn. The 307th Engineer Battalion supported the withdrawal by blowing the bridges over the Salm River, laying minefields, and establishing roadblocks. The 325th and 504th withdrew without incident. The 508th, however, was attacked in great force by the 9th SS Panzer Division in the vicinity of the bridges over the Salm River. It also had a platoon on Thier Dumont as a covering force that was cut off during the withdrawal. It managed to return, however, without the loss of a single trooper.

I was with the 508th as its columns began to move north, and I stayed with them until about 10:00 P.M., when I decided to go to the 505th. The movement of the 505th was not difficult; it simply had to hinge its movement on Trois Ponts and withdraw its right flank back to the new line. The 508th, incidentally, had a withdrawal march of about seven miles. Close to 11:00 P.M. I started to drive back, in an open jeep, to the 505th area. I met a platoon of paratroopers deployed along the road. They told me that they had reports of a large German force in the area and that they were looking for them. I went to the Regimental Command Post and there discussed the situation with Colonel Ekman.

An unusual situation was developing. Earlier in the night a jeep driver had reported that as he was driving in the vicinity of Basse-Bodeux he encountered troops wearing full field equipment walking in the woods toward the east. They hit the ground and took cover and acted very evasive as his jeep neared them. Another trooper, a telephone lineman who was out checking his lines, reported that his jeep had been shot up by what he assumed were Germans in our rear area. The regimental commander asked me for a decision on what to do. He estimated that a force of approximately five hundred Germans was moving about in the rear of the regimental area. He could stop his withdrawal and deploy his regiment to search out and destroy the Germans, or, if I desired him to do so, he could ignore the Germans and attempt to continue his withdrawal. He had left three platoons of infantry on the Salm River as a covering force, and they were beginning to receive considerable pressure from what was left of the 1st SS across the river.

It seemed to me that the most important thing was for the regiment to be in position on the new line at daylight and to be prepared for a very heavy fight. We had identified at least four divisions that we could expect to move against us, and we could not afford to have an entire regimental sector in chaos and involved in scattered small-unit fighting when daylight came. I therefore ordered him to move on with his withdrawal without delay. Several hours before daylight one of the platoons on the Salm River, just north of Grand-Halleux, was attacked from the rear by a German force of great strength—approximately eight hundred men. A heavy fight ensued. A number of Germans were killed and wounded, as well as a number of troopers of the division. Among those rescued at this time was an American major of the U.S. 30th Division. (The 30th Division was the first division that bottled up Peiper at La Gleize.) He had been captured in earlier fighting at La Gleize by Peiper's force. They took him with them as they withdrew, and apparently they had been shot up a bit by random encounters with the 505th as they made their way during the night. Most of them, however, escaped across the river to rejoin their division, including Colonel Peiper.

So on December 25 we realized that we had just succeeded in withdrawing through a hostile force which was itself withdrawing. It had been a novel tactical experience. At daylight of that Christmas Day, all the regiments were in their new positions, well organized and ready for whatever might eventuate. (*Fig. 19.*)

It did not take long for the Germans to regain contact.

Two days later an attack was made by the 62nd Volksgrenadier Division in the 505th area. The German division was roughly handled by the 505th. It was a poor division, not well trained, and its patrols frequently wandered into the 505th area only to be destroyed. The 9th SS came up on our center against the 508th and 504th, and it was of much better quality.

The 9th SS Panzer Division was charged, by its Corps headquarters, with breaking across the Salm River at Salmchâteau and Vielsalm, and there rolling up the southern wing of the division along the river. The night of the withdrawal its 19th Panzer Grenadier Regiment attacked with great spirit, whooping and yelling. There were only two platoons of the 508th near the Vielsalm bridgehead; one managed to stop the Grenadiers before they could reach them and the other was engulfed. Under the capable leadership of First Lieutenant George D. Lamm, they fought their way out and back to the regiment. The German 19th Panzer Grenadier Regiment had earned a reputation as the best in the 9th SS Panzer Division. It was an aggressive regiment and followed rapidly the 508th in its withdrawal. The remainder of the 9th SS was strung out for miles, caught up in the chaos of the German rear area.

On the night of December 25 the 19th hit the 508th again, this time on its left flank with two battalions in the attack. After a three-hour fire fight they were beaten back. Again they regrouped, were reinforced, and were joined by the remainder of the 9th SS in an all-out divisional attack on the night of December 27. The division used as the main axis of its thrust the road from Lierneux to Habiemont and hit the 504th in front of Bra and the 508th in front of Erria. The Panzers came in screaming and yelling in a mass attack. There were far more Germans in the attack than we had ever seen before. The 504th stopped them in their tracks. The 3rd Battalion of the 508th was overrun. The battalion commander, Lieutenant Colonel Louis G. Mendez, borrowed a reserve company from an adjoining battalion and the following morning during darkness counterattacked through the town of Erria, capturing a number of the Panzers still asleep in their bedrolls. The American position was restored.

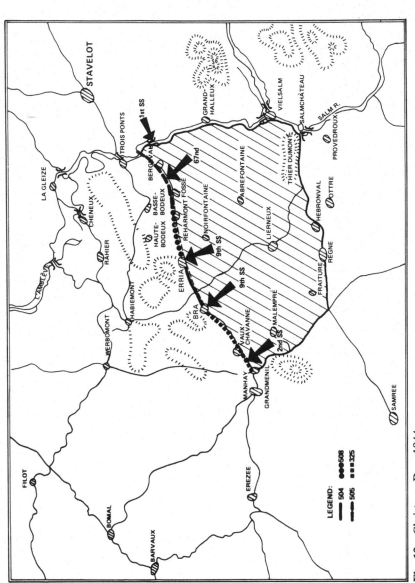

Fig. 19   Christmas Day, 1944

I did not hear of this attack for several hours; I then went at once to the town of Erria. It consisted of a cluster of a half dozen or more stone farmhouses surrounded by fields enclosed by stone walls. It was ideal for defense. The troopers told me that they had never been in a situation like it. The Germans came across the open fields, screaming and yelling, and the paratroopers just kept cutting them down. The Germans finally engulfed the troopers, who stayed in their places continuing to fight them at close quarters. After Mendez restored the situation, they counted 62 dead Germans in one field in front of their machine guns. The troopers informed me that the Panzers they captured told them that they had attacked American troops in that manner in the past and that the Americans had broken and run. According to the official German account of the 1st Battalion of the 19th Panzer Grenadier Regiment, the unit was "cut to pieces" by the American defenders. As far as the 82nd was concerned, that brought the German offensive phase of the Battle of the Bulge to an end.

It seemed to me that the Von Rundstedt offensive was waning in its intensity. Already we had engaged four of their best divisions and defeated them decisively. The latest, the 9th SS, came on with great élan, well supported by artillery, and they had hardly made a dent in our positions by the time the battle was through. Other German divisions continued to flow toward the west, but the numbers available for the western thrust toward the Meuse diminished seriously as the Germans attempted to turn to the north toward Liège and the final objective of Antwerp. Blocking them, after December 19, had been the 82nd, then the 3rd Armored Division, then the U.S. 84th Infantry Division, and finally Major General Ernest Harmon's 2nd Armored Division (Hell on Wheels). Nevertheless, the reconnaissance elements of the westernmost German division, the 2nd Panzer, reached a point within a few miles of the Meuse. With their gas tanks going dry and the long, tenuous supply route behind them under constant air attack during the day, they lay vulnerable to Harmon's final counteroffensive, which was launched on Christmas Day.

During Christmas week, when our front was quite stable, I was invited to the First Army Headquarters to dinner with General Hodges and his staff. It was a very pleasant affair. Everyone was relaxed. The first phase of the Battle of the Bulge was over, and now it was only a short time until we would go on the offensive. The dinner conversation seemed to return again and again to Montgomery, Patton, and the daily newspaper *Stars and Stripes.* The staff spoke of Montgomery with amusement and respect. They obviously liked him, and they respected his thorough professionalism. One officer described him to me as "optimistic, meticulous and precise, and cautious." They were a bit unhappy about Patton because he seemed to be getting all the publicity—Patton and Bastogne. One would think that that was where the Battle of the Bulge had been decided and that Patton had been the victor. It had begun to irk First Army staff. They were aware, and the record now shows, that it was the First Army that took the brunt of Sepp Dietrich's 6th Panzer Army attack and then Manteuffel's 5th Panzer Army as they sought to break through in the direction of Liège. The fighting had been bitter from the outset and very costly, not only to all the combat divisions but to all the higher headquarters, who were constantly, day and night, confronted with the most difficult tactical decisions as they sought to cope with the German onslaught. Yet, when *Stars and Stripes* arrived daily, it was full of stories about Patton and his Third Army and how the defenders at Bastogne were winning the Battle of the Bulge. The story that was the straw that seemed to break the camel's back was of an incident that had occurred just before I arrived. General Patton had called his chaplain in and ordered him to pray for good weather. Reluctant to engage in such an enterprise, the chaplain protested, and Patton, with characteristic profanity, ordered him to go ahead and write a prayer. He proceeded to do so, and it was reproduced in a box on the front page of *Stars and Stripes.*

> Almighty and most merciful Father, we humbly beseech Thee, of Thy great goodness, to restrain these immoderate rains with which we have had to contend. Grant us fair weather for the Battle. Graciously hearken to us as soldiers who call upon Thee that, armed with Thy power, we may advance from victory to victory, and crush the oppressions and wickedness of our enemies, and establish Thy justice among men and nations. Amen.

That was it. The First Army insisted that, from then on, there be a separate *Stars and Stripes* that would print more First Army stories. The first issue was out shortly.

Actually, Patton had been doing extremely well. On thinking over his situation in early December, he decided that there was a possibility of a German attack somewhere in the vicinity of the boundaries between his Army and the First Army. It was the area where Bradley was taking what he later described as "a calculated risk." So Patton directed his staff to give some thought to the prompt organization of a counterattacking force if such an eventuality occurred.

He followed the initial successes of the Von Rundstedt offensive with intense interest and began to anticipate a role for the Third Army. He early decided that there were two battles, the main one being fought against the First Army on the north, and a holding action to prevent the intervention of the Third Army on the south. On December 18 he had a phone conversation with Bradley in which Bradley told him he might have to help Hodges' First Army. It was followed by another call from Bradley at 11:00 P.M. He told Patton that Eisenhower would be in Verdun the following morning and that Patton was to be there for a meeting at 11:00. Patton immediately called for a meeting of the Third Army staff for 8:00 A.M. The staff assembled exactly on time, and Patton at once posed several alternatives to them. It was finally agreed that the III Corps, which had now come under his command as a consequence of the German drive to the west, would be the basis of his counterattack. Out of the staff discussions came agreement on three tentative plans. Each was given a code word so that Patton, talking to his Chief of Staff on the phone, could authorize the launching of the undertaking without delay. His staff meeting was over at 9:15, and he met with Eisenhower, Marshal Tedder, General Devers, and members of the SHAEF staff at 11:00 A.M.

Eisenhower told Patton that he wanted him to go to Luxembourg to take charge of the battle, and asked Patton when he could start. Patton replied, "As soon as you are through with me." He had left his headquarters prepared not to return if the demands of the battle so dictated. Eisenhower then asked him when he would be ready to attack. "The morning of December 22," Patton replied, "with three divisions." A Patton aide, Colonel Codman, who was present, reported that "there was a stir, a shuffling of feet as those present straightened up in their chairs. In some faces, skepticism, but through the room the current of excitement leaped like a flame." Eisenhower considered Patton's reply fatuous, but Patton assured him that at that very moment his staff was making detailed plans and that the operation could be launched on schedule.

Actually, it jumped off at 6:00 A.M. on December 22. At the outset, the going was a little slower than Patton had anticipated; nevertheless by Christmas Day they were close to Bastogne and, as Patton described it,

"Christmas dawned clear and cold; lovely weather for killing Germans, although the thought seemed somewhat at variance with the spirit of the day."[21] The following day, December 26, contact was established with the 101st Airborne Division and the relief of Bastogne was accomplished. Patton at once moved to widen the base of contact and to prepare for an attack by his Third Army in the direction of Houffalize and St.-Vith. It had been an amazing performance. He had disengaged three divisions actually in combat and launched them over one hundred miles of icy roads straight into the German offensive. The rapidity and violence of his attack took the Germans by surprise and completely upset their time table. Of all the army commanders, only Patton could have carried out such an operation.

In the meantime a reorganization took place in the higher command that was to have repercussions in Bradley's headquarters and in the press. A few days after the German offensive had been launched, it became apparent in SHAEF that two major battles would ensue, one on the north that would involve Montgomery's Army Group as well as Simpson's Ninth U.S. Army and Hodges' First Army. The battle on the south would be fought by Bradley's Army Group with Patton's Third Army. With each passing day the communications between Bradley and his Ninth and First Armies were becoming increasingly difficult. On Tuesday evening, December 19, Major General Kenneth W. D. Strong, Chief of Intelligence on the SHAEF staff, went to Major General J. F. M. Whiteley, who was Deputy Chief of Staff for Operations, with the suggestion that it might be wise to put the First and Ninth U.S. Armies under Montgomery's command, thus taking them from Bradley. At first it was assumed that the Germans were attacking through Liège to the Channel ports and that the battle would swing in that direction, to the north. As the Germans were turned back, however, and continued to thrust steadily westward, it became increasingly clear that there were two separate battles, and thus there was need for recognition of this in the command structure.

The two staff officers went to see Lieutenant General Walter Bedell Smith, Eisenhower's Chief of Staff, with the suggestion. His initial reaction was one of great anger, since he saw in it another proposal to place the U.S. armies under Montgomery's command. The more he thought

[21] George S. Patton, Jr., *War as I Knew It*. Boston: Houghton Mifflin Co., 1947, p. 202.

about it, however, the more sense it seemed to make. Smith telephoned Bradley to discuss the idea. Bradley's reaction was interesting and eminently sensible. "Bradley was none too sympathetic toward the idea, but did concede that Montgomery would be more apt to throw British reserves into the battle under such a command arrangement."[22] The matter was brought to General Eisenhower's attention the following morning, and he approved of it. Thus a line was drawn from Givet on the Meuse River to St.-Vith. The armies north of that line would be under Montgomery's 21st Army Group, including, of course, the two U.S. armies, the First and the Ninth.

Montgomery lost no time in taking control of the battle. He had already had his phantom teams distributed at the various headquarters, keeping the situation under surveillance. About 2:30 the morning of December 20 a British major presented himself at First Army Headquarters to tell General Hodges that Montgomery was moving his 30 Corps to the west and behind the Meuse if needed. The 30 was a splendid corps. I had fought with it in Holland, and General Horrocks still commanded it; it made a decisive contribution to the ultimate outcome of the battle. Furthermore, the ability of the armies to make such a serious command decision so quickly and of Montgomery to move 30 Corps so decisively was completely contrary to the thinking of the Germans. They had assumed that a decision of this magnitude would have to go to Washington and London and be resolved by the Combined Chiefs of Staff, thus possibly taking weeks. But it had been accomplished in minutes by a few phone calls.

On the evening that I had dinner with the First Army staff, General Bill Kean, the First Army Chief of Staff, talked to me about his initial meeting with Montgomery. Montgomery told the Army commander that he wanted to bring together a corps for a counterattacking force and to get it assembled promptly. He told the First Army that he wanted the most aggressive corps commander they had, at the same time stipulating that he wanted Major General J. Lawton Collins (Lightning Joe). Collins had commanded the VII Corps in the Utah Beach assault; he had moved very rapidly, swung his corps toward Cherbourg, and captured that major port ahead of schedule. Montgomery explained to Kean that he wanted Collins to be a "savage rabbit." When asked what he meant, Montgomery explained that he wanted a corps to occupy a good

[22] *U.S. Army in World War II, European Theater of War,* op. cit., pp. 423–424.

defensive position and not to lose it, but every once in a while, when the moment seemed opportune, the corps was to rush and nip the German Panzers, then fall back to its prepared defensive positions.

General Collins moved promptly, and the corps was being assembled to the right rear of the First Army. One of the divisions given to him was the U.S. 2nd Armored Division, which had been taken from the Ninth Army on the north. Collins reported to the First Army Commander on December 21, and by December 24 he believed he would be ready to attack. Already two of his divisions, the 3rd Armored and the 84th Infantry, were engaged. The 2nd Armored Division was to be on his right, and it, as the tactics developed, was destined to be the "savage rabbit," a role not particularly to its liking. The 2nd Armored had been fighting since Sicily, and it was a veteran, proved division. If it became engaged, it would be certain to want to destroy its opponent rather than withdraw after a short encounter. Already the German 2nd Panzer Division had moved to within a few miles of the Meuse River and seemed to be enjoying considerable freedom of action. The two left divisions of the VII Corps were involved in a heavy defensive action. On December 24 General Harmon, commanding the 2nd Armored, asked permission to commit a combat team of his division against the 2nd Panzer, which had been identified in the neighborhood of the small towns of Ciney and Celles. Harmon had committed another combat command farther to the east.

Some discussion ensued with Army Headquarters, and Army in turn with Montgomery. Montgomery had hoped to organize a corps-size counterattacking force that would be well to the rear and kept free of any involvement until the moment its attack was to be made. Unfortunately, the Germans' successful move west had already involved two of the divisions of the corps, the 3rd Armored and the 84th Infantry. Further, a combat command of Harmon's 2nd Armored became involved, as the First Army front extended toward the Meuse. Montgomery therefore talked about disengaging the 2nd Armored and withdrawing it well to the rear to have it in a position to protect Liège if necessary. But Harmon had tasted battle and found it to his liking. His Combat Command A handled the Germans very roughly, and he had a hunch that the German spearhead, now so close to the Meuse, was bogged down and in trouble. He therefore wanted to attack with his remaining combat command and his reconnaissance battalion.

General Collins had to make the decision. He told Harmon to go.

The attack was launched on the morning of December 25. Harmon had said that he wanted to take the "panzer" out of the German 2nd Panzer Division. The Panzers were overextended, and many of their vehicles were without fuel. After the battle the 2nd Armored Division claimed that it had destroyed or captured 82 tanks, 16 other armored vehicles, 83 guns, and 280 motor vehicles. Harmon had taken the "panzer" out of the 2nd Panzer Division. That was the high point, and the end of the Von Rundstedt offensive. The long-awaited counterattack by the First Army was launched on January 3.

Those of us in the 82nd were eager to get on with it, feeling that we could go just as far as we would be allowed to go, and we also believed that the harder the attack was made right at the outset, the better off we would be. In the first day's fighting the 82nd completely overran the 62nd Volksgrenadier Division and the 9th SS Panzer Division, capturing 2400 prisoners, including five battalion commanders. After a few days the division was told to hold up. It was then that we became aware that the Army's attack plan was based on a huge turning action, pivoted on Stavelot. It was as though a huge stable door were being closed. The movement of the divisions was controlled by phase lines. In the case of the 82nd, we crossed the open ground at our front, made our way through waist-deep snow and tall timber on the high land, and came to the open valley looking across to Thier Dumont and Vielsalm. When the 505th reached this position, they saw a German truck column approaching. They allowed it to come all the way up to their positions and then destroyed it and captured all the Germans. Prisoners told them that they were the Corps reserve that the Germans were committing to restore their positions, but so unaware were the Germans of the plight of the 62nd Volksgrenadier and the 9th SS Panzer that they committed their reserves right into our welcoming arms.

We felt at that point that we could move to Thier Dumont and Vielsalm without opposition, but the attack plan required us to wait until the divisions on our right moved up abreast. It was frustrating, indeed infuriating, to watch the Germans begin to move weapons into positions near Thier Dumont where we could not interfere with them except by artillery fire. We knew they would be there to kill some of our troopers when we once resumed the attack. All of us had hoped that the American attack would penetrate to the vitals of the German defending forces and cut off all the divisions that had moved toward the Meuse, but this was not to be. The 30th Division on our left near Stavelot, for example, did not advance the first day, and our advance was strictly limited. Von Rundstedt, when he became aware of Montgomery's counterattack, referred to it as "the small solution."

The 82nd was given a new parachute regiment for the offensive: the 517th Parachute Infantry, which had landed in southern France in mid-August. It had had limited experience and was put into the attack abreast of the veteran regiments. The 517th seemed to have difficulty getting off its line of departure on the first day. I went out to find out what the problem was. I went through a small Belgian village through which the front line was reported to be. As I emerged from the village a macadam road lay straight ahead. That was the road on which the 517th's leading infantry should have been for the departure of the attack. There was no firing and no one to be seen. Off to the left were open fields and a shallow valley, at the bottom of which was a large red barn and some small outer buildings. To the right of the road the ground rose through open farmland; nearly a quarter of a mile away the heavy timber began and went up to the top of the ridge. I walked down the road with Sergeant Wood, staying close to the embankment so that I could take cover if I was fired upon.

About 400 yards farther on, I came to a dirt road running from the red barn. Where it met the macadam road there was a depression three or four feet deep. Collected in it I found three or four of the troopers of the regiment and a young lieutenant. I asked them what they were doing there, and at that moment a tremendous detonation took place. The thought crossed my mind that it was an antitank weapon of our own that had just fired. Soon there was another detonation, and I began to notice the smell that I once associated with detonating mortar and artillery projectiles. Everybody was cringing and pressing themselves to the ground. I told the lieutenant to get out of there and get going or he would be killed without having accomplished anything.

I then told Sergeant Wood to move down the valley toward the red barn and go back to the village and join me there. I turned and went back up the road to the village at a walk. It was an interesting fact that the Germans would rarely attack one person with such a weapon as a machine gun unless he was very, very close to them, and I never saw them display rifle marksmanship skills at any distance comparable to that of the Americans. Americans have a long tradition of marksmanship, and it manifests itself in how they fight in combat. Wood joined me in the village, and we went on to another area. Some years later I met the lieutenant, then a colonel, at the Infantry School at Fort Benning. He reminded me of our conversation, and he told me that what I said to him was, "Lieutenant, get off your ass and get going," which was probably true, and that is what he did.

But the regiment continued to have problems. The following morning they again seemed to be stalled, and I again went forward to see what the problem was. Having gone through a small Belgian village and having found no infantry, I continued along a road, crossing open fields, toward a group of farmhouses about a quarter of a mile away. In a few hundred yards I came on half a dozen German antitank mines. They were laid on the hard surface of the road, connected to each other by rods and covered by a light snow that had fallen during the night, about an inch or so. Normally, there would have been antipersonnel mines around them, possibly connected by a trip wire, to kill or wound anyone who attempted to remove the mines. Since they were on the hard road surface, I could see no evidence of antipersonnel mines. They may have been on the shoulder, but I was not about to go along the shoulder of the road, so I stepped gingerly across the minefield. I had that eerie feeling that I was out in the area between the Germans and our own infantry. Usually mines are not laid in such a manner unless they are protected by nearby infantry who can fire on anyone who attempts to move them, but no one disturbed me as I went on toward the farmhouses.

As I neared the farmhouses, I heard some American voices. In the kitchen of one of them were assembled about a dozen troopers warming themselves and making coffee. There was no security guard outside, and the German infantry must have been very close. I told them to post guards outside, finish their coffee, and get going.

This was one of the problems associated with attacking during the winter. Usually the attacks jumped off at 3:00 or 4:00 A.M. in pitch-black and extreme cold. After wading through the snow and fighting at the same time, when the men came on any shelter, they were inclined to take advantage of it. It was the sensible thing to do. Actually, in defense we always tried to arrange it so at least a third of the troops would be getting warm while others were in their icy foxholes, thus rotating the units.

I started back the way I had come, and as I neared the minefields, suddenly there was a *pung, pung, pung* sound of 20 mm. projectiles that must have been from a German flak wagon. The Germans had been in the woods overlooking the minefield, and they were now shooting at me and missing, with the projectiles ricocheting off the trees and off the road. They had apparently let me go by the first time.

The 20 mm. flak wagon accompanied German tactical units to protect them from low-level Allied aircraft attacks. Because of the vibration of the weapon and its very high rate of fire, it spewed forth a cone of projectiles that could be quite effective beyond several hundred yards. The gunsight also was most effective at a long range. It was not very useful against an individual at less than 100 yards. Of course, if the individual was hit, he would be blown to smithereens by the large volume of projectiles. But the significant thing about the incident was that there was no infantry protecting the minefield. In the circumstances the 517th should have been attacking aggressively; they had a golden opportunity to move deep into the enemy rear areas before German infantry could be brought up.

Later in the morning I joined an 81 mm. mortar platoon that was in support of an infantry battalion in the attack. Again, the mortars and their folded bipods were stacked as though they were logs beside a Belgian farmhouse. Inside, the crew were enjoying all the comforts of a cozy fireplace. It took only a moment to straighten out the situation, get the mortars in position, and communications opened with the attacking infantry so that they could give them support. But the 517th Parachute Infantry Regiment improved as the fighting went on and became one of our best regiments.

Historically, there has always been much discussion in the U.S. Army about the proper place of a general in battle. Although lip service is paid to the view that the general belongs as close to the scene of action as circumstances will allow, the fact is that very few generals behave this way. There is a school of thought that the general can best take care of his troops and look out for their interests by controlling the battle from his Command Post well to the rear. I find this particularly disturbing because today, with small computers and modern information processing systems, individuals can find many more reasons to rationalize their presence in their Command Post rather than with the troops. There can be no question that the place for the general in battle is where he can see the battle and get the odor of it in his nostrils. First of all, troops should not be given missions that are beyond the possibility of their achievement. There were several situations in World War II of which I am aware and in which this did take place. The senior officers did not make a reconnaissance of the area in which the fighting was to take place. Next, troops must be properly equipped with weapons, transportation, tank support, and bridging, if that is what they need, to succeed at what they are endeavoring to do. And when all these things are taken care of, the general responsible should, whenever the demands upon his time will allow, go to the scene of the action and see to it that the attack is being carried out effectively. If he is able to do this, he is in a position to get to know firsthand the conditions under which his troops are fighting, to see to it that they are adequately supplied and taken care of, and to be sure that the missions given to them are realistic in terms of their capabilities. Furthermore, by his example, he can instill considerable confidence in the troops and elicit from them a desire to perform better. There is no substitute for the general being seen.

This does, however, take considerable practical experience. Nothing annoys troops more than to have the big brass show up near the front, all dressed up and to all appearances different from the combat infantry, thus attracting attention and bringing down hostile fire. I have always believed that it is important for a general with the infantry to look just like the infantry except for his insignia, which can be seen only by troops nearby.

We finally were allowed to resume the attack on January 8, after having been held up for several days. I was out with the infantry when I heard that Colonel Vandervoort had been hit and that he was in an aid station in the town of Abrefontaine. When I got there, he was on a stretcher in an ambulance. He had been hit in the eye by a shell fragment and apparently had lost one eye. I felt very bad about it, because just a day or two earlier we had been talking about bringing Vandervoort to division headquarters. He had been commanding a company and then a battalion since Sicily, and the veterans among us believed that the chances of his luck running out were quite high and that we should make a change.

The following day, accompanied by Captain Hugo Olson, I was again with the infantry, keeping track of the progress and urging them on to get the job done with the least delay. We came out of a cluster of farmhouses and started across a snow-covered field about a quarter of a mile wide. Halfway across the field ahead of us was an infantry platoon in a column of twos. At the far side of the field was a heavy forest. Instinctively, I sensed that the platoon was a good target and that I should avoid them. Actually, they should have been deployed. Still, the

Germans might not have had them under observation, so I moved along and joined the platoon as it entered the forest.

We had barely gotten beyond the tree line when a series of tremendous explosions detonated above and among us. We hugged the ground, which trembled under us. It seemed to last only a short while; then suddenly it stopped and leaves and twigs fell around us and the acrid odor of detonating artillery shells permeated the air. For a second or two it was absolutely quiet, with none of us inclined to rise because of the danger of another concentration of fire being placed on us. Suddenly Olson yelled, "My leg, my leg!" I turned my head slightly, and there was a human leg about six feet away in the middle of the trail. It seemed to have been cut off above the knee, and the red blood was still spurting out of it onto the white snow. I got on all fours. I thought, "My God, Olson's lost a leg." Then, crouched over, I made my way back. Olson appeared to have been hit in the leg, but he had both legs. About eight feet beyond him was a soldier on the ground whose leg had been severed. We quickly took off his waist belt and applied a tourniquet to his thigh and gave him a shot of morphine. We were able to find a jeep and put him aboard and get him back to an aid station. I was happy to learn later that he had survived. Olson had received quite a few fragments in his leg, and he was evacuated. In a month or so he was back. It had been a somewhat costly attack for our veterans, but the division swept on toward Vielsalm and the Salm River, where it was relieved by the 75th Infantry Division on January 9.

I happened to be a few miles back of our front when the 75th arrived. I felt sorry for them in many ways. It was such a fine-looking division, but so green. They had proceeded according to the textbooks, and all trucks were unloaded about ten miles behind the lines, because of the danger of enemy artillery fire. From then on they walked, wearing long overcoats, black rubber overshoes, carrying full field packs and all the equipment, weapons, and impedimenta they believed a combat soldier should have. Some of them placed some of this burden in ration boxes which they pulled along the icy road with a short rope. By comparison, the 82nd was still in its old, faded jumpsuits, wearing long johns, to be sure, but carrying only the essentials for fighting. However, the 75th went into the line, got its first blooding on the Salm River, and developed into a good division.

The 82nd was moved back about twenty miles to some small Belgian villages. We welcomed the opportunity to get cleaned up and get some warm food and particularly to do some training with one of the tank battalions that was billeted near us. We were back in the line on January 28. On that occasion the 1st Infantry Division, certainly one of the best in the American Army, and the 82nd were to lead an assault through the Siegfried Line. We were followed by two other divisions— an unusual deployment. The snow had become so deep that attacking formations, usually a battalion, would have a lead man wade through the snow, which was then waist-deep, for fifty yards or so, to be replaced by another man. Thus the battalions made a few miles a day.

East of St.-Vith we came upon newly constructed log huts that the Germans expected to occupy for the winter. The Germans were surprised by the rapidity of the attack, and we frequently encountered reserve units moving hither and yon in what they thought was the German rear area. As we approached the small town of Herresbach, Major Wellems' battalion of the 504th, the 2nd Battalion, watched a German battalion approach on foot. When they came upon the concealed positions of the 504th, the 504th killed or captured all of them. The 504th then went on to occupy the town. An interesting characteristic of the winter war began to become evident: neither side wanted to destroy the villages with artillery fire, since invariably they used them for shelter. They would encircle them, dig out the occupants with rifles and bayonets, and do everything they could to rout out the enemy so as to have the houses for their own use later.

A representative of the Department of the Army joined us just before this offensive to explain the wonders of the proximity fuse. It was designed, first of all, for use against the Kamikaze pilots in the Pacific War; it would detonate on proximity to a target. It has been given much credit for turning back the Von Rundstedt force, but it really wasn't all that effective. The Germans first referred to it as "the tree chopper." The projectiles would detonate at a certain height above the trees and destroy the tops of the trees, scattering their fragments down among them. Obviously, the safest place to be would be within a dwelling, since the projectile would detonate well above the roof rather than penetrate the building.

The division made its final attack at 4:00 A.M. on February 2. It penetrated through two miles of tank obstacles, "dragon's teeth," in the Siegfried Line and captured numerous pillboxes. Most of them were unmanned. This had been the object of the offensive that had jumped off some time before: the penetration of the Siegfried Line. Again, the division was withdrawn to the small Belgian towns well behind the lines to rest up, refit, and get ready for the next battle, whatever it would be. It turned out to be in the Huertgen Forest area. We had been hearing a great deal about the Huertgen Forest and the horrors of it, and we had been reading in *Stars and Stripes* about the heavy casualties that had been taken there. It proved to be a monster, an ice-coated moloch, with an insatiable capacity for humans.

But before the Huertgen the troops began to hear about the latest brouhaha brought about by the Field Marshal. It was triggered by a press conference that Field Marshal Montgomery held in Brussels on January 7. Actually, it had begun in Sicily, where Patton's Seventh Army fought beside Montgomery's Eighth Army. Little that Montgomery did from Sicily on until the Battle of the Bulge assuaged the Americans or increased their regard for him. Montgomery in his memoirs states that he held the press conference because "of the sniping at Eisenhower which was going on in the British press." He told the Prime Minister of his intention, and he said that he expected to "show how the whole Allied team rallied to the call and how teamwork saved a somewhat awkward situation." In his press conference he described the situation created by the Germans which, in his opinion, "looked as if it might become awkward," and then went on to say "as soon as I saw what was happening, I took certain steps to insure that if the Germans got to the Meuse they certainly would not get over that river . . . merely precautions, that is, I was thinking ahead." He then went on to say that "national considerations were thrown overboard," and described the battle as "one of the most interesting and tricky that I have ever handled." He spoke highly of Eisenhower and the American troops and omitted Bradley.

When the reports of his press conference reached Bradley's headquarters, according to Bradley, his "staff exploded with indignation." Bradley asserts that the Montgomery statement came to his staff via the BBC. Chester Wilmot, in *The Struggle for Europe,* states that the broadcast they had received came from the Germans. It had been contrived by Goebbels and had given a slant to the statements of Montgomery that was certain to infuriate the Americans. If this had been his intent, he certainly succeeded. Bradley quickly realized that he had to say something for the record; furthermore, the American people and the American troops had to hear his version of the battle. Two days later, on January 9, he had his own press conference, in which he made a very thoughtful, noninflammatory statement that seemed to settle the issue for the time being.

Nevertheless, the British press went on merrily criticizing Ike and hailing the achievements of Montgomery. The British press began to suggest that the time had come, at long last, for Montgomery to be put in over-all charge of the land battle. They did not seem to realize that at this juncture in the war, immediately following the reports of the casualties in the Battle of the Bulge, the American people were less inclined than ever to put their troops under British command. The Von Rundstedt offensive itself had been a shock, the casualties quite enormous, and the reaction in Congress and back home was for Eisenhower to take and keep firm control. Not knowing the details of what discussions might be taking place between Montgomery and Eisenhower in Paris, and reading the reports of the British press, General Marshall, on December 30, had telegraphed Eisenhower as follows:

> They may or may not have brought to your attention articles in certain London papers proposing a British deputy commander for all your ground forces and implying that you have undertaken too much of a task yourself. My feeling is this: under no circumstances make any concessions of any kind whatsoever. I am not assuming that you had in mind such a concession. I just wish you to be certain of our attitude. You are doing a grand job, and go on and give them hell.[23]

As seen by Bradley and Patton, Montgomery was far from the Great Captain that the British press would have one believe. They remembered past battles: Sicily, Falaise, and particularly MARKET-GARDEN, which they considered to have been a debacle. Furthermore, he had failed to open the port at Antwerp, and due to that failure, all the Armies suffered serious logistics shortages. He continually seemed to want more and yet seemed to accomplish less. They went along with Eisenhower's decision to place all the troops north of the German offensive under Montgomery's command in the Battle of the Bulge—that is, the U.S. First and Ninth Armies. They did it reluctantly. They did it reluctantly because it was obvious that the battle was totally in the sector of General Bradley's Army Group. Both Bradley and Patton believed that by mounting a major offensive north toward Houffalize and St.-Vith with Patton's Third Army they could destroy the German

---

[23] Dwight D. Eisenhower, *Crusade in Europe.* New York: Doubleday & Co., 1948, p. 356.

armies that were attacking General Hodges. Bradley's headquarters was the logical one to carry out such a battle plan. American divisions were involved in the execution of the battle, and their commanders were all known personally to Bradley and his staff. He could have easily asked for the movement of the British 30 Corps to the Meuse as a backup force. He then could have maneuvered and fought his First and Third Armies as a nutcracker crushing the German armies between them. But they went along with the Eisenhower plan, as Bradley expressed it, because this was one way to ensure the commitment of the British reserves.

Early in the battle Patton was convinced that Montgomery's view was that Patton was incapable of launching an offensive and Hodges' First Army could not launch a counteroffensive for weeks. They were aware, too, as the Von Rundstedt offensive reached its high tide, a few miles from the Meuse, that Montgomery was directing Hodges' First Army to disengage the VII Corps and move it thirty miles to the rear to protect Liège and to be available as a counterattacking force. Actually, at that very time, Harmon, with Joe Collins' approval, and at odds with Montgomery's intentions, launched the first counteroffensive that was to destroy the Von Rundstedt troops. Even as this began and Bradley linked up with the Bastogne garrison, Bradley kept urging Bedell Smith at SHAEF to make Montgomery launch a counterattack without delay. With the Third Army attacking toward Houffalize and St.-Vith and the U.S. First Army attacking from the north to link up with it, they could have cut off thousands of German troops and destroyed them. Instead, Montgomery chose to wait until January 3, more than a week after Ernest Harmon's first successful attack, and then the Montgomery plan envisioned a tidy battle, phase line by phase line, that would slowly close the door of the barn by pushing the Germans back on their supply bases and their frontier.

It was little wonder therefore that Bradley's headquarters and Patton's took a very dim view of Montgomery's claims on January 7. Montgomery apparently had no intention whatever of exacerbating the feelings of his American fellow combatants. But the extent that he did so is clear evidence of his failure to understand the American psychology and the attitude of the American commanders. And he did not appreciate how responsive the Supreme Commander, an American, had to be to the people back home.

The British and the American troops always fought well side by

side. Nevertheless, there was, underneath the surface, considerable misunderstanding about their methods of command. I recall quite vividly
having a final meeting with General "Boy" Browning, commander of the
British Airborne Corps, when the battle in Holland was over; he suggested to me that our troops had fought well but that I had given too
much authority to my subordinate commanders. In the U.S. Army a
battle commander is given his mission and the available resources, and
he is then expected to get the job done. Unit commanders are encouraged to use their initiative. I was startled when I first heard a
subordinate commander in a briefing at British 30 Corps headquarters
say that a certain task was "unacceptable." This would be unthinkable
in the American army. Commanders and staffs may discuss every aspect
of a battle plan, limited only by time, but once the decision is made by
the commander, it is then up to the subordinate to carry it out. He may
ask to be relieved, which is also almost unthinkable, but he is expected
to do his best to carry out the decision. This was demonstrated dramat-
ically in Sicily when Patton, having been ordered to make a major
amphibious landing without any ports and with an inadequate road
network, replied that he would do his damnedest to carry it out.

As a consequence of this practice, American commands right down
to the platoon level tend to demonstrate considerable resilience and
independence. They are particularly good in a catch-as-catch-can type
of battle; this is true especially in the airborne units. They like to feel
that they have the initiative to maneuver and seek to take advantage of
any tactical opportunity that the enemy opens up to them. In defense
they are resourceful, give ground grudgingly, and are prepared to counterattack at the first opportunity. It is part of the national psychological
make-up that manifests itself in so many aspects of the Americans' lives,
including business and management of our national affairs. The "set
piece" event is rarely to their liking. I do not believe that Montgomery
understood this, and when a protracted series of events forced American
units to withdraw, he thought that they should be given a week or more
to tidy up and be prepared for a very conservative, albeit costly, phase
line by phase line counteroffensive. Every echelon of the battle command, from Bradley on down, sensed, if they did not at once discern
clearly, the Montgomery attitude, and they found it quite incompatible
with their own point of view, their own background, and their own
training.

Three days after being replaced by the 99th Division, the 82nd

Airborne Division was en route to the Huertgen Forest. On February 8 it opened its Command Post in the midst of the forest in the small town of Rott. Three miles to the northeast the XVIII Corps opened its Command Post in the town of Zweifall. The 82nd was to continue to be assigned to the XVIII Corps. Within a few hours after opening in Rott, I stopped at Corps headquarters to get an outline of our next mission. Then, traveling by jeep, I started through the Huertgen Forest to the clearings on the far side where our new jump-off positions would be. I learned my first lesson about the Huertgen. It couldn't be traversed by jeep. The mud was too deep and the jeep bellied down.

The Huertgen Forest is part of a heavily wooded area of about fifty square miles. It begins about five miles southeast of the city of Aachen. As the official *U.S. Army History* described one's first view of it: "Looking east from the little German border villages southeast of Aachen, the Huertgen Forest is a seemingly impenetrable mass, a vast, undulating blackish-green ocean stretching as far as the eye can see. Upon entering the forest, you want to drop things behind to mark your path, as Hansel and Gretel did with their bread crumbs."

After traversing the forest for three or four miles, one comes upon open farming country on higher ground. Two ridges thrust like fingers toward the distant Roer River. On the north was the ridge containing the towns of Huertgen, Menhau, and Grosshau. That ridge extended to the northeast for three miles. To the south was a longer ridge extending from the town of Lammersdorf toward Schmidt. The latter overlooked the principal dam on the Roer River. Between these cleared ridge lines was the deep Kall River gorge. At the base of the northern ridge and just across the Kall River from Schmidt was the German town of Vossenach. The eastern side of the Huertgen Forest was occupied by numerous pillboxes with interlocking fields of fire. This was part of the West Wall, or the Siegfried Line, as we called it. The concrete pillboxes, bunkers, and Command Posts continued southward through Schmidt. Farther to the south and west another line of fortifications extended southward from Lammersdorf. The Siegfried Line stretched directly through the forest in two main defensive lines of the West Wall. They were almost parallel and several miles apart. Each had to be taken in turn, and each contained numerous pillboxes and bunkers.

Although I had seen heavy pillbox fortifications in Sicily, they were nothing compared to those in the Huertgen Forest. In the Huertgen they were huge, frequently consisting of several rooms. They were dark and blended with the trees and landscape around them; usually they were so well covered by leaves and pine needles that they were hardly visible. I was startled when I first realized that I was looking right at one only a short distance away and hadn't realized it was a pillbox. In addition to the pillboxes, concertina barbed wire was stretched across the forest floor. This, with trip wires, antipersonnel mines, and antitank mines, reduced fighting to its most primitive form: man against man at grenade distance.

When we arrived in early February, the Germans presumably had withdrawn to the Roer River line or very close to it. I went to the town of Vossenach (*Fig. 20.*) on reconnaissance. I found no enemy, and, having gone through the town by jeep, reached the trail that crossed the Kall River valley. Accompanied by the Division G-3, Colonel John Norton, and Sergeant Wood, I started down the trail. It was really a reconnaissance, since I did not know what the lay of the land would be, and what, if any, enemy might still be there. Our orders for the following day were to attack across the Kall River valley from Vossenach and seize the town of Schmidt. By now most of the snow had melted; there was only a small patch here and there under the trees.

I proceeded down the trail on foot. It was obviously impassable for a jeep; it was a shambles of wrecked vehicles and abandoned tanks. The first tanks that attempted to go down the trail had evidently slid off and thrown their tracks. In some cases the tanks had been pushed off the trail and toppled down the gorge among the trees. Between where the trail begins outside of Vossenach and the bottom of the canyon, there were four abandoned tank destroyers and five disabled and abandoned tanks. In addition, all along the sides of the trail there were many, many dead bodies, cadavers that had just emerged from the winter snow. Their gangrenous, broken, and torn bodies were rigid and grotesque, some of them with arms skyward, seemingly in supplication. They were wearing the red keystone of the 28th Infantry Division, "The Bloody Bucket." It had evidently fought through there the preceding fall, just before the heavy snows.

I continued down the trail for about half a mile to the bottom. There a tumbling mountain stream about six feet wide had to be crossed. A stone bridge had been over it but had long since been demolished, and a few planks were extended across the stone arches for the use of individual infantrymen. Nearby were dozens of litter cases, the bodies long dead. Apparently an aid station had been established near the creek, and

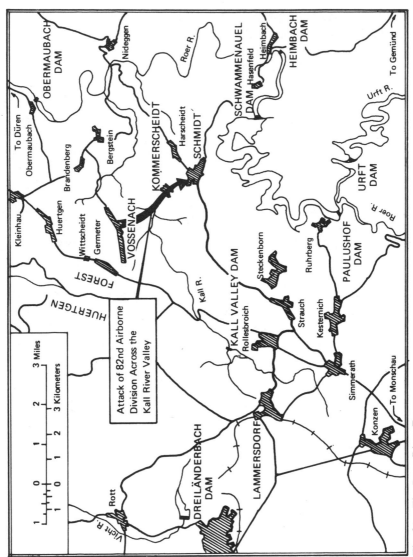

Fig. 20   The Roer River Dams

in the midst of the fighting it had been abandoned, many of the men dying on their stretchers. Off to the right, about fifty yards, a hard road appeared. Across it were about six American antitank mines. On this side of the mines were three or four American soldiers who had apparently been laying the mines and protecting them when they were killed. Beyond the American mines, about ten feet away, was a string of German antitank mines. On the other side of the mines were three or four German dead—a dramatic example of what the fighting must have been like in the Huertgen. It was savage, bitter, and at close quarters.

I made my way up the far side of the canyon. One had to be extremely careful because the trail had not been cleared of mines. I assumed that the woods were infested with mines and therefore I did not even get near the edge of the trail. As we approached the top, all the debris evinced a bitter struggle. There were many dead bodies about, an antitank gun or two, destroyed jeeps and abandoned weapons. At the top of the trail was a wide clearing. A few miles away could be seen the small German town of Kommerscheidt. So far, we had not been challenged by any Germans, although I knew they were supposed to be in the town of Kommerscheidt and in the town of Schmidt, beyond. The sun was setting, and I was anxious to get back to the other side of the valley before darkness. As darkness descended over the canyon, it was an eerie scene, like something from the lower levels of Dante's *Inferno*. To add to the horrors, a plaintive human voice could be heard calling from the woods some distance away.

We continued on down and up the other side, reaching Vossenach in the darkness. During the night troops were moved up, and I went back down the trail with the leading battalion not long after daylight. I remember vividly the lead battalion stopping for a short break. A young soldier, a new replacement, was looking with horror at the dead. He began to turn pale, then green, and he was obviously about to vomit. I talked to him, calmed him a bit, and assured him that we never abandoned our dead, that we always cared for them and buried them. I knew his state of mind. Every young soldier first entering combat is horrified by the sight of dead bodies that have been abandoned for some time. They always equate themselves with the dead they see and think that it could happen to them.

Soon the battalion continued down the trail and up the other side. It attacked across the open land, seized Kommerscheidt and then Schmidt.

The fighting had been moderate to heavy, and after capturing Schmidt, the batallion continued to receive artillery fire.

It seemed obvious to me that the regiment could not be supplied across the Kall River canyon, certainly not if the enemy interfered or if artillery fire covered the trail. In addition, the trail was impassable for vehicles. A catastrophe must have occurred there in the fall of 1944. I could not understand why the bodies had not been removed and buried. Neither Corps nor Army headquarters must have been aware of the conditions in the canyon. Otherwise, the bodies would have been buried and the disabled tanks recovered.

As soon as I returned to the Command Post, I called the Chief of Staff of V Corps and explained the situation to him, emphasizing the need for an alternate supply route. There was a good one from Lammersdorf to Schmidt, and that was under V Corps. He listened to my story, then laughed and asked, "Have you tried pack mules?" It made me furious. There is nothing that angers a combat soldier more than a higher headquarters staff officer belittling the problems of the combat infantryman. It is as old as soldiering.

My favorite description of a staff officer from a higher command is that in Shakespeare's *Henry IV*. Technology, as so often happens, has outdated his skills. Nevertheless, with an attitude of disdain, he visits a commander, Hotspur, who, weary of battle, wounded, and leaning on his sword, describes the visit:

> But I remember, when the fight was done,
> When I was dry with rage and extreme toil,
> Breathless and faint, leaning upon my sword,
> Came there a certain lord, neat and trimly dress'd,
> Fresh as a bridegroom; and his chin new reap'd
> Show'd like a stubble-land at harvest-home;
> He was perfumed like a milliner;
> And 'twixt his finger and his thumb he held
> A pouncet-box, which ever and anon
> He gave his nose and took't away again;
> Who therewith angry, when it next came there,
> Took it in snuff; and still he smiled and talk'd,
> And as the soldiers bore dead bodies by,
> He call'd them untaught knaves, unmannerly,
> To bring a slovenly unhandsome corse
> Betwixt the wind and his nobility.

. . . .

To see him shine so brisk, and smell so sweet,
And talk so like a waiting-gentlewoman
Of guns and drums and wounds—God save the mark!—
And telling me the sovereign'st thing on earth
Was parmaceti for an inward bruise;
And that it was great pity, so it was,
This villanous salt-petre should be digg'd
Out of the bowels of the harmless earth,
Which many a good tall fellow had destroy'd
So cowardly; and but for these vile guns,
He would himself have been a soldier.[24]

The following morning I went to Lammersdorf and met the Commander of V Corps and the Commander of the division whose headquarters was in that town. Obviously the attack on Schmidt should have been made straight down the ridge from Lammersdorf. Lammersdorf and Schmidt are connected by a paved road, the terrain was a mixture of woods and open farmland, good tank country, and it would have been a much simpler tactical undertaking than crossing the Kall River. The question in my mind was how in the world had they ever gotten involved in attacking across the Kall River valley? Why not stick to the high ground, bypassing the Germans in the valley, and then go on to the Roer River? I raised this question with a Corps staff officer present, but he brushed it aside. I asked why in the world they had attacked through the Huertgen Forest in the first place, but apparently that was a "no-no" question.

By this time they were talking about seizing the dams at the Roer River now that we had Schmidt. Based on my experience in airborne operations, I suggested that a dam is much like a bridge. Any amount of fire power can be brought to bear on one end of it and you will never own it. Instead an offensive should have been made up the other side of the dam and a coordinated attack made against both ends of the dam at once. This too seemed to be a not-to-be-talked-about subject.

In the meantime I noticed that the Corps Commander and the Division Commander were bent over a map. The Corps Commander occasionally drew a short line, a quarter to a half of an inch, with a blue grease pencil. It represented an infantry battalion, and he was suggesting to the Division Commander a tactical scheme by moving battalions about. I had the strangest feeling when I realized how remote they were

[24] *Henry IV*, Part I, Act I, Scene iii.

from the realities, from what it was like up where the battalions were. The thought crossed my mind that the disaster that had befallen the 28th Division in the Kall River valley might have had some relationship to the lack of understanding in higher headquarters of what the actual situation on the ground was. It turned out to be true, as I learned later.

In twenty-four hours the road from Lammersdorf to Schmidt was open and we pushed down closer to the Roer River. In the process we uncovered a much better road across the Kall River, easily traversed by jeeps. I was told that our next mission was to cross the Roer River itself. It was rapidly flowing and turbulent, and I did not relish the prospect. It was not too wide, but wide enough in any circumstances to be difficult—about fifty yards. The first problem was that it was dominated by high ground on the far side that in turn was occupied by dug-in German infantry. They had artillery which they used with more skill than I had seen since Normandy. Obviously the crossing would have to be made at night, with the initial wave crossing in inflated rubber boats, while our own troops on the launching shore tried to keep the German infantry fire down with suppression fire.

Once the infantry was on the far shore, they would have to spread out rapidly, destroying any Germans encountered and capturing a bridgehead. While that was going on, the technique was to get a line across the river well anchored on the far side. We could then begin to ferry troops across with a rigid boat. If all went well and a good bridgehead was established, a footbridge could be put across and finally a pontoon bridge if a linkup could be made with a suitable road network on the far side. I began to experiment with rubber rafts in the Kall River near the Roer, and it was disastrous. The river was flowing so fast that it tossed the rafts about like corks, and the rafts collapsed, and the troopers were thrown overboard into the icy water.

During the next few days I attended a meeting at the XVIII Corps headquarters where the Division Commander of a new division was present. He was obviously eager, and when he heard some of our plans to make a night crossing of the Roer, he expressed some envy, hoping that his division would get the chance to make the crossing. His wish was granted. On February 17 we pulled out of the line and his division took over. We were delighted to give him the mission, and it was the subject of much raillery among the staff.

Our winter war was over.

Spring of 1945

We were ordered back to Sissonne, France—to our old billets. We were all pleased at the prospect. The winter fighting had opened huge gaps in our ranks, and we looked forward to having our new replacements join us. As soon as they did, we began intensive training. In the meantime as many troopers as we could spare were sent on furloughs. We opened a War Room and began to follow closely the day-to-day fighting at the front. Weapons were repaired and replaced, ammunition and food distributed, and soon we were ready for whatever came next.

Looking back on the winter war, I realize that one battle made an indelible impression on my mind. It was our battle for Schmidt beyond the Huertgen Forest. Reconstruction of the battle was almost too much to contemplate, but as a soldier, I kept thinking about it. How could they have gotten themselves into such a predicament and why had the battlefield been abandoned so completely for so long? The Huertgen was an incredible battle area with its concrete pillboxes deeply imbedded in the surface of the forest, the whole landscape covered by German machine-gun and artillery fire. It was into this that the 9th Infantry Division drifted on September 19. In less than four weeks the division lost 4500 men, one casualty per yard gained. As the official history— *U.S. Army in World War II, The Siegfried Campaign*—sums it up, "The real winner appeared to be the vast, undulating blackish-green sea."

The 9th Infantry Division was followed by the 28th Division, which made the first attack across the Kall River valley to seize Schmidt. They captured Schmidt and within days were routed, more than 200 men captured by the Germans and the remainder driven back in complete disorder. The regimental commander was directed to report to Division Headquarters. Although he was physically exhausted and had been twice wounded by artillery fire, he started down the trail of the Kall

River gorge. He was in bad physical shape when the Engineers on the trail found him and put him in a jeep. He must have been a sight to see when he walked in on Major General Norman D. Cota, the Division Commander—covered with mud, twice wounded, unshaven, and staggering from exhaustion. It was too much for General Cota. At the sight of him Cota fainted.

Before the engagement was through, the 28th Division suffered more than 6000 casualties. The 28th was followed in turn by the 4th, the 8th, the 83rd, and a combat command of the 5th Armored Division. Tragically, before it was over, not only were the casualties appalling, but the battle turned out to be not so much to capture the Huertgen as to capture the dams over the Roer River on the far side of it. In retrospect, it was a battle that should not have been fought. Once we were into it, the higher command did not seem to appreciate the incredible conditions under which the infantrymen had to fight. Unlike other battles in Europe so far, we sacrificed our ground mobility, our tactical air support, and we chose to fight the Germans under conditions entirely to their advantage—where they had strong fortifications and were on ground they knew very well. The Germans agreed. In an interview after the war General Major Rudolph Gersdorff, Chief of Staff of the German Seventh Army, said, "The German Command could not understand the reason for the strong American attacks in the Huertgen Forest . . . the fighting in the wooded area denied the American troops the advantages offered them by their air and armored forces, the superiority of which had been decisive in all the battles waged before." But the Huertgen was over, and I think it fair to say that little was learned from it and less understood.[1] It had been our Passchendaele.

The return to Sissonne was a welcome respite from the horrors of the Huertgen. A breath of spring was in the air. Veterans were coming back from the hospitals daily, and replacements and parachute volun-

---

[1] In the spring of 1976 I had occasion to visit the Command and General Staff School at Fort Leavenworth, Kansas. They had made a thorough study of the fighting in the Huertgen Forest and the battle for Schmidt. It was presented to the students as a case history early in the course. One of the purposes of the presentation was to drive home to them the need for senior commanders to learn firsthand the battlefield conditions under which their troops might fight. The junior troop leaders who fought in the Huertgen were courageous and resourceful. Some of the regimental commanders were outstanding in every respect. But the more senior officers frequently lacked the firsthand knowledge of the conditions under which the troops were being compelled to fight. They had fought the battle on maps. And battles are not won on maps.

teers were arriving. A parachute jump school was opened, hard training was resumed, and morale soared.

One of the first missions assigned to us was to participate in a parachute assault on Berlin. It was a sobering prospect, especially to the veterans with four parachute combat jumps. But at the same time it *was* exciting. This was to be the final battle, and to be in at the finish, after the long road from North Africa, was very much to our liking. The capture of Berlin was part of Operation ECLIPSE. It was an operation that the high command had anticipated carrying out in the event that the collapse of Germany appeared imminent. General Lewis Brereton, Commanding General of the First Allied Airborne Army, first received orders from SHAEF to plan for the Airborne capture of Berlin on November 20, 1944. And even though ECLIPSE had been about for some time, it was not taken seriously by all echelons of the command until March 1945. With the XVIII Airborne Corps and the First Allied Airborne Army, plans were made for the landing of two American divisions and one British brigade. The American 82nd planned to land two parachute regiments just south of Tempelhof airfield. These regiments were to move to defensive positions well south of Tempelhof and block any German efforts to recapture the airfield. A third regiment was to seize the airfield and move into the city to gain contact with the other airborne formations.

In the midst of this planning, I was pleasantly surprised to learn that Arie Bestebreurtje, who had parachuted with me into Holland, was to join us. Bestebreurtje, who was a Special Forces Agent, was considered to have special knowledge of Berlin. During the war he had entered Berlin via Switzerland as an agent. As a teen-ager he had lived in Berlin and knew the Tempelhof area intimately. Early in March he received secret instructions to rendezvous with an American staff car near Namur, Belgium, in the middle of the night. He was ordered to remove all insignia from his uniform except rank, and the instructors impressed upon him the secret nature of his mission.

When he arrived in Sissonne we took him to the War Room and then through another door where, in great secrecy, the Berlin planning was under way. A curtain covered the map so that it could not be seen through the open door of the second room. On his arrival the map was uncovered, and a detailed discussion followed. He impressed upon us the character of the buildings around the Tempelhof airfield, the "Mietskasernen." Each was a little fortress. And it seemed likely that their capture, if the Germans decided to offer any resistance, would be a difficult and costly task.

Concurrently with our planning, General Ridgway was considering the administrative aspects of the operation. On March 8, 1945, he sent a memorandum to the First Allied Airborne Army in which he wrote, "It is believed that the reaction of the German mind will be tremendously influenced by the personal appearance of individual soldiers who participate in Operation ECLIPSE . . . it is the intention of this headquarters to take into ECLIPSE a dress as well as a field uniform."

At about this time I found an abandoned military airfield not far from Sissonne, and rehearsals for the Berlin operation were commenced at once. Somehow, because of our past combat experience, we assumed that the most difficult operation would be seizing and organizing the defense of Tempelhof. Our first rehearsal made it quite clear, however, that the most difficult task would be receiving and processing the cargo that would be airlanded there. We devised a scheme, and actually carried it out in rehearsal, whereby planes arrived at very brief intervals, taxied off the runway, did a 180-degree encirclement of the field, parked and there unloaded, and immediately took off to bring in more cargo. In an hour or so we had cargo piled so high around the field that we had to stop the operation. We then began to analyze the cargo that had to be flown in and to re-establish priorities. It was obvious that the critical problem was the removal of the cargo from the field, not flying it in.[2]

So far in World War II the division had planned and carried out four major airborne operations. In addition, we had planned several that had not been executed, notably the capture of Rome. We were confident

[2] Preparation for the airborne seizure of Berlin was a closely guarded secret. Only those with an absolute need to know were allowed to have access to detailed planning. To the junior officers and NCOs, the training was considered to be routine. Despite the care with which we guarded our preparations, the Soviets were aware of our intentions. I was startled to learn from Cornelius Ryan, who interviewed a number of the senior Soviet officers in Moscow in April 1963, that Marshal Stalin told them of the plan of the Allies. As soon as he received Eisenhower's message of March 28 declaring his plan to meet the Red Army south of Berlin, and the low priority Eisenhower gave to Berlin, Marshal Stalin called in his two marshals who were capable of a rapid seizure of Berlin; Zhukov and Konev. He told them that Berlin was Eisenhower's main aim and that "two Allied airborne divisions are being rapidly readied for a drop on Berlin." He then pitted one marshal against the other, challenging them to see who could get to Berlin first, ahead of the Americans. I discussed this interview with Cornelius Ryan on several occasions. There is no question about the Soviets' having the information. It was Marshal Vasili Sokolovsky who told Ryan of the information given to Zhukov. Sokolovsky was Zhukov's Chief of Staff whom I got to know very well in Berlin after the war.

about the Berlin operation. Not only did we have the experience, but we now had a seasoned well-trained division. In addition, we had acquired quite a few panzerfausts and a full complement of 57 mm. antitank weapons.

Although Berlin loomed large among the many problems besetting Eisenhower in the spring of 1945, it was only one of a mélange of many problems. The command problem, the acceptance or rejection of a British deputy to control the land battle, had been an irksome and persistent one, but it was only part of the over-all problem that one encountered when dealing with the British. As the American buildup continued through the fall of '44, Winston Churchill was loath to accept a secondary role in the war. Field Marshal Sir Alan Brooke noted in his diary of November 18, 1944, "Winston hated having to give up the position of the predominant partner which he held at the start. As a result, he became inclined at times to put out strategic proposals which he knew were unsound, purely to spite the Americans."

Field Marshal Montgomery never liked being in a position subordinate to the Americans. In fact, he didn't like being subordinate to anyone. But he looked forward, as did Prime Minister Churchill and Field Marshal Brooke, to being on center stage in the last great battle, the battle of Berlin. Again referring to this attitude in his diary on January 2, 1945, Brooke, in remembering a conversation with Churchill, was to note, "He then propounded strategies based on insuring that British troops were retained in the limelight, if necessary, at the expense of the Americans." Montgomery communicated almost every day with Brooke, and he was well aware of the desires of Churchill. He, too, wanted to be in the limelight when the last battle was fought, and that meant, to him, the capture of Berlin.

To do this, however, provided all other aspects of the tactical situation at the time would favor it, it would be necessary for the British to have twenty-four additional U.S. divisions, or two field armies. Furthermore, they would require a massive amount of U.S. logistical support. This meant that "The Plan" that they had been recommending had to be carried out without deviation and that the U.S. Ninth Army and U.S. First Army had to be placed under British control. Montgomery's persistence in being given command of the land battle intensified after the Battle of the Bulge to the point where Eisenhower had to recognize it for what it was: either Montgomery would continue to command his Army Group and stay where he was and Eisenhower would remain as Supreme

Commander, or Eisenhower would place the problem before the Combined Chiefs of Staff and either Montgomery or Eisenhower would have to go. When this information was brought to Montgomery from Eisenhower's headquarters by Montgomery's Chief of Staff, General de Guingand, Montgomery backed down gracefully and wrote a brief note to General Eisenhower accepting his position.

The Prime Minister, however, thought of a new scheme. He would bring Field Marshal Sir Harold Alexander from the Mediterranean, where earlier he had been a supporter of Eisenhower and very highly regarded by Eisenhower. The Prime Minister would suggest that Eisenhower's deputy, Air Marshal Tedder, be replaced by Alexander. Thus we would have a topflight soldier deputy to Eisenhower and in a position to command all the land forces. The British sounded out Eisenhower on the idea, and he agreed in principle that he would not object to Alexander's replacing Tedder. He appeared not to realize what the Prime Minister was attempting to accomplish. General George Marshall, however, understood. En route to the Malta Conference, General Marshall met General Eisenhower in Marseilles in late January 1945, where they spent a day going over Eisenhower's problem. At that time, General Marshall told Eisenhower that in no circumstances should he accept Alexander, and, indeed, if he did, Marshall would resign as Chief of Staff of the U.S. Army. This was the stiffening that Eisenhower needed, and in a rather long cable to the Prime Minister, Eisenhower explained why Alexander would not be acceptable. Immediately following the Marseilles conference, the Combined Chiefs of Staff met in Malta. They were en route to Yalta, and there the British insisted on a reaffirmation of The Plan. Eisenhower's Chief of Staff, General Bedell Smith, briefed them, and the British were reassured.

While General Eisenhower had a number of serious, conflicting problems as we entered the month of March, one of them, in particular, could not be shared with the British, and that was the redeployment of individuals back to the United States, and the planned redeployment of combat formations to the Pacific to take part in the war against Japan. As early as February 1945, at the insistence of the War Department, General Eisenhower's headquarters began to develop plans to accomplish these missions. The attitude of the War Department was that the war in Europe would soon end, and when it did, all General Eisenhower would need would be sufficient troop strength to occupy a conquered Germany. His troop strength was approaching three million Americans organized into sixty-one combat divisions, as well as many service and combat support units. As the fighting began to slow down, he worried about those who would not be fully engaged in combat and thus be idle, and he had to begin to meet demands from the Pacific theater.

Thus, as his eager combat formations raced for the Elbe, and, it was hoped, beyond, stretching themselves well beyond their strong bases of logistic support, Eisenhower's command was being drawn in the opposite direction toward the Pacific. And while this was going on, plans were being made for the redeployment of high-point personnel. These were individuals who had been in combat for long periods, and those who had been wounded, among other criteria. I remember the impact that this program had on the 82nd Airborne Division. It was quite devastating, and I am sure that other formations had the same experience. Individuals with high points were deployed out of the division back to the United States, regardless of the role they occupied, whether as machine gunners or clerks; it made little difference. Thus combat formations lost their integrity very quickly. To be sure, this did not happen until VE Day, but there was much talk about it, and we were aware that it would happen.

In fact, on a warm spring day, while we were still at Sissonne, I assembled the entire division and talked to them about our training so far and probable missions that lay ahead of us. I made mention of Berlin, but I also thought it well to suggest to them that we might be considered for that other war, the Pacific war. Already there were beginning to appear rumbles of complaint in the press about European combat divisions having to go to the Pacific to finish that war, and I thought it well to soften the blow if it was to come. The A-bomb saved us from that, but that was not until August. By the end of March the redeployment problem had become a very serious matter, and in early April Eisenhower established a formal headquarters in Europe to process and administer individuals and troop formations leaving the theater for movement to the Pacific.

On March 7 General Eisenhower had a dinner for several senior airborne officers at his home in Rheims. I was among those present. It was a very pleasant evening. In the midst of dinner he was called to the telephone by General Bradley, who told him that he had captured a bridge over the Rhine River near Remagen. This was exciting news. Ever since we had begun planning in London for the Normandy assault, a crossing of the Rhine had been the object of much concern. Historically, a military crossing of the Rhine was of the greatest importance. However, the location of the river crossing, and the bridgehead, had to bear some reasonable relationship to the plans of the highest headquarters for the final battle of the war. What troubled Bradley was whether or not sending reinforcements across would be committing Eisenhower to a course of action that he might not want to take. But Eisenhower told Bradley to put everything across that he had—four divisions, which would be increased soon to five. So we were across the Rhine, and the end could not be far away, or so it seemed.

As it turned out, Bradley's call to General Eisenhower was precipitated by a heated discussion that was taking place in Bradley's headquarters that very evening. By chance, General Eisenhower's G-3, the man in charge of plans and operations, Major General "Pinky" Bull,[3] was at Bradley's headquarters the evening of March 7. When Bradley received the call from General Hodges, the commanding general of the U.S. First Army, telling him that he had captured the bridge, Bradley's reply, according to his memoirs, was:

> "Hot dog, Courtney, this will bust him wide open. Are you getting all your stuff across?"
> "Just as fast as we can push it over," replied Hodges.
> Standing nearby was "Pinky" Bull; he wasn't so sure.
> "Sure, you've got a bridge [Brad], but what good is it going to do you. You're not going anywhere down there at Remagen. It just doesn't fit into The Plan."[4]

This was the Churchill-Brooke-Montgomery plan, which envisioned making a major effort across northern Germany, striking directly for Berlin. This was opposed to the so-called broad-front strategy of Eisenhower, which envisioned pressing the war vigorously against the Germans on a very broad front, while at the same time preserving the final

[3] Major General Harold Roe Bull, USMA 1914, was well known in the peacetime Army and highly regarded. He was a career infantry officer, and in 1941 was Commanding General of the 4th Infantry Division. Because of his outstanding record as a trainer, he was moved to G-3 of the War Department General Staff. I joined him in London in November 1943 when we were planning for the Normandy operation. He continued as Eisenhower's G-3 throughout the war. He was a dedicated, capable soldier who, no doubt, would have achieved high command if he had not been retained on Eisenhower's staff. "Pinky" alluded to his florid complexion. After the war he served as Commandant of the War College from 1949 to 1952, after which he retired. He died on November 1, 1976.
[4] Bradley, op. cit.

option as to when and where to end the war until the tactical situation became clearer. The seizure of the crossing at Remagen suggested to General Bradley a third possibility, a "Bradley Plan" that envisioned a direct thrust to the east to link up with the Soviets.

This would obviate the need to give American divisions to Montgomery and would also relegate Montgomery and his Army Group to a secondary role.

The capture of the Remagen bridge and Eisenhower's prompt decision to exploit the crossing was a historic event of extraordinary importance. It would allow General Eisenhower to give free rein to his own generals: Bradley, Patton, Hodges, and Simpson. Further, it would allow Eisenhower to pursue the strategy that would bring about the destruction of the German armed forces at the earliest possible date. Finally, it would resolve the conflict that had been raging, ever since the Normandy landings, between the Americans and the British on how to end the war. But for it to be carried out successfully, it was important that the details of the plan not be disclosed to the British until it was an accomplished fact. Otherwise, Prime Minister Churchill, Field Marshal Brooke, and Field Marshal Montgomery would strongly object to the abandonment of The Plan, to Berlin, and to the casting of the British into a secondary role in the final battle with the primary mission being given to Bradley's Army Group.

In the meantime Montgomery's 21st Army Group closed up on the Rhine. It consisted of the British Second Army, the Canadian Twelfth Army, and the U.S. Ninth Army. The U.S. Ninth had been given to Montgomery to enable him to achieve a crossing of the Rhine River when he was ready to make that effort. The U.S. First, which had been temporarily assigned to Montgomery during the Battle of the Bulge, was reassigned to Bradley's 12th Army Group, which now consisted of the U.S. First Army and the U.S. Third Army. If the situation evolved as Eisenhower and Bradley hoped it would, the Ninth Army was to be reassigned to Bradley's Army Group after the Rhine crossing had been accomplished and the pocket of Germans who were surrounded as a consequence of that crossing was eliminated. In addition, Bradley was to be given the newly formed U.S. Fifteenth Army.

As Montgomery moved on with his planning to achieve a crossing of the Rhine, he developed an early plan in late January 1945. The plan envisioned a typical Montgomery set-piece battle that would force a crossing of the Rhine River north of the Ruhr early in the spring. The first instructions to the U.S. Ninth Army in effect placed an Army Corps under Sir Miles Dempsey's Second Army for the attack. There was no role envisioned for the U.S. Ninth as a whole, and its commander, General William H. Simpson, and his staff were dumfounded, for they had trained and led the Army and they intended to fight it as an Army. The protests were widespread, and Montgomery quickly changed his plans so as to include the Ninth Army headquarters in the offensive. Nevertheless, it was quickly seen by the Americans as another attempt to use their troops under British command and thus to give credit to the British for the victory that the Americans would achieve.

As the offensive toward the Rhine rolled on, the U.S. Ninth Army proved to be combat-tough and aggressive. It reached the Rhine in early March and prepared to force a quick crossing before the German resistance could build up on the far side. This was in keeping with American combat doctrine, which allowed a maximum of initiative to subordinate commanders in order that they might take advantage of local situations as they encountered them. Montgomery, however, denied it permission to cross and instead held it in readiness for the set piece that was to follow in late March.[5] This, too, did not go down well with the Ninth Army. After that they were restless to go back under Bradley's American command.

In the meantime Bradley steadily built up his troop strength in the Remagen bridgehead. He ordered his combat divisions to advance about 1000 yards a day, depending upon the terrain, so as to deny the Germans the opportunity of laying extensive minefields in front of them.[6]

On March 20 General Bradley and General Eisenhower went to Sous-le-Vent, near Cannes, for a short vacation. They were accompanied by two other officers and, according to Kay Summersby Morgan, in her last book, *Past Forgetting,* she and three other WACs accompanied the party. For some time General Bedell Smith, Eisenhower's Chief of Staff, had been urging Eisenhower to take a rest. Before leaving his headquarters, General Eisenhower issued orders to "Pinky" Bull to prepare the detailed and final plan for an advance by Bradley's Army

[5] As Simpson approached the Rhine, he made plans for a crossing. He presented them to Montgomery and was turned down. The official history of the Ninth Army reads, "So the course of history as it might have developed had the Ninth Army leapt the Rhine early in March will never be known. Of one point Ninth Army men are certain—it could have been done and done successfully."
[6] Conversations with General Omar Bradley at his home in Beverly Hills in August 1975.

Group directly to the east. This was the "Bradley Plan" that envisioned abandoning Berlin to the Soviets and moving eastward with all the U.S. armies under Bradley's command for a linkup with the Soviets. Generals Eisenhower and Bradley spent several days together before they returned to their troop commands.[7]

On the night of March 22–23, using the leading elements of the U.S. 5th Infantry Division, Patton crossed the Rhine near the small town of Oppenheim, midway between Worms and Mainz. Oppenheim was not directly connected to a good road network, and it was assumed that the Germans would be taken by surprise. They were. Patton asked Bradley to say nothing about the crossing, because there were not many Germans in the vicinity and he did not want to alert the German higher command. The next day Patton asked Bradley to announce it—he wanted the world to know of it before Montgomery made his crossing, which was scheduled for March 23.

After months of preparation, Montgomery staged a spectacular crossing of the Rhine north of the Ruhr on the night of March 23–24. At 9:00 P.M. Lieutenant General Brian G. Horrocks' 30 Corps entered the Rhine River southwest of the small town of Rees. In less than seven minutes they touched down on the far shore. Montgomery's crossing was well under way. The following morning the British 6th Airborne Division and the U.S. 17th Airborne Division landed in the enemy rear areas. The landing was made at 10:00 A.M. in the face of intense small-arms fire and light ack-ack. The air column was two hours and thirty-two minutes long. It consisted of 889 escorting fighters, 1696 transport planes, and 1348 gliders, bringing altogether 21,680 paratroopers and glidermen to the battlefield. This was followed closely by 240 four-engine Liberator bombers, dropping 582 tons of supplies. Another 2153 fighter aircraft either maintained a protective umbrella over the target area or ranged far over Germany in quest of any German planes that might seek to interfere. High-ranking observers were present in abundance; General Brereton, commanding the First Allied Airborne Army, watched from the west bank of the Rhine, as did Prime Minister Churchill; the Supreme Commander, General Eisenhower; and the Chief of the Imperial General Staff, Field Marshal Sir Alan Brooke. It was a spectacularly staged, typical Montgomery set piece.

Never having viewed an airborne operation as a spectator, I flew up

[7] I discussed this vacation with "Pinky" Bull in November 1975, and he remarked rather dryly, "They didn't get much rest."

from Sissonne in a DC-3, a troop carrier transport. We flew over the operation at about 2000 feet, and it was an awesome spectacle. At one time I counted twenty-three transports or gliders going down in flames, trying desperately to make it back to the west bank. To many the question that immediately arose was, "Was it necessary? Could not the ground troops have achieved the same objectives at less cost?" The casualties in the U.S. 17th Airborne Division on the first day were 159 killed, 522 wounded, and 240 missing. There were 50 gliders lost, 44 transports destroyed, and 332 transports damaged. Among the pilots of the 9th Troop Carrier Command, 41 were killed, 153 wounded, and 163 missing. Again the Americans were impressed by the contrast between how Patton and Hodges got across the river, on the run as it were, and the manner in which Montgomery took so much time and so many resources to prepare for his set piece. They believed also that if Simpson had been allowed to go, he would have crossed the Rhine—in Montgomery's sector—weeks before Montgomery's crossing was made.

Shortly after Montgomery's crossing of the Rhine, the 82nd Airborne Division was moved up to the Rhine River, north and south of Cologne. The first warm breath of spring touched the flatlands west of Cologne, and extensive tulip beds were in full bloom.

On the way up to our new front I talked to the Commanding General of the newly established U.S. Fifteenth Army, Major General Leonard T. Gerow. He told me that he wanted us to be aggressive, to seek contacts with the Germans across the river, and to identify the formations opposing us. I assured him that we would.

One of our first responsibilities in the vicinity of Cologne was to take over a camp of 10,000 Russian prisoners, most of them civilians. They had been shipped back by the German armies and put into a barbed-wire compound on the outskirts of Cologne. They were highly organized. A Russian Army major was in charge of the camp. There was an information center, with maps, where they kept track of how the war was going, and they were a spirited lot. We could not remove the barricades and turn them loose on the civilians who lived in Cologne, but that was just what they wanted. Revenge was foremost in their minds, and while we were quite in sympathy with their feeling, we could not have rioting and chaos on our hands. On one occasion I had to go to the camp at 2:00 A.M., and with an interpreter I got on top of the hood of a jeep and harangued the crowd for about an hour, trying to explain to them why we were doing what we were doing, and why it was in the common good to bring the war to an end quickly with no rioting and confusion in the rear areas. We, of course, took over the responsibility for their medical care and for feeding and sheltering them. Gradually more and more displaced persons began to come under our responsibility. It was the beginning of what was to be a serious problem in the immediate postwar period.

Fraternization also loomed unpleasantly. Higher headquarters was adamant on the point of no association between the troops and the Germans. After the long trek all the way from North Africa, some of the frauleins looked quite attractive. But the higher command was afraid that the troops would be politically contaminated. The GIs reasoned that as long as they kept on their airborne caps and their jump boots, as tokens of their patriotism, they should be allowed to do anything, or almost anything. Some months later, when we were on occupation duty in Berlin, I tried to explain this to General Patton by saying, "General, you know the troops really aren't fraternizing." He turned to me abruptly. "Gavin, you're as nutty as a fruitcake." I said nothing more to him. The higher command's agitation about the fraternization problem gradually began to diminish and in time seemed to go away.

Our front on the Rhine River extended ten or twelve miles north and south of Cologne. All the bridges at Cologne were destroyed. Most of downtown Cologne was flattened also. For many blocks there were high piles of rubble, out of which grew tall weeds. Strangely, the cathedral stood intact. Even many of the windows were unbroken. Inside the cathedral the Germans had built brick walls around the statues, many of them out on the main floor of the cathedral. To the best of my knowledge, they were all spared.

As the retreating Germans reached the Rhine, they found that they could not get their tanks across the river, so they abandoned them by the hundreds, although they were still in good working order. One Tiger was left standing in the square in front of the cathedral. We decided to use it to test our various antitank weapons, including the German panzerfaust, as well as our bazooka and the 57 mm. The panzerfaust was by far the best weapon, if one was ready to wait until the tank was within approximately fifty yards. Remembering the instructions of General Gerow, I began to consider the possibilities of patrolling against the Germans on the far side of the river.

Actually we were confronted by 325,000 Germans in the Rose Pocket, and it was a mixed bag of all types of units. When sector assignments were made, the 505th was south of Cologne, extending down to Bonn, and the 504th was north of Cologne, extending northward about ten miles. They at once began night patrols across the river. It proved to be difficult and at times costly. The river was flowing rapidly, and a patrol sent across was very vulnerable, particularly as it approached the far shore. With characteristic disdain for the danger, Colonel Tucker of the 504th followed a better idea. During the course of a night he sent two companies of infantry across to seize the small German town of Hittdorf. They encountered little opposition and no serious problems. By daylight they owned the town and were well organized. It was Tucker's intention to use this as a base for patrolling operations; thus he would not have to send men in rowboats across the river every night. It was a fine idea except that it drew upon him the wrath of all the Germans in the Rose Pocket; specifically, he was attacked by the 3rd Parachute Infantry Regiment and after an all-day fight backed up into the last houses on the riverbank. During the following night he withdrew his forces.

The next morning Hitler announced that a bridgehead that the Allies had attained for the purposes of putting a pontoon bridge across had been destroyed. Our Corps Commander, General Ernest Harmon, heard about it and called me on the telephone at once. We had a long, serious talk. I insisted that we didn't want to sit and do nothing, and if the Germans were on the other side we wanted to attack them. He told me that his orders were to incur no casualties in the 82nd, since there was still an airborne assault envisioned for us. We were presumed to be up there on what amounted to occupation duty. The words "airborne assault" had a particular meaning to me. They could mean only the airborne capture of Berlin. And if that was to be my next mission, I wanted to have available every man I could get my hands on.[8]

By late March Eisenhower had three well-established bridgeheads over the Rhine: Montgomery's north of the Ruhr, Hodges' at Remagen, and Patton's farther south. Patton's staff was convinced that the problem of a Rhine crossing from here on out would be one for the engineers, not for the infantry, since Patton could cross the Rhine almost at

[8] Years later—in 1976, to be exact—in a letter exchange with General Harmon, I learned that he had been told, in secret, that the 82nd Airborne Division was earmarked for an airborne assault on the mainland of Japan. We were one of the divisions scheduled for redeployment to the Pacific. And we were totally unaware of it.

will. The next task confronting Eisenhower was the rapid encirclement of the Ruhr. This was undertaken at once and completed on April 1; the mopping-up took a couple of weeks longer. Three hundred and fifty thousand German troops, including Field Marshal Model, had been taken in the pocket—it was a greater bag than that taken by the Russians when they encircled German Field Marshal Friedrich Paulus opposite Stalingrad. It also resulted in a gap 250 miles wide being torn in the German defenses. Bradley thought of Hodges' First Army and Patton's Third Army as two very powerful horses he could drive ahead and keep under control, bringing up Simpson's Ninth Army on his left when it was detached from Montgomery, and getting protection from the U.S. Seventh Army on his right.

The situation was now rapidly coming to a head. On March 24 Bradley and Eisenhower had met Montgomery at his headquarters. Eisenhower used the occasion to familiarize Montgomery with his concept of how to bring the war to an end. Implicit in Eisenhower's message to Montgomery was the view that he intended to advance to the east when the Ruhr pocket mop-up was completed. At that time he intended to take the U.S. Ninth Army from Montgomery and return it to General Bradley's Army Group. It at once raised questions in Montgomery's mind, for he readily saw the implication that the seizure of Berlin, as his and Eisenhower's prime objective, might be abandoned. Eisenhower tended to assure him on this point, professing to be open-minded concerning the concluding phase of the war.

On March 25 Eisenhower again was in Montgomery's headquarters to meet Prime Minister Churchill and Field Marshal Brooke. Winston Churchill made it clear that he foresaw Berlin as the final objective. Eisenhower did not entirely agree; he demurred, but was noncommittal. His position was somewhat similar to that explained to Montgomery the preceding day—he said that his mind was open and that he was prepared to move on Berlin if this was how the tactical situation evolved. However, ever since his meeting with Bradley at Sous-le-Vent, he had been moving aggressively forward in planning to bring the war to an end by an advance to the east to link up with the Soviets.

The following day, March 26, he attended what must have been a very important meeting. Bradley, Patton, and Hodges all met with General Eisenhower at the U.S. First Army's headquarters. Here the details on Bradley's main thrust in the direction of Dresden-Leipzig, rather than going for Berlin, were hammered out. The first cabled suggestion from Washington in support of Eisenhower's thinking came the following day, March 27, in a message from General Marshall. The significant paragraph read as follows:

> From the current operation reports it looks like the German defense system in the West may break up. This would permit you to move a considerable number of your divisions rapidly eastward on a broad front. What are your views on the possibility and soundness of pushing United States Forces rapidly forward on, say the NÜRN-BERG-LINZ or KARLSRUHE-MUNICH axes? The idea behind this is that in a situation where GERMANY is breaking up, rapid action might prevent the formation of any organized resistance areas. The mountainous country in the south is considered a possibility for one of these.

Marshall's letter raised two important points: the first was the need to consider a thrust to the east and possibly southward; in the second he opened the possibility of a German national redoubt.

The idea of a German "National Redoubt" was to become quite pervasive through all echelons of the Allied command in Europe, and a matter of growing concern. It was not only talked about in all the high commands, but it became a matter of much discussion in *Stars and Stripes*. It was talked about by everyone, from privates to generals. In a message to the War Department on March 20, Eisenhower, after discussing what were essentially clean-up operations, observed that "we could launch a movement to the southeast to prevent Nazi occupation of a Nazi citadel."

This was reinforced the following day by a message in which he envisioned the advantage of attacking in the southern areas with the comment "that an early junction with the Russians there would prevent the establishment of a Nazi fortress in southern Germany." In the end, however, the National Redoubt proved to be illusory, and after the war Bradley was to lament:

> Not until after the campaign ended were we to learn that this Redoubt existed largely in the imagination of a few fanatic Nazis. It grew into so exaggerated a scheme that I am astonished we could have believed it as innocently as we did. But while it persisted, this legend of the Redoubt was too ominous a threat to be ignored, and in con-

sequence it shaped our tactical thinking during the closing weeks of the war.[9]

Returning to the planning, Eisenhower and his senior generals continued to work out the details of the final attack toward the east, thus abandoning the plan that envisioned Montgomery's seizure of Berlin. The American generals had the strength, and they intended to use it to win the war in the manner they considered to be in the U.S. interest, and in conformity with Eisenhower's mission.

In the meantime the American generals saw to it that their divisions were so involved that they could not readily be taken away from them. "We all felt," wrote Patton afterward, "it was essential that the First and Third Armies should get themselves so involved that Montgomery's plan to use most of the divisions on the Western front, British and American, under his command . . . could not come off. . . ."

At the end of March the Allies had four and a half million men in combat. They were organized into 90 divisions, of which 25 were armored and 5 airborne. As the multiple drives beyond the Rhine began, Montgomery's 21st Army Group controlled 30 divisions (including 12 U.S. divisions in the U.S. Ninth Army). Bradley's 12th Army Group had 34 divisions, including 6 in his new army, the Fifteenth. Devers' 6th Army Group, on the south, had 12 U.S. Divisions and 11 French divisions.

In late March the Red Army was on the Oder River, 30 miles from Berlin. The nearest Allies were 250 miles from Berlin. The time had come for Eisenhower to disclose his hand, to explain what his intentions were in bringing the war to an end. He also had to think seriously of the forthcoming meeting with the Russian armies, since the dangers of tactical aircraft engaging each other's forces, and the likelihood of artillery fire involving both sides, as well as infantry confrontations, were very real.

On March 28 Eisenhower sent a message to Marshal Stalin by way of our military mission in Moscow, which was headed by Major General John R. Deane. He outlined his plans for the immediate future and his intention to drive directly east to Leipzig. Implied was the abandonment of Berlin.

[9] Bradley, op. cit., p. 536.
    In an interview given to Cornelius Ryan after the war, Eisenhower, referring to Lübeck, on the north, and the so-called Redoubt area, stated, "I deem both of these to be more important than the capture of Berlin."

This came as a bombshell to Prime Minister Churchill and Field Marshals Brooke and Montgomery. An intensive exchange of telegrams, involving all the concerned headquarters, followed. Eisenhower stuck to his plan, reaffirming his intention to hold in the central area once he reached the Elbe and to clean up his flanks. By the latter he referred to linking up with the Soviets on the south, denying the Germans any chance to establish a redoubt. On the north he intended to cross the Elbe and strike in the direction of Lübeck, thus sealing off Denmark from Soviet occupation. The 82nd was destined to take part in this action.

Meanwhile, the 82nd Airborne Division continued in its occupation role along the Rhine River north and south of Cologne. We received word of the death of President Roosevelt on April 12. It came as a shock to all of us. An appropriate ceremony was held wherever the troops could be assembled. About the third week in April I received an alert to be prepared to move to the north and to rejoin the British Second Army under Ridgway's XVIII Airborne Corps.

I was directed to assemble the division on the west bank of the Elbe River, well south of Hamburg, near the small German town of Bleckede. Once the division was withdrawn from its front and organized for the move, I hurriedly went to the new area to learn what our next mission was to be.

On the afternoon of April 29 the 82nd Airborne Division was strung out, moving by truck and rail, more than 200 miles from Cologne. By darkness the 505th Parachute Infantry, less one battalion, was expected to arrive at the Bleckede ferry site. General Sir Miles Dempsey, Commanding General of the British Second Army, and Lieutenant General Matthew Ridgway, Commander of the U.S. XVIII Corps, came to my Command Post to discuss the proposed crossing with me. General Dempsey was most anxious that the crossing be made as soon as possible in order to cut off the Russian advance toward Denmark. About twenty miles to our left the British had established a bridgehead over the Elbe, but if we used it, it would delay our meeting the Russians by another five or six days, and we most certainly would be too late to intercept them. We had to make a hasty crossing and establish our own bridgehead at Bleckede.

Across the Elbe the Germans could be seen digging in and organizing their defenses. General Ridgway offered to reinforce me with troops from another nearby division, the U.S. 8th Infantry, as well as engineer support with boats and amphibious vehicles. It appeared to be a feasible undertaking, although a bit marginal, and plans were made accordingly. An assault force crossed at 1:00 A.M. and took the Germans completely by surprise. I crossed with the leading wave. Most of the Germans were routed out of their foxholes along the dikes of the river by troopers with flashlights and M-1 rifles. Our only surprise was the use of magnetic sea mines by the Germans. They planted the mines along the roads, preset to detonate when a specific number of vehicles had passed. The first one that went off was at the actual ferry site on the German side of the river. I was about 100 yards away, and it tossed a jeep high into the air, turning it over several times. We had never seen anything like it, and it took us some time to figure out what sort of explosion it had been. The Germans also were expending their last artillery ammunition, and unusually heavy concentrations came down on us. But the veteran 30.5th cleared its bridgehead and was well consolidated by daylight, and at once the advance to the south began. On the night of April 30 the 504th arrived and was committed on the right of the 505th, both continuing to advance all day, May 1.

There were rumors from prisoners and civilians that the Russians were not far away. How far we did not know. In anticipation of something unusual happening, I was up before daylight on May 2 and rode out in a jeep with a reconnaissance platoon. It was a lovely spring morning. The fields were freshly green, and flowers and chestnut trees along the road were in full bloom. The streets and roads were deserted as we entered the first small German town. Ahead of us on a cobblestone street, as we approached a Y in the road, about half a mile away I saw a German soldier on a motorcycle scoot to the left across the street. His leather coat glistened in the early-morning sunlight. The other leg of the Y-shaped road intersection led to the left, where he could be intercepted. Pounding over the cobblestones, we drove up that streeet as fast as we could. When he came in sight, we fired at him from the bounding jeep and missed, the bullets ricocheting off the cobblestones through the trees, causing a shower of leaves and flower petals. We soon overtook him, and as he caromed into a ditch beside the road, we took him prisoner. He was the last German in the war we were to see running away.

By late morning large groups of Germans began to appear in patches of woods on the horizon. They seemed to be milling about indecisively and to be not particularly desirous to fight. It was an eerie sight for those of us who had fought for more than three years all the way from Africa, for the mere sight of that bucket helmet meant certain death unless one reacted instantly and instinctively, taking cover and firing. So, taking our lives into our hands, we drove right up to them. They wanted to surrender. As we went on, their numbers increased by the hundreds and then thousands. Finally, by midafternoon, I arrived at the charming German village of Ludwigslust in Mecklenburg. The streets were jammed with retreating German soldiers and their camp followers. Young and old, crippled and wounded, robust and ailing, men and women, but mostly men, were trying to get through the town to go to our rear. Adding to the confusion were civilians and shopkeepers, piling whatever they owned in wagons and small handcarts, their faces stricken with fear for what would happen if the Russians were to capture them.

Our troopers were attacking just beyond the town and more were coming up. I was standing near the curb of a main street intersection, wearing a parachute jumpsuit faded from three years of war, carrying an M-1 rifle over my shoulder, looking like any other GI in the 82nd, except for the two stars on my collar and on my helmet. An American GI came up to me and said that there was a German general looking for the American general who was in charge. I told him to send him over. He arrived, rather haughtily, I thought, and a bit threadbare, but otherwise impeccably attired in the field gray uniform of the Wehrmacht. It was set off by the red collar tabs and insignia of a general, and an Iron Cross dangled at his throat. When told that I was the American general, he looked at me with some disdain, saying that I couldn't be; I was too young and did not look like a general to him. It took only a moment to change his mind. The General said that he represented Lieutenant General Kurt von Tippelskirch, commanding the 21st German Army Group, and that he wanted to talk terms with me. Earlier I had been urged by Colonel Charles Billingslea, Commanding Officer of the 325th Glider Infantry, who had just occupied the Palace of Ludwigslust, to use it for a Command Post if the need arose. I had not yet seen it. We had already discussed the need for a suitable Command Post, since it was to be, for us, the last of the war and the occasion would be a historic one. I told the General that I would be happy to see General von Tippelskirch at the Palace that evening. He suggested eight o'clock, and we agreed.

The movement of the prisoners and refugees continued all that day and all the next day. We had never seen anything like it. We told them just to throw away their weapons and continue to our rear. By day's end we counted more than 2000 trucks and more than 125 half-trucks and tanks, not to mention thousands of rifles, machine guns, and artillery pieces abandoned in the ditches along the road. Two Hungarian cavalry regiments with splendid-looking horses and equipment came by and offered to fight with us against the Russians. A trip through a few miles of the division area took hours because of the confusion that went on day and night. I remember, in particular, one poignant scene. Some troopers had found a concertina, and as they watched some rather grim-looking soldiers of the super-race march by, they played "Lilli Marlene." Tears rolled down the cheeks of the Germans. The troopers knew "Lilli Marlene" well enough; they had heard it on the radio many a night as they lay on the ground in North Africa and as they fought through Sicily and Italy. So, as the Germans cried, they bent over with laughter, holding their sides. The whole scene seemed to be unreal.

In the meantime Von Tippelskirch came to my Command Post in the Palace, which, as it turned out, was a resplendent building, the like of which we had not seen at any time during the war. In front was a huge courtyard, and the building itself was handsome and somewhat modern as European castles go. The high-ceilinged rooms had what appeared to be quilted silk wall covering. Life-size oil paintings of the former residents were hung on the walls, and lovely chandeliers scintillated as the evening light reflected in the mirrors and from highly polished parquet floors. Von Tippelskirch offered to surrender his army group to us, making a specific point that he would surrender to me and that I was to tell the Russians to cease their attacks. Of course, I had no control over what the Russians would do, although I had already established contact with them, so I told him he would either surrender unconditionally or I would continue to attack until I joined the Russians. The surrender document was typed while he and his staff stood about. When he signed it, he added in longhand, in very soldierly fashion, I thought, that it was to be effective upon entry into the American lines. The meeting had been cold and very proper. By the time we reached Germany, there was much ill feeling on the part of the troopers toward the German military establishment.

It turned out that one of Von Tippelskirch's most able and attractive staff members spoke fluent English. After some conversation he asked one of our staff if he could spend the night in the Palace. I heard the conversation and told him that if he spent the night in the American lines, it would be as a prisoner of war. He then replied that he wanted to be sure that we took good care of the Palace, that it had once been his home. I asked him if he knew how the Germans had taken good care of Coventry. We had trained near Coventry before going into Normandy and knew of the devastation wrought by the Luftwaffe there. He replied, "Not especially, but I know what the Allies did to Cologne." I assured him that we, too, were aware of the condition of Cologne, that we had just come from there, and that we had walked all over the high piles of rubble out of which weeds were growing in what once had been the lovely downtown part of the city. He said no more.

Many years later we corresponded, and I returned to him a military sword that I had taken from the Palace. He is now a successful banker in Hamburg.

On that eventful day a complete army group surrendered to the 82nd Airborne Division, more than 150,000 troops with all of their impedimenta.[10] At dawn the next day I learned that the Mayor of Ludwigslust and his wife and daughter had committed suicide. I was shocked and puzzled. I could think of no reason for their suicide. From the day we crossed the German frontier, we had been anxious that our troopers behave properly and that they be in no way abusive to non-combatants. It was difficult to understand why, when the war came to an end, these three would commit suicide. It was two days later that we discovered the reason.

One could smell the Wobelein Concentration Camp before seeing it. And seeing it was more than a human being could stand. Even after three years of war it brought tears to my eyes. Living skeletons were scattered about, the dead distinguishable from the living only by the blue-black color of their skin compared to the somewhat greenish skin, taut over the bony frames of the living. There were hundreds of dead about the grounds and in the tarpaper shacks. In the corner of the stockade area was an abandoned quarry into which the daily stacks of cadavers were bulldozed. It was obvious they could not tell many of the dead from the living.

Wobelein had been a transfer camp built hastily to hold the overflow of thousands of political prisoners who had to be moved west in front of

---

[10] I discussed this in an interview with General Omar Bradley in 1975. He said that there was much laughter in his 12th Army Group headquarters when they heard of the accomplishment of the 82nd Airborne Division. Montgomery had been complaining that the German opposition was too great for him to cross the Elbe River. When the 82nd crossed it, it advanced thirty-six miles the first day and captured more than 100,000 prisoners.

the inexorably rolling Russian armies. Unlike Auschwitz and Buchen-
wald, it did not have gas ovens and similar killing devices. However, in
its own unsophisticated way, it manufactured its own horrors. I had
learned quickly in early May that each small German town had its own
critical food supplies, such as flour, grain, and canned meat. They were
kept under lock and key and under the control of the Mayor. As each
German town was entered, this was the first question raised by the
authorities. What would happen to the control of the food? Ludwigslust
was no exception. Evidently, however, the Mayor allowed the inmates at
Wobelein to starve rather than share his food supplies.

The camp contained political prisoners of all ages. One of the first
tarpaper-covered shacks that we entered had been occupied only by
Jews. The enclosure contained about 4000 political prisoners, of whom,
in the final weeks of the war, almost a quarter had died of starvation.
One Jewish boy named Paul was from Budapest. He had been thrown
into a concentration camp at ten, and four times he had been to the gas
chambers and four times they had withdrawn him at the last moment.
One was Peter G. Martin, a sixty-seven-year-old Paris works manager,
who two years earlier had made the mistake of questioning Nazi politics.
We found a Dutch boy who had been taken shortly after our landings in
Holland in the fall of '44 for being in disagreement with the German
occupation policies in Holland. We made the mistake, at first, of getting
black bread and cans of meat from the warehouse and delivering them
directly to the camp. The inmates stormed and clawed the wagon and
stepped on each other in the stampede as they fought for food. One
frenzied man got up off his sickbed, the lousy straw that they slept on,
ran a few yards, and dropped dead of convulsions. We stopped the
distribution of solid food, and, as quickly as we could organize it, hundreds of cots were placed in a hangar at a nearby airfield. Doctors were
brought in and intravenous feedings began. It was a sad sight, and I
went by the hangar almost daily until the people were ready for more
solid feedings and movement. The dead we buried in the park in front of
the Palace, where we required the leading German citizens to dig the
graves and place the bodies in them. The entire population of the town
was required to attend the burial service.

So we had come to the end of the war in Europe. It had been costly.
More than 60,000 men had passed through the ranks of the 82nd Airborne Division alone. We had left in our wake thousands of white
crosses from Africa to Berlin. And when it came to an end, there was

not a man in the ranks of the 82nd Airborne Division who did not
believe that it was a war that had to be fought. The powerful
Wehrmacht and Luftwaffe had rampaged across the face of Europe,
living off the land, looting and destroying as they went, and sending to
concentration camps those who did not meet the standards—political,
racial, or whatever they were—of the super-race. More than six million
human beings had lost their lives at the hands of the executioners of
Hitler's "final solution." And even then the gas ovens were being en-
larged when we overran the concentration camps.

Within twenty-four hours I met the Russians. Earlier I had sent an
armored cavalry unit that had been attached to the 82nd Airborne Division, under the command of Captain William Knowlton, to find the
Russians. It was a hair-raising experience for him, but he made his way
through the skeptical Germans and finally established contact with the
Russians and was able to communicate to me that he had done so.[11]
The day after the surrender of Von Tippelskirch, I made my way with a
Russian interpreter, a sergeant from the 82nd Airborne Division, toward
the Russian lines. After we left the front of the 82nd, there was absolute
quiet; the area was abandoned with no evidence of war except the piles
and piles of weapons in the ditches beside the roads. As I approached
the small German town of Grabow, four or five miles away from my
own front, I could hear the sounds of a few weapons firing and vehicular
movement. As I entered the town square of Grabow, I saw that Russian
soldiers had a hogshead of wine in the square. They had fired into it
with their pistols, and as the wine spurted out, they caught it in their
helmets and drank it. One soldier had smashed the window of a nearby
store, stepped through the broken glass, and held up a blue gown that
had been on display. To say that they were celebrating without restraint
would be an understatement. The thought occurred to me that they
might not know my uniform and that I soon could have a problem on
my hands, for they were all getting very drunk. We asked one of those
who appeared to be sober about higher headquarters, and he indicated
that it was somewhere down the road, so we continued. About a mile
away a Russian truck chockablock with standing soldiers approached.
As it neared me, for no reason at all, it drove up on the shoulder of the
road, which was a steep slope, six or eight feet high. Slowly the truck

[11] Captain William A. Knowlton, " 'Your Mission Is to Contact the Russians,' "
The Reader's Digest, August 1945.

toppled over on its side and out tumbled all the Soviet troops, happy and laughing and obviously unconcerned.

I thought of stopping to offer to help, but no one seemed a bit interested. And there was some risk in stopping, since they did not know me, so I continued to the next small town, a couple of miles away. There on the main street were two very prim-looking, Tartar-featured, stocky, tough soldiers guarding the front of a building. They had Russian tommy guns slung across their chests and looked at me rather menacingly. I inquired about the nearest Russian headquarters, and that building turned out to be the Command Post of the Russian division commander I was looking for. I went into the living room of the house and introduced myself. Maps were spread on the table, and we went about explaining our dispositions. The thought crossed my mind that this must have been what it was like in 1939 when the Russians met the German army in Poland. I suppose I thought along these lines because the Russians acted distrustful, as though we were combat enemies. All we wanted was to get our dispositions understood, bring the war to an end, and go home. But it had been a good meeting, and the Russian general accepted my invitation to visit me the following day.

As was the case with most American combat divisions, we had a roisterous meeting with the Russians. At first they were obviously suspicious of us, but in the next weeks the evening receptions and the vodka seemed to remove all barriers. There was much celebrating and many toasts. However, as the days went by, I noticed that the senior Russian generals were accompanied by their political commissars. The Russians began to behave a bit more quietly and more seriously and, in fact, almost became unfriendly. By then a couple of weeks had passed, and it was time for us to leave. But before the division left, we received our first orders to return our high-point personnel to the United States for discharge from the Army. Although the men were all delighted to go home, it was a sad parting for many of us. We had been together since Africa, and through much, and once the old-timers left, the division would never be the same, or so we thought.

Our next move was to eastern France in the vicinity of Epinal. There we received replacements, underwent intensive training, and prepared for the occupation role we were to fill in Berlin itself. We moved to Berlin in July, just as the Potsdam Conference came to an end.

The occupation of Berlin was a new experience for us. To begin with, as the senior U.S. Army officer, I was also the senior American member of the Kommandantura, the government body for the city of Berlin. Our first task was, of course, to clean up the city, remove and bury the bodies, and feed and care for the living. There were estimated to be more than 3000 bodies in the subway system alone. It had not only been destroyed by bombing, but had been flooded as well. It was a tremendous task. Food was rationed, and the old and the children received barely a starvation diet. Plans were made to cut down the trees in the nearby forest to provide fuel for the coming winter. Some factories began to operate again.

I recall one of the first problems was the organization of workers' unions. I had been in Berlin several months when this problem became serious. I was sure I would receive instructions from either the Department of the Army or the State Department as to what our policy would be. No instructions were forthcoming, however. As the son of a coal miner, I was quite familiar with unions, their organization and procedures. At an early Kommandantura meeting, therefore, I proposed that the workers have elections to choose their leaders. The Russians strongly opposed this. They said, "How do you know they will elect reliable people?" They said the only way to do it was to choose the leaders and put them in responsible positions. It was the first of many confrontations between our capitalism and "communism," as practiced by the Soviets.

Soon unfavorable stories began to appear in the press about the brutality of the Soviet occupation. The Russians complained bitterly to me about them. I assured them that our press was a free press and would report only the news as it occurred. The Russians said that there should be a news bureau that would put out only the "reliable news." Numerous other minor difficulties seemed to exacerbate our co-existence. The Soviets had combat troops in their sector, and they seemed to be given to holding up any German at pistol point and removing his watch or whatever else the German had on his person that they fancied. The Soviet soldiers frequently were in civilian clothes and could not be readily identified as soldiers.

Soon they began to raid across the border into our sector. The first time a Soviet soldier drew his pistol and fired into the ground—for emphasis, as the Soviets explained it to us later—he was killed by an American paratrooper. This raised all kinds of trouble, since the Americans believed that when a weapon was drawn and fired in their direction, they were entitled to shoot back and, indeed, were expected to. The Soviets insisted that this was outright murder, that their soldiers were inclined to use pistol fire to punctuate their conversations for the purpose of emphasis. It created quite a problem during the first few weeks, until the Soviets found out that the paratroopers were not only good shots but would react instantly when a weapon was drawn on them.

As summer neared an end, General Eisenhower established an office in the city and organized the Office of Military Government, United States (with the unpleasant acronym, OMGUS). The division staged a review on Tempelhof airfield for General Eisenhower, and he seemed pleased. In fact, he was so pleased that he invited Marshal Zhukov to visit the 82nd and receive a review also. At General Eisenhower's suggestion, I sent an invitation to Marshal Zhukov to receive a review of the 82nd Airborne Division on the following Saturday and to bring with him whatever staff he desired. I asked him for lunch also. He promptly replied, saying that he would bring along twenty-eight members of his staff. Fortunately, I was living in the former home of General Heinrich Brauchitsch, and we had a dining room large enough to accommodate the group. Sometime earlier I had called on the Commanding General of a Russian combat division nearby and had asked him to have lunch with me at my home on that very day. Assuming that he would join us, I did not withdraw the invitation. When he arrived, I saw him outside the house on the lawn, visibly quite agitated. I went out to talk to him through an interpreter, and when he learned that Marshal Zhukov was in the house, he actually trembled. He would not enter the house in any circumstances. With apologies he departed. When I went back into the house, I noticed that when Marshal Zhukov came into a room everybody disappeared. I was invariably left standing, drinking, and talking to him by myself. Such was the degree of fear that he seemed to cause among his subordinates. He apparently had the right of life or death and did not hesitate to use it in combat to get results. His combat record was well established in the Red Army, and he was thoroughly respected. Personally, I found him to be a very warm, intelligent, and witty man. He loved to tell stories. At the same time, I could see that he was one of the toughest individuals I had ever encountered.

Our relations with the Russians continued to deteriorate. One Russian general I had known in Mecklenburg seemed to go out of his way to be unpleasant when we were together in public. In December I finally received orders to return to the United States with the division. Before I left, he invited me to his quarters. We went out on the porch, where there appeared to be some privacy, for a drink. We talked and drank for several hours. He was a well-read man, kind and intelligent. He told me that he had been embarrassed to have behaved as he had, but that he had strict orders that in no circumstances should he fraternize with us. Because we had been such good friends in Mecklenburg, he felt that he had to lean over backward, as it were. He wanted me to understand that. It was my first encounter with clear evidence of what the Cold War was to be.

Berlin seemed to be a magnet for visitors. Members of Congress, ministers from some of the countries the Germans had overrun, high-ranking military officers all wanted to see Berlin. We quickly decided that this wasn't war—it was something entirely different—and that we had better be prepared to put our best foot forward. The 82nd Airborne Division organized an honor guard, selecting the most decorated combat veterans—all more than six feet tall—and placing them in one company, the Honor Guard Company. Among the first visitors the Honor Guard received was General George Patton. We were very proud of his comment to the Honor Guard: "In all of my years of service, this is the finest honor guard I have ever seen."

A few days earlier, at a meeting of the Kommandantura, the Russians had announced that in the forthcoming victory parade either they or the Americans would lead the parade—no one else. I took exception, pointing out that the British had fought as long as anyone else and that they were entitled to lead. The French also were entitled to lead the parade. I therefore suggested that we draw lots, or even that we go in alphabetical order, using the French language, as is sometimes the diplomatic practice, to establish precedence. The Russians strongly objected.

Apparently my Russian counterpart's orders from Marshal Zhukov were not to be violated. He suggested that we go see Marshal Zhukov in Potsdam. The Kommandantura went there in a body and met with the Field Marshal. It was a pleasant enough meeting. Observing the Kommandantura at work was an interesting example of the style of our separate services. I had no instructions whatever, and I didn't try to obtain any. I knew that I was free to do what seemed to be appropriate. My Russian counterpart, however, could not do anything but what the Field Marshal told him. When Marshal Zhukov told me what I was to do, I declined. He then told me that he was going to get in touch with General

Eisenhower. I told him that that was fine with me, but I saw no reason to change my position. That was the end of the discussion. Several days later I received some very nice candid photographs taken during the conference, although no cameraman had been visible.

The day before the parade was to take place, General George Patton, resplendent with twenty stars and his ivory-handled pistols, arrived. The following morning we all assembled in the reviewing stand. As it turned out, leading the parade meant one thing to the Soviets and another to us. It is the Russian custom for the officer receiving the review to ride around and inspect the troops before the parade starts. This to them was leading the parade. They didn't care who marched first. In our Service it is well established by regulations who shall lead a parade, and it is the senior Service; they stand on the right of the line and they lead in the march. At about the dramatic moment when the parade was to start, Marshal Zhukov jumped into his huge Ziv. He was covered with medals down his chest to his waist on both sides of his tunic. At once George Patton jumped into a car with me in his wake. As Zhukov rode around taking the review, Patton and I rode in a car beside his. It all went off very well, a bit to my surprise, and Zhukov seemed in very good spirits. The troops looked superb, and it was a happy day all around.

The morale of the division had never been better by summer's end in 1945. Not only had it performed well after Berlin, but it had proved to be an outstanding occupation division. Airborne warfare was entirely new in the U.S. Army, and we were certain that there would be an airborne division in the postwar Army. We were sure, too, that it would be the 82nd.

Then came the blow. In early October we received a cable from Washington informing us that the division was to be disbanded in Europe, that it was through. Another division had been chosen for the peacetime Army, one that had far less experience than the 82nd. It was shocking, and we were in despair. I at once got in touch with several people in Washington who, I thought, might be helpful. But I was afraid that my efforts would be to little avail. In the midst of this, I received an anonymous letter signed simply, "A lieutenant." His concluding paragraph read: "And we know that somewhere there will always be an 82nd Airborne Division. Because it lives in the hearts of men. And somewhere young men will dare the challenge to 'Stand up and hook up' and know that moment of pride and strength which is its reward."

In late November we were notified that the division would not be disbanded. Not only that—it would return to the United States shortly after the first of the year and it would march up Fifth Avenue in New York. We were, of course, elated, and we at once began preparations for the move and the parade.

In the midst of all this, on Sunday, December 9, early in the afternoon I received word from a member of the division staff that General Patton had been in a car accident. As we learned more of the details, it did not seem to be too serious. The car had been traveling at thirty miles an hour and hit the rear of a truck that had slowed down. No one else in the car was hurt, but Patton was reported as being in critical condition. We followed what we assumed was his recovery in *Stars and Stripes* and expected at any time that he would be out of the hospital. It seemed incredible when we learned on the morning of December 22 that he had died the afternoon of the day before. Evidently he had been paralyzed from the neck down throughout his hospitalization. It could not have come as a greater shock to us. His spirit and enthusiasm had seemed unquenchable. When I learned that he was to be buried among the soldiers who had been killed in battle, it reminded me of a refrain from an old West Point song, "Benny Havens' Oh!"—"May we find a soldier's resting place beneath a soldier's blow."

Our division was already moving to its staging areas in northern France, whence it would return to the United States. It marched up Fifth Avenue early in January. Thus the 82nd Airborne Division marched into history.

Berlin in Retrospect

(*All the messages quoted in this chapter are official messages, copies of which have been obtained from the National Archives in Washington, D.C.*)

In June 1961, when the late President John F. Kennedy visited with Nikita Khrushchev in Vienna, Khrushchev declared that "Berlin is a bone that must come out of the Soviet throat."[1] Khrushchev then went on to say that he was determined to settle the Berlin issue for all time and that the Allies would be out of it by the first of December. It was a bitter moment for the President, who had been elected on a platform espousing the cause of peace, and who was now told that he was confronted with the likelihood of war. He promptly sent military reinforcements to Europe. As Ambassador to France, I was called upon by many ambassadors stationed in Paris who wanted to know whether or not President Kennedy really would go to war with the Soviets over the Berlin issue. I assured them that he would.

Berlin has been a bone in our throats, too, ever since the spring of 1945 when the Soviets captured it. In the very beginning it caused problems as the 82nd Airborne Division was moving into Berlin on occupation duty in early July 1945. A parachute infantry regiment left Magdeburg on a train bound for Berlin. Twenty-four hours later it was lost somewhere in the Soviet Zone, and the Soviets did not know where it was. I went looking for it in a light plane and finally located it, but I was impressed by the degree to which Berlin had been isolated at

---

[1] *Time* magazine, June 16, 1961.

According to *Newsweek*, June 19, 1961, President Kennedy, in reporting to the members of Congress on his trip, reported that Khrushchev said, "Berlin is a cancerous sore in the throat that has to be cut out."

the end of a long and tenuous communication line with the West. It was obvious then, as it is today, that access to Berlin is clearly subject to Soviet control and Soviet interruption. For a while Berlin was a gateway to the West for Eastern Europeans who wanted to flee across the border between East and West Berlin. The Berlin Wall put an end to that. Aside from these physical aspects of the Berlin situation, psychologically, it was and is the capital of Germany. When the degree of German interest in Berlin is aroused, the Soviets can interrupt its communications with the West at any time. In 1953 only a gigantic airlift kept the city alive. But in the spring of 1945 the paratroopers had been ordered by General Eisenhower to be ready on short notice to capture Berlin. They were confident that it could be done and regretted the decision that came in late April to cancel the operation.[2]

Could we have captured Berlin? Should we have captured Berlin? To the paratroopers it was a simple decision: go or no go—seize Berlin or not—and they were sure they could capture it. In recent years a great number of messages that were exchanged between the higher commanders have become available. Some of them were "Eyes Only," "Top Secret," between General Eisenhower and General George C. Marshall. It is quite clear now that it was a very complicated issue, involving the senior generals and their willingness to serve with one another, the logistics situation, the desire of the British to be on center stage in the last battle, using American combat divisions if necessary, and whether Field Marshal Montgomery, having been given all he asked for, could move with the rapidity and skill the situation certainly would call for. In addition, there was a great deal of pressure placed on General Eisenhower by the War Department to ready U.S. divisions for shipment to the Pacific. Finally, there was the likelihood of combat in the streets of Berlin with the Soviet troops, plus the question of whether or not it should be risked in view of President Roosevelt's high hopes for the postwar United Nations.

Berlin did not seem very important when we were in London preparing for the Normandy landings. In the first place, we did not know the direction the armies would take if they did succeed in establishing

---

[2] The latest treatise on the subject is " 'A Might Have Been'—Operation Eclipse" in the *Armed Forces Journal* of May 1976. It was written by Colonel Barney Oldfield, who participated in the planning for the capture of Berlin. It is a well-written, persuasive piece which concludes that the seizure of Berlin "was the key to the West having the initiative in Berlin, and not having used it to that end, we have never had the initiative there."

themselves on the Normandy coast. Besides, we had many other problems to contend with. Eisenhower's mission, given to him before he left England, was quite simple:

Land on the Normandy coast.
Build up the resources needed for a decisive battle in the Normandy-Brittany region. . . .
Pursue on a broad front with two army groups, emphasizing the left to gain necessary ports and reach the boundaries of Germany. . . .
Launch the final attack as a double envelopment of the Ruhr, again emphasizing the left, and follow this up by an immediate thrust through Germany, with the specific direction to be determined at the time.
Clean out the remainder of Germany.[3]

There was no mention of Berlin.

It was the surprise crossing at Remagen that for the first time suggested the possibility of a plan other than that of reinforcing Montgomery and giving *him* the mission of seizing Berlin. It posed the possibility of allowing Bradley and his army commanders to make an early thrust to the east. Bradley was a superb technician and tactician. He probably had more influence in developing the final battle plan for Eisenhower than anyone else in Eisenhower's command. He knew exactly what his combat divisions could do, and he handled his army commanders with consummate skill. Less than two weeks after the crossing at Remagen, he spent two or three days at Sous-le-Vent in a private meeting with General Eisenhower. That meeting enabled them to hammer out all the details about how they would bring the war to an end. Once the Ruhr pocket was taken care of, they would then move forward rapidly to the Elbe, hold on that river line, advance on the right toward Leipzig to break up the German armies, deny them the opportunity to establish a redoubt, and meet the Russians. As soon as practicable, they would tidy up the left flank by thrusting toward Lübeck and cutting off Denmark from Russian occupation.

Militarily, the plan was simple, but its execution was another matter. It was imperative that it be kept from the British, and that the British be kept in the dark as to what Eisenhower's real intentions were. This was one of the reasons the airborne plan to capture Berlin was kept alive long after there was any need for it. In a personal interview with Gen-

[3] Eisenhower, op. cit., pp. 228–229.

eral "Pinky" Bull, Eisenhower's G-3 and Chief of Plans, I asked him how it was possible to develop such a plan within the SHAEF staff and not have the British learn of it. He answered by explaining that such a plan, as one of many contingencies, was known to quite a number of the staff, but as it became more likely that it would be used, discussion of it was restricted to fewer and fewer senior people.

I discussed this with Sir Kenneth Strong, then Major General Kenneth Strong, Chief of Intelligence on Eisenhower's staff.[4] He said that he discussed General Eisenhower's plan with him several times. He was fully informed of General Eisenhower's intentions and his strategic thinking. He, General Strong, had great respect for the Germans' resilience, and he cautioned Eisenhower right up to the very end to take no chances. He said that Eisenhower frequently mentioned to him the worries he had about readying troops for movement to the Pacific. Eisenhower was also concerned about some of the divisions which were already idle, and he was sure that they would be causing trouble. Strong said also that there was a very real risk of fighting breaking out in the streets of Berlin between the Americans and the Russians if Eisenhower sought to take it from them at the last moment. In fact, it was his personal opinion that an attempt to seize Berlin would have resulted in open conflict between the Americans and the Russians. Once in the course of his discussions Eisenhower asked him, "If I were to seize Berlin at a very great cost in lives and a day or two later we were ordered to withdraw to comply with the postwar occupation plan, what would the troops think of it and what would the American people think of it?"

Bradley had already cautioned Eisenhower that it would probably cost 100,000 lives to take Berlin, adding that it would be "a pretty stiff price to pay for a prestigious objective." In addition to these considerations, there was genuine doubt that Montgomery's set-piece battle style would be anywhere near adequate to deal with the rush of events if they decided to close on Berlin. There was concern that if Montgomery had been given all he asked for, and the American armies held back, Montgomery might not have succeeded in capturing Berlin, after all. Then Eisenhower would be left with the problem of the southern flank and the probable establishment of a German redoubt.

Eisenhower was aware also, in a limited way, of the results of the Yalta Conference. He knew that President Roosevelt's policy—antici-

4 Meeting in London on September 17, 1976.

pating the United Nations—seemed to be one of mollification of the Soviets. With this background, why should Eisenhower risk fighting the Soviet troops in the streets of Berlin and placing in jeopardy the prospects for peace with the Soviets after the war, and the future of an international peace-keeping body? Finally, the problem of preparing higher commands and troops for movement to the Pacific was becoming more troublesome with each passing day. This in time became a major effort, and on April 9, 1945, a headquarters was formally established to control the troop movements westward. With all this, the logistics situation was still tenuous because of the rapid advance of the armies to the east.

In any case, whether or not to seize Berlin was not Eisenhower's decision to make. The decision had to be made by the Combined Chiefs of Staff. No doubt, it being a matter of great political importance, the Combined Chiefs would have had to consult their own heads of state before arriving at a decision to pass on to Eisenhower.

Under these conditions, Eisenhower put the final touches to his plan to thrust directly eastward toward Leipzig in late March. He frequently consulted his G-2, General Strong, and his G-3, General "Pinky" Bull, worked out the details. The entire plan was closely held, and neither Field Marshal Montgomery, Field Marshal Brooke, nor Prime Minister Churchill had an inkling of it until Eisenhower was prepared to disclose his intentions to Stalin. General Strong, quite properly, did not give any of the information to his British colleagues. Evidently his relations with Montgomery were not very good. On one occasion he had pointed out to Eisenhower's Chief of Staff, General Bedell Smith, certain shortcomings in Montgomery's conduct of a battle. Montgomery became aware of this, and thereafter Strong was *persona non grata* in Montgomery's headquarters. So the planning went on, and the troops moved aggressively toward the Elbe River, and when it was clear to Eisenhower that the war could be brought to an end and the German armies destroyed, he sent a telegram to Stalin outlining his intentions. It was sent on March 28 via the U.S. Mission in Moscow headed by Major General John R. Deane. Important paragraphs of it follow:

Personal Message to Marshal Stalin from General Eisenhower:

1. My immediate operations are designed to encircle and destroy the enemy forces defending the Ruhr, and to isolate that area from the rest of Germany. This will be accomplished by developing offensives

around the north of the Ruhr and from Frankfurt through Kassel, until the ring is closed. The enemy enclosed in this ring will then be mopped up.

2. I estimate that this phase of operations will terminate in late April or even earlier, and my next task will be to divide the enemy's remaining forces by joining hands with your forces.

3. For my forces the best axis on which to effect this junction would be Erfurt-Leipzig-Dresden; moreover, I believe, this is the area to which the main German governmental departments are being moved. It is along this axis that I propose to place my main effort. In addition, as soon as the situation allows, a secondary advance will be made to effect a junction with your forces in the Regensburg-line area, thereby preventing the consolidation of German resistance in a redoubt in southern Germany.

4. Before deciding firmly on my future plans, I think it most important that they should be coordinated as closely as possible with yours both as to directions and timing. Could you, therefore, tell me your intentions, and let me know how far the proposed operations outlined in this message conform to your probable action?

5. If we are to complete the destruction of the German armies without delay, I regard it as essential that we coordinate our action and make every effort to perfect the liaison between our advancing forces. I am prepared to send officers to you for this purpose.

General Deane promptly replied to Eisenhower, stating that the U.S. and British ambassadors in Moscow were trying to arrange for a meeting with Stalin on the night of March 29 in order to give him the message. He went on to ask for more information, saying, "It would be helpful if we could have some additional background information in case he wishes to discuss your plans in more detail. Suggest, if possible, that you send, with least delay, a brief message to us indicating (1) the present composition of the armies, (2) a little more detail on the scheme of maneuver, (3) which army or armies you envisage making the main and secondary advances, following the accomplishment of the first objective, (4) brief current estimate of enemy dispositions and intentions."

General Eisenhower dispatched complete answers to the questions raised by General Deane. The Combined Chiefs of Staff, however, were not going to tolerate any more direct communications between Eisenhower and Stalin. They so instructed Eisenhower, and he, in turn, told Deane that he must withhold from Stalin the detailed information that he had just sent to him, directing him to deliver the earlier message. Then, on March 31 Eisenhower sent a detailed message to the Combined Chiefs of Staff. He began by pointing out that he had carried out their instructions. "Further details requested by General Deane had already been dispatched. On receipt of your cable I told him he must *not* pass them on to Marshal Stalin."

In Eisenhower's cable to Marshal Stalin on March 28, it should be noted that no mention was made of Berlin. However, it was clearly implicit in the message that he intended to move directly to Leipzig and thus abandon Berlin.

In his cable to the Combined Chiefs of Staff on March 31, Eisenhower was more explicit, and he stated:

> BERLIN as a strategic area is discounted as it is now largely destroyed and we have information that the Ministries are moving to the ERFURT-LEIPZIG region. Moreover, it is so near to the RUSSIAN Front that once they start moving again, they will reach it in a matter of days.

Interestingly enough, the day before Eisenhower sent the telegram to Stalin, Field Marshal Montgomery had developed his own plan for the employment of his armies, including the U.S. Ninth Army. Among other things, this plan urged a rapid thrust to the Elbe River.

> The operations will be conducted with speed and violence by the armored columns; foremost commanders must always be quick to bypass resistance with the leading troops, and to push on deep into enemy rear areas; if a column is held up on one route, another one must push on.
>
> This is the time to take risks and go "flat out" for the ELBE.
>
> If we reach the ELBE quickly, we win the war.

A copy of it was sent to Eisenhower's headquarters on March 28, the very day that Eisenhower's telegram went to Stalin. It seemed to baffle Prime Minister Churchill, and he inquired why Montgomery had one plan and Eisenhower another.

Montgomery's directive was so worded as to suggest a dash and verve that would not be in keeping with his methods earlier in the war, certainly not his counterattack in the Battle of the Bulge. It seems strange also that he sent it, since Eisenhower had informed him several days earlier that the U.S. Ninth Army was to be removed from his command after the Ruhr pocket was reduced. Perhaps he suspected that Eisenhower was thinking of another plan and he wanted to produce his own, once again, and force the issue.

The British were upset by Eisenhower's cable to Stalin. Field Marshal Brooke was to note, with irritation, in his diary: "To start with, he has no business to address Stalin directly. His communication should be through the Combined Chiefs of Staff; secondly, he produced a telegram which was unintelligible and finally what was implied in it appeared to be entirely adrift and a change from all that had been previously agreed on."

The British at once got in touch with the Combined Chiefs of Staff, objecting to the contents of Eisenhower's telegram of March 28 and to the procedure that he adopted. A memorandum from the British representation on the Combined Chiefs of Staff to General Marshall stated "that the British are concerned at the contents of Eisenhower's telegram both as regards the procedure which has been adopted by General Eisenhower and, what is more important, the change of plans which is implicit in his message to Marshal Stalin." The British further expressed the view "that the main thrust should be made across the open plain of Germany with the object of capturing Berlin."

Eisenhower also had a message from Prime Minister Churchill, and he, in turn, sent a personal message to the Prime Minister on March 30, explaining in detail his intentions. By this time Prime Minister Churchill realized that this was a matter that had to be resolved between him and President Roosevelt.

Ever since Yalta Prime Minister Churchill had been distressed by the turn of events. Since Yalta it had become increasingly apparent that Stalin was violating, or disregarding, the promises that he had made there. It was apparent that Stalin had no intention of recognizing the government of Poland that Winston Churchill and President Roosevelt had urged upon him. "Before the end of March the Yalta agreement had been broken or discredited by the Russians in every important case which had, so far, been put to the test of action."[5] President Roosevelt, on the other hand, had not been well and had not been able to follow closely political developments in Europe after Yalta. Furthermore, he was most anxious to obtain the Soviet agreement to participate in the international conference that would follow the war, and he seemed in-

5 Wilmot, op. cit.

clined to mollify the Russians in order to obtain their participation. On April 1, out of his deep concern for what would happen after the war, Prime Minister Churchill sent a top-secret personal message to the President. Since it persuasively and eloquently outlines the British point of view, the important parts of the cable follow:

> I am however distressed to read that it should be thought that we wish in the slightest degree to discredit or lower the prestige of General Eisenhower in his increasingly important relations with the Russian Commanders in the field.
>
> All we sought was a little time to consider the far-reaching changes desired by General Eisenhower in the plans that had been concerted by the Combined Chiefs of Staff at Malta and had received your and my joint approval. The British Chiefs of the Staff were naturally concerned by a procedure which apparently left the fortunes of the British Army, which though only a third of yours still amounts to over a million men, to be settled without the slightest reference to any British authority.
>
> . . . .
>
> At this point I wish to place on record the complete confidence felt by His Majesty's Government in General Eisenhower, our pleasure that our armies are serving under his command and our admiration of the great and shining qualities of character and personality which he has proved himself to possess in all the difficulties of handling an allied command. Moreover, I should like to express to you, Mr. President, as I have already done orally in the field to General Eisenhower, my heartfelt congratulations on the glorious victories and advances by all the armies of the United States centre in the recent battles on the Rhine and over it. . . .
>
> Having dealt with and I trust disposed of these misunderstandings between the truest friends and comrades that ever fought side by side as allies, I venture to put to you a few considerations upon the merits of the changes in our original plans now desired by General Eisenhower. It seems to me the differences are small and as usual not of principle but of emphasis. Obviously, laying aside every impediment and shunning every diversion, the allied armies of the north and centre should now march at the highest speed towards the Elbe. Hitherto the axis has been upon Berlin. General Eisenhower on his estimate of the enemy's resistance, to which I attach the greatest importance, now wishes to shift the axis somewhat to the southward and strike through Leipzig, even perhaps as far south as Dresden. He withdraws the Ninth U.S. Army from the northern group of armies and in consequence stretches its front southwards. I should be sorry if the resistance of the enemy was such as to destroy the weight and

momentum of the advance of the British Twenty-first Army Group
and to leave them in an almost static condition along the Elbe when
and if they reach it. I say quite frankly that Berlin remains of high
strategic importance. Nothing will exert a psychological effect of
despair upon all German forces of resistance equal to that of the fall
of Berlin. It will be the supreme signal of defeat to the German
people. On the other hand, if left to itself to maintain a siege by the
Russians among its ruins and as long as the German flag flies there, it
will animate the resistance of all Germans under arms.

There is moreover another aspect which it is proper for you and
me to consider. The Russian armies will no doubt overrun all Austria
and enter Vienna. If they also take Berlin, will not their impression
that they have been the overwhelming contributor to our common
victory be unduly imprinted in their minds, and may this not lead
them into a mood which will raise grave and formidable difficulties in
the future? I therefore consider that from a political standpoint we
should march as far east into Germany as possible and that should
Berlin be in our grasp we should certainly take it. This also appears
sound on military grounds.

The Prime Minister's cable was received by the War Department at
the same time that it was delivered to Admiral William Leahy in the
White House. The War Department drafted a reply in which they fully
supported Eisenhower's plan. In part, it was not well written, and Field
Marshal Alan Brooke referred to it as "that rude message." In the meantime the British Chiefs of Staff developed a rather lengthy paper again
justifying their point of view. It was dispatched to the Combined Chiefs
of Staff on April 4, and it concluded: ". . . the obvious psychological
and political advantages in reaching Berlin as soon as possible seem to
the British Chiefs of Staff to point to the desirability of Anglo-American
forces capturing Berlin as soon as possible."

The Prime Minister seemed more aware of what was happening than
his military subordinates. He realized that Eisenhower had other responsibilities, that he had to be prepared to send troops to the Pacific, and
that he was acting with considerable prudence. And so, in concluding
this particular episode, he sent a personal message again to President
Roosevelt on April 5:

I still think it was a pity that Eisenhower's telegram was sent to Stalin
without anything being said to our Chiefs of Staff or to our deputy, Air
Chief Marshal Tedder, or to our Commander in Chief, Field Marshal
Montgomery. The changes in the main plan have now turned out to be
very much less than we at first supposed. My personal relations with

General Eisenhower are of the most friendly character. I regard the matter as closed and to prove my sincerity I will use one of my very few Latin quotations, "Amantium irae amoris integratio est."[6]

A copy of this was promptly sent, "Personal, Top Secret, Eyes Only," from General Marshall to Eisenhower for his comment. Specifically, he was asked, "Was Tedder informed or consulted in the matter?" The following day, April 7, Eisenhower, with some asperity, replied to Marshall, "For His Eyes Only":

> I hope it will not be forgotten that some of the ablest members of my staff are from the British Army. Such men as Tedder, Morgan, Whiteley, and Strong possess great ability and are absolutely unimpeachable in their objective approach to every question. Tedder was freely consulted in developing the outline of our major plan and on the necessity of communicating with the Russians in the attempt to achieve coordination. Due to his absence from headquarters he did not see the exact terminology of the message. He completely agreed in principle with the action taken.

Actually, Tedder, in his memoirs written after the war, states flatly that he was never informed of the message that was to be sent. General Strong, for his part, did see it and helped prepare it and was fully supportive of General Eisenhower in what he was attempting to accomplish. It was, however, kept from Field Marshals Montgomery and Brooke and the Prime Minister. The most charitable thing that one could say was that Eisenhower was not entirely candid with the higher members of the British command.

In the meantime a message arrived at Eisenhower's headquarters from General Deane in Moscow. The meeting with Stalin was held on the evening of March 31. Present were the American and British ambassadors and Molotov. The message read in part:

> After Stalin had read Eisenhower's message, we pointed out the operations described in the message on the map. Stalin immediately reacted and said that the plan seemed to be a good one, but that he of course could not commit himself definitely until he had consulted his staff. He said that he would give us an answer tomorrow. *He seemed to be favorably impressed with the direction of the attack* in Central Germany and also of the secondary attack in the south.[7]

[6] Lovers' quarrels always go with true love (or are a part of love).
[7] Italics mine. J.M.G.

The message went on to discuss the shifting of German troops, whether or not Germans were being withdrawn from Norway, numbers of divisions on different fronts, and so forth. The final paragraph stated:

> Stalin had apparently been considering Eisenhower's message all through the discussion, and at this point he reverted to it and said that *the plan for Eisenhower's main effort was a good one* in that it accomplished the most important objective of dividing Germany in half. He felt that the Germans' last stand would probably be in the mountains of western Czechoslovakia and Bavaria.[8]

It should be realized in reading the foregoing that Stalin had already alerted his two crack Army Group commanders, Marshal Zhukov and Marshal Konev, to ready their forces for an immediate assault upon Berlin, pitting one marshal against the other to see who could develop the plan that would permit the Soviets to capture Berlin at the earliest possible date.

So far, Stalin's agreement with the Eisenhower proposal was verbal, as he expressed it at the meeting with General Deane on March 31. The following day, April 1, he sent a "Personal and Top Secret" telegram to General Eisenhower. He acknowledged receipt of Eisenhower's telegram of March 28 and went on to say:

> Your plan to cut the German forces by joining up the Soviet forces with our forces entirely coincides with the plan of the Soviet High Command.
> I agree with you also that the place for the joining up of your forces and the Soviet forces should be the area near Erfurt, Leipzig, Dresden. The Soviet High Command considers that the main blow of the Soviet forces should be delivered in that direction.
> Berlin has lost its former strategic importance. The Soviet High Command therefore plans to allot secondary forces in the direction of Berlin.

It is interesting to note that two weeks later, after a long evening meeting with Marshal Stalin, U.S. Ambassador Averell Harriman reported that Stalin had told him that the Russians were planning an immediate renewal of their attack directed against Berlin. But then, seemingly as an afterthought, Marshal Stalin told him the main blow would be in the direction of Dresden, as he had already told Eisen-

[8] Italics mine. J.M.G.

hower. This message was sent on April 16. In fact, Stalin was now ready to launch his major all-out assault to capture Berlin.

In the meantime General Marshall, again quoting the efforts of the British Chiefs of Staff in their memorandum to the Combined Chiefs on April 5, fully supported Eisenhower, pointing out:

> Eisenhower's dealings with Marshal Stalin have been directed to him in his capacity as Commander in Chief of forces on the eastern front and not as that of Chief of State. Possibly it might be desired that Eisenhower should communicate with Antonov, the Chief of Staff. Experience, however, has shown that contact on any lower level than Stalin is impracticable because of the inevitable incidental delays. In view of the present state of the battle, review of operational matters by Committee action is impracticable. Only Eisenhower is in a position to make decisions concerning his battle and the best way to exploit successes to the full.

After a week had elapsed, at which time Eisenhower must have been vexed and troubled by the commotion caused by his cable to Stalin, Eisenhower sent a personal "Eyes Only, Urgent," cable to General Marshall.

> I give you the following background in my reluctance from the military viewpoint to lay down Berlin as a major objective of our operations. In the first place, through bombing, as well as through partial transfer of German governmental officers, Berlin has lost much of its former military importance. . . . I believe that my central thrust should be in great strength to the area including Leipzig. You will note that in Stalin's reply to my message he agreed that the best place for us to meet was in the Dresden-Leipzig-Erfurt area.

So now General Eisenhower was using Stalin's statement of his intentions to support his own plan, whereas Stalin was making every effort to seize Berlin as rapidly as possible.

Eisenhower then, quite properly, pointed out that:

> If the Combined Chiefs of Staff should decide that the Allied effort to take Berlin outweighs purely military considerations in the theater, I would cheerfully readjust my plans and my thinking so as to carry out such an operation.

There is no record that the Combined Chiefs of Staff acted on this offer. In fact, it is quite possible that General George Marshall, who was the senior U.S. member of the Combined Chiefs of Staff, decided not to forward Eisenhower's suggestion to the Combined Chiefs, since the situation had quieted down considerably and Eisenhower was well on the way to having his own way in bringing the war to an end. Nevertheless, Eisenhower's point was well made. If Berlin was to be captured, then Eisenhower had to be so directed by the Combined Chiefs of Staff. If they refused to give such a directive, the only prudent course he had, in view of all other considerations, was not to take Berlin.

In the meantime the SHAEF staff had been studying the possibilities of what specifically would occur when the Armies reached the Elbe River. In a paper dated April 9, entitled "Operations After Reaching the River Elbe," it states:

> On completion of the operations covered in our present directives Northern and Central Groups of Armies will be on the ELBE, while Southern Group of Armies may have begun an advance on the axis NÜRNBERG-REGENSBURG-LINZ. The enemy pocket in the RUHR may not yet have been eliminated.
>
> At this stage, if the Russians have not advanced from their present positions, in the centre only some 60 miles will separate our forces. Clearly the immediate and overriding task would be to close this gap and completely divide the enemy's forces. . . .

In the midst of all this intense activity among the higher commanders, the Allied combat divisions continued to march eastward. On April 11, after an all-day march of 57 miles, the Second Armored cabled back, "We're on the Elbe." It was 8:00 P.M. and they had covered 200 miles in the past fourteen days. The Ninth Army itself had covered 226 miles in the past nineteen days. As the Army History of the Ninth Army was to say, "The only things that moved faster than the Ninth Army in those nineteen days were a few fleeing remnants of the broken, battered, and beaten German Army." On April 13 the U.S. 83rd Infantry Division had established a bridgehead across the Elbe River. The Second Armored also had a bridgehead, but was unable to get heavy armor across the river and for tactical reasons considered it best to withdraw its infantry. However, Simpson was absolutely confident that he could move his Army across the Elbe and go on to Berlin. By April 15 Simpson's IX Corps' zone had expanded the bridgehead on the Elbe to thirty square miles. And on that day Simpson went back to Bradley's 12th Army Group Headquarters in Wiesbaden and presented his plan for the continued expansion of his bridgehead over the Elbe and a strong drive on Berlin. Bradley told him that by direction of the Supreme Allied Commander, the Ninth Army was ordered to hold the line of the Elbe and await the advance of the Russian forces.[9] As the offi-

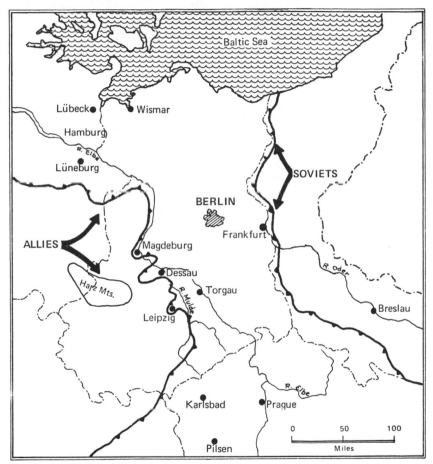

Fig. 21   April 16, 1945

[9] In the third week of April First Lieutenant Arthur Hadley, who was a member of the Second Armored Division (he is now a successful American author), went forward from his division bridgehead over the Elbe. He was in a tank, and he was followed by a jeep with several newspapermen. They moved in the direction of Berlin. They soon encountered a few Russian soldiers. They had neither heavy weapons nor radios. The newspapermen, after talking to the Russians, decided to go into Berlin and invited Hadley to come along. His orders forbade him to go any farther. The newspapermen drove directly into the city. They were Ernest Leiser of *Stars and Stripes* and Mack Morris of *Yank*.

cial Army History was later to describe it, "Their Supreme Commander had already made and would soon reaffirm the decision that was to turn their holdings into a bridgehead to nowhere." This was as close to Berlin as we were to get. (*Fig. 21.*)

The Soviets launched their final Berlin offensive on April 16, a month earlier than originally planned. On April 25 they announced that Marshal Zhukov's forces had joined those of Marshal Konev northwest of Potsdam. Thus Berlin was lost. On May 2 the city surrendered to the Russians.

I discussed the Berlin situation with Willy Brandt on March 10, 1977. At that time he was in Boston to speak to the World Affairs Council. We had both been in Berlin in the summer of 1945. In the course of our discussion he told me that he had talked to President Eisenhower about Berlin in 1958. Eisenhower told him that if he had it to do over again, he would do things differently. I asked him if Eisenhower meant that he would have taken the city, and he replied, "Oh, yes, but Eisenhower said that he had been given bad political advice." This is strange, since Eisenhower's senior political adviser was Robert Murphy, and he was of the opinion that capture of the city would be of a certain political advantage to us. Eisenhower's view, however, seems to confirm a statement made by him on July 29, 1952, when he was a Presidential candidate. Meeting with some Republican advisers, he told them that he had made a secret flight back to Washington from London early in 1944. The purpose was to protest "vigorously to Franklin D. Roosevelt against the Allied plans for the postwar division of Germany that left Berlin isolated inside Soviet-occupied territory." He then went on to say, "In talking to Mr. Roosevelt about these things, he just laughed, 'I can handle Uncle Joe.' That is exactly what he told me."[10]

Eisenhower went on to say that he renewed his protest in early 1945 to President Roosevelt, and also to British Prime Minister Winston Churchill. He insisted that his western forces were in a strong position and that blueprints for dividing Europe between the Western Allies and Russia should not be made until the end of the war. Again, he said, "They didn't listen to us." These remarks were made in the Brown Palace Hotel in Denver. They are of considerable political significance. Mr. Eisenhower asked that his remarks be kept secret unless the Demo-

[10] "Why Ike Didn't Capture Berlin: An Untold Story," *U.S. News & World Report,* April 26, 1971.

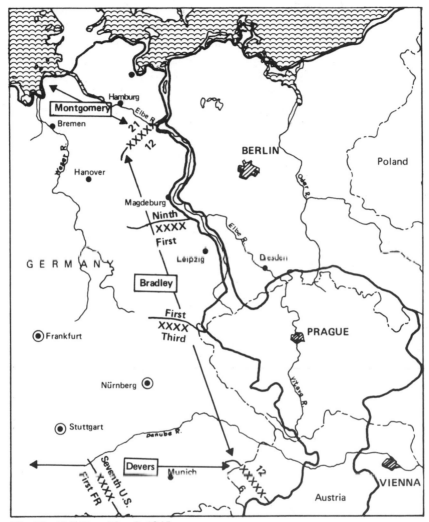

Fig. 22   V-E Day, May 8, 1945

crats made his role in the Berlin episode a major issue in the election campaign—in which case they would be used in a Republican counter-attack.[11] That need, apparently, never arose. Oddly, this presentation to his political advisers was very much at variance with the attitude of his Supreme Headquarters staff during the summer of 1944, after the Normandy landings. For example, on September 24, 1944, a SHAEF

[11] Ibid.

Planning Staff memorandum stated, "Our main objective must be the early capture of Berlin, the most important objective in Germany."

Finally, if General Eisenhower was convinced that Berlin should not be allowed to go to the Russians, he should have taken the matter up through the Combined Chiefs of Staff, asking for authority, even as late as the spring of '45, to seize Berlin if it was within his grasp. The Combined Chiefs would then take the matter up with their heads of state, President Roosevelt and Prime Minister Churchill, and they, in turn, would see that the proper directives went to Eisenhower through the Combined Chiefs; so reporting that the matter was taken up directly with President Franklin D. Roosevelt would seem to have been for political purposes and, in fact, to be hardly more than political rhetoric.

There was one final effort made by the British to get the Americans to move forward to seize a political objective. It began in the last week of April when the British Foreign Secretary raised the issue with Prime Minister Churchill. Churchill, in turn, put it to the President. "There can be little doubt," he said, "that the liberation of Prague and as much as possible of the territory of western Czechoslovakia by your forces might make the whole difference to the postwar situation in Czechoslovakia and might well influence that in nearby countries. Of course," he added, "such a move by Eisenhower must not interfere with his main operation against the Germans, but I think the highly important political consideration mentioned above should be brought to his attention." As the official British history expressed it, "The suggestion, however, was not welcome in the United States. Marshall had already told Eisenhower on the 28th [April] that such a proposal might be made, and in passing it on for his comments, had declared: 'Personally and aside from all logistic, tactical, or strategic implications I should be loath to hazard American lives for purely political purposes.' "[12] Eisenhower concurred and in his reply the next day stated, "I shall not attempt any move I deem militarily unwise to gain a political prize unless I receive specific orders from the Combined Chiefs of Staff." Such orders were never given and, of course, never received by Eisenhower.

Through all this period, Patton was straining at the leash. His Army had been built up to 540,000, its largest size since the war began. He was anxious to advance into Czechoslovakia and impatiently awaited

[12] L. F. Ellis, *Victory in the West*, II. London: Her Majesty's Stationery Office, 1968, p. 332.

authority to go ahead. Finally, on May 4, Bradley gave him the green light.

> Patton's eagerness kept puzzling Bradley, so now he asked, "Why does everyone in the Third Army want to liberate the Czechs?"
> Patton said nothing about the Russians. "Oh, Brad," he answered, "can't you see? The Czechs are our *allies* and consequently their women aren't off limits. On to Czechoslovakia and fraternization!" he yelled into the telephone. "How in hell can you stop an army with a battle cry like that?"[13]

The problem was not on the battle front but in Washington. President Franklin Delano Roosevelt had been his own Secretary of State, and when he became incapable of making decisions, action originated neither in the White House nor in the State Department.

One of the last State Department officers to meet with President Roosevelt before he left the White House to go to Warm Springs, where he was to die, was Ambassador Robert D. Murphy. He anticipated being appointed political adviser to General Eisenhower in Germany and he looked forward to an interesting discussion with the President. It was on an evening late in March, and as he described the meeting in his memoirs: "When Roosevelt was wheeled into the second floor study of the White House that evening, his appearance was a terrible shock; he was a mere shadow of the buoyant man who talked so confidently to me the previous September." And then he went on to write, "But Roosevelt was in no condition that night to offer balanced judgments upon the great questions of war and peace that had concerned him for so long. His conversation illumined for me why the Army during this period was making decisions which the civilian authority of our government normally would have made, such as the ones related to the capture of Berlin."[14] He goes on to give credit to General Marshall for protecting the President and for taking this responsibility. Under normal circumstances the State Department would have played a more active role in the decision-making process, but in a sense President Roosevelt had also been his own State Department. Referring to it in his memoirs, Murphy wrote, "The situation demonstrated a weakness

[13] Farago, op. cit.
[14] Robert D. Murphy, *Diplomat Among Warriors.* New York: Doubleday & Co., Inc., 1964.

which exists in our government structure despite our superb Constitution."[15]

Two weeks later Robert Murphy was in London, where he was to be United States Political Adviser for Germany. In that capacity he followed closely the events in the Allied Armies. On April 16 he wrote from London to the Director of the Office of European Affairs in the State Department, Mr. H. Freeman Matthews.

> Dear Doc:
> Just a word about the current trend. Apparently there is on the part of some of our officers no particular eagerness to occupy Berlin first. It is not at all impossible that our forces may linger along the Elbe "consolidating" their position. This will be true in the event there is substantial German resistance. One theory seems to be that what is left of Berlin may be tenaciously defended house by house and brick by brick. I have suggested the modest opinion that there should be a certain political advantage in the capture of Berlin even though the military advantage may be insignificant.

This seems to be the only expression of interest on the part of a representative of the State Department on the importance of seizing Berlin. All the cables from Eisenhower to Washington went to the War Department to General George C. Marshall. Cables from the Prime Minister to the President were delivered to General Marshall as promptly as they were received at the White House. Marshall, in turn, had replies drafted which he cleared with Admiral Leahy in the White House. The State Department, in effect, was not in the communications network and hence was not concerned with Berlin. General Marshall, for his part, was deeply preoccupied with the problems of the Pacific Theater: Chiang Kai-shek, General MacArthur, and General Stilwell. Berlin, in retrospect, seems not to have been of great importance to him. At least the Berlin situation is not discussed in any of the documents I have been able to find in the State Department. One of the troublesome problems was that Secretary of State Cordell Hull resigned on November 21, 1944. His Undersecretary, Edward R. Stettinius, who was confirmed as

[15] In an interview I had with Ambassador Robert Murphy in December 1975, he told me of a conversation he had with President Roosevelt earlier when President Roosevelt told him to report directly to him. Murphy pointed out that, as he was an officer of the State Department, it would put him in a difficult position. President Roosevelt replied, "Don't worry, I'll take care of Cordell," referring to Secretary of State Cordell Hull.

Secretary of State on November 30, 1944, seemed, if anything, to be more remote from the conduct of the war than his predecessor. The only reference to Berlin in the papers of Edward R. Stettinius is in his book, *Roosevelt and the Russians,* published by Doubleday & Co. in 1949. With some indignation he makes the comment, "I know of no evidence to support the charge that President Roosevelt agreed at Yalta that American troops should not capture Berlin ahead of the Red Army. General Eisenhower has written that the decision that American troops should not push into Berlin was taken in March, 1945, solely on military grounds."

In conclusion I would like to touch upon two aspects of the Berlin problem: a possible tactical solution, and the significance of the absence of State Department participation in the final decision-making process.

Every soldier I know of who has analyzed the fighting during the month of April 1945 is troubled by the fact that Eisenhower's armies stopped on the Elbe. All the junior commanders I knew assumed that we would go on as long as we could until contact with the Russians was made. During March, however, Eisenhower seemed apprehensive about making contact without stopping on some well-defined line, such as a river. But this was of no express concern whatever in the British Second Army when the U.S. XVIII Corps and the 82nd Airborne Division were told to move until they gained contact with the Russians. Although that operation was on a smaller scale, it followed the conventional tactical practice of sending out a reconnaissance force to make the initial contact. In an approach to Berlin, this could have been done by a mechanized cavalry command without larger forces becoming heavily engaged. Such a command, well equipped with communications, could promptly withdraw if the need arose. On the other hand, if the tactical situation suggested, the command could hold all it had seized until reinforced.

The question, therefore, is why Eisenhower did not make a reconnaissance in force in the direction of Berlin, and even through Prague. He was just as much entitled to occupy Berlin as the Soviets, and he might well have suggested such a course of action to the Combined Chiefs of Staff. It is possible that the request for authority to undertake such a move had to go through the War Department and the office of General George Marshall, and Eisenhower did not do so because of earlier understandings with General Marshall regarding the termination of the war. Or, possibly, he was once again too remote from the tactical realities of the battlefield. But as commander of the Allied military force, he had a responsibility to recommend the most effective way of bringing the war to an end. If then he had been ordered to stop his advance, he could have brought his forces to a halt whenever and wherever he was told to do so.

Far more troublesome was the role of the Department of State. Knowing that the war would come to an end, sooner or later, the Department of State should have prepared a plan that had the concurrence of the War Department and the approval of the White House. By not having developed a plan, it was forced to acquiesce in the course of action proposed by the War Department. In other words, it subordinated itself to the wishes of the War Department in carrying out foreign policy.

In subsequent years this condition has been allowed to grow in an alarming manner. Military people can always rationalize almost any problem's becoming military and thus susceptible to a military solution. They dislike interference on the part of the State Department when that Department sees serious political consequences stemming from the use of military force. I have discussed problems of this nature in the Pentagon, and with the Joint Chiefs of Staff, on many occasions. I remember quite vividly a senior officer in the Pentagon referring to State Department officers who were raising questions about the political aspects of Alaskan statehood. The General referred, rather derisively I thought, to State Department people as "those field marshals in striped pants." Actually, it was the generals who were wearing the striped pants. The State Department acquiescence in the policies of the War Department was a most alarming portent of what was to come. Later, less than ten years after the war, the State Department concurred in the Pentagon's policy of depending upon the big bomb to solve all our foreign policy problems: massive retaliation at a time and place of our choosing. The State Department translated this into a foreign policy described as "brinkmanship." Obviously this was not a policy. It was a slogan.

It was not long thereafter that the State Department acquiesced in the Pentagon's desire to intervene in Southeast Asia. As a general who opposed the Southeast Asian involvement from the outset, I found this deeply disturbing. Surely there must have been, among the more thoughtful people in the State Department, some who saw the ultimate consequences, from a political if not military point of view, of our venture. Ultimately, this proved to be one of the greatest foreign policy and military disasters in our nation's history.

But the abandonment of foreign policy initiative to the War Department at the time of Berlin, and afterward, is profound in its implications. There have been outstanding State Department people who have opposed such policies, such as George Ball and Averell Harriman, among others. And there have been State Department junior officers who have given up their careers because they believed that they could not continue to serve with the policies of the Department. This has resulted in considerable paralysis and ineffectiveness that has troubled every President in recent years. President John F. Kennedy was very much concerned about this, and in my last conversation with him on October 21, 1963, when we were discussing a forthcoming visit of General de Gaulle, he tilted his head toward the State Department and said to me, "But first I must straighten out that State Department." Earlier, in the summer of 1961, President Kennedy is reported to have remarked to Hugh Sidey of *Time,* "The State Department is a bowl of jelly."[16] The condition of the Department, whether it began with World War II, or much earlier, as believed by many, is one that must be corrected as a matter of highest priority.

The Department needs additional foreign service officers. They need them so that they can send their people back to school in mid-career on a scale comparable to the advanced educational training provided by the Pentagon for its career people. In addition to postgraduate educational work, after the State Department people have been out of school for some years, they need career training in business and commerce, for example. In short, they need help and an opportunity to prepare for the roles that they must be able to fill. Sending State Department people to the National War College, and the war colleges of the separate Services, as now is the practice, is hardly adequate. Indeed, in the long run it may be harmful.

The journey to Berlin began when the mood of the country was far from sanguine about entering the war. It was carried on courageously by Americans in all walks of life. It ended with many well-founded suspicions of the Soviets' postwar intentions. It also ended with many questions about why we allowed the Eastern European countries to lose their independence to Soviet aggression. In the postwar period, there-

[16] Smith Simpson, *Anatomy of the State Department.* Boston: Houghton Mifflin Co., 1967, p. 228.

fore, we began to question our State Department's ability to develop a diplomatic strategy that would provide security for the free world, and peace and prosperity at home. But these matters are beyond the scope of this book.

It had been a long and costly journey, and when we overran the concentration camps and looked back with a better understanding of where we had been, we knew it had been a journey worth every step of the way.

INDEX

328 INDEX

Moran, Lord, 152
Moravec, Frantisek, 200
Morgan, Frederick E., 83, 307
Morison, Samuel Eliot, 13n.
Morocco: French, 9; Spanish, 8–9
Morris, Mack, 311
Moscow, 283, 301, 302, 307
Mostaganem (Algeria), 58
Mueller, Josef, 199
Mulloy, Lieutenant, 179
Munich (Germany), 199, 282
Munroe, Charles E., 51
Murphy, Robert D., 62, 312, 315
    and n., 316 and n.; quoted, 316
Mussolini, Benito, 16
My Three Years with Eisenhower
    (Butcher), 198n.

Namur (Belgium), 269
Naples, 49, 55, 56, 58, 62, 65n., 70,
    71, 72–73, 74, 78, 82
Napoleon, 71, 139
National Guard, 3, 64
National Redoubt, German, idea of,
    282
Neuville-au-Plain (France), 98, 111,
    112, 113
New York Sun, 186
New York Times, The, 187
Newsweek, 297n.
Nicolson, Nigel, 47, 48n.
Night Drop (Marshall), 115n.
Nijmegen (Holland), 144, 146–51
    passim, 155, 157, 158, 160–66
    passim, 169, 170, 171, 172, 177,
    180, 183, 185, 186, 187 and n.,
    190, 191 and n., 193, 197, 225
Niscemi (Sicily), 34, 35, 36, 38, 39,
    40, 41
Nocera (Italy), 55, 58
Nogues, Auguste, 9
Normandy invasion, 53, 78, 79, 80
    132 *passim,* 133, 136, 137, 202
    and n., 225, 239, 298–99; and
    hedgerows, difficulties presented
    by, 121, 122; pathfinder personnel

in, 99–100; and SHELLBURST,
    130; Task Force A in, 100; 21st
    Army Group in, 81–82, 93, 130.
    See also OVERLORD, Operation
North Africa, 10, 15, 18, 44, 51, 53,
    54, 58, 59, 68, 184, 194, 232, 238,
    239, 269, 279
North African Air Corps, 59
North African Theater of Opera-
    tions, 13n.
Norton, John, 50, 71, 143, 150, 153,
    218, 261
Norway, 84, 308
Noto (Sicily), 39
Nürnberg (Germany), 209, 282,
    310

Oakley, Lieutenant, 114
Oder River, 283
Office of Military Government,
    United States (OMGUS), 293
OKW (German high command),
    63, 198, 199
Oldfield, Barney, 4, 5, 298n.
Olson, Hugo, 103, 106, 109, 110,
    116, 153, 172, 176, 205, 253, 254
Oosterbeek (Holland), 138, 183
Oppenheim (Germany), 277
Orgaz, Luis, 9
Orleans Gap, 92, 93
Orne River, 84
OSS (Office of Strategic Services),
    62, 200, 203
Ostberg, Edwin J., 108, 109
Ottre (Belgium), 230
Oujda (Algeria), 7, 8
OVERLORD, Operation, 77, 78, 80,
    83, 84, 123; battle force assem-
    bled for, 80; and D-day, 99, 100,
    101, 120, 122; drop zones for, 91,
    94, 98, 113; and Hill 110, 90, 91,
    92, 98, 119; and liberation of
    Cherbourg, 119; Phases I and II
    of, and Montgomery, 123; and
    Rommelspargel (Rommel's aspar-
    agus), 92, 94, 95, 96; troop car-